CONSTRUCTIVE THERAPIES

Also by Michael F. Hoyt, from Guilford

The First Session in Brief Therapy
(1993, coedited with
Simon H. Budman and Steven Friedman)

CONSTRUCTIVE THERAPIES

Edited by
Michael F. Hoyt

THE GUILFORD PRESS
New York   London

© 1994 The Guilford Press
A Division of Guilford Publications, Inc.
72 Spring Street, New York, NY 10012

Printed in the United States of America

This book is printed on acid-free paper.

Last digit is print number: 9 8 7 6 5 4 3 2 1

Library of Congress Cataloging-in-Publication Data

Constructive therapies / Michael F. Hoyt, editor.
     p. cm.
  Includes bibliographical references and index.
  ISBN 0-89862-094-5
  1. Brief psychotherapy. 2. Solution-focused therapy.
I. Hoyt, Michael F.
  [DNLM: 1. Psychotherapy, Brief.   WM 420 C758 1994]
RC480.55.C66   1994
616.89—dc20
DNLM/DLC
for Library of Congress
                                94-14220
                                  CIP

To Jennifer,
who usually sees the light
while I'm still cursing the darkness

Others seek; I find.
—PABLO PICASSO

"A warrior is aware that the world will change as soon as he stops talking to himself," he said, "and he must be prepared for that monumental jolt."

"What do you mean, don Juan?"

"The world is such-and-such and so-and-so only because we tell ourselves that that is the way it is. If we stop telling ourselves that the world is so-and-so, the world will stop being so-and-so. At this moment I don't think you're ready for such a momentous blow, therefore you must start slowly to undo the world."
—CARLOS CASTANEDA

What is by now evident and clear is that neither future nor past exists, and it is inexact language to speak of three times—past, present, and future. Perhaps it would be exact to say: there are three times, a present of things past, a present of things present, a present of things to come. In the soul there are these three aspects of time, and I do not see them anywhere else. The present considering the past is the memory, the present considering the future is expectation.
—ST. AUGUSTINE

To the extent that therapist and client deny the client's power, the client is a victim. To the extent that they believe he has power which is not his, as in changing someone else, the client is both grandiose and a victim.
—ROBERT AND MARY GOULDING

Each person is a unique individual. Hence, psychotherapy should be formulated to meet the uniqueness of the individual's needs, rather than tailoring the person to fit the Procrustean bed of a hypothetical theory of human behavior.
—MILTON H. ERICKSON

Contributors

TAPANI AHOLA, MA, Codirector, Brief Therapy Institute, Inc., Helsinki, Finland

RICHARD CHASIN, MD, Codirector, Family Institute of Cambridge, Watertown, Massachusetts; Associate Clinical Professor of Psychiatry, Harvard Medical School at Cambridge Hospital, Cambridge, Massachusetts

GENE COMBS, MD, Codirector, Evanston Family Therapy Center, Evanston, Illinois; Faculty, Chicago Center for Family Health, Chicago, Illinois

STEVE DE SHAZER, MSW, Senior Research Associate, Brief Family Therapy Center, Milwaukee, Wisconsin

VICTORIA C. DICKERSON, PHD, Codirector, Bay Area Family Therapy Training Associates, Cupertino, California; Teaching Faculty, Mental Research Institute, Palo Alto, California; Adjunct Lecturer, John F. Kennedy University, Campbell, California; Adjunct Lecturer, Santa Clara University, Santa Clara, California

YVONNE M. DOLAN, MA, private practice, Denver, Colorado

RICHARD FISCH, MD, Director, Brief Thearpy Center, Mental Research Insitute, Palo Alto, California; Clinical Associate Professor of Psychiatry Emeritus, Stanford University, Stanford, California

JILL FREEDMAN, MSW, Codirector, Evanston Family Therapy Center, Evanston, Illinois; Faculty, Chicago Center for Family Health, Chicago, Illinois

STEVEN FRIEDMAN, PHD, Coordinator, Mental Health Training, Harvard Community Health Plan, Braintree, Massachusetts; Senior Lecturer, Lesley College Graduate School, Cambridge, Massachusetts

BEN FURMAN, MD, Codirector, Brief Therapy Institute, Inc., Helsinki, Finland

ERIC GREENLEAF, PhD, private practice, Berkeley, California

MICHAEL F. HOYT, PhD, Director, Adult Psychiatric Services, Kaiser Permanente Medical Center, Hayward, California; Clinical Faculty, University of California School of Medicine, San Francisco, California; Continuing Education Faculty, California School of Professional Psychology, Alameda, California

PATRICIA O'HANLON HUDSON, PhD, Director, The Hudson Center for Brief Therapy, Omaha, Nebraska

SCOTT D. MILLER, PhD, Problems to Solutions, Inc., Chicago, Illinois

WILLIAM HUDSON O'HANLON, MS, The Hudson Center for Brief Therapy, Omaha, Nebraska

JANE E. PELLER, MSW, Codirector, Consultations: A Center for Solution-Focused Brief Therapy, Chicago, Illinois

SALLYANN ROTH, LICSW, Codirector, Family Institute of Cambridge, Watertown, Massachusetts; Lecturer on Psychiatry, Harvard Medical School at Cambridge Hospital, Cambridge, Massachusetts

JOHN L. WALTER, MSW, Codirector, Consultations: A Center for Solution-Focused Brief Therapy, Chicago, Illinois

JOHN WEAKLAND, ChE, MFCC, Codirector, Brief Therapy Center, Mental Research Institute, Palo Alto, California

JEFFREY L. ZIMMERMAN, PhD, Codirector, Bay Area Family Therapy Training Associates, Cupertino, California; Teaching Faculty, Mental Research Institute, Palo Alto, California; Clinical Faculty, Stanford University, Stanford, California; Adjunct Lecturer, John F. Kennedy University, Campbell, California

Acknowledgments

First, kudos to all the authors who contributed to this book. It has been a privilege to work with such constructive, creative, and cordial colleagues. Thanks also to the many patients and clients whose experiences and wisdom are reflected in the following pages. I am also grateful to Seymour Weingarten, Editor-in-Chief at The Guilford Press, for his fine guidance; and to Sherran Boll, for her secretarial assistance.

Many other people deserve thanks as well, including Simon Budman and Steven Friedman (my coeditors for *The First Session in Brief Therapy*), all my colleagues at Kaiser Permanente (especially Bob Rosenbaum, Gerson Schreiber, and Norm Weinstein), plus Jeffry Ordover, Evan Garelle, Mary Goulding, Michael White, Jeffrey Zeig, Michelle Weiner-Davis, Eve Lipchik, and Carl Whitaker. My special gratitude to those friends—all passed, none forgotten—who in their different ways have provided support and encouragement: Dennis Farrell, Lloyd Churgin, Richard Centers, Ed Holcomb, Susan Stieg, John Long, Irving Janis, Lewis Wolberg, and Bob Goulding.

Finally my deepest appreciation to Jennifer Lillard, my wife, and to Alexander Hoyt, my son, for their love and forbearance.

Contents

CHAPTER 1

Introduction
Competency-Based
Future-Oriented Therapy

MICHAEL F. HOYT

In recent years there has been a psychotherapy movement toward a "new direction" (O'Hanlon & Weiner-Davis, 1989), one that invites fuller appreciation of human agency and potential. This new direction focuses more on the strengths and resources that patients/clients[1] bring to the enterprise than on their weaknesses or limitations. Similarly, more emphasis is put on where people want to go than on where they have been. While not ignoring the painfulness and seriousness of some situations, the shift has been away from conventional psychiatric patholo-gizing and toward a more optimistic view of people as unique and resourceful creators of their own realities (for better or worse).

While some theory is provided to enhance comprehension and cohesion, this is not a "theory" book. Rather, it is a "how to" book, a user's guide. The purpose is to promote skills in competency-based future-oriented psychotherapy. Chapters have been prepared by experts in different areas of practice. Each author describes and demonstrates methods that utilize client resources in building solutions and solving problems, briefly reviewing the theory/rationale of a given approach and then presenting transcripts and related case material to illustrate how the work is actually done. No single chapter (or book) can fully teach a method of psychother-apy, of course, but the hope is that readers will, through transcripts and commentaries, get a sense of what actually happens and what characterizes a particular approach.

[1]The terms *patient* and *client* will be used interchangeably throughout this volume, the choice being at the discretion of particular authors. Each term carries certain connotations, the former sounding more medical and emphasizing suffering, while the latter tends to be more egalitarian but may seem to be more business-related than health-oriented (Hoyt, 1979, 1985). Whatever terms are used, it is important to be aware of their implications for the emerging therapeutic alliance, particularly the development of power and role expectations.

1

LOOKING FOR SOLUTIONS:
HOW YOU SEE IS WHAT YOU GET

Different paradigms or reality constructions carry with them different "analogies" (White & Epston, 1990) or "observing positions" (Gustafson, 1986) through which we order and attempt to influence experience. As seen in Table 1.1, moving from an understanding based in the physical and biological sciences to one based on social science leads us into radically different ways of construing problems and solutions, of helping people change how they perceive their world and conduct themselves.

Underlying these different constructions is the construction that we are constructive, that we are engaged in a building process—whether we know it or not. "Patients have problems," as Milton Erickson said, "because their conscious programming has too severely limited their capacities. The solution is to help them break through the limitations of their conscious attitudes to free their unconscious potential for problem solving" (Erickson, Rossi, & Rossi, 1976, p. 18). Following Erickson, the essential paradigmatic shift is from deficits to strengths, from problems to solutions, from past to future (Fisch, 1990; Hoyt, in press-a), utilizing whatever the patient brings in the service of healthful change (de Shazer, 1988). As discussed in Chapter 2, this change in orientation results in the therapist truly functioning as a mental health (not mental illness) professional.

A variety of terms—such as *solution-oriented, solution-focused, possibility, narrative, postmodern, cooperative, competency-based, constructivist*—can be found on signposts marking this territory.[2] They have their differences, to be sure, although in clinical practice all have certain common characteristics: a respectful partnership between therapist and client, an emphasis on strengths and resources, and a hopeful eye toward the future.

Each, in its own way, is *constructive therapy*, the *building of solutions*, with language or "conversation" (de Shazer, 1991, 1994; Friedman, 1993; Gilligan & Price, 1993) being the map if not the territory. The shift toward some typical solution-building terms may be seen in Table 1.2.

WHAT'S AHEAD

Chapter 2, "On the Importance of Keeping It Simple and Taking the Patient Seriously," reports an interview with Steve de Shazer and John Weakland. Each is a leading figure in the field, and a far-ranging discussion ensues with emphasis being placed on the value of careful listening that respects patients' goals and self-determination, on identi-

---

[2]An extensive bibliography is provided in the Appendix to supplement the reference section of each chapter.

TABLE 1.1. Table of Analogies

Analogies drawn from	Social organization constructed as	Problems constructed as	Solution constructed in terms of
1. Positivist physical sciences	Elaborate machine, constituted by mechanics and hydraulics	Breakdown, reversal, insufficiency, damage	Isolating cause, precise analysis, repair, reconstruct, correct
2. Biological sciences	Quasi-organism	Symptomatic of underlying problem, serving a function, having utility	Identifying pathology, correct diagnosis, operating and excising pathology
3. Social sciences			
(a) Game theory	Serious game	Strategies, moves	Contest, countermoves, strategizing
(b) Drama	Living-room drama	Roles, scripts, performances	Revising roles, selecting alternative dramatic form
(c) Ritual process	Rite of passage	Transition— separation, betwixt and between, re-incorporation	Mapping, drawing distinctions around status 1 and status 2
(d) Text	Behavioral text	Performance of oppressive, dominant story or knowledge	Opening space for the authoring of alternative stories

Note. From White and Epston (1990, p. 6). Copyright 1990 by Dulwich Centre, Adelaide, South Australia. Reprinted by permission.

fying what works (exceptions, the "difference that makes a difference") rather than engaging in obfuscating theorization (see Whitaker, 1976). Interviewing for the purpose of helping patients reach their goal is primary.

Chapter 3, "Solution Talk: The Solution-Oriented Way of Talking about Problems," is by Ben Furman and Tapani Ahola. As in their acclaimed *Solution Talk: Hosting Therapeutic Conversations* (1992), the

TABLE 1.2. Solution-Building Vocabulary

In	Out
Respect	Judge
Empower	Fix
Nurture	Control
Facilitate	Treat
Augment	Reduce
Invite	Insist
Appreciate	Diagnose
Hope	Fear
Latent	Missing
Assets	Defects
Strength	Weakness
Health	Pathology
Not yet	Never
Expand	Shrink
Forward	Backward
Future	Past
Collaborate	Manipulate
Options	Conflicts
Partner	Expert
Horizontal	Hierarchical
Possibility	Limitation
Growth	Cure
Access	Defense
Utilize	Resist
Exception	Rule
Difference	Sameness
Solution	Problem

authors highlight the constructive nature of therapeutic language, presenting a compilation of solution-oriented conversational themes they frequently employ. Each theme is discussed and illustrated with a refreshing case example, and a wide variety of sample questions are provided that might be used to facilitate open and salutary discussion.

In Chapter 4, "Narrative Intentions," Gene Combs and Jill Freedman, authors of *Symbol, Story, and Ceremony: Using Metaphor in Individual and Family Therapy* (1990), emphasize the importance of language, and make explicit their intention to help clients create a more useful narrative: "we in no sense want to imply that what therapists think and do is the most important aspect of what happens in therapy. It is simply the side for which we bear responsibility. Our intention is to engage in collaborative, horizontal relationships in which people choose stories they prefer and make their own meanings about those preferred stories" (p. 70). With special acknowledgment to the influence of Michael White (1989; White & Epston, 1990), the authors describe methods for emphasizing a client's personal agency and deconstructing a "problem-saturated narrative," and then illustrate their work in a case example as they help "Jessica" to "re-author" or "re-story" her life into a more self-empowered and satisfying direction.

Chapter 5, "Some Questions (Not Answers) for the Brief Treatment of People with Drug and Alcohol Problems," by Scott Miller, applies many of the concepts of solution-focused therapy to work within the substance abuse area. Miller, coauthor of *Working with the Problem Drinker: A Solution-Focused Approach* (Berg & Miller, 1992), describes and illustrates the use of outcome questions, instance/exception questions, scaling questions, and endurance and/or externalization questions (including an interesting discussion of the disease model of alcoholism, following Bateson, 1972).

Chapter 6, "'On Track' in Solution-Focused Brief Therapy," is by John Walter and Jane Peller. Known for their highly instructive *Becoming Solution-Focused in Brief Therapy* (1992), here the authors present several examples of how therapy can be briefer if the goal is recognized as simply helping the client get back "on track" rather than having him or her stay in treatment until all the work is completed. This respects clients' capacities to carry on the work themselves at their own pace. In addition to the fine examples provided by Walter and Peller, the "on track" metaphor can be particularly useful in many "recovery" situations where the process might get "stuck" (Hoyt, 1990, in press-a, b) or bogged down in "either/or" thinking (Lipchik, 1993), such as problems of guilt or "codependency" (Blackstone, 1987; Nylund, 1992).

In Chapter 7, "Basic Elements in the Brief Therapies," Richard Fisch—senior author of the highly influential *Tactics of Change: Doing Therapy Briefly* (Fisch, Weakland, & Segal, 1982) and coauthor of *Change: Principles of Problem Formation and Problem Resolution* (Watzlawick, Weakland, & Fisch, 1974)—returns to the theme of the de Shazer and Weakland interview reported in Chapter 2: keeping it simple and getting the work done as briefly as possible. Fisch advocates narrowing the database to current and interpersonal descriptions with a clear task orientation and a well-defined stopping point, and illustrates how language directed toward the past and toward putative intrapsychic processes, often confounded by vague treatment goals, tends to work against parsimony.

In Chapter 8, "Single-Session Solutions," I note that many patients are able to successfully complete their treatment in one session, particularly if the therapist is open to this possibility and helps the patient make the most of the session. After reviewing earlier studies of single-session therapy (some done in collaboration with Moshe Talmon and Robert Rosenbaum) and noting that most effective single-session therapy is actually not time-limited therapy—it is open-ended and the patient gets what is needed and elects to stop after one visit—I present a variety of successful one-session treatments. The widely different methodologies used in these cases result in patients accessing inner strengths and revising the stories that structure their functioning.

Chapter 9, "Coauthoring a Love Story: Solution-Oriented Marital Therapy," is by Bill O'Hanlon and Patricia Hudson. Each an authority in his or her own right (Hudson, 1993; O'Hanlon, 1987; O'Hanlon & Weiner-Davis, 1989; O'Hanlon & Hexum, 1990; O'Hanlon & Martin, 1992), they have also coauthored *Rewriting Love Stories: Brief Marital Therapy* (Hudson & O'Hanlon, 1991). In their chapter, they present a lively consultation session in which they actively work with a couple to help them change the "doing and viewing" that impedes their relationship. Avoiding the communication pitfalls of blame, invalidation, closing down possibilities, and vagueness, O'Hanlon and Hudson use a wide variety of solution-oriented methods—including acknowledgment, humor, appropriate self-revelation, "videotalk" clarification, normalization, reframing, encouragement, searching for past solutions that may be used again, and instructive storytelling—which contribute to a successful outcome.

Chapter 10, by Sallyann Roth and Richard Chasin—"Entering One Another's Worlds of Meaning and Imagination: Dramatic Enactment and Narrative Couple Therapy"—further develops an approach described by Chasin, Roth, and Bograd (1989) and elaborated by Chasin and Roth (1990) in *One Couple, Four Realities* (Chasin, Grunebaum, & Herzig, 1990). The authors present a novel and constructive way of helping couples to build better solutions (realities). Through a series of carefully described and illustrated guided interactional "role-playing" exercises, partners have a chance to (re)enact emblematic past and future scenes, crafting them so as to produce new and inspiring experiences, which can produce powerful and enduring changes in how they see themselves and their partners.

In Chapter 11, "Possibility Therapy: Constructing Time-Effective Solutions with Children and Families," Steven Friedman—coauthor of *Expanding Therapeutic Possibilities: Getting Results in Brief Psychotherapy* (Friedman & Fanger, 1991), coeditor of *The First Session in Brief Therapy* (Budman, Hoyt, & Friedman, 1992), and editor of *The New Language of Change: Constructive Collaboration in Psychotherapy* (1993)—applies the principles of what he calls "possibility therapy" to a variety of clinical situations. In cases varying from delayed toilet training and childhood nightmares to adolescent drug abuse and stealing, Friedman illustrates ways of maintaining a collaborative posture, keeping assumptions simple and staying focused on the client's goal, emphasizing strengths and resources, and introducing novelty. In each case he successfully shows how "the therapist guides and structures the therapeutic conversation such that the family, rather than becoming immersed in problems and constraints, is afforded opportunities to re-vision their predicament in ways that emphasize possibilities and offers hope for the future" (p. 248).

Chapter 12, "Solving the Unknown Problem," by Eric Greenleaf, describes a unique and highly creative form of "solution building." He provides the annotated record of a hypnosis consultation group "passing the trance" from one member to another, gazing into a faceted crystal as they "consider solving an unknown problem that has been interfering in life" (p. 253). Like a jazz ensemble, what results is a kind of "reflecting team" (Andersen, 1991) of the unconscious, a form of "group dreaming" (Greenleaf, 1973) or psychodramatic communication, with images and metaphors emerging that members are able to apply beneficially to various problems. This concept of "solving an unknown problem" suggests looking in the cupboard to see what spices and stuff might be found, the "main course" only being known once the available ingredients are located.

In Chapter 13, "Solution-Focused Therapy with a Case of Severe Abuse," Yvonne Dolan—author of *A Path with a Heart: Ericksonian Utilization with Resistant and Chronic Clients (1985)* and *Resolving Sexual Abuse: Solution-Focused Therapy and Ericksonian Hypnosis for Adult Survivors* (1991)—presents the case of a stalking, rape, and assault survivor. Emphasis is placed on the importance of treating the "rigid associational compartmentalization" that often results as a defensive response to traumatic stress, lest the survivor be left unable to access and utilize much needed internal resources and thus be particularly vulnerable to psychological retraumatization. Solution-focused techniques, such as the use of scaling questions and the writing of postcards and letters to help identify and later elicit resources, are successfully illustrated.

Chapter 14, "Tales of the Body Thief: Externalizing and Deconstructing Eating Problems," is by Jeffrey Zimmerman and Victoria Dickerson. Acknowledging the strong influence of Michael White and David Epston (1990) as well as Carol Gilligan's understanding of "voice" for women and adolescent girls (Gilligan, Rogers, & Tolman, 1991), the authors present excerpts from several cases that illustrate a "process of interviewing [that] has the effect of deconstructing these [oppressing anorexic] practices by bringing forward the cultural, social, and familial contexts that helped create and support them. . . . Raising questions for the client about her interest in challenging the problem and helping the client to notice unique outcomes . . . leads to a conversation about ınorexia and the beginning of a new story" (p. 297). Numerous ˷ʃ̣ ıfic questions and intervention strategies are clearly described, the overarching goal being to encourage the patient to reclaim her voice and begin to narrate her own story in a way that does not require unhealthy eating patterns.

An Appendix follows the last chapter, containing an extended selected bibliography.

TOWARD THE FUTURE: DOING WHAT WORKS

Suppose tonight, while you're sleeping, a miracle occurs . . . and when you awaken you find you are helping clients in a more positive and effective way than before! How will you notice your practice has changed? What new skills will you be using? Perhaps the pages that follow will help inform your answer. Readers are strongly encouraged to adapt and cross-fertilize as appropriate and to follow-up on references, apply their own experiences, and learn more than is printed. The invitation is extended.

REFERENCES

Andersen, T. (Ed.). (1991). *The Reflecting Team: Dialogues and Dialogues about the Dialogues*. New York: Norton.

Bateson, G. (1972). *Steps to an Ecology of Mind*. New York: Jason Aronson.

Berg, I. K., & Miller, S. D. (1992). *Working with the Problem Drinker: A Solution-Focused Approach*. New York: Norton.

Berne, E. (1972). *What Do You Say After You Say Hello?* New York: Grove Press.

Blackstone, P. (1987). Loving too much—disease or decision? *Transactional Analysis Journal, 17*, 185–190.

Budman, S. H., Hoyt, M. F., & Friedman, S. (Eds.). (1992). *The First Session in Brief Therapy*. New York: Guilford.

Chasin, R., Grunebaum, H., & Herzig, M. (Eds.). (1990). *One Couple, Four Realities: Multiple Perspectives on Couple Therapy*. New York: Guilford.

Chasin, R., & Roth, S. (1990). Future perfect, past perfect: A positive approach to opening couple therapy. In R. Chasin, H. Grunebaum, & M. Herzig (Eds.), *One Couple, Four Realities: Multiple Perspectives on Couple Therapy* (pp. 129–144). New York: Guilford.

Chasin, R., Roth, S., & Bograd, M. (1989). Action methods in systemic therapy: Dramatizing ideal futures and reformed pasts with couples. *Family Process, 28*(1), 121–136.

Combs, G., & Freedman, J. (1990). *Symbol, Story, and Ceremony: Using Metaphor in Individual and Family Therapy*. New York: Norton.

de Shazer, S. (1988). *Clues: Investigating Solutions in Brief Therapy*. New York: Norton.

de Shazer, S. (1991). *Putting Difference to Work*. New York: Norton.

de Shazer, S. (1994). *Words Were Originally Magic*. New York: Norton.

Dolan, Y. M. (1985). *A Path with a Heart: Ericksonian Utilization with Resistant and Chronic Clients*. New York: Brunner/Mazel.

Dolan, Y. M. (1991). *Resolving Sexual Abuse: Solution-Focused Therapy and Ericksonian Hypnosis for Adult Survivors*. New York: Norton.

Erickson, M. H., Rossi, E., & Rossi, S. (1976). *Hypnotic Realities*. New York: Irvington.

Fisch, R. (1990). The broader implications of Milton H. Erickson's work. *Ericksonian Monographs, 7,* 1–5.

Fisch, R., Weakland, J. H., & Segal, L. (1982). *The Tactics of Change: Doing Therapy Briefly*. San Francisco: Jossey-Bass.

Friedman, S. (Ed.). (1993). *The New Language of Change: Constructive Collaboration in Psychotherapy*. New York: Guilford.

Friedman, S., & Fanger, M. T. (1991). *Expanding Therapeutic Possibilities: Getting Results in Brief Psychotherapy*. New York: Lexington Books/ Macmillan.

Furman, B., & Ahola, T. (1992). *Solution Talk: Hosting Therapeutic Conversations*. New York: Norton.

Gilligan C., Rogers, A., & Tolman, D. (1991). *Women, Girls, and Psychotherapy*. Cambridge, MA: Harvard University Press.

Gilligan, S., & Price, R. (Eds.). (1993) *Therapeutic Conversations*. New York: Norton.

Greenleaf, E. (1973). Senoi dream groups. *Psychotherapy: Theory, Research and Practice, 10,* 218–222.

Gustafson, J. P. (1986). *The Complex Secret of Brief Psychotherapy*. New York: Norton.

Hoyt, M. F. (1979). "Patient" or "client": What's in a name? *Psychotherapy: Theory, Research & Practice, 16,* 16–17.

Hoyt, M. F. (1985). "Shrink" or "expander": An issue in forming a therapeutic alliance. *Psychotherapy, 22,* 813–814.

Hoyt, M. F. (1990). On time in brief therapy. In R. A. Wells & V. J. Giannetti (Eds.), *Handbook of the Brief Psychotherapies* (pp. 115–143). New York: Plenum.

Hoyt, M. F. (in press-a). Brief psychotherapies. In A. S. Gurman & S. B. Messer (Eds.), *Major Systems of Psychotherapy*. New York: Guilford.

Hoyt, M. F. (in press-b). Is being "in recovery" self-limiting? *Transactional Analysis Journal.*

Hudson, P. O. (1993). *Making Friends with Your Unconscious Mind: The User Friendly Guide*. Omaha, NE: Center Press.

Hudson, P. O., & O'Hanlon, W. H. (1991). *Rewriting Love Stories: Brief Marital Therapy*. New York: Norton.

Lipchik, E. (1993). "Both/and" solutions. In S. Friedman (Ed.), *The New Language of Change: Constructive Collaboration in Psychotherapy* (pp. 25–49). New York: Guilford.

Nylund, D. (1992). Escaping a co-dependent lifestyle: A systemic/cybernetic approach. *Family Therapy Case Studies, 7*(1), 41–47.

O'Hanlon, W. H. (1987). *Taproots: Underlying Principles of Milton Erickson's Therapy and Hypnosis*. New York: Norton.

O'Hanlon, W. H., & Hexum, A. L. (1990). *An Uncommon Casebook: The Complete Clinical Work of Milton H. Erickson*. New York: Norton.

O'Hanlon, W. H., & Martin, M. (1992). *Solution-Oriented Hypnosis: An Ericksonian Approach*. New York: Norton.

O'Hanlon, W. H., & Weiner-Davis, M. (1989). *In Search of Solutions: A New Direction in Psychotherapy*. New York: Norton.

Walter, J. L., & Peller, J. E. (1992). *Becoming Solution-Focused in Brief Therapy*. New York: Brunner/Mazel.

Watzlawick, P., Weakland, J. H., & Fisch, R. (1974). *Change: Principles of Problem Formation and Problem Resolution*. New York: Norton.

Whitaker, C. A. (1976). The hindrance of theory in clinical work. In P. J. Guerin (Ed.), *Family Therapy: Theory and Practice* (pp. 154–164). New York: Gardner Press.

White, M. (1989). *Selected Papers*. Adelaide, South Australia: Dulwich Centre Publications.

White, M., & Epston, D. (1990). *Narrative Means to Therapeutic Ends*. New York: Norton.

CHAPTER 2

On the Importance
of Keeping It Simple and
Taking the Patient Seriously

A Conversation with
Steve de Shazer and John Weakland

MICHAEL F. HOYT

The solution of problems and the problems of solutions have long been the focus of attention for John Weakland and Steve de Shazer. One of the contributors of the original double-bind hypothesis (Bateson, Jackson, Haley, & Weakland, 1956), Weakland is Codirector of the Brief Therapy Center at the Mental Research Institute in Palo Alto, California. He is coauthor of *Change: Principles of Problem Formation and Problem Resolution* (Watzlawick, Weakland, & Fisch, 1974), *Counseling Elders and Their Families: Practical Techniques for Applied Gerontology* (Herr & Weakland, 1979), and *The Tactics of Change: Doing Therapy Briefly* (Fisch, Weakland, & Segal, 1983). de Shazer is Senior Research Associate at the Brief Family Therapy Center in Milwaukee, Wisconsin. Like Weakland, he is a major figure in the development of brief therapy and the shift toward a constructivist perspective. His books include *Patterns of Brief Family Therapy* (1982), *Keys to Solution in Brief Therapy* (1985), *Clues: Investigating Solutions in Brief Therapy* (1988), *Putting Difference to Work* (1991), and most recently, *Words Were Originally Magic* (1994).

The following conversation took place during the afternoon of December 3, 1992, in Phoenix, Arizona, where we were all participating in the Fifth International Congress on Ericksonian Approaches to Hypnosis and Psychotherapy.

HOYT: I think it's appropriate that we're meeting here at the Erickson conference, especially since the theme is "The Essence of the Story."

11

And that was the first thing that I wanted to ask. What do you think is the essence of being a brief therapist?

DE SHAZER: My first immediate thought is that "essence" is a muddling word. Because when you talk "essence," that means you also talk something about "nonessence." And you've got me, Michael. That, to me, is unanswerable because of that.

HOYT: Maybe I should take out the question about the essence and ask it the other way. What is brief therapy?

DE SHAZER: Oh, shit. I think that made it worse! (*laughter*)

WEAKLAND: About the essence, I'll say one thing. It's leaving out a whole lot of stuff that a great many people otherwise think is essential.

DE SHAZER: Right.

HOYT: Well said. It's leaving out what many people think is essential, but obviously isn't.

WEAKLAND: Yeah, I guess that it's about *simplifying*. That's probably the essence, if there is such a thing.

HOYT: What's the Ericksonian essence in your work?

WEAKLAND: When I get to the Ericksonian essence, it has really nothing to do with technique. It has nothing to do with theory. It mainly had to do with Erickson was very curious, and he was a hell of an observer, and he looked and listened to other people, and he finally had the guts to draw his own conclusions. That basically is what I think was the essence of Milton and comes at a much deeper level than what he did specifically.

DE SHAZER: I guess my point again is around this point of essence. When you start to look for the essence of Erickson's work or brief therapy, you're always in danger of forgetting the "nonessential" stuff. You automatically point to something that is nonessential when you say something is essential. Automatically. And you're in danger then of sticking something into the "nonessential" box that will prove, in the long run, to be just as essential as anything else has been.

WEAKLAND: You're always in danger of being too sure of yourself before-hand. You're equally in danger of not having the nerve to go with what you think is best.

DE SHAZER: So I think it's a very slippery category because of that. A not-very-useful way of thinking. You can't afford to box things off into this "nonessential" box, because over and over it has proved to be that things we thought were not essential at one point were things that later turned everything around.

WEAKLAND: Also, you can't—it's very similar—but you can't really do the same with big and little, or at least what seems to me to be big things often seem to other people to be little things and vice versa.

HOYT: In your own experience, what did you put in the nonessential box that you then brought back?

DE SHAZER: I started off trying to construct a theory, in the formal sense of the term, looking at Erickson's published cases and there's all these goddamn cases that didn't fit the theory. I mean, the theory worked very well. There were five major patterns. That worked just fine. I simplified it. But, nonetheless, there was always pile number six, which usually contained more cases than the other five. But we thought, you know, it's only a matter of figuring out how the theory works in these other cases.

WEAKLAND: We're going to whittle down that residual category until it's no bigger than all the rest and go from there.

DE SHAZER: I started off, essentially, looking for the essence, a very grand theory. And there are always these weird cases. And then I tried doing my form of brief therapy. And I could get most of my cases to fit into these five patterns, but, goddamn it, even by deliberately trying, I couldn't get all of them to fit. So I swept it off to the side, remembering that all theories are incomplete and incorrect, and that it's okay. It's just that the "weird cases" pile kept growing over the years.

WEAKLAND: That brings a terrible thought to mind. It couldn't have been very far away, but I never saw it this clearly. I have done a certain amount of reading in physics. I never got rid of my original scientific bent. Besides, they have things to say that make more sense than most of the psychologists. And poor old Einstein struggled for many late years looking for the grand, unified theory, and he left a number of other people who were doing it. And I read *Infinite in All Directions* by Freeman Dyson [1988], and I was moved to sit down and write Dyson a letter pointing out that it's never going to happen, because you're putting together new interrelated observations; you're always building new observing tools and taking new angles of observation, so you're always going to have more stuff to interrelate. Therefore, you will never reach the end. Dyson didn't answer. And now that I think of it, we're in the same fix.

HOYT: The more we know, the more ways we can theorize it, but it doesn't necessarily mean . . .

WEAKLAND: We may simplify certain things, but we are never going to reach an endpoint that will encompass everything, unless we just completely stop doing anything.

HOYT: My question really is backwards. Rather than asking what's the essence, meaning pulling all this data together into one, it may be more useful to realize the uniqueness of the experiences.

DE SHAZER: Yeah. Yeah. I think the way I see it now is that every session is somehow a unique event, and that the main thing the therapist has to do is listen and keep it simple. And if you do it, I think, the clients will tell you what to do.

HOYT: That reminds me of my favorite Einstein story. I read that his mother, when he would come home from school each day, would say to him, "Albert, did you ask any good questions today?"

WEAKLAND: This enterprise of therapy is a bitch of a job, because in a number of respects you have to go two directions at the same time, although they stay in close relation to each other. I'm not so sure that this isn't really the essence of living in general, but you have got to have some idea what you're about in a session, but you have to always be prepared to hear something that will tell you that you're headed the wrong way. You have always got to be making contact with your clients, but you've always got to preserve enough distance so that you're not seeing things exactly the same way they are or you're no good.

DE SHAZER: You've got to know where you're going.

WEAKLAND: Yeah. So that you're doing things that are in a sense contradictory or at least headed in opposite directions over and over again. And, I think, probably in a lot of other ways that one could spell out. Maybe the essence is to be ready to live with uncertainty.

DE SHAZER: Exactly. And incompleteness.

WEAKLAND: Yeah. And that is the last thing that most people want to do.

DE SHAZER: Or, as Wittgenstein says, "You've got what you've got, and that's all there is." Just take what you've got, no matter how incomplete and inconsistent and incoherent it appears. You've got what you've got.

HOYT: It isn't even especially this field, but this is one of many fields that people want closure or want the answer, fast answer, slow answer, brief answer, long answer.

DE SHAZER: Ten steps.

WEAKLAND: Yeah. That's right. That's the sort of thing I meant. That's the sort of thing that will sell.

DE SHAZER: Completely muddleheaded. The widest variety of unnecessary and unuseful divergences from figuring out what the hell to do.

HOYT: Many of the different methods that are called techniques or steps may be creative and clever, but they don't seem necessary and may just be imposing . . .

WEAKLAND: Clouding the waters. Some are nice stories, a combination of nice stories and eight to ten steps, and you can just go out and follow them. It's a great sales job.

DE SHAZER: Those ten steps won't lead to stories like that. (*laughter*)

WEAKLAND: You mean, they don't come from the same place? (*laughter*) You see, thinking about first-order and second-order change, although it is useful to diagram or explain certain things, it does not help you help people make specific changes in the midst of practice.

DE SHAZER: There is this group that I call the "weird case" pile. The ones that don't fit the theory.

WEAKLAND: That's where the potential instruction is.

DE SHAZER: Yeah. It's these "weird cases" that don't fit the theory . . .

WEAKLAND: All right, then we're more similar than I thought, but I didn't start with anything like a theory. What I started with was lost in the world and saying, "What the hell is going on out there?" And I didn't understand what was going on in the "normal world," so called, let alone the world of problems.

DE SHAZER: Reading Erickson's papers, my initial response was, "What the fuck is going on here? He's got to be crazy."

WEAKLAND: Oh, God, when I first went down to talk to him, my main reaction was, "That is interesting, but I can't make a fucking bit of sense out of it."[1]

HOYT: Do you remember when you began to see it? Was there a moment or watershed where it clicked?

WEAKLAND: Oh, no. It was very gradual. One of the simplest stories he told, one of the plainest stories he told, it was 20 years I began to think about that again and thought about what it was, which was simply the story about Erickson and the headwaiter and his son and the son's friend who weren't dressed properly. Remember that story?

HOYT: Recount it, please.

WEAKLAND: It was in San Francisco. And Erickson was there for one of those traveling roadshows that they used to put on. And his son was working somewhere near the city, and Erickson invited him to come down and have dinner with him one night. And he came down with a young friend. They went down to the dining room. The two young men were dressed quite casually and, when they got to the doorway of the dining room, the headwaiter said, "I'm sorry, sir, you cannot

---

[1]Transcripts of many conversations with Erickson (involving Weakland, Haley, and Bateson) are available in Haley (1985).

come in. The two young men with you are not dressed properly for the dining room." And Erickson said, "But I am a guest in this hotel and these two young men are my guests." And the headwaiter said, "I'm sorry, sir, but the two young men are not dressed properly according to our rules here. I cannot admit you." And Erickson said, "But I am a guest in this hotel and these two young men are my guests." And this went on very civilly for several more rounds, at which point, suddenly the headwaiter said, "Would you come this way, please," and took them to a nice table and seated them. I can get it, but I don't understand it. I can get it, but don't understand it. The sense I finally made out of it, which wasn't long ago, was . . . well, I connected it up with some things that finally we'd gotten clear on and that helped me to at least get some grasp. Erickson was not arguing. There was no confrontation. There was just a statement of fact. He did not argue with the headwaiter's statement. He just made his statement of fact. He did not escalate; he didn't change the volume of his statement. He just repeated it. But he was clearly prepared to repeat it essentially forever if necessary. And, I'm assuming that meanwhile the pressure was growing on the head-waiter to get on with his business. But the main point was he made no confrontation, no argument; he just stated a fact and kept on stating it. So, but how come . . .

DE SHAZER: So, how come . . . that sounds like more of the same of something that's not working.

WEAKLAND: What's the difference? Well, somebody, I think it was Bateson somewhere, said we have to consider the role of time in these things. That was changing.

DE SHAZER: Ah. That was changing. And there may have been some other things about the situation . . .

WEAKLAND: There may have been some people piling up . . .

DE SHAZER: Ah, the line behind them! This is the whole point I suppose: exceptions. And here's an exception of some sort. Now the easiest thing to do with exceptions is to sweep them under the rug and forget 'em.

WEAKLAND: Furthermore, that's a time-honored procedure in many a field . . .

DE SHAZER: That's how you keep your theory pure.

WEAKLAND: . . . including the cases of cancer that go into remission.

DE SHAZER: Right. For 20 years.

WEAKLAND: Including the "flights into health" that plagued the field of analysis for so long.

HOYT: "Flukes." "Flight into health." "Let's not talk about that one."

DE SHAZER: Right. Keep your theory pure, you see.

WEAKLAND: But it's always those exceptions that seem most interesting. That's probably another example of how my mind is bent.

HOYT: Well, here's an exception that I've been struggling with. I'll read you the quotation. It's in the Preface to *Putting Difference to Work* [de Shazer, 1991, p. xiii]. Steve, you say, "You do not need to know what a problem is in order to solve it." Yet, John, you're giving a workshop [at the Ericksonian Congress] called "What's the Problem?" Why ask, "What's the problem?" if you don't need to know what the problem is?

WEAKLAND: Why not? It doesn't always get in the way of resolving it.

DE SHAZER: Yeah. You just don't need to know what it is.

WEAKLAND: In a sense, you never know what it is.

HOYT: Is the problem the problem they're stating?

WEAKLAND: It's, "What do you see as a problem?"

HOYT: Steve, you wouldn't ask that at the beginning . . .

DE SHAZER: Not usually.

WEAKLAND: I wouldn't usually talk too much about solutions, but I might. I don't think you necessarily need to know what the problem is. I happen to think it's one way to go that can be very simple and productive, and will fit with the inclinations of most of your clients. So why not?

DE SHAZER: I think it's not necessary. And I use the word "necessary" very strongly. It's not necessary.

HOYT: How do you deal with patients, though, that come in, and they're more traditionally oriented and they feel they need to tell their story, and they need to present their problem, give their history, portray their tale?

DE SHAZER: I guess that I have to tell you, frankly, I don't get many of them. My hunch is that it is more of a therapist's concern about what they think the client thinks. I've found that, basically, my clients tend to be veterans, and they've told these stories before. And if I can get in and break into that story with exceptions questions, or a miracle question, we can get beyond it very, very quickly.

WEAKLAND: Okay, then you're saying or implying that a lot of your clients have told that story enough so they're tired of telling it and finding it doesn't go anywhere.

DE SHAZER: Yeah.

WEAKLAND: All right. But let me give you a further answer to my title. It's not aimed at solution-focused therapists. It's aimed at conventional therapists who think they know better than the client what the problem is. That's where it's really aimed.

DE SHAZER: Oh, that's the problem, all right. That's a problem.

HOYT: The psychoanalyst David Malan [1976], in his work on short-term psychodynamic therapy, writes about "valuable false solutions," where, in his model, the patient is doing something useful but not addressing an "underlying" or "more important" issue. Have you ever had instances where someone takes a solution and you feel that solution is going to be so limiting to them or hurtful to them that you'll try to talk them, maybe not out of the solution but try to get them to expand their options?

DE SHAZER: Hum . . . I don't think so.

WEAKLAND: When they're saying it's okay, even though I don't think it might be, as long as they say they think it's okay, and they can convince me that they think it's going to stabilize and continue to be okay, then that's okay.[2]

DE SHAZER: Malan still implies that he knows best. . . . And if we want to get into that frame, that's probably true with every case, then. *His* thing.

HOYT: "Do it my way." That's "The Art of Psychoanalysis," Haley's [1969] paper—the attitude that, "We still haven't addressed this deep enough, long enough, the way I think you should."

WEAKLAND: Yes.

HOYT: Yvonne Dolan, who gave a wonderful presentation the other day, has emphasized in some of her work with clients [Dolan, 1991], how important it is to let them tell their experiences, to validate and hear their history. And Cory Hammond the other day was talking about the importance he saw for abreaction with PTSD folks and MPDs.

DE SHAZER: I have no idea what these initials mean.

HOYT: Multiple Personality Disorder and Post-Traumatic Stress Disorder.

DE SHAZER: Okay.

---

[2]de Shazer (1991, p. 112) has described the general characteristics of well-formed goals, the features of solutions that affirmatively answer the question, "How do we know when to stop meeting like this?" They are: (1)small rather than large; (2) salient to clients; (3) described in specific, concrete, behavioral terms; (4) achievable within the practical contexts of clients' lives; (5) perceived by the clients as involving their "hard work"; (6) described as the "start of something" and not as the "end of something"; and (7) treated as involving new behavior(s) rather than the absence or cessation of existing behavior(s).

HOYT: Is there a time when people need to talk through their feelings with the therapist? "Working through," some people would call it.

WEAKLAND: Oh, yeah. I'll give you an answer to that in my framework. If somebody has kept it all to themselves, then to talk to a therapist is a new behavior.

DE SHAZER: Right.

WEAKLAND: And then it can be useful. If they've talked to three other therapists, let alone six relatives and 42 in-laws, then it don't amount to shit.

DE SHAZER: Then, it's problem talk; it's problem-maintaining behavior already.

HOYT: It's stabilizing rather than progressive.[3]

DE SHAZER: Yes. I guess that I'm going to go more indirectly on an answer for that. Some years ago, we talked to a whole bunch of people that had terminal diagnoses, cancer, from six months to 15 to 20 years before. So they should have been dead a long time. And a common feature we found running throughout the cases was that they didn't talk to other people about the cancer.

HOYT: They didn't create a social world that would reinforce destruction.

DE SHAZER: Yeah, one of them told me very plainly that she got up and went back to work the next day after she got this terminal diagnosis.

WEAKLAND: By God, that's interesting. You'd never find this out from reading Bernie Siegel [1986].

DE SHAZER: We didn't have enough cases, and I couldn't get the funding, but . . .

HOYT: If there's one exception, one . . .

WEAKLAND: It opens the door, but the people who control the money and things won't recognize that it opens the door.

DE SHAZER: They all had goals. They all went back to work. They all followed doctor's orders—until they stopped taking doctor's orders.

HOYT: I saw a tape of Norman Cousins describing an interview with a woman who was eight years after her diagnosis. She was a nice, little, blue-haired old lady, very polite. And she said, "The doctor told me that I had six months to live." And Norman Cousins said, "And what

---

[3]Drawing on the work of Gergen and Gergen (1983, 1986), in *Putting Difference to Work* de Shazer (1991, p. 92) describes three narrative types: (1) *progressive* narratives that justify the conclusion that progress is being made toward goals, (2) *stabilizing* narratives that justify the conclusion that life is unchanging, and (3) *digressive* (or *regressive*) narratives that justify the conclusion that life is moving away from goals.

did you say to him then?" And she said, "I told him to go fuck himself!" (*laughter*)

DE SHAZER: To me, that fits the stereotype of these successes. We had this one, her husband had a terminal diagnosis of some sort. So she had been nursing him. And then she got her terminal diagnosis. And she said to the doctor, "I'm going to outlive that son-of-a-bitch." And she did . . . by 15 years. (*laughter*) Or another one of these. She was lying in the hospital and had just gotten this terminal diagnosis. And the Cancer Institute people come in and say, "I'm sure you're wondering, 'Why me?'" And the woman says, "No, actually, I'm not. Why not me?"

WEAKLAND: Because it makes exactly the same sort of logical sense.

HOYT: Yeah. I see taking history as being very destructive, most of the time. That is, so many people look at the past, and it's problem talk. The emphasis is on history and diagnosis of problems, rather than the future or the resources.

WEAKLAND: I've been more and more convinced that every one of these things is quite unique.

HOYT: Other than the money, what's the biggest impediment? How do you get people to make the shift, get mental health professionals to see it?

DE SHAZER: Well, I think that I have a somewhat facetious answer and that is that they're not "mental health," they're "mental illness" professionals. It's not a mental health industry; it's a mental illness industry.

WEAKLAND: Yes.

DE SHAZER: We're in doublespeak.

HOYT: Yes.

DE SHAZER: But I'm rather puzzled by this in some ways.

WEAKLAND: Would part of that be that people, therefore, that get into it, by and large need dependents?

DE SHAZER: I think they need to see themselves as being wrapped up in something important.

WEAKLAND: Certainly, one line of that is, "Those poor, damaged people need me."

DE SHAZER: Right.

HOYT: Meaning, "and I'm not one of them."

WEAKLAND: That, too.

HOYT: And, "I'm different. I'm one of the healthy, wise ones."

WEAKLAND: Yeah. "Even if I was one before, now I have surmounted that and can bring help to them."

DE SHAZER: What I also think is involved, on another level entirely, is the misapplication of the scientific metaphor to this field. I don't know why Freud abandoned other metaphors. But I've been reading Freud. In his 1915 "Introductory Lectures on Psycho-analysis," Freud says, "The only thing there is, is the talk between doctor and patient." That's the only thing there is. That's all psychoanalysis is. Then he forgot that by the end of the third page, but he talked about that for several paragraphs.[4]

WEAKLAND: It might have changed the course of history.

DE SHAZER: So it was becoming medical, becoming scientific—to me, in an inappropriate way, because that science then got captured by this positivistic mode of science, which we now call "science," which is a very small part of something that might be called science. Science was quite different 200 years ago. And, in our world, research has narrowed down to this A versus B business. And all that complicates the picture.

WEAKLAND: By and large, I have a strong impression that it is only people like psychologists and sociologists who are concerned to be "scientific." Scientists aren't concerned about this. They go ahead and do their work.

HOYT: They're interested in answers.

WEAKLAND: They're interested in problems and answers, and maybe even in procedures, but they don't sit around thinking about "scientific."

DE SHAZER: Right.

WEAKLAND: They don't seem to be worried about it.

DE SHAZER: Yeah. But it becomes necessary to worry about it if you have a misapplied model. So if you are applying some theory of oranges, and you have apples in your hand, then you've got to really worry about your theory, you see.

HOYT: Let me stay with this idea. In training people, what stumbling blocks do you see people having in learning to be solution-focused?

WEAKLAND: Are we getting fresh people or trained, already "properly" trained people?

HOYT: What are the stumbling blocks with each of those two?

WEAKLAND: Getting fresh people, it's a helluva lot easier.

---

[4]Freud's words (1915/1961, p. 17): "Nothing takes place in a psycho-analytic treatment but an interchange of words . . . the patient talks . . . the doctor listens. . . . Words were originally magic and to this day words have retained much of their ancient magical power. By words one person can make another blissfully happy or drive him to despair. . . . Words provoke affects and are in general the means of mutual influence among men. Thus we shall not depreciate the use of words in psychotherapy and we shall be pleased if we can listen to the words that pass between the analyst and his patient."

DE SHAZER: Yeah, usually. I can train an engineer in a relatively short period of time, or a computer scientist.

HOYT: So what's the baggage that "mental illness" professionals need to let go of?

WEAKLAND: I'd say that, just to begin with, there's a body of "knowledge" and a point of view that goes along with it, both of which have been acquired at considerable cost and, therefore, people have got a large investment in it.[5]

DE SHAZER: And people don't, we haven't trained ourselves to pay attention to what works.

WEAKLAND: That is true.

DE SHAZER: And even people who have been in the field for a long time and have lots of "experience" get married to their theories, as we all do. But they won't pay attention to what works. Even stuff they do. So I think that what's really difficult, to me, with the older, more experienced practitioners, usually, is that they know all this stuff about what works but they don't know they know it. And they get hung up on looking at what doesn't work. It's good to know what doesn't work, but it's really helpful to know what does.

HOYT: I think this may be a benefit of this managed-care movement that's come in—even though it has some problems, there is the idea of accountability [Hoyt, in press]. They're not going to pay therapists for long, inefficient treatment. In some way, people are going to have to start looking at what works and what doesn't work. Even if all the altruistic reasons don't motivate people, being told, "We're only going to pay you if it works," may bring people around.

DE SHAZER: Judgments of what works are good. Who's making the judgments? I hope it's the clients.

HOYT: I hope so. That's a good point.

DE SHAZER: I think we have enough evidence from various research projects that therapists are very bad judges of what works. You contributed to that literature and so have I.

WEAKLAND: That's the other end of the thing I'm talking about. It's, "We know better than they do."

HOYT: I was actually the principal investigator on the single-session

---

[5]In his essay "Myths about Brief Therapy; Myths of Brief Therapy," Weakland (1990) describes some of the assumptions and belief systems that constrain practice and often promote unnecessary complexity. In a related vein, Hoyt (1985, 1990, in press) has discussed some of the factors—including the belief that "more is beter," theoretical obligations, financial payoffs, emotional entanglements, and reactance against being required to work briefly—that may interfere with efficient practice.

therapy project with Moshe Talmon and Bob Rosenbaum [Hoyt, Rosenbaum, & Talmon, 1992; Rosenbaum, Hoyt, & Talmon, 1990; Talmon, 1990]. And we asked people, "In terms of the problem that you came in with, are you satisfied or unsatisfied? What do you see as different?" And so it was really client-centered, rather than us giving a rating.

WEAKLAND: That's what makes the difference.

DE SHAZER: It's really amazing to think that you have to ask the customer about whether he got what he wanted or not.

WEAKLAND: Just within the last six months, I've seen a flyer come from some analytic-connected institution in the [San Francisco] Bay Area, in which one of the workshops is titled—let's see how close I can reproduce it—"Resolving the Problem of Desire for Early Termination."

HOYT: I saw that, too.

WEAKLAND: It's dealing with a problem that clients have without even knowing they have it, and it's important to cure that one, or nothing else can be cured.

HOYT: It's to keep them in.

DE SHAZER: Must prevent "flight into health," because they're flying around there with their eyes closed, and they never know what they're going to run into!

HOYT: Do you notice any gender differences? In your clinic, do women want longer or do men want longer therapy?

WEAKLAND: Oh, I've noticed gender differences everywhere.

DE SHAZER: My father told me all about that. He still notices and he's 85!

WEAKLAND: My father didn't tell me a thing, but I notice some myself.

HOYT: People have come up to me at workshops and said—I've heard this on several occasions—"Brief therapy is more of a masculine energy or a male endeavor. It's fixing things. It's problem-solving. It's not relationship and nurturing and holding and unfolding."

WEAKLAND: And you're asking us questions about what's the difficulty in getting people trained in working this way?

DE SHAZER: You've got your answer. Just like every client, you've got your answer already.

WEAKLAND: My God, we've got all this garbage, and they're acting like it's serious.

HOYT: I think it's a confusion of their interests and the client's interests.

DE SHAZER: I hear some of that sometimes, too. And I usually try to have a tape of Insoo [Berg—de Shazer's wife and colleague] along with me in my workshops. And she's pretty obviously different gender-wise, if nothing else. And then they get a little puzzled by that, the people who ask this question, they get a little puzzled. And then they say after I've puzzled them by showing Insoo's tapes, then they say, "What you two do doesn't even look like therapy."

HOYT: So you've heard that too?

WEAKLAND: I see people come up with all sorts of cockamamie ways of saying, "Can I somehow keep from having to take this seriously?" Which I assume means it's making some sense to them, but they're scared of it somehow.

DE SHAZER: That's a pretty common reaction, actually. When people watch our tapes, they frequently find what we do to be unbelievable. I always start my workshops with, "You've got to be skeptical. And you probably can't be more skeptical than I am, and I'm going to remind you to be skeptical, if anybody starts to go too far in the other direction." I always start with this. "If somebody had told me about this model 15 years ago, I would have called the men in the white coats. This can't work. And every day I'm surprised, but it does work. And I still am. It's not logical in some way."

HOYT: I think the simpler you keep it, the more the client's resources can be utilized, and so it's ultimately respectful to let them access what they have.

WEAKLAND: It's a helluva lot more respectful than knowing better than the client what ails them, which I think is the most basic comparison. And it's what the whole damn other psychiatric and psychothera-peutic scheme is based on.

HOYT: What taught you this? Was there a moment when you got it?

WEAKLAND: Jesus, how did I find that out? I think I found that out—I must have gotten primed some by Milton, but I didn't recognize it, and by getting tired by what I knew of psychodynamics. But I think what really did it for me was time with the early family therapists where we started out with something that we thought was new and differ-ent. And within five years, I was starting to read articles like "After Only a Year of Family Therapy, the Nature of the Problem Was Becoming Clarified." And I thought, Jesus Christ, we've gone and copied the worst thing about the analytic movement at several times their pace. And that's what pushed me toward brief therapy. And, brief therapy, one of the main things was, "What's the present problem?" and stopping looking around and behind and under it and second guessing. That's the real thing. I think that's as close as I can come.

HOYT: How would you contrast that to long-term therapy?

WEAKLAND: The essence of long-term therapy is to create the illusion that you can make life not be one damn thing after another.

HOYT: Steve, was there something where you got the power of cooperation, the power of empowerment?

DE SHAZER: I guess it was when we started to listen to the clients and take them seriously, actually. And that was the discovery at some point, and I don't know when it was anymore, but I know it dawned on us in about '82 or started to dawn on us . . .

WEAKLAND: Let me interrupt one second. After he tells you this, you need to go back and ask him one thing, because he said something that sounded very plain and simple, but I think it's very complicated what it means.

HOYT: Let him tell this, and then you ask him.

WEAKLAND: I may forget it. But the phrase is, "Listen to the clients and take them seriously." So ask him about that later.

HOYT: Continue.

DE SHAZER: Somewhere about '82, we started to—let's see, what was the word I want to use—discipline our observations around what clients were telling us were their criteria for improvement and success. And what they said was strikingly different from what even we, as brief therapists, thought it should be. And it was amazing, the "trivial" things they said made the difference sometimes, and that they weren't connected to whatever goddamn complaint they brought in. They'd list 12 criteria for measuring that things were better since the previous session, and 11 of them had nothing to do with the complaint. And it all seemed to me, up to that point, that the job of the therapist was the presenting problem and resolving that. That's the job. Plain and simple. Well, yeah, except if the client doesn't think it's resolved; in other words, it's not resolved. And the strangest things resolve "problems." They all fit the rule in that they're doing something different or at least seeing something different, which is doing something different.

HOYT: We saw that in our single-session project, where not only did the main complaint problem get solved, but 60 or 70% of the patients also described what we called "ripple effects" with other problems clearing up or improving.

DE SHAZER: In our telephone calls to them later on, we found strikingly more oddball things that we couldn't possibly have predicted. And we learned that we couldn't predict anything.

HOYT: Despite that, are there categories of patients that you've found your approach doesn't work with?

DE SHAZER: I wish there was a category like that.

HOYT: Then you could predict it and say . . .

DE SHAZER: Then I'd have a project I could send John to work on. (*laughter*) John would love to have a project like this, wouldn't you? I would love to have a project like that. I would like to say, "This is a special category of something. And this is a 'something.'"

HOYT: Anorexics or tall people or something.

DE SHAZER: Yeah, something that we could identify as a "something." And there seems to be no way to get at that. I have not found it in 25 years.

HOYT: How about the category being people who have desire for long-term therapy or long-term relationship with the therapist—it may not be "therapy."

WEAKLAND: Even that, I think if you assembled what you thought was a bunch of them and started to talk to them a little bit, you would probably find your category falling apart. Rather rapidly.

DE SHAZER: Yeah. We'd have more exceptions to the rule than examples of the rule. I think, for me anyway, our practice suggests that the sooner you can ask the miracle question,[6] the less likely you're going to get into that trouble. The sooner you can get an answer, of course.

WEAKLAND: And the next thing you know, somebody is going to call up and immediately after they say "Brief Family Therapy Center," they're going to ask the miracle question.

DE SHAZER: Well, I don't think it'd work that way, because you have to respond properly. It's not the one step.

WEAKLAND: He's still holding on to some threads of complexity.

HOYT: When you say "respond properly," what's your thought behind that? Is there a certain thing that makes it "properly"?

[6]The Miracle Question: "Suppose that one night, while you were asleep, there was a miracle and this problem was solved. How would you know? What would be different?" (de Shazer, 1988, p. 5). A number of other elegantly simple techniques designed to focus on the construction of useful solutions include the "Crystal Ball Technique" (de Shazer, 1985, pp. 81–92) which has patients visualize successful, complaint-free futures; and various "skeleton key" interventions, such as the "First Session Formula Task" (de Shazer, 1985, p. 137), which tells patients: "Between now and the next time we meet, I would like you to observe, so that you can describe to me next time, what happens in your [family, life, marriage, relationship] that you want to continue to have happen." Rather than tailoring each intervention to the particular client, a generic or invariant task is assigned that paradoxically directs the client toward his/her/their own individual strength, success, and solution.

DE SHAZER: No, it really depends on the client and what they're telling you. You have to respond properly for them. You have to take it seriously. There's a case I had recently, he's a borderline street person and long-term drinker. And I asked him the miracle question. And we had this wonderful discussion for 25 minutes, and he sticks really, really nicely to the topic; what the miracle might be and what he might be doing the day after and all these other things. And I'm going with this and trying to expand it to his wife and so on. And then I asked him one of our scaling questions where a 10 stands for, "He'd do anything to get this miracle to happen" and a zero, "Well, if it happens, it happens." And I say, "Where are you on this?" And he says, "Oh, zero." That's when I said to myself, "Oh, no. Now what?"

WEAKLAND: And he says, "Can't you give me a 0.5?" (*laughter*)

DE SHAZER: Right. Then he says he could not possibly stand the idea of winning $35 million in the lottery. $250,000, that he could handle. But not $35 million. He wouldn't know what the hell to do. So what's the first step? That "zero" meant something entirely different to him than it meant to me. "Oh, no, I'm not going to get my expectations that high." That's what that meant to him.

WEAKLAND: "Well, suppose you woke up one morning and half a miracle would have happened while you were asleep. What would you notice? What would tell you that half a miracle had happened?"

DE SHAZER: Or, in another version, there was this guy in Leipzig recently—he was already in therapy—so I somehow got into asking him scaling questions starting with, "Are things better?" And we talked that around several times and using a scale from –10 to 0, he'd gotten up to –5 sometimes. And we explored when they were. And then I asked the miracle question; he couldn't answer. He had no idea. And so I said, "Well, maybe this miracle brings you up to –5."

HOYT: Brings you to where you are.

DE SHAZER: Well, he reached –5 once in a while. And he says, "Wow, yeah, and it also happens sometimes when. . . ." And he went on to tell us about two more times in his life when he gets to –5. He describes his trip to Cologne, which was a wonderful place for him. He'd never been in the old west part of Germany. He'd never gotten out of the East Zone before in his life. And as he describes this, I say, "You, know –5 sounds an awful lot like 0 to me." Okay, so there's this half-miracle. Sounds good enough.

HOYT: And he's happy?

DE SHAZER: Oh, yeah. He said he could stay at –5 forever and it would be okay.

HOYT: You wanted me to ask about "listening to clients and taking them seriously."

WEAKLAND: Yeah. I think that sounds very simple, but I don't think it is simple. I think we've made a beginning on that right here. I think it's a very complicated operation.

DE SHAZER: Yeah, it is. It's so easy to read into . . . you've got to watch out for this. People, therapists in particular, I guess, are taught to read between the lines . . .

HOYT: "Listen with a third ear . . ."

DE SHAZER: Diagnosis, interpretation, understanding.

WEAKLAND: "Perceptiveness."

DE SHAZER: Yeah. To me, however, the danger of reading between the lines is that there might be nothing there. So you've just got to listen to what the client says. So just stick on the lines of things. The client says that getting out of bed on the south side makes for a better day than getting out on the north side. Well then, goddammit, tell him to get out of bed on the south side. As crazy as it sounds.

HOYT: If it works, don't fix it. Do more.

DE SHAZER: Yeah, do more of it. I had one sort of like that. He moved the bed over so he couldn't get out on the north side. He'd run into the wall trying to get out on the north side of the bed. That would be a different challenge to have, instead of a perceptivity training, to have a "simplicity training" or "beginner's mind"—a "denseness" training.

HOYT: "Keep it simple."

DE SHAZER: "Stupidity training."

HOYT: Maybe the fact that you weren't trained in psychology originally. . .

WEAKLAND: That's a great help.

DE SHAZER: I think that my training in music helps.

WEAKLAND: Ask him a little more about "taking it seriously," because I have this feeling that doesn't just mean one simple thing, that may mean maybe a lot of variations on that point. Taking it seriously. And I got your example; that's clear. But don't think it always means the side of the bed, that sort of thing.

DE SHAZER: Probably not.

HOYT: What else would you think about "seriously"?

WEAKLAND: Well, I think of an interview I had with a couple who came in to see me very concerned about their daughter who was anorexic. She was 30 years old, married with kids, but anorexic. They were very anxious about her, practically couldn't sit still. I had this one interview, after which I was going to be away the next week. Dick [Fisch] saw them the next week. I came back, and Dick started out telling about something disastrous, but he was putting me on. The truth of the matter was, they came in looking and sounding very, very different. And we were both up in the air about what the hell had happened. So I listened to the tape and I'd gone over it again since, and I had another interview with them. And the three sessions were all we had. We wouldn't have needed to have the third, really. So, I tried to figure out what the hell had happened in the interview that I had with them. Basically, I think all that happened was, or the main thing that happened was, I listened to them and I took it seriously, but I took it seriously in a certain way. I was clearly listening to and appreciating their concerns, but I wasn't getting excited. I think that's the main thing. There were a couple other things that went along with that like they'd been running around from one doctor to another. I suggested that "certainly you may want to look for further doctors, but since the ones you've been finding have generally been unsatisfactory, you might want to give it a little more consideration before your next decision on a doctor for her." And I proposed that we could meet in two weeks, since I wouldn't be there, but if they wanted they could meet with somebody else, which was two steps more concretely of the same sort as my general behavior. And as far as I could see, that was it.

HOYT: You took your sail out of their wind. (*laughter*)

WEAKLAND: At least, I kept my wind out of their sail.

HOYT: Yeah, okay. You didn't get on board and go with that problem.

WEAKLAND: No. But at the same time I didn't tell them, "Look, folks, you're making too much out of it. Calm down," or any of that sort of shit.

DE SHAZER: Exactly. A counterexample of taking it seriously is when clients come in and tell you, "This is the problem. And it's a big, heavy, monstrous problem." To you, it looks trivial. And you go and tell these people about all these other people who have more problems, or bigger or more awful ones.

WEAKLAND: Yeah. Yeah.

DE SHAZER: That's a counterexample.

HOYT: "You think you've got a problem . . ."

DE SHAZER: Yeah. A client tells you they've got a problem, then they've got a problem, and you better take it seriously. You also better take it seriously if they tell you they ain't got a problem. That's the other part of it. He comes in and somebody sent him because he drinks too much. He says he doesn't drink too much or it's not a problem. Leave it alone. Take it seriously.[7]

WEAKLAND: You're not going to deal with denial.

DE SHAZER: I'm going to deny the denial. You start to mess with that and you'll never work with him. Certainly, you'll never work with the drinking. If you help him get something out of therapy.

HOYT: What I'm getting from what you're saying is it's best to accept that what the patient is communicating about is accurate. And it's our job to figure out what it's accurate about.[8]

WEAKLAND: That's an interesting way of putting it, rather than converting them.

DE SHAZER: I'm not even sure about the last part . . . just, "it's accurate."

HOYT: It's accurate.

DE SHAZER: Yeah. It's accurate. And that's all there is.

HOYT: But if we're going to be of service to them, not just to take them seriously and listen, what do we add beyond listening?

DE SHAZER: The seriously. Taking them seriously. See, I think a lot of people listen, but they don't take them seriously.

WEAKLAND: I think that's probably true.

DE SHAZER: For example, we recently heard a therapist who reported some nice stories. From the stories, it's clear the therapist listened. But from some of the instructions and steps that then got presented, it is clear the clients aren't being taken seriously.

WEAKLAND: Is it possible that, once again, maybe not as blatantly as some places, we've got a therapist who is doing one thing, and describing it quite differently?

DE SHAZER: My experience of this is, yeah, he does a marvelous job at storytelling, but the theory, the rule-making theory construction stuff is not his ballgame. He's telling us all these rules and steps and stuff he's never done.

WEAKLAND: Okay, but what I'm saying is he doesn't have to tell us the rules one way or the other. What he ought to be telling us is how he does what he does.

DE SHAZER: I was thinking, sitting there, during a couple of these stories— show us two segments of videotape.

---

[7]Solution-focused ways of working *with* the problem drinker are discussed at length in Berg and Miller (1992); also, see Chapter 5 by Miller in this volume.
[8]This is a paraphrase of a statement from Schnarch (1991, p. 344).

HOYT: At least, let us decide what really happened rather than filtering it through a . . .

DE SHAZER: Or, at least, all the points could be made with two videos of about seven minutes each.

WEAKLAND: You don't get either the appreciative audience nor the keynote speaker's fee for 15 minutes of videotape.

DE SHAZER: I know, that's why I don't get those jobs.

WEAKLAND: I seldom get them either, partly because I get up there and I don't have any answers, and I'm struggling with questions in my mind. And I'm not "inspirational," as they say.

HOYT: I think this touches on the "respectfully" and the "seriously," in a way. In the *Difference* [de Shazer, 1991, p. 33] book, you say, "The use of strategy and tactics, meant to suggest careful planning on the part of the therapist, implies at the very least that the therapist and the client are involved in a contest." And you, John, in your Foreword to the book, you stated your disagreement, saying: "At a specific level, I do not think that use of the term 'strategy' necessarily implies a contest between therapist and client; indeed, I would propose that de Shazer carries on his therapeutic conversations strategically" [p. viii]. What's up?

WEAKLAND: Simple. My view is somewhat different, at least from the views that Steve expressed there. My view is expanded a little bit more in the paper at Tulsa last summer [Weakland, 1993], in which I talk about what I mean by "strategic."

DE SHAZER: There's no disagreement with what you mean. It's the word. It's the extra baggage the word carries with it that I'm objecting to.

HOYT: The word "strategic"?

DE SHAZER: Yeah.

HOYT: What is the extra baggage?

DE SHAZER: It's the military metaphor that's attached to it.

WEAKLAND: Oh, but I cannot be responsible for what a bunch of other people are attaching to things always.

DE SHAZER: It comes with it automatically. That's why I like the word "purposeful," rather than "strategic."

HOYT: Were you aware of the military . . . ?

WEAKLAND: I was not aware, if that is what he is referring to.

DE SHAZER: That's what I'm referring to. Trying to refer to.

WEAKLAND: Well, it wasn't referred to sufficiently clearly in that quotation.

DE SHAZER: That could be.

HOYT: You said a "contest" in strategy. Do you mean a "combat" in the way of military?

DE SHAZER: Yeah, contest, military.

HOYT: It's like when people talk about their "therapeutic armamentarium."

WEAKLAND: I never do that.

HOYT: Other people do.

WEAKLAND: Well, what am I going to do then with all of the words that formerly were good words and people have done similar things with them so that they all aren't worth a shit anymore?

DE SHAZER: You have to keep making up new ones.

WEAKLAND: Then they'll do the same thing again.

HOYT: It's hard to be politically correct in these times.

DE SHAZER: We want to be politically incorrect.

WEAKLAND: I'm going to have to move to France and put it up as a project to the French Academy.

DE SHAZER: We have always this competition of winning/losing that gets attached to "strategy," because of this, the implication of underhanded dealings, the backroom dealings, the dirty guys behind the mirror, and so on. Which I think all come out of this military "strategic" word.

WEAKLAND: That's where I would disagree. I think they are there, and I think they get attached to that word, but I don't think they come out of it. I think they come out of something much deeper, which is that therapists want to have power without acknowledging it, influence without acknowledging it. They want to be in there, superior and influential, with perfectly clean hands. And as long as that's the case, they will corrupt the hell out of any word you use.

DE SHAZER: Yeah, probably. That's probably true. And it's probably true with every word, absolutely. So if the word is easier to hear—I'm using the word "purposeful"—it's less distracting than the word "strategic." When I stopped using the word "strategic" and started using the word "purposeful," I got into less problems with my audience.

WEAKLAND: Okay.

HOYT: It's more "user friendly." It doesn't set off the "Is this manipulation? Is this somebody getting over on someone?"

DE SHAZER: Right. It's clearly manipulation. It's got purpose behind it.

HOYT: Okay. In terms of listening to them seriously, that's what I was trying to get at. The purpose is to take them seriously, but the purpose is still to have influence?

DE SHAZER: No, the purpose is to reach their goal. And it's therapists . . .

HOYT: Is this one of those kinds of binds that we started talking about, like connection versus independence? It's like in one way, we're empowering them, but we're influencing them.

WEAKLAND: We care about influence. Yeah, but that's okay. This is the old hypnotic argument, where on the one side you have all those people who say, "You hypnotize somebody, you make them dependent." And on the other side is, "It depends on what you do with the hypnosis with the subject." You may use it to empower them. You may make them dependent, but it's not inherent in "hypnosis." Just as there's nothing inherent in "influence." It depends on what kind of influence it is.

DE SHAZER: There's always influence.

WEAKLAND: Sure.

DE SHAZER: You can't not influence.

HOYT: Is there an inherent language paradox here? To "influence someone" implies having a power over them, but you want to influence someone to be more powerful.

DE SHAZER: I think that in any conversation, everybody is influencing everybody else.

WEAKLAND: Always.

DE SHAZER: And "power" is a bad concept.

WEAKLAND: I think "power" is a bad concept because it is generally not very useful. But I don't think that it is an idea that will corrupt the world like Bateson seemed to think toward the end.

DE SHAZER: No, I agree that the idea of unilateral control is not possible.

WEAKLAND: No, that's true.

DE SHAZER: Stalin proved that.

HOYT: But constructing a reality that's going to make a difference is different than power; it's constructing.

DE SHAZER: And it takes at least two people to construct a reality. One person, by himself, might construct this reality, but it would probably be a psychotic one. It takes two to make it a viable reality.

HOYT: If you mean a social reality.

DE SHAZER: Yeah.

WEAKLAND: Is there any other?

DE SHAZER: There is no other.

HOYT: Semantically, there's not. But what I do in my head is real in my head, to me.

DE SHAZER: Yeah. But I don't know about. . . . See, that's the whole point.

HOYT: You know the one about the three baseball umpires that are disputing? This is my favorite constructivist story. The first one says, "I call 'em as I see 'em." And the second guy says, "Well, I call them as they are." And the third guy says, "They ain't nothing until I call 'em!" And that's, I think, what we're saying. Until we call them, it's not. Things come into reality by being said.

DE SHAZER: Right. Wittgenstein goes into all this stuff about the slipperiness of a private language. You can't depend on it. You can't count on it. You can't count on anything inside until you bring it out, test it out. Then, as soon as you do that, you're changing it.

HOYT: Where is our field going? Do you have any prediction? Any sense of it?

DE SHAZER: I'm no good at predicting. I know that. I've proved that to myself beyond a shadow of a doubt.

WEAKLAND: I may make an attempt at describing where it is, if I get geared up between now and April, or at least where I see it is. Where it's going, I don't think I'd try that.

HOYT: Where do you think it is?

WEAKLAND: Well, in terms of some things we know and some confidences we have, at the best, it is a helluva long way from the old days; but in terms of how it has become bureaucratized, stupefied, taken over, the extent to which people are willing to accept, both practically and intellectually, a sort of second or third place role for it, it's gone way the hell downhill. People work in a hospital at a level more or less that of a nurse in relation to the doctor, that sort of thing, when it should be changing the fundamentals of the whole field.

DE SHAZER: I think that we see some . . . there is some more, maybe a warped picture. There's more change to the whole field in Europe than there has been in the United States. There's more influence of systems theory in Europe. They take it a little more seriously. Well, like, family therapy became a method in the United States. Brief therapy is a method on the menu.

WEAKLAND: I see the main change having taken place when things just got far enough so you could begin to sell family therapy and make some sort of a living at it.

HOYT: That was the beginning of . . .

WEAKLAND: That was the beginning of, "Let's see where we can make a quick sale. Let's 'establish standards,' certifications, freeze them." I mean, once you've established them, you've largely frozen them, whether you do that deliberately or not.

DE SHAZER: Narrow the pool of potential influence in the field, by saying, "Well, you are left-handed, you can't come in. We don't allow left-handed people any more."

WEAKLAND: And worse yet is if you're left-minded.

DE SHAZER: Yeah.

WEAKLAND: Say a little more about what goes on in Europe. Usually, all I hear is what I hear from Paul [Watzlawick], and mainly what Paul will say is, "A great deal is going on that you should know about." We say, "We're open." Then he says, "But you don't read German."

DE SHAZER: There's lots going on in Germany that nobody knows about. I think that there's more within the various mental health professions. There's more influence of systemic thinking, rather than in family therapy being one approach on the menu. There's less rigidity about some of these things. I have to go in another direction somewhat. In the United States, I think that brief therapists are still seen as a radical nut fringe. On one hand and simultaneously on the other, we're both archconservative and archradical. And family therapy has become this something that is organized and run by this organization over there. And hypnosis is organized and run by this organization over here. And somehow these two are different. I don't know how, but anyway. In Europe, although they have separate societies—there's an Ericksonian Society and so on and so on—there seems to be a wider variety of people who are in these various societies, and they don't seem to have any feuds (this is a general rule; there are exceptions) the same as they are in the United States about territory and right and wrong. There are some other feuds, but they're different. There are some right and wrong difficulties, but there's no such thing, for instance, as a one-model allegiance. It's an allegiance to a way of thinking.

HOYT: Maybe that's even a reflection of multiculturalism, all the different languages and . . .

DE SHAZER: Well, I can just stick within Germany and say that. So I don't know that it's that. I think that they take the idea of general systems theory more seriously. Not completely, but more seriously. And I think John and I are pretty radical on that. We probably took it more seriously than most people, word for word sometimes.

HOYT: Is there something about "American character," to use that broad stereotype, that makes people here want simple answers or ten-step programs? Or 12-step? (*laughter*)

DE SHAZER: Or 12-step or 5-step. I'm not sure I'd go that direction in describing the difference. I think that our psychotherapy business became overattached to the medical establishment. Part of it is that, and then it becomes this organization stuff. [Murray] Bowen was right. We shouldn't have organized at all. If nothing else, one thing I've always agreed with him about, maybe the only thing I've agreed with Bowen about, is we shouldn't organize this field. Don't do it! And he was saying—well, I don't know when he started saying that—but the first time I heard it, I agreed completely. Don't do it! Don't do it!

HOYT: I don't know how we're going to take it back. I think, if anything, we're getting more organized in the managed-care movement and the licensing bureaus and the different schools of therapy and the certification and education business.

DE SHAZER: And it's all the same kind of thing. And the Europeans, they like to have these little certificates, too. But it's educational, rather than job training.

WEAKLAND: Now, why are the psychiatrists in Europe doing therapy instead of giving pills and doing esoteric biochemical and brain anatomy research?

DE SHAZER: I'm not sure. Obviously, it's not all of them, but more than I meet here in the United States. I think they see themselves as doctors, and they're healing. I suspect medical training is different. These guys all, the ones I'm thinking of in particular, see themselves as healing, and they're afraid of medicines. They stay away from pills.

HOYT: In the front of [Furman and Ahola's] *Solution Talk*, Carlos Sluzki [1992] writes a Foreword, and he has sort of a warning. He talks about, if you really take the solution approach, how radical it is. He puts it in the tradition of antipsychiatry and R. D. Laing and David Cooper.

DE SHAZER: I'm anti antipsychiatry, too.

HOYT: But he says, if you really take this seriously, it's going to raise hell in traditional institutions. How you talk about people, what you chart, what you do; the whole egalitarian versus authoritarian structure breaks.

DE SHAZER: I agree completely.

WEAKLAND: Oh, yeah, if you take our version seriously, that would happen.

DE SHAZER: Any version.

WEAKLAND: And frankly, I think that's what should happen.

HOYT: I wanted to ask you just a couple more questions. My question is, What's your cutting edge? What are you interested in now? What are you investigating? What's got you excited?

WEAKLAND: Not a helluva lot, to tell you the truth. I'm tired. I've been seeing things going the way we've been talking about for many a year, and I've been putting my oar in to try to see things go differently. And I feel like I've been swimming upstream against a current that's probably faster than my stroke is.

HOYT: What would you want people to take from your work?

WEAKLAND: What would I want them to take from my work? I think that's fairly simple. Which is you look around the world, try to understand behavior, look at how people are dealing with each other first, and don't get away from that until you've given it a good look.

DE SHAZER: Don't let the theory get in the way. Theories will blind you.

WEAKLAND: Also, don't let the theory that "everything is individual" get in your way. Don't let the theory that "everything is genetic" get in your way. Look at what the hell people are doing right here and now where you can look at them.

DE SHAZER: Don't even let the theory of "everything is not individual" get in your way.

WEAKLAND: Okay. Fair enough.

DE SHAZER: It might be individual this time.

HOYT: What in Zen they would say, "Have a beginner's mind."

DE SHAZER: Yeah.

WEAKLAND: I think this emphasis is still fair because it is very plain that the medical way of looking and the individual psychology way of looking have gotten tremendous emphasis and support compared to anything that's gone with looking at the way people deal with each other on all fronts.

DE SHAZER: Absolutely. They also say in Zen, "Before enlightenment, a mountain is a mountain. After enlightenment, a mountain is a mountain."

HOYT: What mountains are you climbing?

DE SHAZER: John's swimming this river; I'm climbing a mountain.

WEAKLAND: He's got a better deal. Unless it's a new volcano, that mountain isn't rising up as he's climbing.

DE SHAZER: But some of the side trails are so interesting.

WEAKLAND: That's always a possibility.

DE SHAZER: And you go back down to see something.

HOYT: There's also the pleasure in climbing, not just to get to the top.

DE SHAZER: And I like to take a walk around it now and then. I don't have any particular place I'm going.

WEAKLAND: I think you asked the question. I'm not excited about this, but there's a couple things I'd like to see happen. I would like to see a few more young people interested in things I'm interested in that would be likely to hang around our Institute. And I would like to see three, two, or even one person on our board of directors who would read that little piece by Carlos [Sluzki] and be in favor of it. I might think there might be some future in the Institute.

DE SHAZER: You know, 22 years ago, we could have had a Brief Therapy conference in Palo Alto, and we could have all fit into a VW bus. We'd need a little bigger bus now. It's grown faster than the population growth curve. But I think it's important for the field for there to be some outside to the field. And I think you've done it and our group has done it. We've been outside and inside simultaneously. We've been out in the margins. Not quite family therapy. And we're not quite brief therapy, MRI style, and you're not quite brief therapy, Milwaukee style. We're sort of always around the edge of things. Well, Insoo says I'm completely untrained, which is true. And John's completely untrained.

WEAKLAND: Well, yeah.

DE SHAZER: And the field has to keep somebody out there; there has to be an outside, somebody in the margins. Family therapy would not have been an idea, much less a fact, if there had not been some outsiders. You, Jay [Haley], Gregory [Bateson]—untrained therapists.

HOYT: Do you see these outsiders today?

DE SHAZER: Well, they're being legislated out of existence.

WEAKLAND: Because they're trying, certainly working very hard, giving them a bad time, if there are any out there.

DE SHAZER: I'm looking for them. You've got to get those people. You've got to keep getting them in somehow, so they can take a look at things. If you legislate everything and train everybody in the orthodoxy, then you're closing out. You've got to kill the field in order to save it, so to speak.

WEAKLAND: This is one time I think that might be apt.

HOYT: Are you writing another book?

DE SHAZER: Am I writing a book? Yeah, sure. I'm always writing a book.

HOYT: What's your next thought? What's it on?

DE SHAZER: I have no idea.

WEAKLAND: He'll tell you that after it gets written.

DE SHAZER: Yeah, when it's done. My basic writing method is to sit down and write, and it's free form, so to speak, in my own way of doing free form. And then I edit. Chop, chop, cut, paste. So I really don't know where it's going.

WEAKLAND: By God, that explains some things.

HOYT: You'll see when you get there. You may have a solution without knowing the problem. What would you want people to take out of your work, Steve, if you wrote no more?

DE SHAZER: I know what I don't want, and that's for anybody to develop some sort of rigid orthodoxies. I'm afraid of that. I'm always afraid of that. For me, it's a big point of concern. That there's a right way to do this and this. And to see my descriptions—and they've done this to me; I've probably done this to myself—to see my descriptions as prescriptions. So what I'd like, I suppose, is what I said earlier about listen and take them seriously. The "take them seriously" part. That's what I want people to take out of it is to take it seriously. And I suppose that the break between "problems" and "solutions," certainly that part. But I ain't dead yet.

WEAKLAND: Well, I'll tell you what I'd like to leave as a message: "Stay curious." And everybody is rushing like hell to try to get away from that.

DE SHAZER: Or, to put it another way, if the choice is between the therapist or the client being stupid, it should be the therapist. (*laughter*)

HOYT: Well, gentlemen, I think we've done it. I thank you both.

REFERENCES

Bateson, G., Jackson, D. D., Haley, J., & Weakland, J. H. (1956). Toward a theory of schizophrenia. *Behavioral Science, 1*, 251–264.

Berg, I. K., & Miller, S. D. (1992). *Working with the Problem Drinker: A Solution-Focused Approach*. New York: Norton.

de Shazer, S. (1982). *Patterns of Brief Family Therapy: An Ecosystemic Approach*. New York: Guilford.

de Shazer, S. (1985). *Keys to Solution in Brief Therapy*. New York: Norton.

de Shazer, S. (1988). *Clues: Investigating Solutions in Brief Therapy*. New York: Norton.

de Shazer, S. (1991). *Putting Difference to Work*. New York: Norton.

de Shazer, S. (1994). *Words Were Originally Magic*. New York: Norton.

Dolan, Y. M. (1991). *Resolving Sexual Abuse*. New York: Norton.

Dyson, F. J. (1988). *Infinite in All Directions*. New York: Harper & Row.

Fisch, R., Weakland, J. H., & Segal, L. (1983). *The Tactics of Change: Doing Therapy Briefly*. San Francisco: Jossey-Bass.

Freud, S. (1961). Introductory lectures on psycho-analysis. In J. Strachey (Ed. and Trans.), *The Standard Edition of the Complete Psychological Works of Sigmund Freud* (Vol. 15). London: Hogarth Press. (Originally published 1915)

Gergen, K. J., & Gergen, M. J. (1983). Narratives of the self. In T. R. Sabin & K. E. Scheibe (Eds.), *Studies in Social Identity*. New York: Praeger.

Gergen, K. J., & Gergen, M. J. (1986). Narratives form and the construction of psychological science. In T. R. Sabin (Ed.), *Narrative Psychology: The Storied Nature of Human Conduct*. New York: Praeger.

Haley, J. (1969). The art of psychoanalysis. In *The Power Tactics of Jesus Christ and Other Essays*. New York: Avon Books.

Haley, J. (Ed.). (1985). *Conversations with Milton H. Erickson, M.D.* (Vols. 1–3). New York: Triangle Press.

Herr, J. J., & Weakland, J. H. (1979). *Counseling Elders and Their Families: Practical Techniques for Applied Gerontology*. New York: Springer.

Hoyt, M. F. (1985). Therapist resistances to short-term dynamic psychotherapy. *Journal of the American Academy of Psychoanalysis, 13*, 93–112.

Hoyt, M. F. (1990). On time in brief therapy. In R. A. Wells & V. J. Giannetti (Eds.), *Handbook of the Brief Psychotherapies*. New York: Plenum.

Hoyt, M. F. (in press). *Brief Therapy and Managed Care: Selected Papers*. San Francisco: Jossey-Bass.

Hoyt, M. F., Rosenbaum, R., & Talmon, M. (1992). Planned single-session psychotherapy. In S. H. Budman, M. F. Hoyt, & S. Friedman (Eds.), *The First Session in Brief Therapy* (pp. 59–86). New York: Guilford.

Malan, D. H. (1976). *The Frontier of Brief Psychotherapy*. New York: Plenum.

Rosenbaum, R., Hoyt, M. F., & Talmon, M. (1990). The challenge of single-session therapies: Creating pivotal moments. In R. A. Wells & V. J. Giannetti (Eds.), *Handbook of the Brief Psychotherapies* (pp. 165–189). New York: Plenum.

Schnarch, D. M. (1991). *Constructing the Sexual Crucible: An Integration of Sexual and Marital Therapy*. New York: Norton.

Siegel, B. S. (1986). *Love, Medicine and Miracles*. New York: Harper & Row.

Sluzki, C. E. (1992). Foreword. In B. Furman & T. Ahola, *Solution Talk: Hosting Therapeutic Conversations* (pp. v–ix). New York: Norton.

Talmon, M. (1990). *Single Session Therapy*. San Francisco: Jossey-Bass.

Watzlawick, P., Weakland, J. H., & Fisch, R. (1974). *Change*. New York: Norton.

Weakland, J. H. (1990). Myths about brief therapy; myths of brief therapy. In J. K. Zeig & S. G. Gilligan (Eds.), *Brief Therapy: Myths, Methods, and Metaphors* (pp. 100–107). New York: Brunner/Mazel.

Weakland, J. H. (1991). Foreword. In S. de Shazer, *Putting Difference to Work* (pp. vii–ix). New York: Norton.

Weakland, J. H. (1993). Conversation—But What Kind? In S. Gilligan & R. E. Price (Eds.), *Therapeutic Conversations* (pp. 136–145). New York: Norton.

CHAPTER 3

Solution Talk
The Solution-Oriented Way of Talking about Problems

BEN FURMAN

TAPANI AHOLA

The term *brief therapy,* in its broadest sense, refers to any form of psychotherapy that aims to solve clients' problems in a significantly briefer period of time than is characteristic for traditional psychodynamically oriented, long-term therapy. Particularly within the family therapy movement, the term has been used to denote a distinct therapeutic tradition pioneered by Milton H. Erickson and further developed and elaborated by a number of groups and individuals. Major contributions to this field include, among others, the brief therapy approach of the Mental Research Institute (MRI) in Palo Alto (Fisch, Weakland, & Segal, 1982; Watzlawick, Weakland, & Fisch, 1974); the approach known as strategic therapy described by Jay Haley (1987) and Cloe Madanes (1982, 1984); the Milan approach of systemic family therapy (Boscolo, Cecchin, Hoffman, & Penn, 1987; Palazzoli, Boscolo, Cecchin, & Prata, 1978, 1980); Ericksonian hypnosis and brief therapy (Haley, 1973; Zeig & Lankton, 1989); solution-focused brief therapy developed by Steve de Shazer and the team at the Brief Family Therapy Center in Milwaukee (de Shazer et al., 1986; see also O'Hanlon & Weiner-Davis, 1989); and the therapeutic approaches of Michael White in Australia and David Epston in New Zealand (Epston, 1990; White & Epston 1990). All of these approaches are in some ways different from each other, yet they have much in common. One could argue that these brief therapies are characterized by a pragmatic stance that is focused on the future rather than the past.

The purpose of brief therapy is not to "understand" the cause of a given problem, but to find fertile ways of thinking about it and practical ideas to deal with it. Conventional psychiatric explanations involving presuppositions of underlying psychological problems, personality disorders, family disturbance, or any form of pathology are not favored. Either they are replaced with more acceptable explanations or the question of the cause of the problem is ignored altogether.

THE SOLUTION ORIENTATION

We believe that, whenever they meet with the intention of solving problems or resolving conflicts, people should feel comfortable and at ease. For this reason, we deliberately promote such an atmosphere by behaving informally ourselves: we offer coffee to clients, we use their first names, we readily give compliments, we encourage openness, and we encourage laughter by kidding and joking (Furman, 1990; Furman & Ahola, 1988). In our view, the conductor of the session should lead the conversation in such a way that the emphasis is on solutions rather than on problems. By this, we mean that the problem and other issues should be discussed in a manner that tends to generate and encourage optimism, collaboration, and trust in one's own resources. We have learned to talk with and about clients and their problems in a way that is respectful of all parties involved, including those not present at the session. We have developed a style of working with people that could be characterized as the joint negotiation of solutions. We use the term *solution talk* to refer to this manner of talking. (See Furman & Ahola, 1992, for a more thorough exploration of this concept.)

What follows is a compilation of solution-oriented conversational themes that we frequently use in our sessions. Each section includes an illustrative case sketch or story drawn from our experience with clients or other people. We have also included a compilation of specific questions that can be used to evoke the respective themes for conversation.

Inventing Names and Labels

When people talk about a problem, they need to call it by some name in order to avoid repeatedly giving a lengthy behavioral description of what actually happens. Names are useful in the sense that they allow us to refer to a complex problem with just one or a few words; unfortunately, however, names and labels also have their drawbacks. A name for a problem is rarely just an innocent description of the problem without any embedded implications of its origins, prognosis, or treatment. For example, the terms *borderline personality disorder* and *having trouble* can both be used to refer to an adolescent with multiple problems. The terms create very different impressions about the problem. Likewise, the term *depression* can be used to refer to the condition known in psychiatry as *major depression*, but there are many alternatives, such as *down in the dumps* or *being blue*. It is possible to develop even more inventive names, such as *doing one's life inventory*, *hatching*, or *latent joy*.

Case Example

We were invited to consult with a young woman who had recently divorced her husband and had been seeing a therapist for some months. After establishing that she had made much progress, we asked her what she wanted to achieve with her therapy. She said she wanted to be able to stand on her own feet. That, in turn, meant to her that she would not lose her temper with her four-year-old son, and she would be able to set limits with her former husband when he came around her house and behaved as if he still lived there. When asked what word she would like to use to describe this kind of behavior, she found it hard to answer. We asked if she knew of anybody who was like she wanted to be. She thought for a while, then said with a smile, "Kevin Costner." Since Kevin is a male name, it was agreed upon that her goal was to become "Kevina." When asked what she felt she had been like before she undertook her Kevina project, she said, "Roger Rabbit."

Sample Questions

- Do you have any nickname for this problem?
- Perhaps we should start by giving this problem a nice, optimistic name. What could it be?
- What would the old generation before the time of psychiatry and psychology have called this kind of problem?
- Well, we could use the term *weak ego* to describe this problem, but wouldn't saying "the person's strong ego is dormant" convey the same thing and yet sound nicer?

Comment

The main function of the new name is to help the client and other people involved with the problem get rid of the various negative implications associated with the conventional name. However, a well-chosen new name can simultaneously serve the purpose of making discussion of the problem easier and of acting as a springboard for creative new solutions. It should be emphasized that the new name for the problem should not undermine the seriousness of the problem. For example, one should not call drug abuse "exploring" or domestic violence "being temperamental." The new name should not become an excuse not to do anything about the problem, but should be a mutually agreeable term that enables people to become active in solving it.

Making Up Explanations

Diagnosis and explanation are overlapping concepts, since the name used in talking about a problem often implies ideas about its cause. Just like names, explanations can also stand in the way of solving problems. Causal explanations, particularly conventional psychological explanations, often imply blame, that is, they may be perceived as accusations. Blaming has the effect of destroying collaboration and creativity, as people unavoidably become defensive or angry.

In order to avoid what could be called the "accusatory explanations trap," one can deliberately bypass the whole issue of the cause of the problem by focusing on other themes instead, such as positive future visions, progress, or solutions. Another possibility is to talk about explanations in a solution-oriented way.

Case Example

"Jan," a boy of 12, was making trouble at school, as well as at home. His parents were at odds with him, and the family therapy he was attending with them was not giving results. In the consultation, we found out that the boy had a friend who was in even deeper trouble than he was. Some two years ago, this friend had been placed in a foster home due to alcoholism and other problems in his biological family. He had become Jan's best friend, and the two had been hanging out together ever since. Jan's parents, as well as the therapist, were convinced that the other boy was bad company for Jan. We suggested that Jan had taken this other boy under his wing and that his problems were due to the fact that he was so committed to helping the boy that he was willing to do almost anything, even things that parents and teachers would not approve of. This suggestion rang a bell in Jan. He told all of us about the many ways in which he had been helping this other boy. At the end of the session, it was agreed that family therapy should be discontinued and that the two boys could instead come together so the therapist could help them help each other in more productive ways. Jan was more happy about this agreement.

Sample Questions

- Let's invent a creative or playful explanation to account for why there is this problem. That might help us to think of new kinds of solutions. Do you have any suggestions for an entirely different kind of explanation?

- Let's imagine—even for a just few minutes—that your problem is not caused by any emotional problem but by the fact that you have excessive sexual energy. I know this may sound weird, but suppose there were some truth to it, what should you do to solve the problem?
- I have a hunch that may sound odd, but I'd like you to think about it, because I see some evidence to support it. Namely, that under the surface you have already become cured of this problem but for one reason or the other, you have not yet made this internal change public. What do you say? I'm not all wrong, am I?
- You may be right in thinking that her running away from home with this boyfriend of hers is caused by her going through a difficult independence phase. However, there is another possibility that she is dedicated to helping this boy get back on his feet. Sometimes, young women become like that. It's called the "social-worker phase." What do you think? If that were the case, what should you do?
- Suppose your problem is not psychological, but that it has more to do with vocational planning. If that were the case, you would not need psychotherapy but something else, instead. What would it be?

Comment

When problems need to be explained in one way or another, it is advisable to favor explanations devoid of the idea that the problem is caused by another problem or a disturbance that is difficult to solve or cure. Instead, one should favor solution-oriented explanations which may assume that the problem is just an accident or a bad habit. Solution-oriented explanations, can also be based on the idea that the problem has the function of helping one to achieve something or to learn or grow in one way or another. One should never oppose clients' views about the cause of the problem, because this will usually force them to defend their position and, thus, become even more fixed in their point of view. The new explanation should, therefore, be brought up as no more than an experiment or an alternative way of looking at the problem. Another possibility is to suggest it indirectly in the form of a story about someone else with a similar problem.

Viewing the Past

The belief that current problems are caused by negative past experiences is widespread, not only among professionals, but also among lay people. It is, for example, commonplace that when clients come in for therapy or consultation, they begin their story by relating past negative experiences, as if it were self-evident that these experiences caused the current problems. For example, while writing this very chapter, we received a call from a school nurse who wanted to refer to us a ten-year-old boy who refused to go to school. Among the first things that the nurse told us was that the boy's father had died of cancer. In spite of the fact that six years had passed since the father's death, and the boy had apparently overcome the loss quite well, both the boy's mother and the nurse seemed to be convinced that the father's death somehow explained the school-related problems.

The view that past negative experiences are the cause of current problems is, however, not the only one. One can think of one's past negative experiences as psychological trauma that have caused one trouble, but one can also think of them as ordeals that have brought about something positive. For example, if a person complains that her mother was extremely dominating, she may easily be led to believe that her mother's dominating behavior is responsible for some of her problems. On the other hand, she might also be willing to consider the possibility that her mother's dominance is actually not related to her problems at all, but, rather, is the reason for some of her resources.

Case Example

The client was a young woman suffering from depression, anxiety, and excessive use of alcohol. She told us that she was working in her father's company along with her two brothers and that, as long as she could remember, her father had picked on her and treated her unfairly as compared to her two elder brothers. She was bitter as she related incidents from her past where her father had required much more from her than from her brothers. She also complained that her father was much harder on her about her alcohol consumption than he was with her brothers, even though they drank "twice as much." She was plagued by the question of why her father had always been harder on her.

Tapani said that what she had been telling us about her relationship with her father reminded him of his relationship to his late supervisor and director of the abuse service he worked for. "You know, I used to have this director who was constantly picking on me. For two years, I thought that he was deliberately intimidating me. Gradually, it dawned on me, however, that he had chosen me as his crown prince and that he was educating me to become his follower. It was awful until I realized his intention. After he died, I worked for five years as the director of that place. I don't know about your father, but could it be that he plans to make you his follower in the company?"

The client, who had been listening very attentively said, "My God, I never thought about it like that. Could be . . . I don't know. I'll have to think about it." The follow-up a few weeks later revealed that the client was doing better and that she was enjoying a much improved relationship with her father.

Sample Questions

- If there were a way to find out whether your past experiences are related to your current problems, and it was found that your problem has nothing to do with your past, would you approach your problem differently?
- Is there anything that you have learned from all the things that you have had to go through that could be of use in solving this problem?
- It may be fortunate that you have had such an eventful childhood. Isn't it true that a person who has gone through as much as you is more likely to be able to solve these kinds of difficult problems than, for example, a person with a happy childhood?
- Do you think that a difficult childhood makes one stronger or weaker?
- Let's imagine that ten years have passed. You haven't had your problem for quite some time now, and, as you look back on your past, how would you say that past experiences helped you in overcoming your problem?

Comment

The idea that a client's past has contributed to his or her resources rather than problems should be introduced in a cordial manner, preferably in the form of a story or a gentle allusion. It should be the client's task—not the therapist's—to review his or her life in accordance with this more positive way of thinking.

Linking with Other Problems

When people turn to professionals for help, they usually have other problems in addition to the presenting one. In such situations, therapists are likely to make the assumption that the presenting problem and the concurrent problems are somehow interconnected. One may think, for example, that the presenting problem is caused by one of the other problems or that there is an underlying disturbance, which is responsible for causing or maintaining the various concurrent problems.

When approaching problems in a solution-oriented way, one refrains from assuming causal relationships between various coexisting problems. For example, a child who has problems at school may also have problems at home. In such instances, there is a temptation to assume that school problems are a result of problems at home. It is suggested here that, instead of making this presupposition, it may be more useful in terms of creating solutions to presume that the child just happens to have problems both at school and at home without there needing to be any causal connection between the two.

Case Example

A teacher consulted us about a seven-year-old boy who was behaving disruptively in the classroom. She said that there was nothing she could do to help the child since she knew the reason for his behavior. She had heard through the grapevine that the boy's mother was suffering from a fatal brain tumor. She also asked us if it would be possible to apply a solution orientation to such a case. We asked her to invite the boy, along with a few classmates, to the session. The teacher took the challenge and invited the boy and three of his friends to a consultation meeting.

At the session, we discussed the problem of disruptive classroom behavior in ways that were both funny and entertaining. For example, the boys had a good laugh when their teacher role-played for them what she considered disruptive behavior. We called this behavior "the Disruption Ghost" and invited everyone to join in a discussion about how to get rid of such a ghost. At the end of the session, Tapani, together with the four boys, carried the Disruption Ghost (who was played by Ben) out of the room. During the session, it never came out which one of the boys was the disruptive boy, since he was not singled out. Everyone had lots of fun, and the boys worked well as a team. When we discussed the session after the boys had gone back to school, the teacher revealed to the group which one of the boys was "the boy." Only at this point did we reveal to the training group that we had been aware of the fact that the boy's mother was seriously ill. We then turned to the group and asked whether they thought what we did was the right thing to do. Everyone agreed that helping the boy solve his school problems by allowing him to reconnect with his classmates was probably the best way for the school to help the boy survive the ordeal he was going through in his family.

Sample Questions

- You seem to have several concurrent problems. Is it okay with you if we focus on this one first and look at the others later, if needed?
- There are several problems that you have mentioned. Which one of them would you like to solve first?

- Solving any one of your problems is likely to have a positive effect on the other problems. Which one do you think is most potent in this respect?
- You know the old question about the chicken and the egg? Do you think it applies to your problems?
- You have mentioned a number of problems. Which one of them has taught you the most? Can you use what you have learned, thanks to this problem, in solving some of the others?

Comment

Sometimes, therapist and client disagree on the way in which concurrent problems are causally linked to one another. In such instances, the therapist should either adopt the client's point of view, or if this is not possible, openly discuss the differences in opinion in terms of its possible consequences.

Eliciting Resources from Clients

Everyone has some resources, such as skills, capabilities, talents, interests, admirable character traits, and so forth that can be utilized in solving the problem. However, these resources may go unnoticed unless the therapist deliberately focuses on finding out about them. A person with a good sense of humor can be coached to use his wit and humor in solving his problem; another person who is skillful in writing can be helped to take advantage of that skill; a good planner can use that talent.

Case Example

We consulted with a teenage girl who was having serious problems at school and who had a bad habit of losing her temper. When asked about her hobbies, we found that she spent a good proportion of her free time at the stables taking care of horses. When she was reminded of the fact that even horses sometimes become unruly, her father looked at her meaningfully and said, "Do you want to tell about what happened at the stable the other day?" First she said, "No," but it did not take more than a few seconds for her father to talk her into telling us. She then told us about how she had managed to calm down three frightened horses at once. After ending her story and answering a few questions, she received well-deserved applause from our group. When we started to talk about her problems in terms of a girl who sometimes gets unruly and needs to be calmed down, she became a motivated and resourceful participant in the discussion.

Sample Questions

- If I had to go through what you have gone through, I probably would not have made it. How did you survive so well? Where did you find the strength?
- You managed to avoid the problem for so long. What resources did you use to do it?
- Is there anything you are good at? How could that skill be used to solve this problem?
- What is your best personal characteristic? In what way have you used that characteristic so far in handling this problem? What else can you do that would allow you to use that trait in solving the problem?
- Are there any similar problems that you have solved before? Could you think of using a similar type of solution in this case?
- Who do you think would be able to solve this problem? What do you imagine he or she would do?

Recognizing Clients' Expertise

As experts in the field of therapy, professionals sometimes fail to recognize that clients are often experts on their own problem. They have already tried numerous solutions, and this has given them a clear idea of what kind of solutions do not work in their case. They have heard innumerable suggestions from relatives and friends and also from professionals. This has made them experts on the more traditional ways of approaching the problem. Often, clients are surprisingly well-acquainted with the literature on their own problem, and they may have met and talked to many other people with similar problems. Milton Erickson had a point when he asserted that clients know the solution to their problem, even if they do not know that they know.

Also, family members may often be seen as experts. If they have had or continue to have similar problems as the client, they may have a lot to say not only about how the problem might be solved, but also about how it should *not* be solved. For example, the parent of a drug-abusing adolescent may have substance abuse problems himself or herself. In such cases, there is a temptation to blame the parent for the child's problem. However, it may be more useful for the purposes of therapy to think of the parent as a person with firsthand experience and, therefore, as an expert on problems related to substance abuse.

The belief that clients know what will not be helpful to them and that, in the back of their minds they somehow even have an idea of how their problem should be solved, allows therapists to "consult their consultant," as White and Epston (1990) have expressed it, or to obtain supervision "free of charge" from the client, as we like to say.

Case Example

"Ahmed," who had emigrated to Finland from an Arab country, was invited by a social worker employed at the foreigners' crisis center to come in for joint solution negotiation with our training group. Ahmed was in a difficult spot. He had met his Finnish wife some years ago in central Europe. They had studied there, but both had given up their careers in order to move to Finland to start a family. Soon after he emigrated, however, Ahmed's wife decided to leave him. Ahmed was shocked. All he wanted to do was to find a way to keep his wife, who seemed quite determined to end the marriage.

Ahmed came to the meeting, but, as he became aware that there were several strangers in the room, he refused to come in. We went out and found him sitting in the lobby. We found out that he spoke some Finnish, and we said that we understood him, that talking about one's problems before a group of people is probably not his way of solving problems. We then asked him how a problem like his would be solved in his own country. He said, "Not like here," and proceeded to explain that, in his own country, he would go to a friend, and they would drink coffee and talk things over. He would then go back home to his wife, and the problem would be solved.

"Is there any such person in Finland?" we asked him.

"Yes, there is Yusuf," he answered. "He is a medical student in another town in Finland."

"Suppose we had a chance to talk with Yusuf. We would ask him what we should say to you about your problem. What advice would he give us?"

"He would say, 'Don't ask questions. Just let him speak what he needs to speak.'"

Immediately after Ahmed said this, he decided to come in and talk with the group after all. We had an interesting session, which provided many ingenious strategies for Ahmed to use in his attempt to win back his wife.

Sample Questions

- Let's suppose that a friend of yours with a similar problem as yours came to you and asked for advice. What would you tell him or her?
- Suppose one day you received an invitation to give a lecture to professionals about the kind of problem that you have had to live with. What would you tell them?

- I have a suggestion about what you could do, but you are probably the best person to foresee what would happen.
- Suppose, after this meeting, you feel that we have had a successful conversation. What topics do you imagine that we will have discussed?
- Which one of your own solutions has so far proven to be the most effective? What else have you thought you might like to try?
- Could we make a list of solutions that you have tried or have found not applicable in your case?

Sharing Personal Experiences

How much therapists should reveal about their personal experiences to their clients is a question that is often discussed by psychotherapists. In our opinion, revealing personal information to clients may be useful when the information revealed fosters optimism and creativity in clients. Stories about how one once had but then overcame or adjusted to a similar problem to that of the client are useful in many ways. They can offer clients hope and new ideas, they can help to establish rapport between therapist and client, and they can help clients feel more normal as they realize that even therapists have similar problems.

Case Example

We were asked by the staff of a children's daycare center to see "Tim" and his mother, because Tim was still soiling his pants at the age of five. We suggested that, instead of arranging a meeting with the family, we would come to the daycare center and discuss the problem together. The meeting was held within a week. Present were the mother, the director of the center, two members of the staff, and us. Tim was out playing with the other kids. We started by drinking coffee and socializing for a while. We then said that we already knew what the problem was and that we would be curious to know if anyone present had any personal experience with this kind of problem. One of the staff members, an elderly lady, said that her granddaughter had had the problem of wetting her pants, and she had solved the problem by having her teach a doll to use the potty. When the doll had used the potty, it was given a hug by both the granddaughter and the grandmother. We then asked her if she thought a similar kind of approach could be used in helping Tim overcome his problem, and she said that she had not thought about it but that it might be a good idea. Since mother also seemed fond of this idea, it was decided that Tim should have a teddy bear, both at home and at the kindergarten, and he could teach it how to use the potty.

- Has anybody in this group had a similar experience that he or she would like to share?
- If you feel like sharing an experience from your own life that you think might be of help, please do. Remember that you don't have to say it was you, you can say it was your neighbor.
- This has been a touching discussion with you today, and I suspect that it has had an impact on all of us. Would some of you (participants) want to share your personal experience and, if so, would you (clients) be interested in hearing what they have to say?

Comment

At the end of any session where there are several people present, we usually ask not only the client but also the other participants to share their personal experience of having taken part in the session. This question often inspires participants to share their feelings, to speak about what they learned themselves, or to articulate their respect for the clients. Such sharing at the close of the session usually has a powerful and positive effect on clients.

Generating Creative Solutions

One of the most challenging tasks of any discussion about a problem is that of generating solutions. When such a discussion is solution-oriented, the atmosphere tends to inspire the creation of solutions. When working in large groups, we often divide the group into smaller groups, and ask each group to suggest solutions for the client.

Case Example

A general practitioner who participated in one of our training groups brought an acquaintance, "Sara," a middle-aged woman who suffered from her husband's paranoid jealousy. He guarded her every step and provoked constant arguments, which had sometimes escalated to violence on his part. Recently, there had been many rows about the fact that Sara wanted to begin taking summer adult education classes at the local university. Sara's children knew about their father's jealousy, and Sara often talked on the phone with her daughter and gave a report of the situation at home. When asked if there had been any progress in the problem, she said that, recently, her husband had apologized for one of his unfounded suspicions.

When Sara had explained the problem in some detail, we asked her if she thought that there was a need to understand why her husband was so jealous, or would it be okay with her if we skipped the question "why" and focused directly on solutions instead. She said that she had thought about the question "why" so much that, for her, it would be a relief to drop the issue and just hear suggestions about what to do about the problem.

We divided the group, which that day consisted of some 40 trainees, into several small groups. Each small group was given the task of suggesting a solution to Sara, who herself became a member of one of the groups. After half an hour, the groups met again to give their reports. As the groups reported their suggestions, we wrote them down on a flip chart.

The first suggestion was that Sara should ask her husband if he would promise to keep a secret. If he said yes, she should then reveal to him a true secret that no one else knew about, not even her best friend. When she asked for a rationale for the task, she was told that sometimes when a spouse, say a husband, is jealous, it may be that he has the feeling that she is sharing more secrets with someone else than with him. In such cases, the sharing of one or more important secrets with him can reverse this feeling.

The second suggestion was based on the fact that Sara's husband had recently apologized for his behavior. It was argued that this was a sign that there was a great chance that the time was ripe for a joint family negotiation about the problem without any professionals, where the spouses, both of their adult children, and also Father's sisters, who knew about the problems, would be present.

The third suggestion was founded on an intervention developed for a jealous husband at the Family Therapy Institute of Washington. According to this suggestion, Sara should begin to hide small notes in her husband's pockets, briefcase, and other inventive places. The notes should say sweet things, such as, "I love you" or, "You are my sweetheart."

There were about a dozen more suggestions, some of them humorous and inventive, others more straightforward. After collecting the suggestions, we asked Sara what she thought about them. She said that there was only one suggestion that suited her. It was the suggestion that she should assemble the family to talk openly about the problem. She added, however, that some of the other suggestions might be helpful for a close friend of hers who also had a jealous husband.

Sample Questions

- If you were to try something different next time the problem appears, what would you do?

- Let's find a creative solution to this problem. We could even invent something a bit absurd. What could it be?
- In what way would you imagine this kind of problem would be solved in a country where there were no psychotherapists or other professionals?
- We have a suggestion for you. . . . What do you think of it? Would you be willing to try it? What do you assume would happen if you did?
- I know another person with a similar problem who did something like this. . . . Do you think that something similar could be of help in your case?
- Perhaps the suggestions that you have heard from us so far are not directly applicable in your situation. In that case, we would be interested in hearing from you, after some time, about any solutions that you come up with yourself.

Comment

When clients do not "buy" the suggestions of helping professionals, this should be seen as evidence that they know best themselves what is appropriate and what is not appropriate for them. When clients comply with the suggestions of professionals and come back reporting that there was no progress, this should be seen as an invitation to generate new solutions.

Creating Positive Future Visions

In our view, the single most useful issue to be talked about with clients is how they view the future without the problem. The creation of positive future fantasies has many advantages. Talking about what one hopes for the future generates optimism. It also helps people set concrete goals for themselves, which seems to be a prerequisite for change. Positive visions also have the power to change the way people view the present and the past. When people are helped to foresee a good future for themselves, they automatically begin to view their present difficulties as a transitory phase, rather than as an everlasting predicament. The vision of a positive future also sheds new light on past and present problems. It becomes possible to view them in a more favorable light, not merely as meaningless suffering but rather as difficulties that in the long run, contribute to their ability to achieve their goals. Future visions also help people to think about possible solutions, to see changes that are already happening, and to recognize how various people could contribute to bringing about the desired outcome.

Case Example

We consulted with a man who was recovering from several years of excessive consumption of alcohol. We asked him to imagine how his life would seem, after about a year, if he could continue with his newly found sobriety. The question appeared difficult for him to answer, so we asked him if he could think of inviting people for a sobriety party after a year. He said that he could well think of doing something like that, since only a few weeks ago he had had his one-year sobriety celebration at Alcoholics Anonymous. We proceeded to construct a fantasy about the two-year celebration. This celebration was to be held in his home, and also other people than A.A. friends would be invited. We then talked about who would be invited and what he might want to tell those people about his life and more recent progress. We asked him if he would want to invite his parents. He said that they were both dead. "But if they could come as angels?" we continued. "If that would be possible, they would both be welcome to join me." We discussed for a while what he would tell his parents about how he was getting on with his life. Many things emerged, one of them appearing to be more relevant than the others. It was the vision that he was busy taking care of his grandchild, who would be then almost one year old. We also asked him if, in his speech, he would want to thank his parents for something. He found it easy to thank his mom. He said that his mom had given him hope, without which he would not have survived his years of continuous heavy drinking. When asked what he would want to thank his father for, he went blank and said, "My father was an alcoholic. He drank until he died at the age of 78. It's difficult for me to think of what to thank him for." "He lived a long life for an alcoholic, didn't he?" we asked. "He sure did," said the client. "He must have had an exceptionally tenacious liver," we said half-jokingly. "That's right, I remember that people always wondered about how his liver could take all that booze," he said. "In that case, perhaps you could thank him for the fact that you inherited from him a liver that helped you survive through the years of drinking." "Never thought about it like that, I bet I could," said the client with a smile.

Sample Questions

- Let us imagine that this meeting is over. Suppose that, as you leave, you find that the meeting has been useful for you. In that case, what questions would you have had answered?
- Let us presume that we meet again after one year and this problem is gone. How does your life look then?
- Let us imagine that a miracle takes place and suddenly one day

the problem is over. How would you notice it's gone? How would other people notice that a change has taken place? What positive things will begin to happen when the problem is no longer there? Have any of these changes already begun to take place?

- When the problem is finally over, who else but yourself will thank you?
- Let us make up a fantasy that we are in the future and the problem has been gone for quite some time now. We just happen to bump into each other. I become curious and ask you how you are. What do you respond? I become even more curious and ask you what made the change possible. What do you answer?

Comment

Most clients enjoy fantasizing about a positive future. Sometimes, however, a client may seem unwilling to collaborate. In such cases, it is advisable to explain to the client, in detail, the purpose of creating future fantasies. If the client is still reluctant, it may prove useful to utilize circular questioning, that is, to engage whomever is present in the meeting to begin making up positive fantasies about the future. Collective fantasizing about the future usually compels even the most reluctant client to become engaged in the process. Another approach that can be used when people do not seem to be interested in talking about a positive future is to engage them first in the creation of a pessimistic future vision and invite them to create the optimistic vision only after the disastrous vision has been completed.

Focusing on Exceptions and Progress

It is amazing how often people answer in the affirmative when asked whether there is any recent progress in their problem. It has been estimated by Steve de Shazer and his group (Weiner-Davis, de Shazer, & Gingerich, 1987) that up to 80% of all clients coming in for consultation in a private outpatient clinic report positive changes between the time they set up the appointment and the actual interview. Deliberately focusing on even small signs of progress helps to create a positive atmosphere for the session. It tends to help identify workable solutions, already found by the clients, and opens up the question of how various persons have contributed to the positive changes already made.

Another way of eliciting an atmosphere similar to that described above is to focus on exceptions or periods when the problem was temporarily gone. For example, as a rule, even the most severe drug addicts can recall periods when they were off drugs for a time, and any quarreling couple can remember at least some instances when they were able to resist the temptation to enter into a row, despite the fact that all the necessary ingredients were present. Focusing on exceptions allows people to see that the problem is not ever-present, and that it may be possible to think that they themselves have more control over the problem than is at first apparent.

Case Example

My (T. A.'s) son was ten years old at the time he became interested in soccer. There were 40 boys, and they had been divided into two teams. The coach of the soccer club had picked the best boys for his team, and the less talented boys, including my son, were placed on the second team. Since there was nobody to coach this second team, I was asked to do it. For the sake of my son, I could not turn down the request, even though I had no previous experience in soccer.

Standing at the side of the field for the first time, I had no idea what to do. I observed the more experienced coaches shouting and yelling to the boys things like, "Watch the wings!" and, "Pass the ball, don't hatch it!" Soon, I found myself doing the same thing. I stood there shouting and yelling to the boys things that they should do or things that they should not do. It soon became evident, however, that in spite of the fact that I was doing what was expected of me, I was not being very helpful. No matter how much or how loud I yelled, the boys did not pass the ball to each other. Gradually, I began to feel like a fool.

After a few times, I decided to apply what I had learned in my work with clients to coaching the boys. I shut up and let the boys play without yelling. They played much the same as usual, and, when we had our meeting during half-time, I told them, "Boys, I'm proud of you. I saw that many times you were about to pass." Many of the boys eagerly agreed and said that indeed they had been about to pass and went on to explain why they had not been able actually to do so. During the second half, the boys passed the ball significantly more than before, and, when the game was over, I acknowledged their accomplishment.

Another thing I said to the boys was that it is useful to have the opportunity to play on a team that often loses. I explained to them that, at some point in their careers, many excellent soccer players have played on losing teams and claimed that losing teams tend to generate a far better team spirit than winning teams. The boys liked my ideas. They grew fond of soccer, and I grew fond of them. At the time I am writing this, a year has gone by since we started to play together. I have become a soccer enthusiast and, believe it or not, the team is now winning more and more matches. (A version of this story appears in Furman and Ahola, 1992, pp. 107–108.)

Sample Questions

- Have there been situations or times when the problem has been absent? How do you explain that?
- We have found that often when we meet people the desired change has already begun to take place. Have you found that progress has already begun to happen?
- Let's suppose your problem at its worst rated a 10. What number is it now? How do you explain this change?
- Have there been any situations where the problem has not occurred, despite the fact that you expected it to occur? How do you explain those situations?
- Have there been situations when you have managed to resist the temptation to react as you usually do? How did you do that?

Distributing Credit

The identification of exceptions or signs of progress allows one to begin to look at how various people have contributed to the changes. Such a discussion confirms the change by inviting people to construct reality so that the desired change is already happening. It also enhances collaboration, since the very act of thinking about how people have contributed to the solution automatically abolishes blame and encourages respect and thankfulness. Even in cases where collaboration is already in jeopardy, it becomes possible to regain it by sharing credit for progress.

Case Example

I (B. F.) was teaching a course on solution orientation for a group of a half-dozen teachers at a special school. Most of the pupils in this school had multiple problems, and many of them lived in a nearby children's home. We were drinking coffee in the teachers' room and discussing what we should do. One of the teachers suggested, in a slightly provocative manner, that I should teach a class for his students. I asked him on what subject. He said, in a more provocative way, "Well, you must have something you can teach." I asked him, "Would it be all right if I did whatever I pleased with the kids?" He readily agreed. So, the whole group went together into the teacher's class, which consisted of eight 13-year-old boys. I began by introducing myself to the boys and told them why I was there. I made contact with the boys by learning their names and joking a little bit with them. After this, I gossiped to the boys that I had heard from their teacher that the class had made significant progress this spring. The boys started to smile and look at each other.

I then picked one of the boys and asked the others what progress they had seen in him. They said that he had calmed down, that he did not attack others the way he used to, and that he was quieter during lessons. I said, "Do you mean that he doesn't blow his top as easily as he used to?" They all agreed that that was the case. I then asked the boy to explain what had made the change possible.

"It's because Steve has stopped picking on me," he said.

"Do you mean that you have become buddies?"

"Yes, Steve has even helped me with math."

I then shifted to another boy and found out that he had begun to attend school more regularly than before. I asked him why, and he said, "Before, I didn't see much point in going to school."

"And what made you change your mind?"

"Because I need the final certificate."

"What do you need that for?"

"I need to get a good job. I'm planning to become a cook."

"That's quite an accomplishment. I have noticed many times that when people begin to have future plans, it's a sign of real progress. Whom would you give credit for this?"

"I don't know."

"You must have done a lot yourself to accomplish that. How has your teacher been of help?"

"It's more fun to be in his class."

"How come?"

"It's easier to understand here."

"How is that possible?"

"Our teacher explains things three times if we don't understand."

"And what if one does not understand even the third time? Doesn't he become nervous?"

"No, if that would happen, he would go to the blackboard and explain it again, drawing on the board."

"Wow, that means that he's really a patient person."

All the boys unanimously stated, "Yes, he is."

"What about your parents, Paul? What have they done to help you?"

"They've demanded more from me."

"Has that been a good thing for you?"

"It was not nice in the beginning, but it has been more okay lately."

The teacher added, "I think it has been a very good thing."

In this way, we talked about each one of the boys. One hour was not enough, so we decided to continue after the recess. Later, the teacher came and thanked me and said that he had been amazed that the boys not only talked but even talked openly. I said that it was my experience that most people are willing to talk even about personal matters when the discussion focuses on progress rather than on problems.

Sample Questions

- How should this change be explained? What have you done yourself? How has your family contributed? What have professional helpers done to help you?
- Your child has made rapid progress during the time she has been here in treatment. What have you done that would explain these changes?
- Suppose you wanted to thank all the people who have been of help, so far. What would you tell each one of them?
- Let's imagine that, in the future, when this problem has been gone for some time, you decide to arrange a party to celebrate the change. Whom would you invite? How would you give credit to these people?
- Is there anybody you feel has not helped you in any way in solving this problem? Is there any way of thinking that even that person has in some way contributed? How would you say that to him or her?

Comment

Sometimes, a person may not be able to think that a certain other person could have contributed to the change. In such instances, it is possible to bring up the idea that, sometimes, even negative experiences with people can be of help in solving a problem. Even if one is not able to see it now, it may become possible afterwards to construe negative experiences as ordeals that taught one something important or that provoked one to become more determined to solve the problem.

Viewing the Problem as a Friend

When we suffer from a problem, we usually view the problem as an enemy, a nuisance that brings us nothing but trouble. However, later on, we may be able to see that the problem, in addition to bringing us a great deal of suffering, also helped us in a way that may not have been evident at the time. Problems can be of help to us by making it easier for us to solve other problems or by teaching us something valuable that we may not have otherwise learned.

Case Example

We received a phone call from "Mike's" aunt, who wanted to refer him to us for psychotherapy. She told us that Mike was a 17-year-old high-school student who had apparently been doing well until about a month ago, when he attempted to kill himself by taking an overdose of sedatives. There was no history of psychiatric problems, and, thus, Mike's suicide attempt had come as a shock to everyone.

The aunt also told us that, some months earlier, Mike had been told that the man he knew as his father was actually his stepfather. The aunt thought that this, along with the stress of preparing for final exams in high school, had triggered the suicide attempt. We said we would be willing to meet with Mike, but that he would have to call us himself to make an appointment.

A few days later, Mike called, and we agreed upon an appointment the same week. Mike was an easygoing, pleasant young man. He told us about how busy he now was with his studies, and we also spoke about his girlfriend, with whom he had been going steady for about a year. What had happened a month ago seemed a thing of the past.

We told Mike what his aunt had told us and said that we'd be interested in hearing what he had to say. He told us about his recent meeting with his biological father. He also told us the details of his suicide attempt. There was no doubt that Mike had planned to die.

Everyone, according to Mike, seemed to believe that the reason he had wanted to kill himself was his disappointment regarding his biological father, but Mike did not agree. We were interested in hearing Mike's own story.

"You don't have to tell us if you don't feel like it," we said. However, before long, Mike told us the following story.

When he was still a little boy in primary school, he had had a good friend, whom we will call Joe. Mike and Joe had been best friends even before they went to school, and they were always together. Then, for no apparent reason, Joe abandoned him and started to mix with other boys instead. This incident broke Mike's heart. He felt that there was something very wrong with him. He never spoke about this misery to anyone, but, secretly, he started to harbor thoughts of self-reproach and suicide. The memory of being rejected by Joe and the related suicidal thoughts had been with Mike all these years. According to him, the suicide attempt was not the result of a crisis precipitated by current problems—as everybody seemed to think—but the fulfillment of a plan that he had secretly harbored for years.

When Mike had told his story, we asked, "What about now, after your suicide attempt? Have you spoken about these things to your family?"

"I've spoke with my father (meaning stepfather) more than ever."

"So now he knows all about Joe and the suicidal thoughts that you used to have, but you kept secret from everyone?"

"Yes."

Mike had recently spoken not only with his stepfather, but also with his mother and girlfriend about many things he used to keep inside. In a way, by virtue of his suicide attempt, he had gone through a rite of passage. A reserved young man, who used to keep his tormented thoughts and feelings inside, had become able to open his heart to his close ones.

"This may seem odd to you, Mike, but we feel that your suicide attempt cured you. You used to suffer from the problem of keeping important thoughts and feelings inside you, and, now, in a way thanks to your suicide attempt, you have become able to speak. Once you had to speak of suicide, you found you could speak about anything. Your problem of keeping things to yourself seems to have disappeared as you have become able to tell others whatever you need to tell them. Well, what do you say? Could this be what happened?"

"Yes, it's true," said Mike.

We talked for a while about how Mike had, in many ways, grown more mature after his suicide attempt. We then explained to him our own dilemma, "You know Mike, we may be having a new problem here. How will we be able to convince your family? They expect you to start psychotherapy, and now we've come to the conclusion that your suicide attempt was all the psychotherapy you needed. What would your stepfather think of this?"

"Oh, I think he would agree. I've been talking with him so much lately."

"Well, what about your mother and aunt? If you explain this to them, would they think that we don't take this seriously?"

"I can explain it to her. I think she would understand, too."

We said that, in light of what had transpired during the session, we could see no indication for psychotherapy. We thanked Mike for an interesting discussion and walked him to the door. He seemed pleased and thanked us as he put on his coat. We said he knew our number, if he ever needed our help, and wished him luck with his final exams.

After the session, we began to have second thoughts. Was the view that Mike's suicide had been a self-cure appropriate, or had we simply been too eager to make therapy brief, inventing a far-fetched story that no one would take seriously? We knew that many colleagues would shake their heads in disapproval. Some might even accuse us of joining Mike in his denial of underlying problems.

A year later, when we were writing down this story, we decided to call Mike again to see how things had developed. Mike's mother answered the phone. She told us that Mike was off somewhere helping his father. She said that it was most considerate of us to call. She went on to say that she and her husband had at first been doubtful of our recommendation, but that they had gradually changed their minds as they found that things were going really well. Mike was described by his mother as "a sunny boy." He was studying computer science at the university, had many friends, and planned to go to the army for the compulsory one-year period the next fall. (A version of this case appears in Furman and Ahola, 1992.)

Sample Questions

- There is a saying, "In every cloud there is a silver lining." Does it apply in any way to your problem?
- Many people believe that problems and suffering are not in vain. What do you think?
- If this problem has taught you something important about life, about yourself, or about other people, what could it be?
- You know, sometimes, it is impossible to see what one learns from problems until much later. Let's imagine that some years from now we meet and I ask you that question. What do you think you would answer?
- Suppose, one day, you have children or grandchildren, and you want to teach them something very important about life that this problem of yours has taught you. What do you think it might be?

CONCLUSION

Conventional psychotherapy is based on the assumption that the presenting problem is not the real problem, but is merely a symptom of a more encompassing underlying psychological or interpersonal problem. In the early days of brief therapy, this presupposition was replaced with the ingenious idea that it is not the problem that is the problem, but the way people go about attempting to solve it. Gradually, however, the field of brief therapy, at large, has witnessed a shift from emphasizing what people do about problems to what people think about them. It has become evident that one's attempted solution is always contingent upon how one defines and explains the problem. A change in the way one thinks about a problem can bring about a drastic change in the way one attempts to solve it.

The growing awareness of the importance of the way one thinks about a given problem has paved the way for a new view of therapy as an art of helpful conversation. Therapy is no longer thought of as a technology for change but, rather, as an event where professionals and clients jointly search for productive ways of thinking and talking about problems. According to this emerging view of helping, it becomes the responsibility of the helper to direct the conversation in such a way that the emphasis is on resources and solutions rather than on problems. The purpose of solution talk is to provide people with a pleasant experience that turns problems into challenges, fosters optimism, enhances collaboration, inspires creativity, and, above all, helps them to retain their dignity.

ACKNOWLEDGMENTS

Readers familiar with the work of Steve de Shazer, Michael White, and David Epston will find that many of the ideas presented in this chapter appear in their writings. Needless to say, we have been greatly influenced by their ideas. We also feel indebted to many others, particularly John Fryckman, who brought family therapy to Finland; Judith Mazza, who taught us strategic therapy; Richard Belson, who encouraged us in the use of humor; Frank Farrelly, who gave us permission to be provocative; Carlos Sluzki, whose warmth and encouragement have been of major value to us; Lynn Hoffman, for being our "intellectual lover"; Harold Goolishian and Harlene Anderson for introducing the ground-breaking concept of problem determined systems; William O'Hanlon for the idea that several solutions can be suggested to clients rather than just one; Peter Lang and Martin Little of the U.K. for teaching us to take into account the larger system; Karl Tomm for introducing the idea that all questions are leading questions; and our colleagues Eero Riikonen, for providing numerable inventive solution-focused questions, and Kimmo Karkia, for coining the catchphrase "Glasnost therapy."

REFERENCES

Boscolo, L., Cecchin, G., Hoffman, L., & Penn, P. (1987). *Milan Systemic Family Therapy*. New York: Basic Books.

de Shazer, S., Berg, I., Lipchik, E., Nunnally, E., Molnar, A., Gingerich, W., & Weiner-Davis M. (1986). Brief therapy: Focused solution development. *Family Process, 25*(2), 207–221.

Epston, D. (1990). *Collected Papers*. Adelaide, South Australia: Dulwich Centre Publications.

Fisch, R., Weakland, J. H., & Segal, L. (1982). *The Tactics of Change: Doing Therapy Briefly*. San Francisco: Jossey-Bass.

Furman, B. (1990, May/June). Glasnost therapy: Removing the barriers between clients and therapists. *Family Therapy Networker*, pp. 61–63, 70.

Furman, B., & Ahola, T. (1988). The use of humor in brief therapy. *Journal of Strategic and Systemic Therapies, 7*(2), 3–20.

Furman, B., & Ahola, T. (1992). *Solution Talk: Hosting Therapeutic Conversations*. New York: Norton.

Haley, J. (1973). *Uncommon Therapy: The Psychiatric Techniques of Milton H. Erickson, M.D.* New York: Norton.

Haley, J. (1987). *Problem Solving Therapy: New Strategies for Effective Family Therapy* (2nd ed.). San Francisco: Jossey-Bass.

Madanes, C. (1982). *Strategic Family Therapy.* San Francisco: Jossey-Bass.

Madanes, C. (1984). *Behind the One-Way Mirror: Advances in the Practice of Strategic Therapy.* San Francisco: Jossey-Bass.

O'Hanlon, W., & Weiner-Davis, M. (1989). *In Search of Solutions.* New York: Norton.

Palazzoli, M., Boscolo, L., Cecchin, G., & Prata, G. (1978). *Paradox and Counterparadox.* New York: Jason Aronson.

Palazzoli, M., Boscolo, L., Cecchin, G., & Prata, G. (1980). Hypothesizing, circularity, neutrality: Three guidelines for the conductor of the session. *Family Process, 19*(1), 2–12.

Watzlawick, P., Weakland, J. H., & Fisch, R. (1974). *Change: Principles of Problem Formation and Problem Resolution.* New York: Norton.

Weiner-Davis, M., de Shazer, S., & Gingerich, W. (1987). Using pre-treatment change to construct the therapeutic solution: A clinic note. *Journal of Marital and Family Therapy, 13*(4), 359–363.

White, M., & Epston, D. (1990). *Narrative Means to Therapeutic Ends.* New York: Norton.

Zeig, J. K., & Lankton, S. R. (Eds.). (1989). *Developing Ericksonian Therapy: State of the Art.* New York: Brunner/Mazel.

CHAPTER 4

Narrative Intentions

GENE COMBS
JILL FREEDMAN

When we present examples of our work to other therapists they often ask about particular moments in the therapy: "How did you know to ask that?" or, "Why did you do that?" While there are many different ways to answer such a question, we believe that *narrative intentions* are a major influence on the moment-by-moment choices we make in working with people.

In the pages of this book, although the authors have come together because of shared assumptions and values, one can find various sets of intentions. For example, some therapists intend to engage in conversations through which solutions will be constructed. Others intend to converse in ways that focus on the meaning of what people say, believing that a careful focus on meaning cannot help but engender the dissolution of old meanings as new ones emerge. While our work is informed by many of the intentions one can find in this book, our central intention is to collaborate with people in developing new narratives about themselves and the worlds they inhabit.

A guiding metaphor, such as narrative, is no small matter. We recently presented a videotape of a small segment of our work to a group of colleagues, each of whom uses a different model of therapy. To our way of thinking, what happened on the tape was that a couple, Jan and Arthur, came to therapy with their lives situated in a story of misunderstanding and disappointment. They described several incidents in which misunderstanding and disappointment had come between them. However, they also mentioned in an offhand way a task they had completed together. We talked with them about this achievement, asking how they had accomplished it and what it meant about them that they could accomplish it. They described the process they used in working together and agreed that it showed they could cooperate and even be creative with each other. We asked about other times in their relationship when they had cooperated and been creative with each other, and they recounted several such incidents. We wondered what difference it would make to know that they could accomplish things through cooperation and do so creatively. They said it would mean that not only could they work together to deal with misunderstandings, but they also could look forward to doing anything they decided to do together. When we fast forwarded to the end of the tape, the two were excitedly recounting incidents in which they had worked together and planning shared projects for the future.

To our way of thinking, they had begun to "restory" their relationship. What started as a story of misunderstanding and disappointment was becoming a story of cooperation and creativity. When we showed this tape excerpt, we expected that our colleagues would see and hear the kinds of things we have just described.

The first person to comment said, "I don't know what to make of your tape. I'm used to helping people understand problems and you hardly talked about the problem at all. I kept waiting to get back to the problem."

Several people joined in a discussion of what the problem "really" was. The problems they saw did not have to do with stories of misunderstanding and disappointment but with a variety of other things such as legacies from families of origin, life-cycle phases, and diagnostic categories.

This discussion was interrupted by another colleague who said, "I thought there was quite a lot of talk about the problem, but no goals were set. I was confused about how you could decide on a direction without setting goals."

Later, as the two of us discussed the experience, we agreed that we did not recognize our work in their comments. Our colleagues, guided by different metaphors, did not see or hear the tape as we did. We, in turn, did not see or hear what they did. Luigi Boscolo once told us, "You can only see what you see." We would add that the metaphors that guide one's intentions shape both what one sees and what one does.

We come to narrative therapy by way of the world of Ericksonian therapy (see, e.g., Combs & Freedman, 1990). In my (J. F.) early training in Ericksonian approaches, I remember being taught the presupposition that everyone has all the resources he or she needs to reach his or her goals. One of the people in the training program had a hard time believing this idea in relation to some of the people at the agency where he worked. He explained his difficulty to the trainer and asked if the presupposition was really true in every case. The trainer considered the question for a moment and then answered, "I don't know if it's true or not. What I do know is that I get farther with people if I believe it."

The narrative analogy, like any other map or model, is a metaphor.

Our intention in this paper is not to establish it as a "right" or "true" map for understanding people's experience or for guiding our intentions in psychotherapy. What we hope to illustrate is how far we get and in what directions we go when we let this particular metaphor guide our intentions.[1]

We will give an overview of our intentions and the actions that flow from them. Then we will describe the work we undertook with a particular person and comment on how narrative intentions influenced our contributions to that work.

A NARRATIVE MAP AND HOW IT SHAPES OUR INTENTIONS

We base our therapy on the notion that people make meaning of their lives by organizing key events into stories, which they then incorporate into a larger life narrative (E. Bruner, 1986; J. Bruner, 1986; Geertz, 1986; White & Epston, 1990). Such stories are social constructs (Gergen, 1985; Hoffman, 1990), arrived at through interaction and experience with other people in a particular historical–cultural context. Furthermore, as Michael White (1991, p. 28) writes,

> Not only do these stories determine the meaning that persons give to experience, . . . but these stories also largely determine which aspects of experience persons select out for expression. And, as well, inasmuch as action is prefigured on meaning-making, these stories determine real effects in terms of the shaping of persons' lives.

People who come to therapy can be viewed as living in stories where choice is restricted and available options are painful or unfulfilling. Our work involves facilitating experience of new stories—life narratives that are more empowering, more satisfying, and give hope for better futures.

This narrative metaphor is a constant influence on what we notice, what we are most interested in, the kinds of questions we ask, and the ideas that we have during therapy. When people experience themselves as inhabiting more meaningful stories, their ongoing perceptions, choices, and behavior will change more or less automatically. For this reason, we focus on expanding and enriching meaning more than on encouraging new behavior.

Our role in this process mainly involves listening and asking questions.

[1]Many people's ideas inform our work. We want to clearly acknowledge Michael White as being especially important in shaping our ideas and practices. We want to note that many people currently use a narrative metaphor with intentions and related actions that differ from ours. We are not trying here to represent the full range of narrative intentions, only to acquaint the reader with how the narrative metaphor shapes our current work.

This helps us stay as much as possible in a position of "not knowing" (Anderson & Goolishian, 1990). Asking questions rather than making interpretive, diagnostic, or interventive statements invites people to clarify and redirect our understanding at each turn of the conversation.

Although this chapter focuses on what therapists think and do, we in no sense want to imply that what therapists think and do is the most important aspect of what happens in therapy. It is simply the side for which we bear responsibility. Our intention is to engage in collaborative, horizontal relationships in which people choose stories they prefer and make their own meanings about those preferred stories. White and Epston (1990, pp. 148–149) describe it this way:

> As a general rule, persons cannot see unique possibilities for their lives if others are standing in front of them, blocking their view. . . .
>
> Supporting persons from behind is not problematic in this way. The therapist can achieve this position in a general sense by working to identify unique outcomes and by directly engaging the person in the performance of new meanings around these. Thus, the person is encouraged to be the privileged author of the new story.

Deconstructive Listening

Narrative intentions lead us to listen to what people tell us as stories (therefore, not as chief complaints, information to be "gathered," matrices within which resources are embedded, lists of symptoms from which to make diagnoses, surface hints about what the core problem "really" is, or anything else except stories). Since each person has lived experience that does not fit with the problem-saturated story that he or she has brought to therapy, it is tempting to immediately begin asking about such exceptional experience. However, doing so can lead people to feel that the seriousness of their problems is not understood or that their versions of reality are not valued. Listening carefully to people's stories and striving to understand their experience helps both to develop trust and rapport and to have some ideas about the particular constraints their stories carry.

As important as it is to listen to problem-saturated stories, it is even more important not to let our listening reify undesired meanings. We have come to refer to the special kind of listening required for accepting and striving to understand problem-saturated stories without reifying them as *deconstructive listening*.

In academic circles, the word "deconstruction" immediately brings to mind the work of Jacques Derrida (e.g., 1988), which explores, among other things, the slipperiness of meaning, examining and illustrating how the meaning of any symbol, word, or text is inextricably bound up in its context. Deconstructionists believe that it is fruitless to search for the "real" meaning of any text. Any narrative is full of gaps and ambiguities. Deconstructionist scholars focus on these gaps and ambiguities to show that the officially sanctioned or generally accepted meaning of a given text is but one of a great number of possible meanings.

Listening deconstructively to people's stories requires situating oneself in the belief that the stories people tell have many possible meanings and that the meaning a listener makes is often not exactly the same as the meaning that the speaker has intended. This belief leads us to listen for gaps and ambiguities in meaning and, when we hear them, either to ask people to fill in details or to tell them the meaning we are hearing and ask how it fits with their intended meaning.

Listening deconstructively begins with the "not-knowing" attitude that we have already mentioned. When therapists successfully cultivate a not-knowing attitude, therapy is conducted in an atmosphere of wondering, of, "What if . . . ?" or, "Could it be that . . . ?" This is very different from therapy conducted in an atmosphere of searching for clues to the one correct diagnosis or offering interpretations of the deep truth.

The dominant stories in Western culture still value decisiveness, action, and certitude. In our experience, this makes it difficult for therapists to stay in a not-knowing position. However, at least until the dominant stories change, it also makes it more likely that therapists who work in an atmosphere of not knowing will provide novel experiences for the people with whom they work. Such an atmosphere invites people to entertain the belief that they are the experts in regard to their life stories.

Our not knowing is colored by two beliefs or attitudes that we find compellingly useful in inviting people to deconstruct unsatisfying life narratives. The first of these is that life narratives are constructed bit by bit over time by people in interaction with other people; that is, they are *socially constructed* (Berger & Luckmann, 1966; Gergen, 1985). This belief leads us to interact with people in ways that invite them to relate to their life narratives not as passively received facts, but as actively constructed stories. Such interaction begins to deconstruct the "factity" of their narratives.

The second belief that colors our not knowing is Michael White's idea (1987, 1989; see also Tomm, 1989) that people are separate from their problems; that is, people are not the problem but the problem is the problem. Thus, when listening to people's descriptions of themselves or each other, we ask ourselves, "What is the problem that leads these people to behave in this way or have this kind of experience?" By "problem" we are not referring to a diagnostic category, but to an externalized and objectified idea, process, or emotion. That is, when a person says something such as, "I'm not a very good person. I seem to always do things wrong," we might begin to wonder if guilt is coloring his or her view of himself or herself. Thus, the person is invited to perceive "guilt" rather than his or her "self" as the problem. With our question, an *externalizing conversation* (White, 1991) is initiated about what he or she finds problematic.

As people tell their stories, we interrupt at intervals to summarize our understanding of their stories so that they can help us track their meaning and so that they can tell us if the meaning we are making fits for them. In responding to our questions and comments, people must examine their old stories in new ways. The beliefs and attitudes that we listen with create a new context, and in this new context, meanings are different. We listen with a thoughtfulness about what constructions are being made as we try to understand each other. As we perceive a possible new construction emerging, we ask if it is a fitting and helpful way of thinking about the story and we make adjustments in accordance with people's answers. Most of this process occurs automatically and subliminally as a result of our beliefs about narrative and social constructionism. It is not a didactic or intellectual process; we rarely, if ever, talk directly about social constructionism or externalization. Instead, we strive to listen closely and carefully with an attitude that is solidly grounded in these notions. When we listen with this attitude we find that, in the act of telling us their "old stories," people begin to view those stories as social constructions that are not fixed truths and, we hope, to entertain the idea that other stories that are just as true might suit them better.

Deconstructive Questioning

So far, deconstruction has been discussed as something that is a natural and inevitable byproduct of our efforts to understand people's life stories through a narrative/social constructionist filter. The primary intention of our questions has been to gain understanding of people's problem-saturated narratives. At some point, usually when it seems that a certain degree of trust and mutual understanding has been achieved, we begin to ask questions of a more purposefully interventive nature. Our intention shifts from that of *understanding* people's problem-saturated stories to that of *deconstructing* those stories. Questions with a deconstructive intent invite people to see their stories from a different perspective, to notice how they are constructed (or *that* they are constructed), to note their limits, or to discover that there are other possible narratives. To accomplish this, inquiry is directed toward the beliefs, practices, and feelings that support a narrative or develop from it.

For example, in the tape of Jan and Arthur, one of us (G. C.) asked this question: "Has disappointment kept you from responding to some things and encouraged you to respond strongly to others?" My intention in asking this question was to invite the couple to consider how the story of disappointment may have directed their attention toward disappointing events. If they adopted this view, they would begin to see how stories of disappointment construct experiences of disappointment, and to entertain the possibility of constructing other stories. Jan and Arthur, in fact, did decide that the constructions they were making were not in their best interest. They then began to identify and make meaning of other, previously unstoried, events.

Listening for and Asking about Openings

Saying that people make meaning of their lives by organizing selected events into stories oversimplifies the situation. People are born into stories; their social and historical contexts constantly invite them to story certain events and leave others unstoried. As a narrative takes shape, it powerfully influences the selections a person makes about what further events should be storied. The countless experiences, actions, and thoughts that remain unstoried are potential "unique outcomes" (White, 1988, 1989), which present possible openings into alternative stories. Narrative intentions lead us to listen attentively for such openings (we are using "listen" broadly here, as an activity for eyes as well as ears) and even to inquire directly about their existence.

In the example of Jan and Arthur, the offhand remark that they had completed a task together was an opening that led to an alternative story of cooperation and creativity. If they had not mentioned this event or if the meaning they found in it did not seem to open onto a story that they preferred, we could have asked, "Have there been times that you have been able to keep misunderstanding and disappointment from dominating your relationship?" or, "When was a time that you felt understood by each other?" Either of these questions might have led to an opening, which in turn might have led to an alternative story.

Developing New Stories

All the previous discussion of listening and questioning sets the stage for our central intention, which is to assist people in developing new stories. Once problem-saturated stories are understood as social constructions, different, more fruitful constructions can be privileged. Unique outcomes constitute openings that, through questions and discussion, can be developed into new stories. Once a unique outcome is "storied" in a meaningful way, its precursors can be found and included in the narrative and its future can be speculated on and included in the narrative. The new meanings embodied in the emerging story can support new perceptions and behaviors, which will affect other people, whose reactions can also become part of the ever expanding narrative.

More specifically, when possible openings are perceived, we ask questions that invite people to develop them into alternative stories. Initially, we ask questions such as, "Does this interest you?" "Did that surprise you?" "Is this something that you want more of in your life?" or, "Do you think this is a good thing or a bad thing?" Questions like these invite people to consider whether something that we see as a possible opening is really new for them and whether it opens in a direction that they prefer over the direction of the problem story. Our questions are invitations, not directives. We know that we want to lead the conversation in the direction of new stories, but we want to stay in a posture of genuinely not knowing what will constitute a meaningful opening or exactly where that opening will lead. Therefore, it is important to notice quickly when people decline invitations, and to listen until openings that interest them occur. To do otherwise involves the risk of becoming yet another source of oppressive restraint.

If the opening seems to be a preferred one, we will ask questions to encourage the development of an alternative story. We do not have a formula to follow in this process. We do keep in mind that stories involve events that happen through time in particular contexts and that they usually include several people. Also, a big part of what stories these events is that people "perform meaning" (Myerhoff, 1986; White, 1991; White & Epston, 1990) on them; that is, they attribute meaning to them and treat them as important. In the following sections, examples are given of some of the different kinds of questions that are useful in restorying. For more thorough accounts of questions that can be used in the reauthoring process, see White (1988) and Freedman and Combs (1993).

Asking How

Once an opening that is both novel and preferred has been negotiated, we want to know how the person brought that opening about. Questions like, "How did you do that?" "What did you do that led you to feel this new feeling?" and, "How did you arrive at this different way of perceiving the situation?" are useful in this regard. Answers to such questions almost always come in the form of stories.[2] Sometimes people give such full answers to these questions that no further work at story development seems necessary for that particular opening.

When we ask "how" we are implicitly inviting people to join us in a

---

[2]You might want to try this yourself. Identify a behavior, perception, or emotion from your recent life experience. Ask yourself how that behavior, experience, or emotion came about. Isn't your answer a story of sorts?

powerful presupposition: that they have *personal agency* in effecting unique outcomes. Narratives without such a sense of agency tend to be narratives of powerlessness and oppression, so we work to coauthor narratives in which people experience themselves as capable, creative, and effective. However, if a person clearly indicates a sense of passivity in regard to a particular unique outcome, that perception can be accepted and used to explore how the problematic story promotes such a sense of passivity and possibly set the stage for its deconstruction.

Detail

Sometimes a person will clearly indicate that an opening is interesting, but will find "how" questions difficult to answer. In such cases, one can ask for more details: "What happened just before that?" "What happened next?" "Where were you exactly?" "Who else was there?" "What did you say?" "What did they say?" "How did it feel to do that?" "What were you thinking as it happened?" "Who was the first person you told about the incident?" Our intention here is to invite the elaboration of enough detail (particularities of action, character, mood, setting, etc.) for the singular event of the opening to become an experientially vivid story.

Performing Meaning

As a story begins to unfold on what White (1988), following Jerome Bruner (1986), calls the "landscape of action," it is useful to ask questions that direct people's attention to the "landscape of consciousness." Bruner has discussed how the interplay between these "dual landscapes" invites empathic and experiential involvement in the lives and minds of the characters in a story. We ask what we (Freedman & Combs, 1993) call *meaning questions*, with the intention of inviting people to enter the thoughts, feelings, and beliefs engendered by the actions they have recounted. Examples of meaning questions include: "What do you make of that?" "What does that tell you about your relationship?" "What did you learn from that experience?" and, "What does that mean to you now?" Again, asking questions out of curiosity rather than out of a push for therapist-preferred meanings creates a context in which the people who have sought our assistance have the greater voice in the reauthoring process.

Extending the Story in Time

Just as Jan and Arthur did not develop the story of their relationship as one of misunderstanding and disappointment from a single incident, the unique outcome of completing a task together was only an opening for an alternative story, not a whole new narrative in and of itself. Connecting that bit of story with others eventually did constitute a new narrative.

Similarly, people are almost always invited to consider the story developed around any particular opening within a broader flow of time. Until such stories are linked into narratives with a past, present, and future (Boscolo & Bertrando, 1992), they are in danger of easily being overshadowed by old, dominant stories.

One way to facilitate the incorporation of a number of stories into the same flow of time is by linking newly storied events to related events that have not yet been storied. One might attempt this by asking, "Was there another time, farther in the past, that this incident reminds you of?" or, "At what stage in your previous history were you most aware of this quality that you are rediscovering in yourself now?" Often, such a question will trigger a memory that can be developed into another bit of new story. When the person connects the stories of the two incidents, it is not uncommon for still other related incidents to spring to mind. As these "preferred" stories are strung together on the time line of a single life narrative, that narrative cannot help but change in ways that the client prefers.

We can also ask how a particular bit of new story influences a person's ideas about the future. Questions like, "How does this incident change your ideas about what might happen in your relationship over the next week?" and, "Now that you know this, what's the next step?" invite people to alter their plans and expectations so that they are more in line with the emerging story. Such alterations increase the likelihood of new life events that will constitute lived experience of the new story. Meaning can be performed on these new life events in future sessions.

CLINICAL EXAMPLE

We would like to say at the outset that while "Jessica" quickly achieved spectacular results, our experience with people is often less dramatic. This story was chosen because in addition to being dramatic, it is very clear, straightforward, and easy to follow. Remember, however, that what follows is a much simplified and "cleaned-up" report that is intentionally edited and annotated to emphasize how narrative intentions on the part of the therapist contributed to a satisfying outcome for Jessica. In this way it is a lot like the kind of "new story" we invite people to construct for themselves.

At the time I (J. F.) met Jessica she had just completed several years of therapy. She felt that her therapist[3] had been helpful and supportive,

---

[3]In many ways I felt that this therapy was really co-therapy. Jessica saw another therapist both before and after our work together. Much of the work we did was built on and later supported by work she did with the other therapist.

but she had not perceived any progress for a number of months and had come to believe that "it had gone as far as it could go." Within a few months of that ending, Jessica heard me give a talk on sexual abuse, which gave her hope that maybe she could go farther. She called me to set up an appointment, explaining that she felt stuck and hoped that I would see her even though she lived three hours away and did not know how often she could come to see me. Our usual practice in setting appointments is to ask people at the end of each session if and when they would like to have another appointment. In Jessica's situation, distance necessitated less frequent sessions than she would have chosen otherwise. One of the ways we accommodated the distance was by incorporating the possibility of brief phone calls between sessions.

The First Session

Jessica was the head nurse for the emergency room of the only hospital in a medium-sized city in southern Illinois. She lived alone in a farmhouse on the edge of town, had a sizable circle of female friends, and enjoyed participating in sports.[4]

In the first session, Jessica told me that she was 35 years old and had never had a romantic relationship. She described growing up in a family where women were treated as the property of men. Her father and uncle touched her, her mother, and her sister in any way they liked at any time they liked. The touching was often rough and often sexual, including having her breast or crotch grabbed while she was helping with kitchen chores and being forced into sexual contact with one man while another looked on.

I asked Jessica what the effects of this abuse were on her, both in the past, as a child, and now, as an adult. She said that, as a child, the abuse brought forth feelings of fear, insecurity, confusion, helplessness, and isolation. She elaborated on these themes in some detail. The effects on her as an adult were an inability to engage in a romantic relationship, difficulty in friendships, and feelings of worthlessness. Again, she gave examples of how these played out in her life.

I wondered, and asked aloud, how she had moved from a childhood of fear, insecurity, confusion, helplessness, and isolation to the different place that she now inhabited. She helped me understand how the present effects (inability to engage in a romantic relationship, difficulty in friendships, and feelings of worthlessness) were the remnants of earlier difficulties. She explained that the feelings of worthlessness were limited

---

[4]We prefer to start therapy, when possible, by learning some things about everyday, nonproblematic roles, activities, and interests. As Dickerson and Zimmerman (1993) point out, it is important to begin by getting to know people as separate from problems and as experts on their own lives.

to social situations. In fact, it turned out that all the effects of abuse had become contextualized and no longer took over her life as they had when she was a child.

Jessica had a Master's degree, and she described her job as head nurse as a good one, which she had held for a number of years. I asked her what it would have meant to her if she had been able to see these things in her future when she was a child. She said that she would have realized that the fear and related feelings were not inherent truths about her. If they were, she would not have been able to accomplish as much as she had professionally. I was very interested in how she had been able to stand up to the effects of the abuse over the years and determine her own career. I hoped we would be able to talk more about this.

Jessica commented that, now that she thought about it, her accomplishments really were remarkable, especially because no one else in her family had ever gone to college or become a professional.

Commentary

In the beginning, we listen to people's existing narratives. As we listen, we orient ourselves to their experiential worlds. The intimate and graphic details that Jessica volunteers are evidence that a relationship of trust and mutual respect is developing. Only as such evidence is perceived do we feel comfortable about inviting much in the way of new story. For people with stories like Jessica's, attempting to change things right away can be experienced as yet one more violation and disqualification by a powerful other. At the same time, it is important to be careful not to reify or replicate the abuse by becoming voyeuristically involved and pushing for more detail than the person freely and comfortably gives (Durrant & Kowalski, 1990).

From the beginning of therapy, we listen deconstructively. For instance, Jessica did not use the words, "the property of men," but our feminist values lead us to hear stories like hers in these terms and to use such terms in therapy as we summarize our understanding of the emerging narrative. When constructions like these are offered in the conversation, people examine their own way of constructing the situation in the light of our constructions (Kamsler, 1990). This kind of comparison is a basic act of deconstruction.

Inquiring about the effects of the abuse is a more active form of deconstructive listening. Jessica is invited to tell a story about "having been affected by abuse" rather than a story about "being an abused person." When Jessica accepts this invitation, she can experience abuse less as a part of her identity and more as a separate entity with which she can struggle. When she compares the past with the present effects of the abuse, Jessica presents what seems like an opening. Using White's (1987) notion of "collapsing time," which involves such comparisons, helped bring forth this opening.

Jessica was asked a "how" question (How had she moved from a childhood of fear, insecurity, confusion, helplessness, and isolation to the different place that she now inhabited?) which invited her to consider her influence in altering the effects of the abuse. Her response indicated that she was interested in this opening and that she had already developed some new story around it, so she was asked a "meaning question" (What would it have meant to her if she had been able to see these things in her future when she was a child?), which invited her to reflect on the meaning of her childhood fears and the like, in the light of the alternative story that she was developing.

Jessica's response to the meaning question presented another opening, which prompted another "how" question (How had she been able to stand up to the effects of the abuse over the years and determine her own career?), asked in a way that implied it could be explored further in the next session and that invited Jessica to develop more new story between sessions. At the end of the session, Jessica began to reflect on her achievements as "remarkable" and, therefore, to story herself as a remarkable person.

The Second Session

At the second session, which we had scheduled for six weeks later, Jessica said she now realized that she was no longer the child that she once had been, and that life was very different for her as an autonomous adult than it had been for her as a dependent child. Now, she felt ready to get married and raise a family. She wanted to work on smiling, because people kept telling her to smile.

I asked if it would be all right to slow things down a little in the session so that I could keep up with her. When she agreed, I asked her how she had come to this realization that she was no longer the child she once had been. She went over some of the same ground as she had in the first session, this time going into more detail about the differences in her past and present experience. This time, she had more ideas about things she had done to create an identity for herself instead of letting the effects of the abuse create her identity. Experiences at school, a place where she excelled, got positive comments, and was treated with fairness, were very important sources of self-knowledge that she used in creating her identity. These experiences of mastery and of being treated as a person rather than as property nurtured a secret part of her. Over time, she was able to develop that part, and it enabled her to stand up to the effects of the abuse and limit their area of influence.

I asked her what the fact that she had accomplished all this meant about her. With some hesitation, looking away from me, she said it meant that she was smart and tough. I said I understood that people outside of her family did not know about her home situation, but I wondered if they had known, who might have predicted that she would be able to stand up to the effects of the abuse and not let it take over her life. She said that teachers and kids at school knew she was smart and tough. Had they known about her situation at home, they would probably have predicted that she would find a way to oppose the abuse and take her life back for herself. Her previous therapist also recognized these qualities in her.

I then wondered aloud, "If we look back over the years at how you have used your strength and intelligence to take charge of your life—you got an education, became a head nurse, and found ways to limit the effects of the abuse—is this readiness to get married that you are talking about the next step?" She thought maybe it was. As we began to talk about what that meant, Jessica acknowledged that it was different to think of herself as someone who could have an intimate life with someone else. Not only was she smart and tough, but now she could begin to imagine herself having warm and tender feelings and connecting with another person. In fact, in her previous therapy, she had felt connected to her therapist and had a variety of pleasant feelings toward her. She could now see that relationship as preparation for other relationships. In friendships with women, she had also experienced some positive feelings and connection, even though these relationships were often rocky.

As we talked more about the possibility of moving into the realm of romantic relationship, we discovered that simply thinking about herself as someone who could operate in that realm was an important step in taking her life back from the effects of the abuse. Because the effects of the abuse had held her social life hostage for so long, there were probably a number of important social experiences that the effects had robbed her of until now. For example, Jessica did not really think of men as people, so making friends with a man might be an important step, and now she knew that her intelligence could help her pick a safe man for the project.

Commentary

Jessica has developed a lot of new story between sessions. She is perceiving herself differently and identifying new and ambitious goals for herself. At times like this, it is important to develop as rich, detailed, and meaningful a story as possible. It is also important to invite, when possible, enhancement of the "personal agency" aspects of the emerging story (Adams-Westcott, Dafforn, & Sterne, 1993). Here, this is accomplished by asking "how" in a way that presupposes personal agency—how she came to the realization that she was no longer the child she had once been.

A wonderful and richly detailed story of standing up to the effects of abuse and creating an identity for herself comes forth in response to the question. This story was always a possible part of Jessica's life narrative, but, until the last six weeks, the events from which it is assembled had been lying around disconnected and gathering dust in seldom-visited memories.

In response to another meaning question (What does the fact that she has accomplished all this mean about her?), Jessica begins to own "smart" and "tough" as real and prominent personal attributes supported by her life narrative. As the interchange continues, Jessica is invited to flesh out the story of how she has been smart and tough enough to stand up to the effects of the abuse. Her attention is directed toward other people who appreciate these qualities and abilities in her. Jessica identifies several members of her "supporting cast," and realizes that the story that she is only now discovering has already been circulated in her past and present social world. All these people genuinely believe her to be smart and tough, and now that she appreciates their knowledge, it will be much harder for the old narrative of fear, insecurity, confusion, helplessness, and isolation to take over.

Before we adopted a narrative map, we worked to help people identify "resources" from nonproblematic life contexts, and to use those resources in problematic contexts. It was quite common for us to search through past experiences for these resources. However, we thought of the resources as states of consciousness and used past experiences only as a way to help people access resourceful states. We made little effort to connect experiences and states through time. Now we think of such experiences as important life events that, when given prominence in a person's life narrative, will alter the meaning of that narrative in satisfying ways. This leads us to expend much more energy on reviewing the past and less energy on helping people "access states."

With the question about "the next step," the idea of wanting a romantic relationship, which Jessica voiced in therapy, is brought up for possible inclusion in the narrative. She is invited to consolidate the developing new story and extend it into the future. She responds by identifying additional personal characteristics and realizing that they are already part of who she has been and will be, thus continuing to revise her life narrative.

In the ensuing conversation, externalizing language is used to invite Jessica to view her narrative as one in which her romantic life has been held hostage by the effects of the abuse. Since she is already, at this point, storying herself as smart, tough, and at least a little experienced in warm and tender relationships, rescuing her romantic life may no longer seem such a daunting job.

The Third Session

In the third session, one month later, Jessica was taken over by distress about events in one of her friendships. In her estimation, a close woman friend often treated her badly—criticizing her, refusing to talk to her—but Jessica had chosen so far to spend time with her anyway. It was after the most recent bout of these incidents that the distress had taken over. The belief that other people they both knew sided with her friend made the distress even stronger.

I wondered aloud if Jessica's implied desire to do something different with this friendship was a part of the previously identified project of rescuing her social life from the effects of the abuse. Considering it in this light, Jessica thought that the way she had been up to now in the relationship was influenced by the effects of the abuse, but now she felt this way of being was intolerable. I reminded her of the personal qualities she had owned more closely—strength, intelligence, ability to have warm and tender feelings, ability to connect—and wondered how these might be useful in this problematic relationship.

She decided to put her professional self—the part of her that had done well at school and work, and whose intelligence and strength she trusted—in charge of setting limits and deciding what she should do to take care of herself in this relationship. I asked if she thought doing this would constitute progress toward being more secure in other relationships. She thought it would.

Commentary

"Taken over by distress" is an externalizing construction. As always, it is important to notice whether or not this construction fits for Jessica. In this case, it seems to.

Jessica is invited to incorporate the current crisis into the narrative she began to build over the course of her first two sessions, a story in which she is a person with certain personal characteristics who is engaged in a project of rescuing her social life from the effects of abuse. In response to this invitation, Jessica comes up with a plan for how to proceed in the problematic relationship. Again, narrative intentions make us want to incorporate significant events into the overall flow of past, present, and future that constitutes a person's life narrative. As she successfully resolves the current crisis, it will become a significant chapter in the story of how she rescued her social life from the effects of abuse.

The Fourth Session

Jessica came to the fourth session (again, one month later) taken over by distress and also by confusion about her relationship with this same friend. She had consistently used her intelligence and strength in setting limits and making decisions. Her friend had countered with criticism and name calling. This brought forth self-doubt for Jessica. She particularly began to experience doubt about whether it was possible for her to be healthy, normal, or playful.

I wondered out loud if there were times when she had been sure of her ability to be "healthy," "normal," and "playful," even for a moment. With some encouragement, Jessica remembered learning a song at school. Her grandmother, who lived out of town, was visiting, and when Jessica came home from school that day her grandmother was there alone. Jessica remembered sitting on her grandmother's lap and teaching her the song; her grandmother looked into her eyes, smiled, and sang with Jessica, clearly enjoying her company.

I asked what her grandmother recognized in her and most appreciated about her. She said "that I am lovable" and explained that being lovable meant many things. She listed them: she was a good person; she was warm; she was fun; she was normal; she was healthy; she was playful; she was receptive; she recognized good things in others.

Then, we spent a long time talking about how her life might have been different if she had lived with her grandmother. We developed the story of those differences through time, starting with when she was very little and coming all the way up to how things might be different for her now if she had grown up living with her grandmother.

I asked her to list again what her grandmother knew about her and wondered what life would be like if she owned those qualities about herself. She was more thoughtful than verbal in response to this last question.

Commentary

In response to a threatened reemergence of the narrative of self-doubt and distress, Jessica is invited to search for previous life experience that contributes to knowledge of herself as "healthy," "normal," and "playful." Any memory of such experience will constitute an opening for story development around these ways of being.

In her search, Jessica discovers a real jewel. She is invited to relive the incident with her grandmother and examine its implications more closely. She accepts the invitation and makes the incident a more real, vivid, and meaningful part of her life narrative. She is then invited to experience the story from her grandmother's point of view. When she does, she gets a new view of herself. She can experience firsthand her grandmother's knowledge of her. This type of story development—incorporating other people's views—can be quite useful and effective.

Jessica is invited to construct and experience an alternative narrative about her whole life. To the extent that she becomes experientially involved in the world of this alternative story, the knowledge that she gains there will be available in this world as well. As we shall see later, the experience of this alternative story is a pivotal event in the therapy.

A further invitation is offered for Jessica to review and incorporate her grandmother's knowledge of her into her current life narrative. She responds by looking thoughtful, but not saying much.

The First Phone Call

Jessica called me five days after the fourth session. She began the conversation by asking, "Do you know what it would be like to wear new shoes, new clothes, new makeup, and new breast implants all at the same time?" This was completely outside of my experience, so I asked her to explain. She told me that on the morning after our session, she drove through McDonald's on her way to work, as she had every morning, to pick up a cup of coffee. She was handed the coffee through her car window, as she had been every morning, and was asked if she would like sugar and cream, as she had been every morning, and automatically said, "No, thank you" (not just, "No," as she had every other morning). She found this quite startling and absolutely normal, at the same time.

She said now that she realized who she was, she knew that she was the kind of person who would say "thank you," and so she did. Hearing herself actually say "thank you" out loud was a startling and clear confirmation of her new identity. She did not remember ever having felt this strong for this many days in a row. She noticed that she was both more concerned about other people and more tuned in to herself. This was scary, too, because of how different it was. She was feeling strong all the time, but was afraid she must be denying other feelings because she couldn't believe she was so strong. She was afraid the changes were not real, and said that may have been why she used those unreal examples— breast implants and so on. But then she said, "The neatest thing about this is I have something to guide me—my new image."

Since the last appointment, she had also stopped smoking; this was because she now knew she was the kind of person who would not smoke. She said two things about stopping smoking that were particularly interesting to me. One was, "Cigarettes are taking my energy and I need it for other things." The other was that, in the past, when she was around people she liked, if they smoked, she smoked. She said that now it was important to be able to stay on her own path and have others go on their own.

She ended the phone call, saying, "Having a new image of myself has affected me in ways I could never imagine. My car broke down, and I didn't meet the man of my dreams, but it's all right."

Commentary

This whole conversation shows how experience of an alternative life narrative can bring forth changes in self-image, beliefs, and behavior. Most of the therapist's energy at times like this is expended in keeping up with all the changes.

The life narrative that was enriched so much in the previous session continues to make gains over the old, less pleasing one. These are changes that one could not have planned or predicted. One of the great joys of working in a narrative mode is witnessing the emergence of the rich and wonderful stories that people author for themselves.

The Second Phone Call

Jessica called again eight days later. She had ended the relationship with her friend because she could not tolerate all the blaming. With everyone else, she reported, she was being her new self and liking it. When she was her new self with her friend, it began to seem like their relationship would end, so she would go back to her "old" self. She now decided that she could not do that anymore, so she had ended the friendship. She felt strong but very sad. She believed that she was mourning the loss not only of her friend but of her old self.

I mused out loud about whether it was possible that the new self had been there all along, hidden under the effects of the abuse. That made sense to Jessica, but she said she was still sad. I said that I was not trying to take the sadness away. I was sad, too, that she had been through all that abuse and had been forced into hiding.

I asked about ways other than the sadness that her experience was different. She answered that she felt safer, more open, and more understanding. She said that this process had worked to give permission to parts of her that had already changed and to those ready and waiting to change, as well as giving her something she could use to live by every day, a new image of herself.

Commentary

As the new story expands and becomes dominant, the narrative of abuse and the effects of that narrative do not completely disappear; they just become less and less dominant. Jessica will probably always be able to access memories of the abuse and of how the effects of the abuse limited her life. However, those memories will be a much smaller part of her whole life narrative. In a complementary way, the "new" story has always been with her.

Her sadness is accepted and affirmed. The subsequent question, about ways other than sadness that Jessica's experience is different, presupposes that as the new story continues to develop her experience of the world is different, and this invites her to story the differences. In so doing, she affirms that a new self-image goes hand-in-hand with her new story.

The Fifth Session

The fifth session was one month after the fourth. Jessica's very positive experience of getting to know herself in new ways had been interrupted and then overcome by a flood of graphic memories of the abuse that she had suffered. The central memory was of her uncle repeatedly thrusting his penis into her mouth while her father looked on. Her voice became very small and shaky as she described this memory. She reported that after it happened she went into the bathroom and washed out her mouth and then rode off on her bicycle.

I was very distressed to hear of this event. I looked directly at Jessica and said, "I'm sorry that happened to you."

Then, with her permission, I read her the notes from our two phone calls after the last session. She seemed to relax and began nodding as I read the notes. I said, "You were telling me in that first phone call that you know the kind of person that you are. If you really owned that new self-image, and looked back through time with the knowledge and feelings that are part of the new self-image, what would you appreciate about the you that went through the abuse?"

"Appreciate?" she asked.

"Yeah, what can you appreciate or learn about the you that survived this abuse?"

As she reviewed the memories, Jessica identified that she was strong and resilient, and after some thought she even realized that she was creative. She silently began to weep. She said that, in the past, when she had these kinds of memories she had felt helplessness, terror, worthlessness, and shame, but she believed that this was the first time she had ever felt grief about everything she had endured. The grief felt like a good, pure feeling, signifying that she was worthy of sadness over something that had happened to her. We agreed that it was a joyful grief.

Commentary

The flood of images from the past is heard and accepted. Telling these gruesome tales from the past to a person in the present, who hears them as stories of the effects of the abuse and clearly separates her bad feelings about the abuse from her good feelings toward Jessica, tends to deconstruct their more horrifying aspects. No effort is made to develop them into more detailed stories. Instead, as Jessica is affirmed and accepted, she is invited to turn her attention back to the new story about herself that she has recently been developing and experiencing.

As Jessica begins to situate herself in the new story, she can experience herself as smart, tough, warm, tender, experienced, and so forth. Only as she shows evidence of "owning" this new identity with its attendant characteristics is she invited to turn her attention back to the memories of abuse, and even then only in a specially structured way.

If she accepts the invitation, she is to "look back through time" and look specifically for things to appreciate about her younger self. Previously, these memories had coached a story of helplessness, terror, worthlessness, and shame. By connecting the memory with the preferred story and asking what she can appreciate about her younger self, Jessica is asked to restory the memories into ones of her capacity to survive and her positive identity. When Jessica looks back at her younger self through the eyes of her present self, she is able to appreciate that her younger self was strong, resilient, and creative in dealing with the effects of the abuse. This sets the stage for "joyful grief."

The Third Phone Call

Three weeks later, Jessica called and said that she was thinking about canceling her next appointment. Her life was not perfect but she was feeling free. Her new image was guiding her, and the power had gone from the memories. Also, her car had broken down on the way home from the last appointment, and she had had to spend the night in a hotel. When things had been really bad, the three-hour drive each way seemed worth it, but now that things were going more smoothly for her, six hours seemed a long time to drive. She canceled the appointment, arranging to talk again a month later.

It seems from this report that Jessica is now rather solidly situating herself in a life narrative that supports a freer, more resourceful past, present, and future self-concept.

The Fourth Phone Call

Jessica called again a month later. She said that before she had seen me she felt stuck, but now she was "over the hump." She liked herself. She was thinking about going back to her previous therapist for support in the new way she was thinking about herself and about life.

I asked her what had been most important in getting over the hump.

She said it was the memory of singing with her grandmother and learning what her grandmother must have felt about her. It completely changed how she knew herself. I congratulated her on knowing herself and said I was curious to hear where her new knowledge might lead her. She thanked me, and we ended therapy.[5]

Commentary

As she wraps things up, Jessica affirms that the memory of singing with her grandmother was an opening that, when storied, helped her to revise her entire life narrative.

Jessica came to see me once more, four years later. We thought of ending our clinical example here, without including the later session, but on further reflection, we decided to include the rest of Jessica's story as we know it without explanatory comments, to show how far she was able to go in rescuing her romantic life from the effects of abuse. It also seems appropriate for her to have the last word about her therapy. It was particularly helpful to me that Jessica returned years later because her description of her life at the later time let me know that the reauthoring had really occurred in an enduring way and that she was living the future she had predicted for herself in earlier sessions.

The Sixth Session

Four years (to the day) after our last meeting, Jessica came to see me again. The first thing she told me was that she was buying a new house. I asked her what meaning this had for her. She said that it meant that she was going for what she wants and breaking family traditions.

She came to consult with me because she was involved, for the first time, in a romantic relationship. Gary, she told me, was different from her family. He was fun-loving, a traveler. He did not have traditional values about relationships between men and women. He was sexual and playful and did not use sex as power.

"If this works," Jessica said, "I will be different from the women in my family." I wondered if there was not a lot of evidence that she already was. She agreed that she was, but said that what worried her was that she reacted to Gary sexually like her sister and mother would. In her family she had learned that women are not supposed to like sex, and now she

---

[5]A colleague told us she would have been uneasy ending the therapy suddenly by phone. She wondered if the car breakdown evoked old terrors, or if fear blocked Jessica from getting closer to me. I did not have these thoughts. To me, it seemed that Jessica had entered a new narrative about herself and her life. Her therapy seemed successful. She did want support, but she knew that she needn't drive three hours each way to get it. Her ending therapy seemed a confirmation of her achievements.

was finding intercourse painful. She reported that she was businesslike and efficient, wanting "to get in, have an orgasm, and get out."

When I asked how she was different from other people in her family, she said that she was the most playful person in her family. She had always had fun at school and work, but in recent years she has also played in other situations. She had taken up a number of team sports and thought that she had more fun in general than she used to. She also had more friends.

These changes led her to see herself as being more active, involved, and free. She listed friends who had noticed the changes and told me that some of her friends predicted that she would become involved with a man.

The preparation she had undertaken for these changes included coming to therapy and taking chances. For instance, she began frequenting a riding stable where she initially knew no one and joined a dart club as its only female member. She discovered that a lot of what is involved in play is being open to whatever pops into your mind. As she said this, she realized that there were precursors in her youth to these events. As a kid, she made something out of nothing and enjoyed daydreams. As a teenager, she got into telling jokes.

I summarized these events chronologically and asked what might come next. Jessica thought becoming more playful sexually and playing without structure would be next, but fear stood in the way of taking the next step and had also kept her from getting very close to Gary.

I wondered if going to a riding stable where she knew no one was an example of her overcoming fear. She agreed it was and added that she had become close friends with a man she met there. Other examples she offered of overcoming fear included being the only woman to join her dart club and telling Gary about her history of being abused and her subsequent difficulties.

I asked Jessica how she was able to overcome fear in these instances. She said that in the case of telling Gary about her history, she knew that because of the trouble she had with intimacy she would lose him if she did not tell him. So she took the risk and stood up to her own fearful internal dialogue. In a larger sense, Jessica said that she knew that a lot of what we fear in this world does not matter that much; she trusted her Higher Power and that helped her overcome fear.

I asked what these examples of taking risks and overcoming fear said about her. Jessica responded, "that I can do it, that there is some part inside of me that is compelled to do it. I guess, also, that I have perseverance and a belief in my own growth and development."

When I asked what difference it would make if she owned these descriptions of herself in the context of her relationship with Gary, she said that owning them could make a difference sexually. She grinned and said, "It makes me want to practice more." She added that she had been trying to please Gary, but this conversation was making her interested in practicing, like she had horseback riding and darts, for fun and so that she could relax. She also said that thinking about it as practicing made her feel like she could be more in charge. She intended to talk to Gary about these ideas.

As the session drew to an end, I asked Jessica if it had been helpful. She said, "Yes. It hadn't occurred to me how much I have changed and accomplished until now."

The Fifth Phone Call

Jessica called one month later. After our session, she had talked with Gary about wanting to practice and be more in charge. They went through some "misunderstandings about this but then things got comfortable." Sex stopped hurting, and Jessica had been enjoying it more and more. She said that it got more playful and sensual. She and Gary had been having other problems, and she did not know if the two of them would end up together, but she felt very pleased with the possibilities she had begun to realize for herself as a sexual and playful person. She hoped the two of them would work things out but, if they did not, she understood that it was not because there was something wrong with her. It was because they did not "fit." She now believed that it was possible for her to have a satisfying intimate relationship.

CLOSING THOUGHTS

We hope that the story of Jessica's therapy illustrates how narrative intentions guide our work and how the people we work with are the privileged authors of their own narratives. We feel privileged to be in on new narratives as they emerge and inspired by the new lives and relationships people author for themselves.

ACKNOWLEDGMENTS

We would like to thank Froma Walsh for her careful reading and suggestions for revisions of an earlier draft of this chapter.

REFERENCES

Adams-Westcott, J., Dafforn, T., & Sterne, P. (1993). Escaping victim life stories and co-constructing personal agency. In S. Gilligan & R. Price (Eds.), *Therapeutic Conversations*. New York: Norton.

Anderson, H., & Goolishian, H. (1990). Beyond cybernetics: Comments on Atkinson and Heath's "Further thoughts on second-order family therapy." *Family Process, 29*(2), 157–163.

Berger, P., & Luckmann, T. (1966). *The Social Construction of Reality.* Garden City, NY: Doubleday.

Boscolo, L., & Bertrando, P. (1992). The reflexive loop of past, present, and future in systemic therapy and consultation. *Family Process, 31*(2), 119–130.

Bruner, E. (1986). Ethnography as narrative. In V. Turner & E. Bruner (Eds.), *The Anthropology of Experience.* Chicago: University of Illinois Press.

Bruner, J. (1986). *Actual Minds, Possible Worlds.* Cambridge, MA: Harvard University Press.

Combs, G., & Freedman, J. (1990). *Symbol, Story, and Ceremony: Using Metaphor in Individual and Family Therapy.* New York: Norton.

Derrida, J. (1988). *Limited Inc.* Evanston, IL: Northwestern University Press.

Dickerson, V. C., & Zimmerman, J. L. (1993). A narrative approach to families with adolescents. In S. Friedman (Ed.), *The New Language of Change: Constructive Collaboration in Psychotherapy.* New York: Guilford.

Durrant, M., & Kowalski, K. (1990). Overcoming the effects of sexual abuse: Developing a self-perception of competence. In M. Durrant & C. White (Eds.), *Ideas for Therapy with Sexual Abuse.* Adelaide, South Australia: Dulwich Centre Publications.

Freedman, J., & Combs, G. (1993). Invitations to new stories: Using questions to suggest alternative possibilities. In S. Gilligan & R. Price (Eds.), *Therapeutic Conversations.* New York: Norton.

Geertz, C. (1986). Making experiences, authoring selves. In V. Turner & E. Bruner (Eds.), *The Anthropology of Experience.* Chicago: University of Illinois Press.

Gergen, K. (1985, March). The social constructionist movement in modern psychology. *American Psychologist, 40,* 266–275.

Hoffman, L. (1990). Constructing realities: An art of lenses. *Family Process, 29*(1), 1–12.

Kamsler, A. (1990). Her-story in the making: Therapy with women who were sexually abused in childhood. In M. Durrant & C. White (Eds.), *Ideas for Therapy with Sexual Abuse.* Adelaide, South Australia: Dulwich Centre Publications.

Myerhoff, B. (1986). Life not death in Venice: Its second life. In V. Turner & E. Bruner (Eds.), *The Anthropology of Experience.* Chicago: University of Illinois Press.

Tomm, K. (1989). Externalizing the problem and internalizing personal agency. *Journal of Strategic and Systemic Therapies, 8*(2), 54–59.

White, M. (1987, Spring). Family therapy and schizophrenia: Addressing the "in-the-corner" lifestyle. *Dulwich Centre Newsletter,* pp. 14–21.

White, M. (1988, Winter). The process of questioning: A therapy of literary merit? *Dulwich Centre Newsletter,* pp. 8–14.

White, M. (1989, Summer). The externalizing of the problem and the re-authoring of lives and relationships. *Dulwich Centre Newsletter,* pp. 3–20.

White, M. (1991, Summer). Deconstruction and therapy. *Dulwich Centre Newsletter,* pp. 21–40.

White, M., & Epston, D. (1990). *Narrative Means to Therapeutic Ends.* New York: Norton.

CHAPTER 5

Some Questions (Not Answers) for the Brief Treatment of People with Drug and Alcohol Problems

SCOTT D. MILLER

I need not to know all the answers but merely to understand the questions.
—REVEREND TOZEN AKIYAMA, personal
communication, Milwaukee Zen Center (1993)

I never learn anything by talking, I only learn things when I ask questions.
—LOU HOLTZ, *The New York Times,* cited in Berg & Miller (1992)

Not long ago, I was supervising a student who was working with a client with a serious cocaine problem. From my vantage point behind the one-way mirror, I watched and listened as the client told of her long involvement with the drug and, despite the many tragic consequences from her use of it, of her failure to make any effort to quit. In the midst of her story, the client suddenly stopped talking and, as if trying to force some great insight into consciousness, looked away from the student–therapist and stared intently at a piece of Chinese calligraphy which hangs on the consulting room wall.

Just as abruptly, the woman then turned back to the student–therapist and, with an expression of complete enlightenment on her face, started to speak. I remember the moment, because the anticipation of her response caused me to lean forward toward the one-way mirror. I was sure that it was going to be one of those "pivotal moments" in therapy, which I had always heard so much about in graduate school but had never seen in my clinical practice. "You know," the woman said with equanimity, "I am in denial!" She then quickly added, "*And I know it!*"

Like this client, my colleagues and I at Problems to Solutions, Inc., are "in denial . . . and we know it!" Indeed, for most of the years that we have been in practice, we have been in denial about what is typically believed to be true about the nature and treatment of people with drug and alcohol problems (Berg & Miller, 1992; Miller & Berg, 1991). In contrast to the field, however, we have very few—if any—answers to the drinking or drug use problems that currently plague our society. Indeed, all we seem to have are questions—questions that we have experimented with and found to be helpful in orienting the problem drinker or drug user toward solution (Berg & Gallagher, 1991). Over time, we have learned that asking the right question often has more impact on the client and the process of change than having the correct answer (Miller, 1992). Questions have proven useful in helping the client establish individualized treatment objectives, identify potential solutions or steps toward those objectives, and initiate and enhance their motivation to change.

In this chapter, four types of questions that have proven useful in orienting clients toward solution will be presented and discussed in detail. They are: (1) outcome questions; (2) instance and exception questions; (3) scaling questions; and (4) endurance and externalization questions. The chapter will conclude with a case example, in which the use of the questions will be illustrated and explained.

OUTCOME QUESTIONS

Outcome questions ask clients to describe what will be different when the problems that brought them into treatment have been successfully resolved (Berg & Miller, 1992; Johnson & Miller, in press). These questions are usually posed during the opening moments of the first treatment contact once the client has had sufficient opportunity to explain his or her reasons for seeking treatment. The best known and most frequently used outcome question is the "miracle question" (de Shazer, 1985):

"Suppose, tonight, after our meeting, you go home, go to bed, and fall asleep. While you are sleeping, a miracle happens, and the miracle is that the problem that brought you here is *solved*. But, because you are asleep, you don't know that the miracle has happened. When you wake up tomorrow morning, what will be the first thing you notice that is different that will tell you that the miracle has happened?"

The most frequent response to the miracle question is a smile and some laughter. Even considering the question seems to inspire hope for a future that is different from the client's present reality. A significant number of clients, however, are initially unable to respond to the question. These clients may fall silent or say that they "don't know" or that they "never thought about it." Given some time to consider the question, however, most clients are able to respond. The therapist must simply be patient and provide the client with an appropriate amount of encouragement and support.

Even with support and encouragement, some clients are unable to answer the question. In such instances, the key is for the therapist to be flexible and to modify the question to fit within the client's worldview. While the miracle question is the one we use the most frequently, it is certainly *not* the only outcome question used to orient the therapeutic discussion toward the client's desired outcome. As with all of the questions presented in this chapter, the miracle question should *not* be viewed as an end in itself, but as a means to an end. The purpose of the question is simply to identify the client's goals for the treatment contact. Therefore, if the client objects to the question or experiences significant difficulty in imagining how a miracle might look, another style of outcome question can and should be asked. For example, while experience indicates that the number is small, some clients do object to what they see as religious overtones in the question. The following dialogue from a recent case can be used to illustrate the process of modifying the miracle question to overcome a client's objections. The client, a 52-year-old man with a chronic alcohol problem, has just been asked the miracle question:

CLIENT: (*looking down*) Well, that's a hard question to answer, I am not the kind of . . . I really don't believe in miracles . . .

THERAPIST: I see, well, I'm glad you're being up front with me.

CLIENT: (*looking back at therapist*) I have seen a lot in my life (*shaking head from side to side*) but never a miracle.

THERAPIST: So, it sounds like your life experience has taught you to be more realistic than that.

CLIENT: I'd like to think so.

THERAPIST: Okay, good. So, let me ask you this, given your life experience, what could you realistically expect to be different in your life in say six months or so that would tell you that our work here has been successful.

CLIENT: (*long pause*) I'd like to think that I . . . or, um, my drinking would be under control.

THERAPIST: Uh huh.

From this point on, an open and free discussion began, with the client adding detail to his hoped-for outcome and goal for therapy. As can be seen, the key to the successful interaction was modifying the question to meet with this client's worldview. This included, but was not limited to, employing the client's words and unique phraseology in the question. Once this was done, the client readily answered the question.

Always being mindful to make adjustments consistent with the client's language and worldview, the therapist can use any of the following questions as substitutes for the "miracle" question:

"Suppose for a moment that our work here together is successful. What will be different in your life that will tell you that treatment has been successful?"

"What has to be minimally different in your life that will tell you that coming to treatment was a good idea?"

"Imagine yourself, for a moment, six months or so in the future, after you and I have worked together and successfully solved the problem that brings you here today. What will be different in your life, six months from now, that will tell you the problem is solved?"

After clients answer the outcome question, the therapist follows up with a series of questions that shape the evolving description into small, specific, behavioral, positive, situational, interactional, interpersonal, and realistic terms (Berg & Miller, 1992; de Shazer, 1991; O'Hanlon & Wilk, 1987). For example, clients are asked:

"What will be the *smallest* sign that this (desired outcome) is happening?"

"What will be the *first* sign that this (desired outcome) is happening?"

"I am not quite sure what you mean when you say (sober, straight, happy, or any other vague or psychological term that the client may use to describe their desired outcome)? How will you know when that is happening?"

"If I had a video camera (or tape recorder) and followed you around when you (were sober, had solved this problem, etc.), what would we see (or hear) you doing (or saying) that would tell us this problem had been solved?"

"When you are no longer (drinking, fighting, in trouble with the law, etc.) what will you be doing *instead*?"

"*Where will you be* when you first notice this happening?"

"*Who* will be the first to notice that this is happening?"

"*What exactly* will others (your spouse, children, employer, friends) notice different about you that will tell them this is happening?"

"What do you know about (your past, your self, your situation, others) that tells you that this could happen for you?"

The follow-up questions serve not only to amplify and extend the discussion of the hoped-for outcome, but also to make that outcome more tangible for the client. Together, the outcome and related follow-up questions usually account for the first 20 to 30 minutes of the initial treatment contact.

INSTANCE/EXCEPTION QUESTIONS

Instance and exception questions usually follow the outcome and related follow-up questions. These questions orient the therapeutic discussion toward times when the desired outcome is already occurring or to times when the problem that the client presents is either absent, less intense, or dealt with in a manner acceptable to the client (Miller, 1992).

Not long ago, instance and exception type questions were the primary focus of solution-focused brief therapy (de Shazer, 1985). As such, at or near the beginning of the initial treatment contact, clients were asked for details about what was different either when they did not drink or use drugs or when they had experienced any of their hoped-for outcome in the past. The reasoning behind this strategic questioning was simple: Find out how clients were successful in dealing with their drug or alcohol problems in the past and get them to repeat those same strategies in the future.

Over time, however, the discussion of instance and exception periods has shifted to later in the session, after the client has had an opportunity to answer the outcome and related follow-up questions. When the outcome questions and follow-up questions are asked first, a large number of clients spontaneously report exception periods without having to be asked directly about such periods by the therapist. More importantly, however, the instances and exceptions clients discuss are more likely to be related to their hoped-for outcomes or goals for the treatment contact. In addition, clients are more likely to be invested in the instances and exceptions that are related to their goals and, therefore, are more likely to try and repeat them in the future.

The client may be asked more directly if he or she does not spontaneously report any instances or exceptions. This is now done, however, *after* the outcome and follow-up questions have been posed. Examples of such questions include:

"I have a good picture of what you would like to be different. Now, in order to get a more complete picture of your situation, I need to know when the last time was that this happened, even just a small bit?"

"When do you already (experience your desired outcome)?"
"When was the last time you (experienced the desired outcome)?"
"When was the last time you thought you might (drink, use drugs, etc.) and didn't?"
"When was the last time the problem did not happen?"
"What is different about those times when the problem does not happen?"

While the instance and exception periods are being discussed, a series of follow-up questions are posed, which seek detailed information regarding what is different about the time when the instance or exception occurs. In addition, information is sought about how the client contributes to the occurrence of the desired outcome or to the problem being absent, less intense, or dealt with in an acceptable manner. This is accomplished by asking the client detailed questions (who, what, when, where, and how) with regard to the instance or exception. Obtaining such information makes the instance or exception more tangible to the client and, thus, easier to repeat in the future. Examples of such questions include:

"Who else noticed the time when the problem did not happen? What specifically did they notice you doing different?"
"Who else noticed the time when (the desired outcome happened)? What would they say you did differently to make that happen?"
"What would (you/they) say was different about that time?"
"When and how often did/does this happen?"
"Where did this happen?"
"How did this happen?"
"What would (you/they) say you need to do to make this happen again (or more often)?"

In all, the questions about instances and exceptions typically account for ten or so minutes of the initial treatment contact.

Prior to moving on to the next type of question, mention should be made of a special type of instance or exception known as pretreatment change. Results of research conducted at the Brief Family Therapy Center found that as many as two-thirds (66%) of clients reported positive, pretreatment change related to their desired outcome for treatment *if asked* about the change by the therapist (Weiner-Davis, de Shazer, & Gingerich, 1987). Coincidentally, outcome studies conducted at the Center found that the same number of clients actually achieved their desired therapeutic objectives (de Shazer, 1991)! Together, this research not only indicates that pretreatment change is prevalent, but suggests that it may be significant in achieving positive therapeutic outcome.

Curiously, little attention has been directed toward understanding and utilizing the factors responsible for extratherapeutic change, despite the fact that experts agree that such change accounts for at least 40% of the variance of total treatment outcome (Duncan, in press; Garfield & Bergin, 1986). In the field of alcohol and drug treatment, extratherapeutic change has been not only ignored, but viewed with suspicion and even labeled dangerous (Johnson, 1973, 1986). Problem drinkers and drug users who report such change are not likely to be supported for their report, but rather punished for it by being told they are "resistant," "in denial," experiencing a "flight into health," or a "transference reaction." This is probably due to the influence of the disease model, which holds, among other things, that problem drinkers and drug users cannot get better without formal treatment. For example, Vernon Johnson, a leading proponent of this perspective, counsels that, "unless the chemically dependent person gets help, he or she *will* die prematurely. . . . [as] it always gets worse if left untreated" (Johnson, 1986, pp. 6–7, emphasis added).

The field of alcohol and drug treatment has only recently been able to loose itself from traditional thinking long enough to begin a systematic study of the significant percentage of clients who manage to overcome serious drug and alcohol problems *without* the benefit of formal treatment. Preliminary data strongly suggest that there are substantial and consistent characteristics that enable certain individuals to overcome drug and alcohol problems without formal or lay treatment (cf. Shaffer & Jones, 1989). Learning how these individuals are successful will, it is hoped, inform drug and alcohol treatment in the future. In the meantime, however, inquiries can be made into how an individual client manages to make changes prior to the initiation of formal treatment, and those change-producing strategies can be incorporated into the treatment process.

SCALING QUESTIONS

Scaling questions usually come near the end of the initial treatment contact, after the client has answered the outcome and follow-up questions, as well as the instance and/or exception questions. These questions help establish a client-determined rating system for assessing progress, identifying achievable treatment goals, and determining and enhancing the client's willingness to work (Berg & de Shazer, 1993).

Scaling questions are first used in the initial treatment contact to establish a baseline against which future progress may be judged. Some typical baseline scaling questions include:

"On a scale of 1 to 10, where 10 is the day after the miracle, and 1 is when this situation was at its worst, where would you say things are today?"

"Let me ask you a numbers-type question. On a scale of 1 to 10, where 10 is when your problem is solved, and 1 is when the problem was at its worst, where would you say you are today?"

Once a baseline is established, scaling questions are next used to help clients identify small, realistic, and concrete steps toward their desired outcome. In particular, clients are asked to describe what differences they will notice when there has been a small increase in the scale. This is followed by questions intended to shape the client's description into specific, behavioral, positive, situational, interactional, interpersonal, and realistic terms. The following interchange from a recent session can be used to illustrate this process:

THERAPIST: Let me ask you a "numbers" kind of question.

CLIENT: Okay.

THERAPIST: On a scale from 1 to 10, where 10 is the day after the miracle, after the problem that brought you here has been solved, and 1 is when this situation was at its worst, where would you say you are today?

CLIENT: (pause) I would say, a 3.

THERAPIST: So, if a 10 is where you would like to be and a 1 is when this situation was at its worst, you would say that you are a 3?

CLIENT: Yeah, I am sort of in limbo . . . kind of waiting for the earthquake to blow.

THERAPIST: (nodding) Okay. What will be different when you have moved up the scale just a little? From, say, a 3 to a 4?

CLIENT: (long pause) If I would . . . if I could just stay away from those drinks.

THERAPIST: Uh huh. So, what would you do instead of drinking when you have moved from a 3 to a 4?

CLIENT: (pause) Well, that's a hard question . . .

THERAPIST: (nodding)

CLIENT: I might work out or get a game together.

THERAPIST: (curious look)

CLIENT: You know, go to the gym, get some guys and play basketball or something.

Finally, scaling questions are used to assess and enhance the client's willingness to work toward his or her desired objective. Clients are asked to state, on a scale from 1 to 10, how willing they are to do whatever it takes to solve their problem. Clients rating high on the scale are met with encouragement, while those rating low on the scale are complimented for their honesty and questioned further about what will be different when they are (or what it will take for them to be) slightly more willing.

ENDURANCE AND/OR EXTERNALIZATION QUESTIONS

Endurance and externalization questions elicit discussion about how the client manages to cope with, endure, and overcome the problems, temptations, and cravings associated with his or her drug or alcohol use on a day-to-day or moment-by-moment basis. Such questions have proven to have special merit in helping problem drinkers and drug users overcome the temptation or craving to drink or use drugs. In the process of answering such questions, problems, cravings, or temptations to drink or use become separate and distinct entities *external* to the client (White, 1984, 1986, 1987; White & Epston, 1990).

The process of externalizing the problem has been used for some time, albeit unintentionally, in the treatment of drug and alcohol problems. For example, the disease model of traditional alcoholism treatment is an externalization of the problem. This was first pointed out by Bateson (1972) in his analysis of Alcoholics Anonymous. In essence, proponents of the disease model convey the message to clients that they are not personally responsible for their drinking or drug use problem. Rather, problem drinkers and drug users are told that they have a primary, progressive, irreversible "disease" called alcoholism or chemical dependence from which they can recover but never be cured (cf. Johnson, 1973, 1986).

The Addictive Voice Recognition Technique (AVRT) of the Rational Recovery movement (Trimpey, 1993) is another example of an externalization procedure similar in process to the disease model of traditional treatment. In AVRT, problem drinkers or drug users are taught that they have an "addictive" voice originating from a primitive part of the brain, which expresses an appetite for a psychoactive substance and directs behavior toward its consumption. Externalization of the problem occurs when clients are taught to believe that they are not personally responsible for the voice urging them to drink or use drugs because it does not stem from higher, conscious, or rational parts of their brain but from a largely unconscious, irrational, and primitive part of their brain.

While actual physical evidence for both of these models is, at best, dubious (Berg & Miller, 1992; Peele, 1985, 1989), they serve essentially the same purpose as the externalization questions. Externalizing tends to decrease the defensiveness and sense of personal defeat often seen in clients who are struggling to overcome drug or alcohol problems while, simultaneously, increasing their motivation to work on the problem. This was demonstrated in a study by Seligman (1990), who found that subjects who blamed outside forces for poor performance tended to try harder than those who blamed themselves.

Externalization and endurance questions usually begin with a brief acknowledgment of the difficult nature of the client's problem and end with a question that highlights the personal competence or strength of the client in dealing with and overcoming the problem. Some examples of such questions include:

"The cravings that you experience sound nearly overwhelming. How do you manage to cope?"

"Given how strong these cravings have been, how have you managed to avoid (using drugs, drinking, etc.)?"

"What have you been doing to fight off the urge (or temptation) to (use drugs, drink, go to the bar, etc.)?"

"Tell me about the last time you were tempted to (use drugs, drink) and didn't?"

"What do you do to overcome the temptation to (use drugs, drink)?"

"How have you managed to overcome (temptations, cravings, withdrawal symptoms) in the past?"

"How have (you, others) kept things from becoming even worse?"

"What are you doing to keep (alcohol, drugs) from getting the best of you?"

"How did you (know, figure out) that would help?"

"If you hadn't been through this experience personally, would you ever have thought you had the strength to survive thus far?"

"Given how bad things have been, how come things aren't worse?"

Despite their obvious utility, endurance and externalization questions are not used in all or even in the majority of cases. At most, the questions are used in between five and ten percent of all treatment contacts, depending chiefly on the presentation of the client. The questions are most likely to be used when a client presents in crisis or when the focus of the treatment contact is on helping the client overcome cravings, temptations, or urges to use or drink. These questions are also used when the client has experienced a setback or relapse. In contrast to the traditional approaches, which focus on identifying what caused the relapse and then learning to avoid those things in the future, the brief therapist uses endurance questions to highlight what the client was doing to be successful *prior* to the setback and how he or she managed to overcome the relapse or setback once it did occur. The following are some examples of questions that can be used when the client has experienced a setback:

"How were you successful in dealing with (alcohol, drugs, etc.) prior to the setback?"

"How did you manage to be successful for so long?"

"What would others (spouse, friends, employer) say you were doing to be successful? How did you do that?"

"How did you manage to stop (drinking, using) when you did?"

"What clues did you have that told you to stop when you did? "What told you it was time to stop? What are you (have you been) doing to become more sensitive to these clues?"

"What would others (spouse, employer, friends) say you did different in order to stop when you did?"

"What have you learned from this episode that you will use in the future?"

"Is this your way of reminding yourself that you still have a problem? How will you remain aware of this in the future?"

CASE EXAMPLE

A 37-year-old man sought treatment for a serious cocaine problem. "Lamont" had recently been released from prison, where he had been incarcerated for some time for his involvement in a drug-related homicide. At the time of the first meeting, Lamont was unemployed and living with his girlfriend. He had decided to seek treatment when his girlfriend threatened to end their relationship because of his use and selling of cocaine. As is typical of most initial contacts, the session began with the therapist asking the client what brought him into treatment. In this instance, Lamont responded with a brief history of his problem:

CLIENT: Well, I got out of the penitentiary and, when I did, I had a positive attitude. I had slowed down a lot. You see, I been selling and using drugs since I was 13 years old. I came up in Detroit, and we was very poor. I sold drugs, for the money to offset my mother's income and to help myself when I was going to school.

THERAPIST: Uh huh.

CLIENT: (pause) I been in and out of jail before, but this time was different. I tried to put things together.

THERAPIST: (nodding) Uh huh.

CLIENT: But, I went back to old ways and now my girlfriend, well, she has never approved of my cocaine usage.

THERAPIST: Your girlfriend?

CLIENT: (nodding) My girlfriend.

THERAPIST: What's her first name?

CLIENT: Barbara. She put up with it, at first, as long as it wasn't in the house, around her, and I showed some amount of control. It's periods of my life where I lose complete control. I say to myself, you know, "I can't do this, I got to pay these bills, I got to get a car." Well, I've lost complete control again, and she is saying that she is going to walk.

THERAPIST: Uh huh. Sounds like you don't want that to happen.

CLIENT: No, I don't.

THERAPIST: Are you saying that you want to change this?

CLIENT: (*nodding affirmatively*)

THERAPIST: Is that right? You want to change this?

CLIENT: (*nodding affirmatively*) Yeah, I do.

As can be seen from this brief excerpt, the therapist initially listened as the client presented his reasons for seeking treatment. During this initial phase of the treatment contact, the therapist is waiting for the client to say that there is a problem that needs to be solved, or to express a desire to be helped or to change his problematic situation. If no request is made, the therapist would simply continue to listen and acknowledge the client's experience. Asking an outcome question before a client states that there is a problem to be solved or requests help is a common error, since these questions assume that the client wants something from the treatment contact. Because, in this case, the client stated that he had a problem and agreed that he wanted to do something in order to bring about a change, the outcome questions were asked. In this instance, the therapist chose the "miracle" question:

THERAPIST: Okay. Let me ask you a question that can be helpful in getting things started. It takes some pretending on your part. Sound okay?

CLIENT: Sure.

THERAPIST: Here's how it goes. Suppose tonight, after you left our meeting, you went home and the rest of the day went by, you go to bed, and you fall asleep. While you're sleeping, a miracle happens. And the miracle is that the problem that brought you here today is solved, just like that (*snaps fingers*). But, because you're asleep, you don't know that this miracle has happened.

CLIENT: (*nodding*)

THERAPIST: When you wake up in the morning, what would be different that would start to make you wonder, "Hey, a miracle has happened here. My problems are solved!"

CLIENT: (*pause*) I wouldn't feel so heavy at heart. I wouldn't punish myself as much as I do. (*tearful*) I wouldn't feel so sad, and I would, you know, cause *I can remember a few times in my life where I have felt elated, and was just happy about life and just sweet, you know.*

As often happens, the client in this case spontaneously mentioned an instance or exception as he talked about his hoped-for outcome. When such an experience is mentioned this early in the treatment contact, however, the therapist should simply make a note to return to it for further exploration after sufficient time has been spent amplifying the rest of the client's answer to the outcome question. Choosing to explore instances and exceptions early on runs the risk of limiting responses to the outcome question, thereby decreasing the number of potential solutions.

In this case, the interview continued with the therapist asking a series of follow-up questions designed to shape the client's answer into small, specific, behavioral, positive, situational, interactional, interpersonal, and realistic terms. The first question in this series was designed to shape the client's hoped-for outcome into more specific terms:

THERAPIST: So, after this miracle, you wouldn't feel so "heavy at heart."

CLIENT: Uh huh.

THERAPIST: What would Barbara see you *doing* that would tell her that you were no longer feeling so "heavy at heart?"

CLIENT: She'd see me doing some of the things that I wanted to do out of life, like things I wanted to do, I have so many things I want to do.

THERAPIST: What would she see you doing?

CLIENT: She would see me doing some volunteering, she would see me putting some of my art work into effect, not just doing it in the house, but showing it to people. She has been trying to get me to show some of my stuff since I met her.

THERAPIST: Okay. She would see you putting it into effect, doing it around the house, showing it to people. Help me understand that. What would she notice?

CLIENT: She would notice me going back down to the Art Fair, or framing, or . . . arranging something, you know, getting something ready to show, or taking something to Detroit or to the Lakefront in Spring. Every Spring here they have an amateur artist show and she has told me . . . she would like to see me with some of my stuff there.

THERAPIST: Okay.

CLIENT: She would just see me *doing*. Instead of seeing me doing, like, drugs, she would see me doing the things that she knows satisfy me.

With a few questions, Lamont makes his description more specific. The discussion continued with Lamont adding detail and becoming even more specific about this aspect of his hoped-for outcome. The therapist then asked additional questions designed to shape the detail into positive, interactional, and interpersonal terms. Thereafter, the therapist helped Lamont to expand his description of the miracle by asking the question, "What else?" For example, "What else will you notice that is different on your miracle day?" After identifying many things that would be different, the therapist asked Lamont "what else?" one final time.

THERAPIST: Okay. Anything else that would be different?

CLIENT: After the miracle?

THERAPIST: (*nodding affirmatively*)

CLIENT: I would be calmer.

THERAPIST: You wound be calmer?

CLIENT: (*nodding*)

THERAPIST: What would you be doing that would give you and Barbara the idea that you were calmer?

CLIENT: Maybe being able to sit down and watch an hour long program without jumping up and running to the bedroom or running to the adjoining room.

THERAPIST: Uh huh. So you would sit with her, be with her. What else?

CLIENT: If a friend calls me, you know, instead of getting hyped about what they're talking about, I'd say, "Well, you know, right now I'm involved in something." Because it's like she feels I put my friends before her. Anytime my cocaine buddies . . . I only have cocaine buddies now, I used to have other friends, but because of my usage, you know, they didn't feel comfortable, they faded away . . .

THERAPIST: What would be different about *that* after the miracle?

CLIENT: I'll have different friends.

THERAPIST: Say more about that.

CLIENT: Like, last night, my friends called and I had an urge to go and smoke some, but I really didn't want to and so I dealt with it.

While expanding his answer to the miracle question, Lamont once again mentions an instance or exception spontaneously. This time, the therapist chose to explore the client's report. As will be recalled, the identification of exceptions to problem drinking or drug use is not enough. First, exceptions and instances must be related to the client's hoped-for outcome. As the discussion of this exception or instance period occurred spontaneously and within the context of the client's answer to the outcome question, one can safely assume that it is related to his goal for seeking treatment. Second, a vital part of using exceptions to generate solutions is that the client must be able to identify how the instances or exceptions came about. In this regard, the therapist pushes Lamont for exact details about how he was able to turn down his friends and overcome the urge to use cocaine.

THERAPIST: (*incredulous*) You didn't do it?

CLIENT: No. In fact, I haven't had anything since the first of the year. Tonight, at midnight, will be my eighth day of abstinence.

THERAPIST: Congratulations!

CLIENT: Thank you.

THERAPIST: How have you done it?

CLIENT: (*tearful*) I'm tired of it disrupting my life. I'm tired of it making me feel the way it makes me feel.

THERAPIST: How did you get yourself to pay attention to that?

CLIENT: 'Cause Barbara said she was going to walk on me.

THERAPIST: Uh huh. And how did you turn that into action? What did you *do* so that you were able to turn your friends down like that and choose to stay with Barbara?

CLIENT: I told myself, "It's just an urge" and then I walked over and watched TV with Barbara.

THERAPIST: And that worked? That helped you?

CLIENT: Uh huh.

THERAPIST: How did telling yourself that "it's just an urge" help?

CLIENT: 'Cause I knew it would pass and, Barbara, she helped me.

This process continued until the who, what, when, where, and how of the exception period were clearly spelled out. Scaling questions were then used to establish a baseline and to help Lamont identify some small, realistic, and concrete steps toward his desired outcome.

THERAPIST: Let me ask you this, if a 10, on a scale of 1 to 10, were "you're there," and a 1 was the farthest you've ever been away from what we've talked about today, on a scale from 1 to 10, where are you today? A 10 is there and a 1 is the farthest you've ever been away from there. Where are you today?

CLIENT: I am a 0.

THERAPIST: Okay. Are you sure?

CLIENT: I feel zero-ish.

THERAPIST: If I asked Barbara where you were, what would she say?

CLIENT: Probably the same, maybe a 1.

THERAPIST: Okay. Then, with a 10 being out there, a 10 being this place, the place you want to be, what would be just a little bit different, say, instead of a 0 you'd be a ½ or a 1? What would be just a little bit different about your life in, say, the coming weeks that would make you start to think, "I'm moving up the scale, I'm moving and getting closer to what I want." It would be just one step now, just a ½ or a 1, not 10.

CLIENT: Stabilize my mind.

THERAPIST: Help me understand that. What do you mean . . . what will be different when you have stabilized your mind?

CLIENT: To be able to say . . . that I'm making some progress on my plans. I haven't, like, drawn out my goal sheet yet. It's formulated in my heart and in my head.

THERAPIST: A goal sheet?

CLIENT: To write down some of this that we've been talking about.

THERAPIST: Where would some of this that we've been talking about be on the goal sheet?

CLIENT: The number one thing is continuing to stay off drugs.

THERAPIST: Uh huh.

CLIENT: (*stands up and turns around*) That and, you see I used weigh 190 pounds, I don't know if you can see?

THERAPIST: You're pretty thin.

CLIENT: I don't weigh close to, nowhere near that.

THERAPIST: So . . .

CLIENT: Starting to eat right, you know, the right kinda food and just eating every meal, every day.

THERAPIST: That would be on your goal sheet?

CLIENT: (*nodding*) This one thing that I had made up my mind this morning to do would be on there: to do some volunteer work.

THERAPIST: Uh huh.

CLIENT: I was watching the news and it was talking about the FOOD-BANK, and I said, "That's good," cause it will help me and somebody else. But, then, I read an article about volunteering for this hospital, I can't remember where it is, but I got it up here somewhere (*points at head*). When I get back home, I'll get the article.

THERAPIST: Wow! Sounds like doing something for others will make a difference for you.

CLIENT: I want to make a difference. If I die tomorrow, I want somebody to say, "He made a difference this way, he helped me, he helped somebody."

THERAPIST: Sure. You want to matter.

CLIENT: (*tearful*) I want to matter! I want to matter! I don't want somebody to say I'm a drug fiend or a drug dealer and that I was nothing! I'm tired of feeling this way and I feel like I need to do something for somebody without wanting money or anything in return.

Following this interchange, the therapist asked Lamont if there was anything else he wanted or needed to say. Asking clients this question is the standard method of closing the interview. The question has proven useful for that handful of clients who wait until the last moments of the interview to provide some crucial piece of information. Lamont was not asked to rate his willingness to work toward his desired outcome. The therapist decided that Lamont's willingness to work was apparent in the way he had concluded his responses to the scaling questions and that the question was not necessary.

When Lamont responded that he did not have anything more to say, the therapist left the consultation room to consult with a treatment team, which had been observing the case behind a one-way mirror. Together, the team constructed a message and homework task that was read to Lamont before the end of the session. The method for constructing such messages is beyond the scope of the present paper but is discussed in detail elsewhere (Berg & Miller, 1992; Molnar & de Shazer, 1987). Briefly, however, the message contained compliments for what Lamont had been doing that was helpful and was related to his desired outcome, as well as an acknowledgment of the difficulties with which he was faced. The homework task was for Lamont to follow through with committing his goals to paper and then choosing one or two of the items to do during the week.

Lamont was seen for a total of six visits over a period of four months. With one minor setback along the way, he managed to take control of his drug use problem during that time. In the end, the outcome he attained was very similar to the one he had described in response to the miracle question. At his second session, for example, Lamont reported that he had contacted a local youth program and was working as a volunteer tutor in their reading program. In a subsequent session, he reported that, together with his girlfriend Barbara, he had looked for and found a new apartment away from the neighborhood and friends, which were such a significant part of his drug use. At a follow-up interview, conducted six months after his final treatment contact, Lamont reported that he was continuing to make progress. He was still drug-free and was now working on arranging financing so that he could attend a local technical college. When asked how he had managed to accomplish all that he had, Lamont responded, "I've kept myself busy trying to organize this stuff and put in my head about the things I want to do. Going at it instead of just sitting around moping and thinking, cause if I think about what I want and do it, then I think it will come back on me. I can see the beauty in my life . . . as long as I choose the beauty, it will be there." Lamont, it seemed, finally mattered.

SUMMARY

The present chapter presents and illustrates the use of questions in orienting the problem drinker or drug user toward solution. As indicated at the beginning, asking the right question often has more impact on the client and the process of change than having the correct answer. However, while the questions presented in this chapter constitute the bulk of therapeutic activity in solution-focused work, the interviewing component is only one part of the solution-focused approach for treating people with drug and alcohol problems. In addition to interviewing, the model has three other parts, which address issues common to any drug and alcohol treatment approach. For example, solution-focused strategies for addressing different levels of client motivation, helping clients maintain the changes they make in treatment, and preventing and/or addressing the recurrence of problematic drug or alcohol use both during and after treatment. Each of these important issues are presented and discussed in detail in the book *Working with the Problem Drinker: A Solution-Focused Approach* (Berg & Miller, 1992), as well as in several articles (Berg, 1989; Miller, 1992; Miller & Berg, 1991).

REFERENCES

Bateson, G. (1972). *Steps to an Ecology of Mind*. New York: Aronson.

Berg, I. K., & de Shazer, S. (1993). Making numbers talk: Language in therapy. In S. Friedman (Ed.), *The New Language of Change: Constructive Collaboration in Psychotherapy*. New York: Guilford.

Berg, I. K., & Gallagher, D. (1991). Solution focused brief treatment with adolescent substance abusers. In T. Todd & M. Selekman (Eds.), *Family Therapy Approaches with Adolescent Substance Abusers*. Boston: Allyn & Bacon.

Berg, I. K., & Miller, S. D. (1992). *Working with the Problem Drinker: A Solution-Focused Approach*. New York: Norton.

de Shazer, S. (1985). *Keys to Solution in Brief Therapy*. New York: Norton.

de Shazer, S. (1991). *Putting Difference to Work*. New York: Norton.

Duncan, B. (in press). Applying outcome research: Intentional utilization of the client's frame of reference. *Psychotherapy*.

Garfield, S., & Bergin, A. (Eds.). (1986). *Handbook of Psychotherapy and Behavior Change* (3rd ed.). New York: John Wiley.

Johnson, V. (1973). *I'll Quit Tomorrow.* New York: Harper & Row.

Johnson, V. (1986). *Intervention: How to Help Someone Who Doesn't Want Help.* Minneapolis, MN: Johnson Institute Books.

Johnson, L., & Miller, S. D. (in press). Modification of depression risk factors: A solution-focused approach. *Psychotherapy*.

Miller, S. D. (1992). The symptoms of solution. *Journal of Strategic and Systemic Therapies, 11*(1), 1–11.

Miller, S. D., & Berg, I. K. (1991). Working with the problem drinker: A solution-focused approach. *Arizona Counseling Journal, 16*(1), 3–12.

Molnar, A., & de Shazer, S. (1987). Solution-focused therapy: Toward the identification of therapeutic tasks. *Journal of Marital and Family Therapy, 13*(4), 359–363.

O'Hanlon, B., & Wilk, J. (1987). *Shifting Contexts: The Generation of Effective Psychotherapy.* New York: Guilford.

Peele, S. (1985). *The Meaning of Addiction.* Lexington, MA: Lexington Books.

Peele, S. (1989). *The Diseasing of America: Addiction Treatment Out of Control.* Lexington, MA: Lexington Books.

Seligman, M. (1990). *Learned Optimism.* New York: Knopf.

Shaffer, H. J., & Jones, S. B. (1989). *Quitting Cocaine: The Struggle Against Impulse.* Lexington, MA: Lexington Books.

Trimpey, J. (1993). AVRT: A brief summary. *Journal of Rational Recovery, 5*(5), 4.

Weiner-Davis, M., de Shazer, S., & Gingerich, W. (1987). Building on pre-treatment changes to construct the therapeutic solution: An exploratory study. *Journal of Marital and Family Therapy, 13*(4), 359–363.

White, M. (1984). Pseudo-encopresis: From avalanche to victory. *Family Systems Medicine, 2*(2), 150–160.

White, M. (1986). Negative explanation, restraint and double description: A template for family therapy. *Family Process, 25*(2), 169–184.

White, M. (1987, Spring). Family therapy and schizophrenia: Addressing the "in the corner" lifestyle. *Dulwich Centre Newsletter*, pp. 14–21.

White, M., & Epston, D. (1990). *Narrative Means to Therapeutic Ends.* New York: Norton.

CHAPTER 6

"On Track" in Solution-Focused Brief Therapy

JOHN L. WALTER
JANE E. PELLER

In our training seminars, where we teach the use of our version of the "miracle question" from solution-focused brief therapy (de Shazer, 1985)—"If a miracle happened tonight and you woke up tomorrow with the problem solved, what would you be doing differently?" (Walter & Peller, 1992)—workshop participants frequently raise questions and objections such as these:

- What do I do when the client says that his or her goal and miracle will be that he or she will no longer be grieving?
- My clients usually state that they will no longer be feeling bad or overwhelmed. How can therapy be brief with that situation?

The questioner usually thinks that grieving takes a long time, that grieving is painful, and that the solution is a time in the future when the loss is resolved and the client no longer feels bad. The questioner then asks how can this therapy be brief or how can we be doing anything more than putting a bandaid on the pain.

Another seminar participant's question might be something like this:

- What do I do when I ask the miracle question and a client says that after the miracle he or she will have made a decision as to whether to stay married or get a divorce?

When the questioner presses the client for a more detailed description of life after the miracle, the client states that he or she does not know

111

the answer to that yet because the decision has not yet been made. Life after the miracle will consist of either being divorced or being married. The client thinks it is not possible to answer the miracle question because he or she does not know as yet what to decide, and if he or she did know that, then therapy would not be necessary. The questioner is usually puzzled as to what to do when faced with such an either/or answer.

Another question might be:

- What do I do when the client says that after the miracle, he or she won't be addicted anymore.
- What do I do then?
- Doesn't that leave the client still powerlessly thinking that life cannot be different until this addiction is changed?
- What will he or she do in the meantime?

The miracle question is a very useful invitation to the client to jump past problem language to "life beyond the problem," and some other language (see also Freedman & Combs, 1993). Frequently, problem language provides no difference for clients and leaves them going around in circles with their thinking and resulting actions. While we have found the miracle question to be very useful in helping clients avoid problem language, they may still have difficulty, as the above examples illustrate, of shifting to some other language. The miracle does not always seem to be enough for the client to escape problem thinking. In such cases, we have found that an additional metaphor, that of being on track, can also be useful.

"ON TRACK" AS A METAPHOR FOR THERAPY

The notion of "on track" has advantages both as a way of thinking of the overall purpose of therapy and as a technique for opening new meaning where clients are stuck in thinking of their goal as an endpoint or in some either/or fashion.

Harlene Anderson and the late Harry Goolishian stated that they thought clients came into therapy because they perceived themselves as being in situations where they were stuck or they seemed to have no other options (Anderson & Goolishian, 1988, 1989). They (1989) further stated that one of the goals of therapy, then, is to facilitate agency, ". . . a sense of competent action; the ability to think and feel that we have a way of doing." Our understanding of this is that if clients come in feeling that they have no options, no possibilities, no way to make a difference in their situation, then hopefully they will leave therapy feeling that they are already doing something or that they now have options that they did not have before. In our words, they would say they were on track. The problem may not be totally solved, but they now think they are already doing some things or thinking in some way that will eventually lead to what they want.

White has also stated that clients come in with problem-saturated stories, stories that do not fit with their being able to have a satisfying experience (White & Epston, 1990). So the task of therapy is the authoring of new stories, which allow for some new meaning or experience. Again, we agree and understand this to mean that a new story allows clients to do something different, to feel that they are on track.

As we discuss in *Becoming Solution-Focused in Brief Therapy* (Walter & Peller, 1992, especially Chapter 4), being on track involves having well-defined goals, ones that meet the following criteria: They are: (1) in a positive representation (describing what clients *do* want rather than what they do *not*, what they *will* be doing rather than what they will *not* be doing); (2) in a process form; (3) in the here and now; (4) as specific as possible; (5) in the client's control (meaning that the action can be started or maintained by the client); and (6) in the client's language. The goal in solution-focused approaches (Berg & Miller, 1992; de Shazer 1985, 1988; de Shazer et al., 1986; Durrant, 1993; O'Hanlon & Weiner-Davis, 1989; Walter & Peller, 1992) is to help clients to a sense of being on track, to a realization that they can now do something whereas, previously, they thought they could not or that they now can do something when before they thought they were stuck. If clients think that they can continue to do what they have begun, or if they think they can do what they have now created as an option for themselves, then they no longer need therapy. They can do these things on their own. In Anderson and Goolishian's terminology, they now have a sense of agency, that they now have a "way of doing."

This notion of on track enables the therapy to be brief. Ending therapy does not have to wait until the problem is totally solved or the goal is totally reached. When clients think that they are on track or that they now have things they can do on their own, they no longer need a therapist. The total resolution of a situation may take months or even years, but the therapy can be brief because the goal is only for clients to feel they are on a workable track.

Lipchik (1993) pursues an aim similar to the on-track metaphor. She helps clients create "both/and" solutions, where they previously thought their options were either/or. Her thinking is that many times clients present situations as if their options are either very limited or nonexistent, while solutions are unrealistically positive. Many times the both/and solutions many times lie somewhere between the worst and the best scenarios. These new solutions allow clients to feel they now have options they did not think they had before. In our words, the clients leave thinking they are on track.

ILLUSTRATIONS OF ON TRACK

"On track" is a working metaphor, which can be used in questions in the situations mentioned at the beginning of the chapter. Those situations were (1) a seemingly long process like grieving, (2) a solution initially phrased in either/or terms, and (3) a solution phrased as an endpoint (like not smoking).

A Long Process—Grieving[1]

Grieving is commonly understood as a long process whose solution will take a long time.

For us, such processes are normal. However, many therapists bring different assumptions to grieving. They believe that therapy is a relationship in which the therapist and client go through the process of venting feelings together. Second, they may assume that there is something problematic about a transitional process and that something about how the person is functioning should be changed. They may also conclude that almost any person needs to be supported through that transitional process. Third, they may assume that there is some finished end to the transition that would then tell the therapist and client when it is time to conclude therapy.

Again, our belief is that therapy is about getting *on track* with living normal processes—not about solving, changing, or completing the process. Normal grieving can last a long time or at least as long as the person determines that he or she needs or wants to grieve. Missing someone or grieving may go on for the rest of a person's life. To us, therapy is not about being with the client while they go through the entire process of "working through" their feelings of loss. Nor is therapy about leading a client through prescribed stages to reach an end goal of "acceptance," as a therapist might if they subscribed literally to the Kübler-Ross model (Kübler-Ross, 1969).

In solution-focused approaches, therapy is about having a conversation in which both therapist and client construct what the client will be doing when he or she is on track to grieving in a way that fits best for him or her. When clients have formulated their process for grieving and think that they are doing that process, then therapy can stop. Our job as therapists is to get out of their way so that they can go through *their* own process for growth. If we were to continue therapy, the client might think that he or she is supposed to do something different or that he or she needs therapy to do the grieving or to do it properly. We assume that,

---

[1]Some of this material was previously published in Peller and Walter (1993). Copyright 1993 by the Eastwood Family Therapy Centre, Epping, New South Wales, Australia. Reprinted by permission.

as they grieve naturally, the process will be self-reinforcing and lead them to a sense of resolution about the loss.

Case Example

A 43-year-old man came to see one of us (Jane) because he was distressed at having "severe" anxiety attacks at least five times a day, each of which lasted for at least five minutes.[2] When asked what he wanted from therapy, he stated that he did not want to be "victimized" by his feelings but instead he wanted to be "in control" of them. Recently, his anxiety attacks had decreased. Instead, they had turned into a "melancholy" feeling, which to him was just as bad as the attacks. He had other presenting problems, as well. He was having trouble at work, he could not concentrate, his friends did not want to talk with him, and he could not sleep.

Throughout the conversation, he told Jane about a nightmare story of how he was brought back to life twice after complications due to peritonitis and how he had to recuperate for three months. Then his father died, and his lover of 13 years was hospitalized and finally died of a heart attack after a liver transplant because of damage caused by alcoholism. This final loss had occurred one month ago, and he was still dealing with getting the estate in order. Given all this, his anxiety attacks and depression sounded appropriate to Jane. In fact, she commented that she was impressed that he was functioning as well as he was. Given the circumstances he had described, she would not have been surprised if he had reported doing much worse.

At the beginning of the conversation, he stated that he felt so bad that on a scale of 1 to 10 (10 being "contented" and 1 being "very bad"), he placed himself off the scale at an average of a negative 2 or 3. However, when he did feel better—a rating of 1 or 2—he thought he was "denying his feelings." To Jane, this all sounded quite normal, and even impressive, since there were times when he could put feelings aside in order to do something else. However, to him, this was "denial" and, therefore, something that was bad or sick. He thought he should try harder to "deal" with the feelings by what he called "soul-searching." When Jane asked how he would do this, he described how he would take time to deal with his feelings and, at other times, he would "celebrate life."

We felt the client was already in the process of grieving, spending time feeling whatever was important for *him* to feel about the losses and, at other times, doing something else to "celebrate the living."

The fact that he was already doing what he needed to do to go through his grieving process but that he did not know that he was on track was a key point in the therapeutic conversation. If he did not know

[2]While we often work together as a team, Jane was working alone with this individual.

what he was already doing that was working or helpful, or what the on-track behaviors would look like, he could not deliberately do them. If he could not deliberately do them, then the solution would be a random occurrence. The therapeutic move at this point in the conversation was to focus on developing a consciousness of what he was already doing or wanted to do that was on track for his grieving process.

Therefore, in Jane's feedback to him, she stated the following:

"I think you have done a tremendous job in pulling through all of these incidents, not just the loss of John, your lover, your father, and almost yourself twice but also the issues with the doctors, hospitals, legal troubles, et cetera. It is very understandable how it can be one big lump of stuff [feelings]. I agree with you that you need time to sort, 'soul search,' so that the other times are not denials but real celebrations of life.

"Therefore, what I would like you to do is take 30 minutes a day of undivided time to let yourself think and 'soul search' about all this. During the rest of the day, when you think of something, just take note of it so that you will remember to think about it during the 30 minute 'soul search' time."

This task prescribed what he had already constructed for himself as his solution, the "soul-searching." He had described "soul-searching" as taking time to deal with his feelings and, at other times, to go on to "celebrating life." The task supported his solution of soul-searching and provided a structure for doing it in a concentrated way.

He came back 12 days later and stated that there had been a big difference since the last session. He had taken the 30 minutes per day to think over situations, to "logically think through" them. He had discovered that he was mad at John, his deceased lover. He was mad that John had died, that John had left the estate in disarray, and that he was left with the responsibility to clean it up. He also had a discussion with his mother, which was very different for him, about the death of his father. He discussed how he felt guilty for not having been available more often for his mother, whereupon they each consoled the other. In addition, an old friend, Bobbie, had come to visit for the weekend from out of town, and they had a good time—the client felt that he was not a burden to his friend. Being a burden was something that he had been concerned about since all the losses had occurred.

There were times when the client had "given in to the depression," instead of fighting it as he had before. Through this giving-in to the feelings, he realized that he "could not be responsible" for others, that he was not going to carry things over, and that he would never have the "naive outlook on life" that he did before the losses. It was time to "celebrate the living," he said. To Jane, these were some very big steps that he had made in 12 days. Most importantly, he had consciously decided when he was going to process the grieving issues, as he experienced them, and he had separated those issues from times when he was going to move on with his life. From Jane's perspective, therapy could have been finished at this point, because he seemed on track.

On the other hand, he was still concerned about times when he felt bitter and cynical. He did not like this about himself, because he had always thought of himself as a caring person. He thought that this bitterness and cynicism were signs that he was not on track with his grieving process. However, to Jane, this sounded like the process of normal grieving and perhaps if he were to view it as such, he would not let it interfere with his grieving. Jane's feedback to him was as follows:

"I am very impressed with how you went about putting structure on the anxiety and depression, so that it became manageable for you. In addition, you then realized that there were times when you were feeling angry and needing to grieve. You also realized that there were other times when you wanted to celebrate the living with others, like Bobbie, your mother, and even yourself.

"This grieving is a needed process for you to have, and I think that when you experience being bitter or cynical it is because you need to do some more grieving but have not let the process happen yet. Given human nature, there will be some days when you will need to grieve more than on other days. It is like being hungry, some days you are more hungry than on other days, and, therefore need to eat more.

"Therefore, each day I would suggest that you just ask yourself: 'How much time do I need today to go through the grieving?'"

This task was designed to allow the client to continue to evaluate and determine what he thought was his normal process for grieving and to develop some criteria for how much was enough.

The client returned in two weeks. He stated that he no longer thought he was in denial of his feelings nor was he upset with experiencing anxiety attacks and melancholy feelings. He stated that he felt much more in control of his feelings, even though he still had feelings of anger, sadness, and melancholy. Since the last session, he decided that in order to celebrate the living he would start some "self-development" projects while also continuing to ask himself daily how much time he needed to "soul-search." One of his self-development projects was to go out with some friends. Not only did he do that, but he even felt good enough that he met someone to date!

The conversation throughout the session was about how he was constructing these images and plans for the future for himself and with other people. There still was one piece that interfered with his constructing this future—his tendency to be bitter and cynical. He decided that, as part of his self-development project, he would overcome this by observing how others "created positives out of negatives," and he thought this would be a good exercise.

In keeping with the rule, "If it works, don't fix it" (Berg & Miller, 1992; de Shazer, 1985; Walter & Peller, 1992), Jane then gave him the following feedback:

"I am very impressed with what you have done in making a conscious effort to initiate positive self-development. It is a very big step from the last time I saw you, because you are beginning to build a future for yourself with others. I really like this idea you have about how to overcome being bitter and cynical, and I would suggest you continue to listen for feedback and watch how others create positives out of negatives."

Jane and the client had planned their last session for three weeks from the last meeting. The client sat down in the chair, and he responded to, "How are you? What is different or better since I last saw you?" with, "I'm fine. I've been so busy I have not had the time to think about anything. When I do think about the past I think the memories must be fading because it just does not have the impact on my life that it had at one time. When I do reflect upon something it is with . . . kind of . . . a bittersweet way." He proceeded to describe how he now was able to "celebrate the living" *and* have times when he thought about the losses.

He felt he was feeling what he needed to and was on track in his grieving process. He stated that he felt satisfied with therapy. He knew that there would still be times of melancholy and/or anger, but he now accepted that those feelings would be all right and on track for his grieving process.

Grieving over losses in one's life is a normal process that takes time. Like this client, people seem to get scared by the feelings they have during that process and, therefore, seek out professional help. What they are looking for is not necessarily a hand to hold but to know that what they are experiencing is normal. We think that it behooves us as professionals to construct mutually with our clients how they are going to know what their track is so that they can naturally and instinctively follow it.

The Solution as an Either/Or Decision

A different situation is presented when a client's goal is in either/or terms, such as a decision to be made. As we stated earlier, clients frequently present their miracles as the result of the decision. For example, someone contemplating getting divorced or staying married may think they have only two options. When asked the miracle question, they talk about life after the miracle in these same either/or terms, either they will be married or divorced. If the conversation ended here, this would make little difference for the client. The client would still be thinking with problem language. This is where the on-track metaphor can open up space for some alternatives.

Case Example

A man in his early forties came to see John. He had been in a long-term growth-oriented therapy for several months before moving to Chicago.

At first, he stated that he wanted to get out of the doldrums. He had been married for seven years and separated for the past year. He still loved his wife a great deal, but they were getting on so badly that they had decided to live separately. He still saw her for dinner, on occasion, just to keep up their friendship and keep each other abreast as to what was happening.

He felt very unhappy and depressed. He thought he needed to make a decision about whether to get divorced or not. His perception of his previous therapist's advice was that he should make a decision. Friends were also urging him to get on with it and make a decision. But, he was feeling increasingly bad. He, too, felt he should make a decision, and he blamed himself for not doing so. He told himself that he must be some sort of wimp for not forcing himself to make a choice.

He thought his wife was in no hurry to make a decision and that perhaps she wanted to get back together. This only made him feel worse, because he felt the responsibility for the decision to divorce would be totally his. The problem was that he was not sure. He loved her a great deal. He thought she was a good person but, for some reason, they had not been getting along. The fact that he cared so much about her, he thought, made it even more difficult. He found it hard to justify divorcing someone whom he still cared about and thought was a good person. Even now, when he talked to friends who knew them both, he thought he was defensive and had a hard time justifying why he and his wife were not working things out.

For now, he did not want to get divorced or make a decision, he just wanted to get back to feeling decently about himself. Others, including his previous therapist, were telling him he would not feel good about himself until he made a decision. However, he thought the opposite. He thought that as long as he was feeling so bad about himself, he could not trust himself to make a good decision about his future.

His stated goal at this time was to be "striving to be happy." When asked, "If a miracle happened tonight, and you woke up tomorrow, and you were striving to be happy, what would you be doing or thinking different?" he said that he would not be debilitated. This meant that he would go out with friends and with this new person he had met. He would get back into exercise and concentrate on his job rather than worry and ruminate about how bad he felt and what decision he wanted to make. He also thought that he would allow himself to feel sad. He wanted to be honest with himself, and that meant that, at times, he felt very sad and cried about his marriage.

John's feedback and reflections to him at the end of the session were these:

"I am very impressed with your honesty and caring in this situation, caring for yourself, for her, and for your girlfriend. I suspect this is such a troubling situation because you do care so much for others and are sensitive to their feelings and not just your own.

"I agree with your idea that you do not necessarily have to make a decision in order to be happy and feel good about yourself at this time. The decision may evolve as well by your doing things for yourself at this time and making yourself happy.

"My suggestion would be, between now and the next time I see you, that you notice what you do that makes you feel better and how you do it."

The client thought this made sense, and he scheduled another appointment.

When he came in for the second and third appointments, he reported that he felt relieved that he did not have to make the decision right away and that he had gotten himself back into an exercise routine and was getting out some. He was concentrating on his work and was actually thinking about sending out his resumé and changing jobs. He had gone out on two dates with his girlfriend and had a good time. He reminded himself that just because she would like him to take quicker action about the divorce did not mean that he had to. He could make this decision in a thoughtful way.

John's feedback continued to be supportive of his making this decision in his own way, that it probably helped for him to be making himself happy on a day-to-day basis and to see what happened. Perhaps, as he thought, the effort to make himself happy would be helpful in making some eventual decision.

John also offered the idea that if he was looking for certainty about the decision that he might have some misconceptions about certainty. Many people think that the amount of certainty they feel about their decisions is a predictor of the rightness of the decision and a predictor that things will work out that way. John said there was no correlation that he knew of that would make that true. There are just as many people who are unsure about the decision they make and the decision turns out to be all right as there are people who are absolutely sure about a decision and the decision turns out to be a mistake.

In the fourth session, the client talked about his recent thinking about whether to get divorced or not. John asked several miracle questions to help him organize or create possibilities. The first question was: "If a miracle happened and things were going more the way you want between you and your wife, what would be different or what would you be doing differently?"

He thought for quite some time and replied that, as much as he liked her, he just could not imagine things ever being the way he wanted with her. She was a very nice person, and he loved her very much, but perhaps they had just grown in different directions. He thought maybe this was nobody's fault but just a fact that she would probably agree to, that they were just going in different directions at this time. He wanted to buy property in the city and get involved in rehabilitating buildings. She wanted to move to the suburbs and begin a family, before it became biologically too late for her to do so.

The second miracle question was: "If a miracle happened tonight, and you woke up tomorrow, and things were going more the way you want either alone or with your girlfriend, what would be different or what would you be doing differently?"

He said he probably would not move any faster with his girlfriend. He knew that she wanted to get married, but he knew that he was not there yet, that it would take some time. He felt bad that she was disappointed about this, but he felt he had to be true to himself.

The third question John asked used the on-track metaphor. It went like this: "Let's say that tonight a miracle happens, and you wake up tomorrow, and you have not made a decision yet, but your sense is that you are on track and making some progress with making some eventual decision, what will you be doing or thinking differently that will tell you that you are on track?"

He again thought for a long time and replied that he would probably be sharing some of these recent thoughts with his wife. John asked how this would be different or on track. He said that he had not shared any of his thinking with her, because he thought it would hurt her feelings. He also had thought that he did not want her to be angry with him. But now he thought he had to be honest with her and with himself. As he thought about it, he concluded that she probably would be hurt only if he blamed her in some way. However, he was now thinking that the problem was not her. He concluded that the two of them were just different and wanted different things at this time. He thought if he said it that way she would not feel as blamed.

He also thought he would be on track if he were taking responsibility for himself and what he wanted. Going back and forth wondering what the two women wanted was only making him feel guilty. If he really wanted what he said he wanted in his life, he should take the steps to make it happen. John asked if this was different. He said this was very different, as well. In the past, he had always let circumstances or others determine what he should do. He was now thinking that it was high time for him to be making decisions "like an adult."

The on-track question did not necessarily mean that he should go with one choice or the other, but it gave him a way to begin constructing a solution "in process." Previously, he thought of a solution as being one choice or the other. The on-track question put "decision" into more of an immediate process, a process he could be part of, here and now. Like many people, he appeared to think of a process as an event that takes place in a split-second of time. The idea of the on-track question was to open up the idea of decision-making as a process that can include many actions or thoughts. He decided that he would know he was on track as he shared with his wife the thinking he had previously held back. He thought he would be on track to an eventual choice as he continued to think about what he wanted versus his guilt for disappointing others and as he took responsibility for creating what he said he wanted.

The on-track metaphor took the solution out of an either/or and into an evolution or process of "making an eventual decision." He now seemed to have a sense of agency—there were things he could do, and he was already on track just by the fact that he was thinking differently.

John's feedback to him was fairly brief:

"It sounds to me that, as painful as this is, that you are learning more about yourself and what you want.

"You also seem to be learning that, as much as we like to think we are rational and logical, sometimes it just comes down to what seems right enough.

"I like your ideas of what would be helpful at this time, sharing with your wife your recent thinking and changing how you think about the situation, to taking responsibility for what you want. Good luck with these ideas and keep your eyes open for what else tells you that you are on track."

The Solution as an Endpoint—Not Smoking

A similar situation is presented when someone presents as a goal the elimination of a smoking habit, a drinking problem, binge eating, or something similar. For them, the miracle is the stopping of a habit, and the way they respond to the miracle question is usually something like this: "I won't be smoking." The on-track metaphor and question enables the conversation to go beyond this rather dead-end response. Again, the on-track inquiry opens up some space beyond the either/or of smoking or not smoking, beyond thinking of nonsmoking as an endpoint to a process.

Case Example

A woman came to see us to stop smoking. She felt, for health reasons and for vanity, that she needed to quit. Being a doctor, she was aware of the consequences of smoking from seeing her patients who had contracted cancer or had other health problems. She was also aware of and becoming more uncomfortable with the smell of smoke on her clothes and in her house.

Working as a team, we asked if there were times now when she did not smoke. She said that when she visits people and the rule of the house is no smoking, she abides by that rule. She also abides by all "no smoking" signs on airplanes or in doctors' offices and so on. We asked how she did that, and she said that, in those situations, smoking was not even an option. In those situations, she might think about smoking but only feel bad and even more desperate to have a cigarette when she left those areas.

She said that she also did not smoke on her job or around her patients. We asked how she decided to do that, and she said that, as a doctor, she was not allowed. She also stated, however, that she did not smoke for the entire eight hours of her shift at the hospital. This was intriguing to us because we assumed that she could go to a smoking area or even go outside. We asked if there were times now when she *could* have a cigarette and she did not. She said, yes, and that she just focused on something else. However, she really wanted a cigarette at those times, and when she was off of work she could hardly wait to get to her car and have a smoke.

She also said she was very afraid of never having a cigarette again, and yet she thought the only way for her to quit was to give up smoking completely.

We asked the miracle question: "If a miracle happened tonight, and you woke up tomorrow, and the problem was solved, what do you think you would be doing or thinking differently?"

She said, "I just won't be thinking about it, and I won't even want to smoke." It seemed that for her the solution so far was in black and white terms of smoking versus not smoking, wanting versus not wanting. We were curious about some other way for her to think about this than in the smoking versus not smoking way. We also wanted to open up some immediate possibilities, and so we asked the on-track question: "If, as you left here today, and you had not quit entirely yet, but you thought that you were on track and making progress, what would you be doing or perhaps thinking differently that would tell you that you were on track?"

She said almost immediately, "If I could leave here and drive the 20 minutes to my job and not smoke, I would think I was making a start."

We asked how she imagined herself doing that. She said that she imagined it would be hard. We empathized with the difficulty. We wondered what she imagined doing at those times when she might be tempted to smoke but did not. She said that she thought she might switch her attention to something else. This, we thought, might be different and helpful. If she shifted her attention to something other than smoking, she might have an easier time.

We thought that integrating the on-track question with some previously mentioned exception might be helpful. We asked how she, as a doctor, would drive the 20 minutes and be on track. We asked, "How would *Doctor* Sue drive the 20 minutes?" She became reflective and said that she would probably think very differently. She would think of her health and just think differently. She said that, as a doctor, she is used to taking charge and being assertive, rather than thinking about how scared she is. She explained that, as a doctor, she was used to being in scary situations where she could "wimp out," but instead took control. So, she thought that during this on-track time she would take charge of the 20 minutes.

We were confused because we thought that during this on-track time she might still be tempted or even want to smoke. We asked how she would handle that. She said she would think of her health and use a "long-term mind set," explaining that, as a doctor, she thinks of the long-term effects and not just the pleasure or pain of the moment.

We reflected that her description sounded like a very different 20-minute car ride. She said, "yes, it did."

This session is an example of using the on-track question to bring the client's solution development into the here and now and more into a process form. Rather than the miracle of no longer smoking or even not wanting to smoke, the on-track metaphor seemed to normalize how she might still be tempted to smoke, yet not do so. The question also invited her into a solution beginning as she left the session. Integrating the on-track inquiry with the exception of her mind set as a doctor seemed to enable her to create a meaning that would make sense to her and enable her to have success even when she might still want to smoke.

CONCLUSION

These cases illustrate how adopting an on-track metaphor can open possibilities for therapist and client in the here and now and in a more process or movement like form. The grieving person was able to construct his own way of grieving and leave therapy still grieving but feeling more in control. The man wanting to make a decision had still not made his decision completely when he left therapy, but he thought he was doing what was helpful in a process of making a decision. Finally, the doctor left still wanting to smoke and still tempted to smoke, but feeling that, as she took charge of her time, she could think of her health within a long-term frame.

All three of these people left therapy thinking that they were on track or that they were involved in possibilities that they did not have earlier. Concentrating on moving them back on track allowed the therapy to be brief.

REFERENCES

Anderson, H., & Goolishian, H. (1988). Human systems as linguistic systems: Preliminary and evolving ideas about the implications of clinical theory. *Family Process, 27*(4), 371–394.

Anderson, H., & Goolishian, H. (1989, November/December) Generation of human meaning key to Galveston paradigm: An interview by Lee Winderman in "Talk About." *Family Therapy News*, pp. 11–12.

Berg, I. K., & Miller, S. D. (1992). *Working with the Problem Drinker*. New York: Norton.

de Shazer, S. (1985). *Keys to Solution in Brief Therapy*. New York: Norton.

de Shazer, S., Berg, I., Lipchik, E., Nunnally, E., Molnar, A., Gingerich, W., & Weiner-Davis, M. (1986). Brief therapy: Focused solution-development. *Family Process, 25*, 207–222.

Durrant, M. (1993). *Residential Treatment*. New York: Norton.

Freedman, J., & Combs, G. (1993). Invitations to new stories: Using questions to explore alternative possibilities. In S. Gilligan & R. Price (Eds.), *Therapeutic Conversations*. New York: Norton.

Kübler-Ross, E. (1969). *On Death and Dying*. New York: Macmillan.

Lipchik, E. (1993). "Both/and" solutions. In S. Friedman (Ed.), *The New Language of Change: Constructive Collaboration in Psychotherapy*. New York: Guilford.

O'Hanlon, W., & Weiner-Davis, M.(1989). *In Search of Solutions*. New York: Norton.

Peller, J., & Walter, J. (1992/1993). Celebrating the living: A solution-focused approach to the normal grieving process. *Case Studies, 7*(2), 3–7.

Walter, J., & Peller, J. (1992). *Becoming Solution-Focused in Brief Therapy*. New York: Brunner/Mazel.

White, M., & Epston, D. (1990). *Narrative Means to Therapeutic Ends*. New York: Norton.

CHAPTER 7

Basic Elements in the Brief Therapies

RICHARD FISCH

Changes in psychiatry, psychotherapy, and counseling may sometimes stem from events having nothing to do, intrinsically, with those fields. For example, the need to return soldiers to the battlefront quickly during World War I and, more so, in World War II, led to the use of rapid "front-line" techniques avoiding the use of longer term therapy. "Scientific" justification for these shortcuts was made acceptable by redefining incapacitated soldiers as suffering from "shell shock" (World War I) or "battle fatigue" (World War II), rather than from the more pessimistic diagnoses of neurotic or psychotic conditions. Currently, changes in health care delivery and the influence of insurance companies has led to a rekindled interest in and use of "brief psychotherapy." If one were to take a historic perspective, one might see that, throughout the history of humankind, "therapy" was *always* brief, however brutal or mystical or naive we might regard methods used by different tribes, societies, or cultures; for example, trepanning by Neanderthal tribes, ordeals during classic periods in Rome and Greece, shamanistic rituals, voodoo ceremonies, hypnosis, to name a few. "Therapy" was brief until the advent of psychoanalytic concepts and practices near the turn of this century. "Therapy" changed from a *doing* modality in which the change-agent (oracle, shaman, mesmerist, etc.) either *did* something to the troubled/troublesome person and/or had the person *do* something, to an insight or *understanding* modality, one which required a stylized conversation, mostly one-sided. The "patient" was required to be more active in the conversation, the therapist more passive, often metacommunicating about the "patient's" comments. Such a modality inherently required a lengthier and more frequent contact between patient and therapist but was "scientifically" justified by the "discovered" findings of such things as "the unconscious" and the role of "unconscious conflict," among others. Without a historic perspective, one is likely to believe that long-term therapy is the benchmark against which all other therapies are to be measured; that briefer methods are the newcomers often regarded as naive or superficial, ignoring the fundamental "discoveries" of psychoanalytic/psychodynamic approaches. To give the reader an idea of the pervasiveness of this tradition, many therapists who do not regard themselves as following psychoanalytic concepts nevertheless believe that the presented symptom or complaint serves some *needed* function for the individual or family, a need that the patient or family members need to understand.

Shifting from history to the present, the increased interest in and development of briefer methods has led to a burgeoning of different schools. Some of the earliest are psychodynamically oriented approaches, such as those propounded by Alexander and French (1946), Malan (1963), and Sifneos, (1972), but these, for the most part, are more focalized uses of psychoanalytic theory and practice, and differ qualitatively from more recent methods such as those developed by Milton Erickson (Rossi, 1980), Jay Haley (1963, 1977), the Mental Research Institute's Brief Therapy Center (Fisch, Weakland, & Segal, 1982; Watzlawick, Weakland, & Fisch, 1974; Weakland & Fisch, 1992; Weakland, Fisch, Watzlawick, & Bodin, 1974) solution-focused therapy (de Shazer, 1985; O'Hanlon & Weiner-Davis, 1989), and White's narrative method (White & Epston, 1990). In this chapter, I suggest some common denominators among those latter approaches, factors that are unrelated or relatively unrelated to their underlying rationales, their models. Subsequently, I present sequences of an initial session held at the MRI Brief Therapy Center, which illustrates those basic features. This effort is not a comparative study of the different schools but rather a "formula" for making therapy shorter, more efficient, and, likely, more effective. In order for a therapist to utilize such elements, she or he will need some "scientific" or "theoretical" justification, and these are provided by the different schools or approaches.

NARROWING THE DATA BASE

In general, the greater one's data base, the longer therapy will take, and, conversely, the narrower the data base the shorter the therapy. "Psychotherapy" is primarily a verbal exchange. The therapist asks questions to elicit information and, at some point or points, makes some comments to the client with the intended or unintended effect of influencing the client in some way. (Some therapists say they don't influence their clients, that change occurs through some mysterious transformation presumed to have welled up inside the client. But if a therapist says anything at all, he or she will unavoidably influence the client; otherwise why be in the room?) The more areas of information sought by the therapist (e.g., childhood experiences, relationships with people not directly involved in the problem, nonverbal communication), the longer will be the verbal interchange with the client, and this length will be compounded since the client's responses to that data will, in turn, be regarded as further necessary data and so on.

How can the data base be narrowed? (It might be useful to keep in mind that the question can be posed conversely; i.e., how can the data base be expanded so as to lengthen treatment?) Therapies that regard the problem as occurring in the present and that regard present or current data as principal will have eliminated a considerable body of data referable to the past, certainly the distant past. If, within that time frame, the therapist concentrates on eliciting descriptive data ("What did you do when . . . ?" and, "And then, what did you say?"), rather than explanatory and inferential data ("Is it that he's lazy?" or, "Why do you feel it's necessary to . . . ?"), it can save considerable time.

Explanatory data lends itself to expansion and connections with other ideas while descriptive data is limited to the event being described; for the most part, it has a logical endpoint. For instance, descriptive data might be: "Mainly, he doesn't do his homework. We'll come home and he's usually sitting watching TV, and if we remind him to do his homework he just glowers at us and goes to his room and turns on his radio." Explanatory data might sound more like the following: "I think his school problem stems from his low self-esteem. That started as far back as whenhe was a toddler. My husband would get so angry with him if he stumbled and knocked something over. You know, John was never a patient man and, throughout Billy's growing up, John was always criticizing him, never giving him credit for anything. Like the time Billy was building a car model. . . . I think he was eight or ten at the time; anyhow, be got a little glue on the workbench and, when John saw that, he flew into a rage. It was so sad to see Billy's look of defeat. But John had been treated the same way when he was a boy. His father was an alcoholic and when John would come home . . ."

Therapists will also narrow their data base if they regard the client's complaint as the only problem to be resolved rather than believe that other departures from "normalcy" also need changing, even if the client is not complaining about them. This latter effort is consistent with those models that have a normative feature, that is, where the therapist operates on the idea that there is an important and objective standard of human behavior, such as "mental health" or "healthy family functioning." Thus, while the client brings in one problem, the therapist can "identify" another or a number of others, which "require" working on, and which, naturally, expand the data base considerably. Focusing only on the client's *complaint* can avoid this elaboration of therapy. It can narrow the data base even further if, in obtaining a statement of the complaint, the therapist asks the client to prioritize among elements in the problem. This kind of effort reduces time in therapy by focalizing the problem to be resolved. This is distinct from the traditions of therapy that tend to broaden out the complaint and, thereby, increase the data base. "What is the *main* thing your spouse does that gets to you?" will focus the client more than, "You say you've experienced this trouble before. When was the first time and how often has it occurred since? Would you say there's a pattern here that needs understanding?"

INTRAPSYCHIC VERSUS INTERACTIONAL CONCEPTS

A therapist can lengthen treatment by viewing the complained-about behavior as stemming from some quirk or pathology lying within the individual. This is not so easy to avoid. It happens to be a major feature of traditional and extant therapies and is the common parlance of everyday conversation and exchange of ideas. ("Oh, he's just an angry person"; "We're developing a profile of the typical abuser"; "You know those car salesmen are just crooks"; "I'm a real procrastinator.") It can prolong treatment in a number of ways: First of all, since it usually involves some concept of pathology, the individual/family members and therapist are faced with implicit pessimism when attempting to change a fixed or pervasive condition, such as the difference between looking at the way a person *is* versus what a person is *doing* in a given context in interaction with others. The task of change will be regarded as more intimidating with the former view and expectations of change—how much and how quickly—will be significantly diminished. Secondly, an individualistic (intrapsychic, monadic) viewpoint limits the therapist's and the clients' options for changing a complained-about state of affairs; since it is presumed that the problem lies within the individual, it follows, logically, that the person must be the main focus of therapy regardless of whether that individual shows sufficient interest in changing or not. (In the latter case, therapists will usually explain non-change in therapy as resulting from the client's "resistance" or "denial.") Metaphorically, the therapist is limited to banging at the same door and cannot exercise the option of looking for and possibly entering other doors. Finally, data referable to a person's "inside" are "softer" than descriptive data. The latter is more easily obtainable when addressing an interactional sequence.

"Well, he walks in the door and asks me 'is supper ready yet?' When I tell him 'No, it's gonna take a little more time,' he blows his cork. 'What the hell do you do all day you can't get a simple meal ready when I'm hungry!?'"

versus

"As soon as he gets home, he's hostile, although I'm not sure if he's been that way at work. Anyhow, he can't even say hello; he just gets extremely impatient, and he wants to put me down, especially those things I do to take care of him. Nothing I say will satisfy him, and he just seems to lose control like I've seen him do with friends when we've visited them."

As mentioned before, it can save a lot of time in therapy to use descriptive data. It is tangible and succinct. Intrapersonal data, instead, is abstract, explanatory, and can more easily be elaborated upon.

INFLUENCING CHANGE: TASK ORIENTATION VERSUS INSIGHT ORIENTATION

Whether it is acknowledged or not, the therapist cannot *not* influence the client. For that matter, it is the function of the therapist to influence the client, presumably in ways that benefit the client, otherwise, why have the therapist present or, at least, why say anything at all? One dimension of therapy—time—will be influenced by the therapist's view of whether the major modality for benefit derives from the performance of some kind of task or from the attainment of insight. (I am using "insight" interchangeably with "understanding," "awareness," or "discovery.")

A task orientation will significantly reduce the amount of time needed in therapy. First of all, the fact that the therapist anticipates that the client will eventually *do* something in relation to his or her complaint automatically circumscribes the areas of information sought; for example, it is not relevant to expend much, if any, time asking about the client's early years. Secondly, further time is saved since preparing a client for a task tends to limit discussion on some, perhaps much, previously gained information. That is, there tends to be a paring down or sorting out of data to information having more and more relevance for the formulation of a task or suggestion. Finally, an action tends toward closure, either of the therapy or some step or phase of it. The client does something, and if it results in a resolution of the complaint or a step in that direction, termination of therapy is soon to follow. In contrast, "insight" directed therapy tends towards expansion; "awarenesses" are built on "awarenesses." (This in addition to the time-consuming task of the client learning the therapist's "language"—*proper* "awareness"—and with minimal and implicit cues from the therapist, since "awareness" is presumed to arise "spontaneously".) For example, in the various psychoanalytic approaches, it goes beyond coincidence that classical Freudian analysands will develop Freudian insights, Horneyian analysands Horneyian insights, Jungian analysands Jungian insights, and so forth; yet, it is likely that neither analysand nor analyst are aware of those means, which influence such outcomes. Task-oriented therapists may differ in their methods of inducing action by the client, principally by utilizing explicit directives or by implication or, sometimes, both. While these are stylistic or tactical differences among the different "schools" of brief therapies, they have in common an intention of getting the client to take some action different from those actions formerly taken in the struggle with the problem.

GOAL ORIENTATION: KNOWING WHEN TO STOP THERAPY

How long or short therapy is also depends on whether the therapist knows when to stop. It may seem trite to say, but if one has no idea of when something is done one runs the risk of going on interminably. Therapy, therefore, can be briefer if the therapist has some rather clear idea of what needs to occur to mark an endpoint of therapy. The lack of such clear indicators is a feature of a number of models, for example, the psychoanalytic schools, the progenitors of "long-term therapy." It can also be a feature of approaches not particularly characterized as "long-term." For example, psychiatrists utilizing an organic/medical model may deem certain criteria as clear indicators for *starting* medications but have less specific criteria for when to *stop*; thus, medications intended for temporary use may be used for years. A frequent dilemma for both the psychiatrist and the patient is that, if the patient is doing well, will stopping the medication bring a relapse? Either the patient or psychiatrist or both may be too uneasy to take the risk. One "solution" to this dilemma is to define a number of problems as "metabolic" or "genetic" flaws, thus justifying lifelong medication.

In summary, then, stylistic, tactical, and/or theoretical differences may be found among most brief therapies, but they are likely to share some basic features. While it is not a complete description of such similarities the preponderance of features of these therapies are a marked narrowing of the data base, utilizing interactional rather than monadic concepts, emphasizing a task orientation, and formulating definable goals of therapy. The following is a composite transcript of an initial session from the MRI Brief Therapy Center, which illustrates these features.

CASE ILLUSTRATION

The transcript is the first session with a 35-year-old woman whose husband was seen alone in the first session of the case. He was 37 years old and described his problem as a "block." He had been out of work in his profession for almost a year and said that he was having trouble doing those tasks required for employment, such as, completing a resumé, contacting potential employers for interviews, and seeking help from friends for other leads. It is customary for us to see the spouse, to determine if the spouse is also a complainant. (I am using "complainant" to define a person who indicates a clear interest in overcoming or resolving the complaint and who views the therapist as a necessary resource in accomplishing that goal. In that sense, it differs from the common usage of an individual who simply registers a complaint.) This was all the more likely since the husband, Robert, had described his wife, Janet, as very upset about his failure to proceed with job seeking. Her upset compounded the problem since he felt pressured by her, as well as guilty over his failure to get on with the necessary tasks. This state of affairs left a pervasive air of tension in their relationship. From his description, it seemed likely she was a complainant, but we also wanted to assess if she might be the better focus for changing a counterproductive loop. It is difficult to make an absolute assessment of who, in an interaction, is the better focus. Some features that can be used are the degree of expressed discomfort about the problem, responding to questions with appropriate information, and following the therapist's suggestions or directives, among others. The "loop" in this case was the husband's putting off tasks to which the wife responded by pressuring him and to which he responded by further inaction, etc. What follows, then, is the second session, the first one with Janet.

THERAPIST: Let me start off this way: Imagine that I haven't seen Robert, I don't know anything about him, and you are coming in here because of some concern you have about him or some problem you are encountering with him. I'm starting off as if it's fresh and, so if I can assume that either or both are the case, that you have some concern I would then start with: Okay, what's the problem or concern you have?

As in any focalized therapy, an initial session will start right away with some form of, "What's the problem?" Since I had seen Janet's husband first, and she had come in at my request, asking her about the problem required some introductory comments. It can also save a lot of time to inform a client that he or she should not make assumptions that the therapist has some relevant prior information ("I'm starting fresh").

JANET: My concern is that I see him immobilized, and I guess the most obvious proof of that is that he was laid off last April and hasn't, in my assessment, hasn't really looked for a job since then. And I think what brought me to a point of crisis was that I saw that no matter what I was doing, no matter what I could think of to do, it didn't seem like I was able to *help him* and that I didn't see him asking anyone else for help. But on a consistent basis what happens is he gets so *demoralized*, actually *immobilized*. It's almost like in *panic* or in *fear* that he doesn't do any of the things that I suspect he's capable of doing.

I have italicized some of Janet's wording to highlight what I call "the client's position." Her phrasing rather clearly indicates that she is not angry with him but feels sorry for him, sees him as having good intentions but being limited in his efforts, and, logically, she sees her involvement in his problem as one of helper rather than victim. It is a useful time-saving aspect of therapy to pay attention to the client's position, since it will help the therapist from making potentially stalemating comments and, more so, to aid in framing suggestions concordant with the client's "reality."

THERAPIST: What would be some thing, or things that he really could do?

JANET: See, I'm in a little bit of a quandary. When we met, I knew that he was having some problem with his studies. It was clear to me, although he wasn't admitting it, that he wasn't going to classes regularly, and he ended up dropping out of the program. So, the quandary is, I don't know what job he should be looking for. However, it is important to have at least some sort of resumé. You need to look through the paper and network with people and ask them if they know of any jobs anywhere. You have to call people and go to interviews. Those are the sort of practical things that I can see, and I want to be supportive of that, but it seems to me that those basic rules you have to do even if you are uncomfortable, and he hasn't been doing that. The issue of the resumé has been an issue since the first week in May and he's made promises to me over and over: "I'll have it by this week and I'll show it to these people"—and I don't think he has a resumé. I find myself thinking: "What are you doing hooked up with this guy? Are we going to be able to have the life together that we wanted to?" Then my concerns get more future oriented.

THERAPIST: It will be very helpful to us to know what doesn't work, and so in terms of what you've done or said in your efforts to try to get him moving, what doesn't work?

With this particular client, little time was needed to obtain a clear picture of her complaint; she responded to questions as asked, rather than going off on tangents and, for the most part, gave clear, concrete examples, which quickly clarified material. Thus, it allowed the therapist to seek information earlier regarding her attempts at resolving the problem, what we refer to as the client's "attempted solution." For our form of doing therapy expeditiously, this feature is the single most strategic factor in our model, since information about the client's attempts provide the guideline of what is to be a *different* effort for the client to make. Clarity about this can save considerable time, since it avoids the potential of misdirection in the therapy, which may result from simply asking the client, "What would be different?" Too often, the client will equate a variant of his or her customary effort as different, in the same way a person talking to another who speaks little English may try to make himself clear by saying the same thing, only louder. A very frequent error made by clients, which illustrates this point, is when they equate keeping silent as the extreme opposite of their previous statements: "Well, when I wasn't getting anywhere telling him why he needed to stop drinking, I went completely the other way; I ignored him."

JANET: It doesn't work to let myself get to the point where what I do is explode or bitch and nag. That doesn't work, in contrast for instance when I . . .

THERAPIST: When you explode, bitch, or nag, what kind of thing would you say, what would you be saying?

JANET: Well . . . it's more the tone of voice.

THERAPIST: Because when you explode, bitch, or nag, you've got to say something—although I know it would have certain decibel levels.

When reporting an event or sequence of interaction, clients will often use "shorthand," that is, a vague summary of what is being said or done. However, this is not usable information and can be misleading, since it leaves it to the therapist's imagination or interpretation what actually occurred. To save time, it is characteristic for us to ask the client for verbatim dialogue. While tonality and other paralinguistics should not be ignored, as a general rule, the content (wording) of a message is more indicative of the thrust of that message.

JANET: "You never do this thing . . ."

THERAPIST: Yeah, I'm not asking for a success story—otherwise you wouldn't be here.

JANET: Probably saying the same thing over and over again: "I can't count on you"—bringing up, bringing up all the times before—and, "You know, you haven't helped me pay the bills this time, and all these days in the last week you haven't helped me clean up the kitchen and blah, blah, blah, blah," bringing in everything including the kitchen sink, the whole complaint. That doesn't work. It also does not work to just . . . this has been the thing that's been difficult for me, it does not work to just leave him alone. There are times when I just get fed up and I think: "Okay, I'm just going to let him stew." That's one way I explained it, or, "I'm just going to give him a break." I find that that doesn't help, either, that I need to be present. Just because I'm uncomfortable, it doesn't work to be invisible myself, to pull away.

THERAPIST: Say nothing?

JANET: So that's the underside of it—that clearly hasn't worked.

As referred to before, this is a common but erroneous assumption made by clients that "giving up" or becoming silent constitutes a difference from what they had been doing before.

THERAPIST: It may not be important right now, but you're implying that if you were going to do anything differently, in the hope that it would be more effective, it would require your saying something, not just like ignoring. . . . Anyway, what else have you . . . ?

Since a major element in shortening therapy is planning to help the client *do* something different, it enhances efficiency by preparing the client for the idea that different action will be expected. Here, the therapist is "planting" such an expectation.

JANET: Let's say, and he's made this a few times, he'd make the agreement of, "Okay, in these seven days this week I promise to do this every day: Make three phone calls, or work on my resumé for half an hour, or go to the job place, and every day I will report to you in the evening about what I've done." That's one way that he's attempted to manage this.

THERAPIST: Will he volunteer that kind of proposal, or would it be something he would come up with at your suggestion, or . . .

JANET: I don't think I've ever suggested that. But he's come up with it in the context of talking with other people about what might help and having me be the helper here. But anyway, that is one thing we've tried. He doesn't report it—he may report for a day or two and then it becomes my responsibility, and I'm not, I don't think I'm really so invested in it, I don't think it's going to work in the first place, and so maybe I don't even ask him about it. I'm not sure we've given it a fair trial, but for me that hasn't worked.

THERAPIST: Okay. But the proposal, as I understand it, is, "Okay, every day I will report to you as to what I've done or accomplished with some particular effort. . . ." When he proposes that, what do you say anyway, by the way?

JANET: I say, "Okay, okay, how are you going to do it?" I try to get clear about when is it you're going to report to me, what is it that you are going to say, what are you agreeing to do.

Here again, is an illustration of the time-saving effect of getting exact dialogue. Janet's comments just before ". . . I don't think I'm really so invested in it . . . and so maybe I don't ask him about it" implies she takes a more passive or less effortful approach to Robert's proposal. However, when describing actual and specific dialogue, this picture is reversed and confirms her "attempted solution," that of being a taskmaster and urger.

THERAPIST: Okay. And you're saying that what has happened in practice is that for a day or two he might say: "Okay. Here's what I've done today," et cetera . . . but then on the third day or so he doesn't and you don't pursue it?

JANET: No, I have sometimes. If I ask him, often what it is that something didn't work out: Either he didn't do what he'd said he was going to do, or he tried to do it and it didn't work. He was discouraged. He might have read the paper for five hours in the morning rather than going out and doing what he said he was going to do. And so he's disappointed in himself and doesn't want to admit it, and when we talk about it, something happens around that that we both get despairing—so that I don't find myself being very peppy: "Well, you know, just go for it tomorrow."

THERAPIST: Again, just so it might save time, could I take it then that the things you've done are the things that everybody else has done like your sister and brother-in-law. They all fit under the general rubric of, "Robert, you can and must make a more effective effort," which didn't work, and everything else would be, in a sense, a variation of that.

Quite often, time can be saved by alerting the client early in therapy to the main direction he or she needs to avoid, what might be called avoiding the main theme or thrust of their attempted (albeit unsuccessful or counterproductive) solution. This helps to serve the client as a guideline for determining what action(s) will be *different*.

JANET: Is that what we've been trying to do?

THERAPIST: Yes. That is, it's being put in different ways, angrily, threateningly, and coaxingly, but my understanding is, they're all different ways of saying, "Come on, get with it . . ." when one sort of boils it down, and that, with Robert, doesn't work. And, let me shift gears again a little bit. You said you've been very frustrated about the situation, and I gather you've been asking yourself: "Why does be sit there?" . . . that is, you said he's immobilized. You commented that it seems to be, by way of explanation to yourself, you know . . . some purpose? I guess mainly what I'm asking you is, what's your own guess, and I'm not marking papers, I don't have any answer to that, but what is your best guess as to why he is not making an effort you think he's quite capable of making?

JANET: My guess is that he's *scared*, that he has a dream of doing important recognized work, that maybe would make him famous, that certainly would have him be powerful, that he's *afraid* he's not going to be able to do that. I see more of a problem being that he's a man and his wife is supporting him. I think that's a big deal, that for him shows up as "this shouldn't be happening," and there's no way around it.

Therapy can be lengthened, if not undermined altogether, if the client flatly rejects a suggestion or task that might have helped them out of their stalemated problem. This danger can be avoided if the therapist takes the trouble to frame the suggestion in a way (wording) that is consistent with the client's frame of reference, the client's "language," or, as we have labeled it, the client's "position." Here, the therapist is checking on Janet's "position" vis-à-vis the problem with Robert. As can be seen from her reply, it confirms the earlier indication that she feels sorry for Robert—that he is willing but unable, rather than he is able but unwilling—and this position lends itself to framing any suggestion as one of "helping" him (as opposed, for instance, to confronting him, or getting even with him).

THERAPIST: Okay, but to whatever degree you're saying that just inherently in the situation "I'm in a one-up position, not only financially, economically," but also you're, I would assume, reasonably satisfied with the kind of work you're doing. So he's way down, so to speak, in both respects: He's not working, but he, you know, imagines what he would like and what's expected financially—same thing—he can't stand working even now. Let me think out loud as if I were you: "Looking back on the things I've been saying, mostly saying to Robert, is what adds up to 'Robert, you've got to get your act together. You can and you must make a more concerted effort in finding a job.' So that's what I've been doing and that's not working. So if I were going to do anything different, what would be different?"

Having received sufficient information regarding Janet's complaint, her attempt at solution, and her "position," the therapist now moves on to address the task of helping Janet with *doing* something—something different.

JANET: What would I do?

THERAPIST: What would you do or say, so it wouldn't be just a variation on the same old theme? That doesn't work. Second thing I'd like you to give thought to is: Okay, if whatever you would be doing, certainly what Robert would be doing by himself, if either or both of those things were appropriately effective, what would be a very first sign where you could say, "By God, it's not big, it's nothing startling, but it sure as hell is different: that immobility is starting to loosen up."

Since the session is closing, the therapist wants to accomplish several things: summarize the direction therapy needs to go, end on an *implicitly* optimistic note, and convey to the client that active participation in the therapy will be expected of her. This last is conveyed through "homework" in this case, thinking actively about the questions being raised and indicating it will be part of her participation next time. As for optimism, it is always conveyed on the implicit, not the explicit, level, and here it is suggested via the question, "How will you know you are *succeeding*?"

SUMMARY

I have suggested that there are some few features of psychotherapy that can influence the length and efficiency of therapy and that these features cut across lines of different models or approaches. While these features are few in number, they are fundamental and can make a strategic difference in the time spent in therapy. I have not presented these features in any tightly organized way, and they vary in their relative specificity; for example, narrowing the data base is rather general, while utilizing a task orientation is much more specific. However, while they are elements commonly found in current brief therapies, each approach will have its own emphases, different criteria for terminating therapy, different tasks for therapist activity, and different vocabularies for the same or similar techniques utilized by other approaches.

One word of caution, however. While the elements I have described are few and, I believe, simply put, they are difficult to implement in clinical practice. They are not technical guidelines for therapy; rather, they are *outcomes* of a *conceptual shift* from "long-term" therapeutic approaches. For example, narrowing the data base depends on what the therapist regards as minimally necessary features in his or her conceptual framework. There does seem to be an attraction for complexity. Developments in psychoanalysis afford an example. Analyses in Freud's time might be as brief as six months or a year. Subsequent "generations" of analysts, however, "found" more and more "necessary" features, which required increased work in therapy and today an analysis of three to seven years is not unusual. There is no reason to believe that "brief" therapies will be an exception to this trend.

ACKNOWLEDGMENTS

I wish to express my deep appreciation to Barbara Anger-Diaz, PhD, for her immeasurable help in preparing this chapter. Without it, this chapter might not have been written.

REFERENCES

Alexander, F., & French, T. M. (1946). *Psychoanalytic Therapy*. New York: Ronald Press.

de Shazer, S. (1985). *Keys to Solution in Brief Therapy*. New York: Norton.

Fisch, R., Weakland, J. H., & Segal, L. (1982). *The Tactics of Change: Doing Therapy Briefly*. San Francisco: Jossey-Bass.

Haley, J. (1963). *Strategies of Psychotherapy*. New York: Grune & Stratton.

Haley, J. (1977). *Problem-Solving Therapy*. San Francisco: Jossey-Bass.

Malan, D. H. (1963). *A Study of Brief Psychotherapy*. New York: Plenum.

O'Hanlon, W. H., & Weiner-Davis, H. (1989). *In Search of Solutions: A New Direction in Psychotherapy*. New York: Norton.

Rossi, E. L. (Ed.). (1980). *The Collected Papers of Milton Erickson* (Vols. 1–4). New York: Irvington.

Sifneos, P. E. (1972). *Short-Term Psychotherapy and Emotional Crisis*. Cambridge, MA: Harvard University Press.

Watzlawick, P., Weakland, J. H., & Fisch, R. (1974). *Change: Principles of Problem Formation and Problem Resolution*. New York: Norton.

Weakland, J. H., & Fisch, R. (1992). Brief therapy—MRI style. In S. H. Budman, M. F. Hoyt, & S. Friedman (Eds.), *The First Session in Brief Therapy* (pp. 306–323). New York: Guilford.

Weakland, J. H., Fisch, R., Watzlawick, P., & Bodin, A. H. (1974). Brief therapy: Focused problem resolution. *Family Process, 13*, 141–168.

White, M., & Epston, D. (1990). *Narrative Means to Therapeutic Ends*. New York: Norton.

CHAPTER 8

Single-Session Solutions

MICHAEL F. HOYT

Hey, man, grab the reins!
—KENNY LEVY, Kauai, 1992

When given a choice, a sizable number of patients may elect a single treatment session and find it useful. This is suggested by the many anecdotal reports scattered through the literature of successful one-visit treatments (Hoyt, Rosenbaum, & Talmon, 1992; Rosenbaum, Hoyt, & Talmon, 1990); by the finding that single-session therapy—one visit without further contacts—is de facto the modal or most common length of treatment, generally occurring in 20 to 50% of cases (Baekeland & Lundwall, 1975; Bloom, 1992; Rosenbaum et al., 1990; Talmon, 1990; Wierzbicki & Pekarik, 1993); and by the findings of three more systematic studies of the effectiveness of single-session therapy (SST):

1. Medical utilization was found to be reduced 60% over five-year follow-up after a single session of psychotherapy in a study done at the Kaiser Permanente Health Plan (the nation's largest health maintenance organization) by Follette and Cummings (1967). A second study (Cummings & Follette, 1976) found the benefits of SST still in effect after eight years and concluded that decreased medical utilization was due to a reduction in physical symptoms related to emotional stress.[1]

2. Significant symptom improvements years later were noted by Malan, Heath, Bacal, and Balfour (1975) in 51% of "untreated" patients, who had only an intake interview (which served to increase their insight

---

[1]This basic pattern, that psychotherapy (not necessarily one session) reduces unnecessary medical visits is called the "medical utilization offset phenomenon," and is one of the most robust findings in the research literature. It has been replicated approximately 60 times (see Cummings, 1991; Holden & Blose, 1987; Mumford, Schlesinger, Glass, Patrick, & Cuerdon, 1984).

and sense of personal responsibility) conducted at the Tavistock Clinic in London, and half of those patients were also judged to have made important personality modifications.

3. Patients and therapists agreed that a single treatment visit had been sufficient in 58.6% (34 of 58) of attempted SSTs in another study conducted at Kaiser Permanente by Hoyt, Rosenbaum, and Talmon (reported in Talmon, 1990). The other patients continued meeting with their therapists. On 3- to 12-month follow-ups, 88% of the SST-only patients reported either "much improvement" or "improvement" in their presenting symptoms since the session, and 65% also reported other positive "ripple" effects, figures that were slightly (and statistically insignificantly) higher than those for the 24 patients seen more than once.

A single session may occur by plan or design, when patient and therapist mutually agree to stop after one session; or by default, usually when the patient does not continue (Hoyt et al., 1992; Rosenbaum et al., 1990; Talmon, 1990). The term *planned SST* (or *deliberate SST*) can refer to any one-visit treatment that is intended to be potentially complete unto itself—the psychological work may go on long past the session, but the session itself is conceived as a "total experience" with a beginning, middle, and end. Planned SST involves the willingness of therapist and patient to engage in a therapeutic experience such that additional treatment sessions may not be required or sought. There is no single theory, method, or goal for successful SST. The search is for a conceptualization that would allow a viable and parsimonious solution. Considering what the patient wants and asking how the patient is "stuck" and what is needed for him or her (or them) to become "unstuck" (Hoyt, 1990, in press) can lead in many directions. The therapist needs to be versatile, innovative, and pragmatic, asking, "What would help this patient today?"

ATTITUDES, INDICATIONS, AND GENERAL GUIDELINES FOR SINGLE-SESSION THERAPY

Single-session treatments should be as varied as the patients and what they come to accomplish. The goal is not a "quick fix" or some mystical "cure," but rather, a search for new learnings, enhanced coping, and growth, a chance for the patient to make a useful shift or pivot. Some people may need reassurance or confrontation; they may need to look at something deeply or to shift perspective. They may need to remember to remember, forget to remember, remember to forget, or forget to forget (Rosenbaum et al., 1990). As Talmon (1993, p. 112) has put it, it may be useful "to include, exclude, or conclude differently." In each case, the intention should be to help the patient to find/create an experience and answer—to build a solution—that works for him or her. The goal is not for therapy to take a single session; the goal is to make the most of each session and for treatment to end as soon as patient and therapist feel ready to carry on. Most effective single-session therapy is actually not time-limited therapy—it is open-ended, and the patient gets what is needed and elects to stop after one visit.

One should set out to do "time-sensitive" therapy (Budman & Gurman, 1988; Budman, Hoyt, & Friedman, 1992), attempting to assist the patient as efficiently as possible. Needing multiple sessions does not mean there has been as "SST failure." Many patients will require more than one visit to accomplish what is needed, for a variety of reasons: there is a lack of achievable goals or no solution is available; more time is needed to learn, relearn, let go, or work through; the patient is trying to change someone else; steps too big are being attempted; reality is too unfriendly; and so forth.[2] What is most important is to make the most of each session, to use the patient's and therapist's skills to move toward an obtainable goal. It is also important to recognize that all of the work may not be accomplished or completed during the single session. The patient may get information and encouragement that helps get him or her "unstuck" (Hoyt, 1990) or back "on track" (see Chapter 6 by Walter & Peller, this volume). Indeed, patients will often acquire or access skills during the treatment meeting that they will then need to practice and apply if effective SST is to occur. A single therapy session may also be part of "intermittent treatment" (Budman, 1990; Cummings, 1990; Hoyt & Austad, 1992) with the provision of help in a single-session encounter encouraging patients to return later as needed. The potential quick utility of treatment may also promote referrals, thus supporting the fiscal viability of SST, while meeting the treatment needs of a larger population.

While there is no single theory or method for successful SST, a constructive, competency-based perspective is apparent in the following summaries based on the outpatient studies done by two psychologist–colleagues and myself (Hoyt, 1990, 1993; Hoyt & Talmon, 1990; Hoyt et

---

[2]The "corrective emotional experience" (Alexander & French, 1946), which may occur when a patient's negative expectations are dramatically disconfirmed can be understood as an event that results in a salutary narrative shift. The old "story" or "beliefs" are seen as no longer tenable. As discussed at length elsewhere (Hoyt et al., 1992, p. 83), this is what happens in Victor Hugo's *Les Misérables*, the classic example of a corrective emotional experience cited by Franz Alexander. As readers of the novel and viewers of the popular musical *Les Misérables* will recall, the Bishop in the story treats the protagonist, Jean Valjean, with unexpected kindness, reawakening in the hero a spirit of goodness. In regular clinical practice, such sudden and dramatic shifts may be hard to come by or be less durable, especially with patients who may have strongly held negative views of self and others. Such folks, who are sometimes referred to as "personality disordered" (Hoyt, 1989), often require more time and support as they revise (learn and test) new schemas and behaviors.

al., 1992; Rosenbaum, 1990, 1993; Rosenbaum et al., 1990; Talmon, 1990, 1993; Talmon, Hoyt, & Rosenbaum, 1990; Talmon, Rosenbaum, Hoyt, & Short, 1990), as well as those of earlier workers in this area (Bloom, 1981, 1992; Rockwell & Pinkerton, 1982; Spoerl, 1975).

Attitudes conducive to the possibility of successful SST include:

1. View each session as a whole, potentially complete in itself. Expect change.
2. The power is in the patient. Never underestimate your patient's strength.
3. This is it. All you have is now.
4. The therapeutic process starts before the first session, and will continue long after it.
5. The natural process of life is the main force of change.
6. You don't have to know everything in order to be effective.
7. You don't have to rush or reinvent the wheel.
8. More is not necessary better. Better is better. A small step can make a big difference.
9. Helping people as quickly as possible is practical and ethical. It will encourage patients to return for help if they have other problems, and will also allow therapists to spend more time with patients who require longer treatments.

Those most likely to benefit from SST include:

1. Patients who come to solve a specific problem for which a solution is in their control.
2. Patients who essentially need reassurance that their reaction to a troubling situation is normal.
3. Patients seen with significant others or family members who can serve as natural supports and "co-therapists."
4. Patients who can identify (perhaps with the therapist's assistance) helpful solutions, past successes, and exceptions to the problem.
5. Patients who have a particularly "stuck" feeling (e.g., anger, guilt, grief) toward a past event.
6. Patients who come for evaluation and need referral for medical examinations or other nonpsychotherapy services (e.g., legal, vocational, financial, or religious counseling).
7. Patients who are likely to be better off without any treatment, such as "spontaneous improvers," nonresponders, and those likely to have a "negative therapeutic reaction" (Frances & Clarkin, 1981).
8. Patients faced with a truly insoluble situation. It will help to recast goals in terms that can be productively addressed.

Those for whom SST is less likely to be adequate and beneficial include:

1. Patients who might require inpatient psychiatric care, such as suicidal or psychotic persons.
2. Patients suffering from conditions that suggest strong biological or chemical components, such as schizophrenia, manic–depression, alcohol or drug addiction, or panic disorder.
3. Patients who request long-term therapy up front, including those who are anticipating and have prepared for prolonged self-exploration.
4. Patients who need ongoing support to work through (and escape) the effects of childhood and/or adult abuse.
5. Patients with longstanding eating disorders or severe obsessive–compulsive problems.
6. Patients with chronic pain syndromes and somatoform disorders.

Creative application of the following clinical guidelines facilitates SST:

1. "Seed" change through induction and preparation. Engage the patient via a presession phone call or letter encouraging a focus on goals and collection of useful information about competencies, past successes, and exceptions to the problem (as with techniques such as de Shazer's Skeleton Key Question, 1985: "Between now and when we meet, I would like you to observe, so you can describe to me, what happens that you want to continue to happen.")
2. Develop an alliance and co-create obtainable treatment goals.[3] When getting started, inquire about change since pretreatment contact and amplify accordingly (see Weiner-Davis, de Shazer, &

---

[3]The negotiation of achievable goals is a major key to working efficaciously, whatever the length of treatment. It quickly and actively involves the patient; engenders hope and energy by envisioning a better, obtainable future; and helps keep treatment brief by establishing a reachable endpoint. Haley describes the importance of framing a problem in such a way that it can be solved: "If therapy is to end properly, it must begin properly—by negotiating a solvable problem. . . . The act of therapy begins with the way the problem is examined" (1976, p. 9; also see Haley, 1989). Writers such as de Shazer (1985) and O'Hanlon and Weiner-Davis (1989), among others, have suggested a number of questions that help client and therapist orient toward better times ahead. Some useful ones include: "What's your goal, and how will we know when you have reached it?"; "What will be some of the first signs that you are doing better?"; "When X is no longer a problem, how will you be functioning differently?"; "How will we know when we can stop meeting like this?"; "Suppose tonight while you're sleeping a miracle occurs and the problem is gone—how will you notice?"

Gingerich, 1987). Introduce the possibility of one session being adequate, and recruit the patient's cooperation.

3. Allow enough time. Most of us work in the 50-minute hour, which is usually adequate; but consider scheduling a longer session to allow for a complete process or intervention.[4]

4. Focus on "pivot chords," ambiguities that may facilitate transitions into different directions. Look for ways of meeting the patient in his or her worldview while, at the same time, offering a new perspective—"reframing" introduces the possibility of seeing and/or acting differently.

5. Go slow and look for patient's strengths.

6. Practice solutions experientially. Rehearsing desired outcomes provides a "glimpse of the future," teaches and reinforces useful skills, and inspires enthusiasm and movement.

7. Consider taking a time-out. A break or pause during a session allows time to think, consult, focus, prepare, punctuate.

8. Allow time for last-minute issues. "Eleventh-hour" questions should be asked about six o'clock, to allow time for inclusion or prioritization. Unaddressed issues may impede a sense of the session being complete and satisfactory.

9. Give feedback. Information should be provided that enhances patient's understanding and sense of self-mastery. Tasks or "homework" may be developed that will continue therapeutic work.

10. Leave the door open. The decision to stop is usually best left to the patient.

EXPERIENCES IN SINGLE-SESSION THERAPY

"More of the same" does not produce change. As the old saying has it: "If you don't change directions, you'll wind up where you're heading" (Hoyt, 1990). Effective therapy involves breaking a pattern, doing something different (de Shazer, 1991). In successful brief therapy cases,

---

[4]A study by Jacobson (1968) at the Beth Israel Hospital in Boston examined the effects of two one-hour-long evaluation interviews. It was found that many patients benefitted significantly from such a brief psychiatric encounter. In his discussion, Jacobson considers what might be the amount of time for a useful "minimal contact" and suggests: "It may be that one-half hour is too short a time to establish a working relationship with most patients, although it may be sufficient to continue one already established. An hour may not be the optimum time either, and more effective interventions might be made with an even longer initial time span. The factors of duration and frequency of interviews, often practiced as 50-minute rituals, require further scrutiny."

including SSTs, something new happens early on (Budman et al., 1992). A powerful ingredient of most successful single-session treatments is a *new experience*, in which the patient passes through his or her habitual, self-limiting patterns of thinking, feeling, and acting. This may be subtle or dramatic, disconfirming counterproductive expectations which the patient used to hold him- or herself back, and resulting in the patient having a sense of increased freedom and hope. There is a change in the patient's "viewing and doing" (Cade & O'Hanlon, 1993; O'Hanlon & Weiner-Davis, 1989). Reframing helps to change "meaning" and to increase perceived options, and practicing a desired outcome in session allows patient and therapist to experience success directly or recognize and correct impediments during a "dry run" rehearsal. A counterproductive "trance" may be loosed or disrupted (Wolinsky, 1991). In successful SSTs, in different ways, the patient has a new and salutary experience. The patient may achieve some insight or awareness into a counterproductive pattern, a vision of how he or she is getting stuck, but that is not all. Patients also experience themselves as different—there is a change in the stories they are constructing and that are constructing/constricting them. This may occur via a mental-imagery exercise, in which the patient has the experience of functioning in the desired way; via a persistent confrontation of defenses, until there is a breakthrough into true and deeper feelings; via a guided transaction, ritual ceremony, or a behavioral rehearsal, in which he/she/they actually act/think/feel differently; or via a problem-solving exercise, in which a useful solution is thought out and practiced experientially. Whatever the method, the new experience is powerful and undeniable, promoting growth, change, and a shift toward new directions.

There follow a number of examples illustrating the narrative shift that frequently occurs in effective SST.

Example 1. A young woman arrived complaining of "panic attacks," states of great anxiety. When asked, she was vague but noted that her worse "attacks" occurred after seeing her sister. She was hazy on details, but persistent confrontation of her defenses (including her helplessness, vagueness, and weepiness) plus appeals to her desire to feel better and not render the therapist "useless"—all techniques best illustrated by the work of Davanloo (1980; Zois, 1992) and other proponents of intensive short-term dynamic psychotherapy—resulted in her becoming more engaged and active. Disallowing her typical defenses first engendered annoyance and then anger toward the therapist, who worked actively to help the patient acknowledge these feelings. When this was accomplished, and when the therapist did not retaliate or attack the patient, she then brought forward and experienced her anger toward her sister and others who had disappointed her. Her "de-repression" of anger and hurt resulted in her having both the insight and the corrective emotional experience of expressing herself without damaging retribution. Her in-session experience led her to change her personal story, to "re-vision" herself as someone who could express anger and be assertive. On follow-up, she described more comfort with self-assertiveness and reported having had no further "panic attacks."[5]

Example 2. The redecision therapy model of Goulding and Goulding (1979) draws on transactional analysis (TA) theory and Gestalt techniques, as well as the Gouldings' own innovations, to rapidly generate powerful and potentially life-changing therapeutic experiences. In the case of "Anne" presented in their professional training videotape, *Redecision Therapy* (Goulding & Goulding, 1988), we see them work with a woman troubled by feelings of incompetency. Rather than working within a psychodynamic transference model, in which the therapist becomes the participant–observer "object," here the patient is encouraged to do two-chair Gestalt work. In a second chair she undergoes a "Parent Interview" (McNeel, 1976) in which she "becomes" her father (extrojecting the introject, if you will) and then engages in a powerful dialogue with him in which she, in essence, experiences and realizes the futility of trying to remain an incompetent child to please her father. Her therapeutic impasse is resolved as she externalizes and disengages from her sense of incompetency. Back in her adult self after the exercise, she processes the experience to gain further insight and a sense of autonomy and self-mastery.

Example 3. Chronic nightmares in 23 patients were successfully treated with one session of desensitization or rehearsal instruction, with seven-month follow-up, according to a recent report by Kellner, Neidhardt, Krakow, and Pathak (1992). Half the patients were instructed to practice progressive relaxation while imagining the nightmare, while the other patients were instructed to write down a recent nightmare, change it and write down the modified version, and rehearse the changed nightmare in imagery while in a relaxed state. In both conditions, patients were seen once and were to practice at home—skills and direction were provided in the therapy session with the patient responsible for applying the task. On follow-up, the two methods were both successful and no one had worsened, whereas in a quasi-control group less change had occurred and two patients had actually worsened. Again, we see that the pattern is altered, that the patients have a new experience, in this instance either

---

[5]Another successful SST approach has been reported by Swinson, Soulios, Cox, and Kuch (1992), who found that patients just beginning to have panic attacks who were instructed to reexpose themselves to the stressful situation until the anxiety decreased did far better on follow-up (in terms of depression, agoraphobic avoidance, and panic frequency) than did patients who were simply reassured.

relaxation and/or a more favorable ending. In clinical practice, I have found it useful to present the two treatment conditions to patients and to have them choose the one they think most likely to work for them. As one might expect, most prefer the more active choice, in which they get to enhance their sense of agency by doing something positive, authoring a new ending.

Example 4. A widower in his late 60s was referred by his internist, who was concerned about the patient's "depression." Less than a year before, the patient's wife had died while undergoing cardiac surgery. He blamed himself for her death, noting that he had advocated she have surgery to restore her capacities for activities that he sought (e.g., sex, travel). Alas, she had not survived the operation, and he was suffering from heavy doses of "survivor's guilt." A long, quiet talk enabled him to see that sometimes bad things happen to good people, that he, too, was a victim—a grieving survivor. Feeling relieved of his guilt, he was able to shift to the more constructive tasks of missing his wife and moving forward in his life. In a somewhat related case, reported in his instructive new book, *Single Session Solutions*, Talmon (1993, pp. 1–4) describes helping a guilt-plagued man by first acknowledging the client's feelings and then facilitating and activating the positive traits that are submerged. He recognizes and reframes the man's depression: "You are feeling this way because you are a very caring, loving, and responsible husband and father. Your depression is your way of expressing to your family your regrets and sorrow for causing the accident." He then goes on to help the client build a better solution, saying: "Now that you have taken full responsibility for causing the accident you are ready today to go back to your regular self . . . I am sure you want to find a renewed way to show them your positive feelings."

Example 5. A couple complained of communication difficulties and unhappiness. Before they could launch into a long and mutually demoralizing diatribe, I interrupted them with the "miracle question" (de Shazer, 1985): "Suppose tonight, while you're sleeping, a miracle happens, and the problems that brought you here are resolved. Tomorrow, when you wake up, how would you notice that the miracle had occurred?" It took some prompting and probing, I promise you, but then the "miracle" did occur: They began to talk about good times, past and future; they began to see each other again as sources of light, not darkness; they laughed and rekindled hope. To help them shift from a problem-saturated story (White & Epston, 1990) to a more hopeful solution-oriented narrative (Hudson & O'Hanlon, 1992; Weiner-Davis, 1992), I pursued my questioning, getting details, encouraging specific plans for fun and pleasure, while cautioning, "Not so fast. Just two steps at a time." At the end of the meeting, they were feeling good, had skills and plans a'ready, and did not think another appointment would be necessary, but agreed to call back as needed.

Example 6. A woman was seriously contemplating a divorce and wanted to "check out" or validate her thinking before proceeding.[6] The story she told certainly made divorce seem reasonable, and she had thought through many of the social, emotional, and financial implications of the decision, but it was an enormous step and she was understandably somewhat trepidatious. Rather than simply say, "Yeah, divorce the bum!" I took two tacks that would more likely enhance her self-determination. First, I had her imagine herself five years in the future, with two scenarios: what life would be like if she remained married, and what life would be like if she divorced. Drawing on all kinds of experiences, memories, and intuitions which I could never know, she got a strong taste of what both paths seemed to offer for her.[7] The second method was quite simple: Near the end of the session, I said, "Imagine you were a 'fly on the wall,' and a woman came in and told me what you've been telling me. Knowing everything you know, what would you think, and how would you advise her?" She was clear in her answer and proceeded accordingly. Drawing her own conclusions from her own (guided) experience allowed her a greater sense of self-empowerment and mastery.

Example 7. A powerful method of "experiential psychotherapy" has been described by Mahrer (1989). Each treatment session (usually one to two hours) is intended to be a complete experience. Each session moves through four steps: (1) attaining the level of strong, full feeling and accessing inner, "deeper" experiencing; (2) welcoming and appreciating the inner experiencing; (3) inner experiencing of earlier life scenes so thoroughly as to transform into a "new person"; and (4) being and behavior change as the "new person" in the extratherapy world. Giving structure and support for the emergence of strong feelings and fantasies produces, in this model, what Mahrer (1989, p. 101) calls "the distinct possibility that at the end of this session the patient can leave the office as a qualitatively new personality with whole new ways of being and behaving in a world that is seen and lived in completely new ways." In a vivid case report, Mahrer and Roberge (1993) illustrate working with a woman, facilitating her feelingful passage through the four steps with her new experiencing resulting in a commitment to carry forward new behavior in life outside the therapist's office.

Example 8. A ritual or ceremony can be used to generate a therapeutic experience that helps a patient to consolidate gains and demarcate a before-and-after change of status (Combs & Freedman, 1990; Hudson & O'Hanlon, 1991; White & Epston, 1990). This might involve a powerful

[6]In Friedman's (1993, p. vi) book, *The New Language of Change*, there is a wonderful *New Yorker* cartoon in which a woman preparing to leave her uncomprehending husband says, "I'm sorry, Herbert, but you're no longer part of the story I want to tell about myself."

[7]This was an adaptation of de Shazer's (1985) "miracle question" and of its progenitor, Erickson's (1954) "crystal ball technique."

but relatively brief "saying goodbye" mental-imagery experience or a more elaborate production such as the case (reported in Rosenbaum et al., 1990, pp. 178–199; and Talmon, Hoyt, & Rosenbaum, 1990, pp. 45–47) in which I facilitated a patient "emotionally divorcing" her abusive father in a ceremony she created. With her husband attending and assisting, the patient read an extraordinary autobiographical plaint, played carefully selected music, and burned her father's photograph in my office. Hypnotherapeutic "inner child" work was also done, in which she visualized her current adult self protecting the little girl she imagined herself to have been. A "Decree of Divorce" was signed and witnessed, followed by a brief celebration. At the end of the session and on follow-up, the patient felt considerable relief in regard to her relationship with her father. She felt that she had completed a chapter in her life. It should be noted, however, that she also continued to have other psychological problems that might benefit from additional therapy. Such a process may require considerable preparation and is not intended to necessarily "resolve" or "cure" so much as to effect a shift or different perspective; nor is it intended to replace other work that may be beneficial.

Example 9. An attractive young woman was on her way out of town, "headed toward a new life," she said. She had been working as an "exotic dancer" at a local adult theater, and she told stories that indicated why she had tired of such an existence. Somehow, she had decided to use her health insurance before leaving town, and she had made an appointment and was in my office. She had no specific goals or agenda, she just wanted to see what the Psychiatry Department might have to offer that could help her. One session might be useful, I thought, to help prepare her for possible subsequent work and to make a referral. I complimented her on her desire to find a life that would be more satisfying to her. Recognizing that she was intelligent and street-smart, I asked if she was bright, and she said, "Yes, why?" I explained that since we would only have one meeting, I wanted to say something that would make more sense to a bright person. She nodded, and I said, "Have you ever seen a really bad bruise? You know, one that aches and turns yellow and green? I work here in a medical center so I see such things. Well, anyway, from what you've told me, I think that in some ways you've been bruised psychologically, from what you've been through. But from what you've told me I can also tell that *nothing is broken, that all the bruises can heal*. Know what I mean?" She nodded again, and one could almost see her self-image revising, from "broken" to "bruised," from "ruined" to "repairable." I went on to suggest that she might want to get into therapy or counseling once she relocated, when she was ready, and suggested it would be good for her to have someone she could get to know and depend on over time. I gave her the names of two counseling centers in the town she was planning to move to. Almost a year later, I got a call from a therapist in another town. Our patient had changed her plans and had relocated in a different area. She was now in therapy.

Example 10. Nelson (1984) has described a method of child discipline in a book far more humanistic than its title might suggest: *The One Minute Scolding.* The progenitor of other "one minute" books, such as Blanchard and Johnson's best-selling *The One Minute Manager* (1982), Nelson presents a structure intended to provide a complete teaching experience (not punishment) in a 60-second framework. His method has several parts: (1) scolding the undesired behavior, (2) a moment of transition, (3) positive affirmation of the child's worth, (4) a quiz, and (5) a hug. Extraordinarily simple, yet grounded in both theory and practice, it provides parent and child with a framework in which the parent first makes a clear statement of feelings about the child's behavior ("I am angry with you. You hit your sister. That's not the way to deal with your frustration, and I get mad at you when you forget that rule. You simply may not hit," etc.). The parent then draws a deep breath and changes the feeling tone, creating a sense of anticipation in the child. The parent then clearly and lovingly reaffirms the child's worth ("You're such a neat fellow. I love you. I know you can do better. Sometimes you remember to be so loving to your sister. I want to be a good mother to you. So you don't have to worry. Every time you forget the rule and hit your sister, I'll scold you. That will help you to remember."). A brief but important quiz then follows, to make sure the child has learned ("Why am I scolding you? Why do I want to help you remember?"). Finally, the lesson ends with a hug, a physical and symbolic gesture that signals the end of the "scolding" and further reaffirms the closeness of the relationship. While this thumbnail sketch is quite superficial, and the method is drawn from the parent–child realm rather than from psychotherapy proper, it is included because it illustrates how narrative can be shaped quickly as a powerful range of feeling and meaning is expressed, compressed, and constructed.

Example 11. Successful one-session resolution of auditory hallucinations is described by Blymyer (1991). Respecting clients' beliefs and operating from the assumption that rapid change is possible, an approach is described that includes the following elements: (1) co-defining with the patient a positive future-oriented outcome ("When the voices stop bothering you"); (2) normalizing the experience and joining with the client ("Did you know that all people hear voices all the time?"); (3) relabeling the auditory experience as an "internal voice" and complimenting the client on being sensitive to this "voice"; (4) finding out what the voices say and looking for interactional complaints that could benefit from intervention; (5) telling stories to illustrate how internal dialogues can change and how they can influence how we feel; (6) asking about exceptions, times when the voices are not present or are not bothersome. Assumptive language ("When the voices are no longer bothering you") and questions about how and when change will be noticed set the stage for (7) exceptions or predictions tasks generally coupled with directing the client to focus on turning on the voice. A story is told to clients about a child who learns to turn off a water tap by first learning to turn it on, and the client is instructed to spend 15 minutes each day working at turning the voice on. Change is anchored when the new behavior is experienced as normal or real, and the change is also anchored by enlarging upon the new occurrence. Basing his report on a series of ten cases, Blymyer (1991) is careful to recognize that speculations about how the successful outcome of rapid resolution of auditory hallucinations come about are just theoretical constructions in their own right. He is also careful to note that resolution of the initial complaint does not necessarily end therapy, and that a change (new behavior) may not be fixed and permanent for all time. Resolving a problem in a hopeful and positive context, however, may provide the groundwork for additional useful work.

Example 12. In *The Times of Time*, Boscolo and Bertrando (1993) provide a fascinating exposition of the many ways variations in senses of time influence intrapsychic and interpersonal constructions of reality and organize and disorganize individual and family functioning. In one section (pp. 19–29), they present an extraordinary one-visit consultation with Nancy, a severely disturbed 22-year-old woman seen in a psychiatric hospital. Relating empathically to the patient and informed by the temporal differences between Nancy and her delusional alter ego "Mildred" (a 15-year-old girl who Nancy felt lived inside of her, enslaving her, burning and cutting her, etc.), Boscolo helps the patient reorganize herself in time. He points both to the past ("You cannot go back in time") and to the future ("So it's possible . . . that when you reach the age of 60, you will have a 15-year-old girl who will tell you what to do or not to do"). He then attempts to help Nancy further collapse the distinction between her "selves" and to develop new and more temporally coordinated positive scenarios, suggesting that Nancy and Mildred have much in common and that they might be able to "start accepting each other" and "to find some way to be together. I think they could become good friends or like two sisters, even better, like *twin* sisters" (emphasis in original). Immediately after the session, the anorexic Nancy requested and ate some chocolate, saying, "Mildred will let me eat, now." She rapidly improved and was soon discharged from the hospital. She reported that Mildred left her soon after she left the hospital, and Nancy was doing fairly well a year later. While this case may have been exceptional, it again points to the powerful effects—even in one session—of helping a patient construct a more functional reality.

Example 13. A full transcript is provided by Yapko (1990) of a single-session hypnotherapy intervention done with a 42-year-old woman named Vicki who was referred for help in coping with terminal cancer. First interviewing the patient in a "spontaneous" conversational manner, the therapist nicely establishes and builds rapport with the patient, while identifying treatment goals, potential pitfalls, and various resources, which are then utilized in the second portion of the session, involving more formal induction and trancework. Numerous suggestions for dissociation, time distortion, appetite enhancement, alteration in kinesthetic awareness, and reframing of uncertainty as being pleasant are all provided within the patient's frame of reference to facilitate her structuring her experience in ways that minimize her emotional shock and physical discomfort. We learn that these suggestions were very helpful until her physical condition became too severe to self-manage.[8]

DISCUSSION: ONCE MAY BE ENOUGH (FOR NOW)

While single-session therapy is obviously not a panacea or even appropriate for everyone, clinical experience and some systematic data suggest that, when given the choice, many patients elect a single treatment session and find it useful, especially if the therapist is open to this possibility and oriented toward maximizing the impact of the session. Therapy should not be "long" or "short." It should be sufficient, adequate, and appropriate, "measured not by its brevity or length, but whether it is efficient and effective in aiding people with their complaints or whether it wastes time" (Fisch, 1982, p. 156). Many people solve psychological problems without professional consultation. For some others, the "light touch" of a single visit may be enough, providing experience, skills, and encouragement to help them get "unstuck" and continue in their life journey. Clinicians make frequent use of single-session consultations (a detailed example is reported in Hoyt and Goulding, 1989), speaking with a colleague to get some ideas, techniques, and motivation to carry on work with a particular client. Patients may at times use our services in a similar manner. If used appropriately, such "ultra brief" treatments can promote patients' sense

---

[8]Another single-session hypnotherapy was recently reported by Greenleaf (1993; also see Chapter 12 by Greenleaf, this volume) of a young woman troubled with fears and fainting spells. After consultation with her neurologist, the therapist took a future-oriented approach that, within the context of a respectful therapeutic relationship, helped the patient visualize and move into a more successful future. For many other examples of hypnotic and directive brief interventions, of course, the casework of Milton Erickson (Haley, 1973; O'Hanlon & Hexum, 1990; also see Lankton & Erickson, 1994) is a source nonpareil.

of self-empowerment and autonomy (versus dependency), as well as conserve limited resources for those truly requiring longer treatments.

Powerful experience produces new learning, not just recognition and explanation (Hoyt, 1986; Whitaker & Malone, 1953). Many effective therapies, whatever their length of treatment, help patients access inner strengths and revise the stories that structure their functioning. This appears to hold across the cases presented here. There are various other methods of potential planned SST—such as eye movement desensitization and reprocessing (EMDR; Butler, 1993; Lipke & Botkin, 1992; Shapiro, 1989, 1991) and many of the techniques of neurolinguistic programming (NLP; Andreas & Andreas, 1989; Bandler & Grinder, 1985) and the Callahan (1992) Five-Minute Phobia Cure—that appear to operate at an energic and/or information-processing level. Another method, based on behavior therapy principles, has been described by Azrin and Nunn (1973) for the elimination of nervous habits and tics. Whatever the putative "mechanism" of change, the patient still winds up with a different construction of reality. Even in the simplest cases of specific skill-training and rational problem-solving, the patient gets to reexperience himself or herself as competent and thoughtful. Never underestimate the power of the "common factors" of respectful listening, seeking strengths, and practical problem-solving (Barber, 1990; Spoerl, 1975; Talmon, 1990, 1993).

Again, it is important to recognize that we are not trying to "cure" patients, nor claiming that one session is enough for everyone, nor saying that as much can be accomplished in one visit as in many. The choice of a single session (or more, or less) should, whenever possible, be left to the patient to make. "Let's see what we can get done today" is much more "user friendly" and likely to succeed than the resistance-stimulating, "We're only going to meet one time." Most effective SST is thus *not* time-limited therapy—it is open-ended. Suggesting the possibility of one session may provide structure and promote change, but it is the patient who may elect to stop (or continue) after one visit.

SST is the modal or most frequent form of psychological treatment. It is probably the oldest, and now appears to be the newest as well. This "discovery" of the potential power of one therapeutic meeting is not just a result of market forces or the development of new treatment methodologies and a shift to a nonpathological model of human functioning. It is also very much a result of the public's desire for efficacious and cost-effective psychological help and a recognition that, with a little guidance, many people can take the ball and run.[9] While traditional training, certain theoretical obligations, and some fee-for-service arrangements may promote extending treatment, the data suggest that brief, even single-session, therapy will be helpful for many people and many people want it (Butler, 1992; Goode, 1992; Zimmerman, 1992).

With so many people needing our services, it is important to remain open-minded and to look for ways to assist patients as efficiently as possible (Hoyt, 1985, 1994). We may have to treat them briefly, even if it helps.

ACKNOWLEDGMENT

Some of the work described here was supported by the Sidney Garfield Memorial Fund (Michael F. Hoyt, principal investigator), administered by the Kaiser Foundation Research Institute. The opinions reported here are those of the author and do not necessarily reflect any policies of Kaiser Permanente. Special appreciation is expressed to my co-investigators, Moshe Talmon and Robert Rosenbaum.

REFERENCES

Alexander, F., & French, T. M. (1946). *Psychoanalytic Therapy*. New York: Ronald Press.

Andreas, C., & Andreas, S. (1989). *Heart of the Mind*. Moab, UT: Real People Press.

Azrin, N. H., & Nunn, R. G. (1973). Habit-reversal: A method of eliminating nervous habits and tics. *Behaviour Research and Therapy, 11*, 619–628.

Baekeland, F., & Lundwall, L. (1975). Dropping out of treatment: A critical review. *Psychological Bulletin, 82*, 738–783.

Bandler, R., & Grinder, J. (1985). *Using Your Brain–For a Change*. Moab, UT: Real People Press.

Barber, J. (1990). Miracle cures? Therapeutic consequences of clinical demonstrations. In J. K. Zeig & S. G. Gilligan (Eds.), *Brief Therapy: Myths, Methods, and Metaphors* (pp. 437–442). New York: Brunner/Mazel.

Blanchard, K., & Johnson, S. (1982). *The One-Minute Manager*. New York: William Morrow.

Bloom, B. L. (1981). Focused single-session therapy: Initial development and evaluation. In S. H. Budman (Ed.), *Forms of Brief Therapy* (pp. 167–216). New York: Guilford.

Bloom, B. L. (1992). Bloom's focused single-session therapy. In *Planned Short-Term Psychotherapy: A Clinical Handbook* (pp. 97–121). Boston: Allyn & Bacon.

[9]In the course of our SST study, my colleagues and I made a "parallel process" recognition that in many ways typifies a very useful attitude for being brief and effective. Sometimes, one or two therapists would observe a case in treatment through a one-way mirror and might phone in suggestions to the therapist. This was seldom helpful if the proffered idea was fundamentally different from what the therapist was attempting to do, such as suggesting Gestalt-type work when the therapist was taking a psychodynamic tack, or suggesting some kind of dynamic interpretation when the therapist was working strategically to change an interactional pattern. We found it much more helpful if we listened respectfully to our colleagues and tried to assist them in where they were going, not where our pet theories or techniques might take them. In similar fashion, we find we do better for patients if we help them get to where their informed choices take them.

Blymyer, D. (1991). The rapid resolution of auditory hallucinations. *Journal of Strategic and Systemic Therapies 10*(2), 1–5.

Boscolo, L., & Bertrando, P. (1993). *The Times of Time*. New York: Norton.

Budman, S. H. (1990). The myth of termination in brief therapy: Or, it ain't over until it's over. In J. K. Zeig & S. G. Gilligan (Eds.), *Brief Therapy: Myths, Methods, and Metaphors* (pp. 206–218). New York: Brunner/Mazel.

Budman, S. H., & Gurman, A. S. (1988). *Theory and Practice of Brief Therapy*. New York: Guilford.

Budman, S. H., Hoyt, M. F., & Friedman, S. (Eds.). (1992). *The First Session in Brief Therapy*. New York: Guilford.

Butler, K. (1992, April 15). Hard times shrink psychotherapy. *San Francisco Chronicle*, pp. 1, A6.

Butler, K. (1993). The enigma of EMDR. Too good to be true? *Family Therapy Networker, 17*(6), 18–31.

Cade, B., & O'Hanlon, W. H. (1993). *A Brief Guide to Brief Therapy*. New York: Norton.

Callahan, R. J. (1992). *Five Minute Phobia Cure: How to Do It*. Videotape. (Available from Dr. Callahan, Indian Wells, CA.)

Combs, G., & Freedman, J. (1990). *Symbol, Story, and Ceremony: Using Metaphor in Individual and Family Therapy*. New York: Norton.

Cummings, N. A. (1990). Brief intermittent psychotherapy throughout the life cycle. In J. K. Zeig & S. G. Gilligan (Eds.), *Brief Therapy: Myths, Methods, and Metaphors* (pp. 169–184). New York: Brunner/Mazel.

Cummings, N. A. (1991). The somatizing patient. In C. S. Austad & W. H. Berman (Eds.), *Psychotherapy in Managed Health Care: The Optimal Use of Time and Resources* (pp. 234–247). Washington, DC: American Psychological Association.

Cummings, N. A., & Follette, W. T. (1976). Brief therapy and medical utilization. In H. Dorken et al. (Eds.), *The Professional Psychologist Today*. San Francisco: Jossey-Bass.

Davanloo, H. (Ed.). (1980). *Short-Term Dynamic Psychotherapy*. New York: Jason Aronson.

de Shazer, S. (1985). *Keys to Solution in Brief Therapy*. New York: Norton.

de Shazer, S. (1991). *Putting Difference to Work*. New York: Norton.

Erickson, M. H. (1954). Pseudo-orientation in time as a hypnotherapeutic procedure. *Journal of Clinical and Experimental Hypnosis, 2,* 261–283.

Fisch, R. (1982). Erickson's impact on brief psychotherapy. In J. K. Zeig (Ed.), *Ericksonian Approaches to Hypnosis and Psychotherapy* (pp. 155–162). New York: Brunner/Mazel.

Follette, W. T., & Cummings, N. A. (1967). Psychiatric services and medical utilization in a prepaid health care setting. *Medical Care, 5,* 25–35.

Frances, A., & Clarkin, J. F. (1981). No treatment as the prescription of choice. *Archives of General Psychiatry, 38,* 542–545.

Friedman, S. (Ed.). (1993). *The New Language of Change: Constructive Collaboration in Psychotherapy*. New York: Guilford.

Goode, E. (1992, January 13). Therapy for the '90s. *U.S. News and World Report*, pp. 55–56.

Goulding, M. M., & Goulding, R. L. (1979). *Changing Lives through Redecision Therapy*. New York: Brunner/Mazel.

Goulding, R. L., & Goulding, M. M. (1988). *Redecision Therapy*. Professional training videotape. (Available from International Transactional Analysis Association, San Francisco.)

Greenleaf, E. (1993). Case report: Isabel. *The Milton H. Erickson Foundation Newsletter, 13*(3), 12.

Haley, J. (1973). *Uncommon Therapy: The Psychiatric Techniques of Milton H. Erickson, M.D.* New York: Ballantine Books.

Haley, J. (1976). *Problem-Solving Therapy*. New York: Harper.

Haley, J. (1989). *The First Therapy Session: How to Interview Clients and Identify Problems Successfully*. San Francisco: Jossey-Bass.

Holden, H., & Blose, J. (1987). Changes in healthcare costs and utilization associated with mental health treatment. *Hospital and Community Psychiatry, 38,* 1070–1075.

Hoyt, M. F. (1985). Therapist resistances to short-term dynamic psychotherapy. *Journal of the American Academy of Psychoanalysis, 13,* 93–112.

Hoyt, M. F. (1986). Mental-imagery methods in short-term dynamic psychotherapy. In M. Wolpin et al. (Eds.), *Imagery 4* (pp. 89–97). New York: Plenum.

Hoyt, M. F. (1989). Psychodiagnosis of personality disorders. *Transactional Analysis Journal, 19,* 101–113.

Hoyt, M. F. (1990). On time in brief therapy. In R. A. Wells & V. J. Giannetti (Eds.), *Handbook of the Brief Psychotherapies* (pp. 115–143). New York: Plenum.

Hoyt, M. F. (1993). Two cases of brief therapy in an HMO. In R. A. Wells & V. J. Giannetti (Eds.), *Casebook of the Brief Psychotherapies* (pp. 235–248). New York: Plenum.

Hoyt, M. F. (in press). Brief psychotherapies. In A. S. Gurman & S. B. Messer (Eds.), *Major Systems of Psychotherapy*. New York: Guilford.

Hoyt, M. F., & Austad, C. S. (1992). Psychotherapy in a staff-model HMO: Providing and assuring quality care in the future. *Psychotherapy, 29,* 119–129.

Hoyt, M. F., & Goulding, R. L. (1989). Rapid resolution of a transference-countertransference impasse using Gestalt techniques in supervision. *Transactional Analysis Journal, 19,* 201–211.

Hoyt, M. F., & Janis, I. L. (1975). Increasing adherence to a stressful decision via a motivational balance-sheet procedure: A field experiment. *Journal of Personality and Social Psychology, 31,* 833–839.

Hoyt, M. F., Rosenbaum, R., & Talmon, M. (1992). Planned single-session psychotherapy. In S. H. Budman, M. F. Hoyt, & S. Friedman (Eds.), *The First Session in Brief Therapy* (pp. 59–86). New York: Guilford.

Hoyt, M. F., & Talmon, M. (1990). Single-session therapy in action: A case example. In M. Talmon, *Single Session Therapy* (pp. 78–96). San Francisco: Jossey-Bass.

Hudson, P. O., & O'Hanlon, W. H. (1992). *Rewriting Love Stories: Brief Marital Therapy*. New York: Norton.

Jacobson, G. (1968). The briefest psychiatric encounter: Acute effects of evaluation. *Archives of General Psychiatry, 18,* 718–724.

Kellner, R., Neidhardt, J., Krakow, B., & Pathak, D. (1992). Changes in chronic nightmares after one session of desensitization or rehearsal instruction. *American Journal of Psychiatry, 149,* 659–663.

Lankton, S. R., & Erickson, K. K. (Eds.). (1994). The essence of a single-session success. *Ericksonian Monographs, 9,* 1–164.

Lipke, H. J., & Botkin, A. L. (1992). Case studies of EMDR with chronic post-traumatic stress disorder. *Psychotherapy, 29*, 591–595.

Mahrer, A. R. (1989). *How to Do Experiential Psychotherapy: A Manual for Practitioners.* Ottawa, Ontario: University of Ottawa Press.

Mahrer, A. R., & Roberge, M. (1993). Single-session experiential therapy with any person whatsoever. In R. A. Wells & V. J. Giannetti (Eds.), *Casebook of the Brief Psychotherapies* (pp. 179–196). New York: Plenum.

Malan, D., Heath, E., Bacal, H., & Balfour, F. (1975). Psychodynamic changes in untreated neurotic patients: II. Apparently genuine improvements. *Archives of General Psychiatry, 32*, 110–126.

McNeel, J. (1976). The Parent interview. *Transactional Analysis Journal, 6*, 61–68.

Mumford, E., Schlesinger, H., Glass, G., Patrick, C., & Cuerdon R. (1984). A new look at evidence about reduced cost of medical utilization following mental-health treatment. *American Journal of Psychiatry, 141*, 1145–1158.

Nelson, G. (1984). *The One Minute Scolding.* Boulder, CO: Shambhala.

O'Hanlon, W. H., & Hexum, A. L. (1990). *An Uncommon Casebook: The Complete Clinical Work of Milton H. Erickson, M.D.* New York: Norton.

O'Hanlon, W. H., & Weiner-Davis, M. (1989). *In Search of Solutions: A New Direction in Psychotherapy.* New York: Norton.

Rockwell, W. J. K., & Pinkerton, R. S. (1982). Single-session psychotherapy. *American Journal of Psychotherapy, 36*, 32–40.

Rosenbaum, R. (1990). Strategic psychotherapy. In R. A. Wells & V. J. Giannetti (Eds.), *Handbook of the Brief Psychotherapies* (pp. 351–403). New York: Plenum.

Rosenbaum, R. (1993). Heavy ideals: Strategic single-session hypnotherapy. In R. A. Wells & V. J. Giannetti (Eds.), *Casebook of the Brief Psychotherapies* (pp. 109–128). New York: Plenum.

Rosenbaum, R., Hoyt, M. F., & Talmon, M. (1990). The challenge of single-session therapies: Creating pivotal moments. In R. A. Wells & V. J. Giannetti (Eds.), *Handbook of the Brief Psychotherapies* (pp. 165–189). New York: Plenum.

Shapiro, F. (1989). Efficacy of eye movement desensitization procedure in the treatment of traumatic memories. *Journal of Traumatic Stress Studies, 2*, 199–233.

Shapiro, F. (1991, May). Eye movement desensitization and reprocessing procedure: From EMD to EMD/R—A new treatment model for anxiety and related traumata. *Behavior Therapist, 14*, 133–135.

Spoerl, O. H. (1975). Single-session psychotherapy. *Diseases of the Nervous System, 36*, 283–285.

Swinson, R. P., Soulios, C., Cox, B. J., & Kuch, K. (1992). Brief treatment of emergency room patients with panic attacks. *American Journal of Psychiatry, 149*, 944–946.

Talmon, M. (1990). *Single-Session Therapy.* San Francisco: Jossey-Bass.

Talmon, M. (1993). *Single Session Solutions.* Reading, MA: Addison-Wesley.

Talmon, M., Hoyt, M. F., & Rosenbaum, R. (1990). Effective single-session therapy: Step-by-step guidelines. In M. Talmon, *Single-Session Therapy* (pp. 34–56). San Francisco: Jossey-Bass.

Talmon, M., Rosenbaum, R., Hoyt, M. F., & Short, L. (1990). *Single-Session Therapy.* Professional training videotape. (Available from Golden Triad Films, Inc., Kansas City, MO.)

Weiner-Davis, M. (1992). *Divorce Busting*. New York: Fireside/Simon & Schuster.

Weiner-Davis, M., de Shazer, S., & Gingerich, W.J. (1987). Building on pretreatment change to construct the therapeutic solution: An exploratory study. *Journal of Marital and Family Therapy, 13*, 359–363.

Whitaker, C. A., & Malone, T. P. (1953). *The Roots of Psychotherapy*. New York: Blakiston.

White, M., & Epston, D. (1990). *Narrative Means to Therapeutic Ends*. New York: Norton.

Wierzbicki, M., & Pekarik, G. (1993). A meta-analysis of psychotherapy dropout. *Professional Psychology: Research and Practice, 24*(2), 190–195.

Wolinsky, S. (1991). *Trances People Live*. Norfolk, CT: Bramble Books.

Yapko, M. D. (1990). The case of Vicki: Hypnosis for coping with terminal cancer. In *Trancework* (2nd ed., pp. 347–404). New York: Brunner/Mazel.

Zimmerman, J. (1992, March 6). Fast Freud. *Pacific Sun* [Mill Valley, CA], pp. 1, 11–14.

Zois, C. (1992). *Think Like a Shrink*. New York: Warner.

CHAPTER 9

Coauthoring a Love Story
Solution-Oriented Marital Therapy

WILLIAM HUDSON O'HANLON
PATRICIA O'HANLON HUDSON

What follows is the transcript of a one-session treatment that we did with a couple. We were leading our annual workshop on marital therapy at the Cape Cod Summer Symposia (1992) and asked participants if they knew any local couples who would like to have a consultation and would be willing to be a demonstration couple for us that week. One of the participants (Linda, who is mentioned several times during the interview) was visiting friends on the Cape and knew that they were considering seeking therapy for their marital conflicts, so she suggested that they take advantage of the offer. They agreed to be observed and audiotaped. After the interview, they stayed to answer questions and participate in the discussion, so their initial reactions to the session are included here.

We have written more extensively about our approach in *Rewriting Love Stories: Brief Marital Therapy* (Hudson & O'Hanlon, 1992), but here we would like to offer a few introductory remarks to clarify our approach.

Perhaps the most surprising thing for many who are exposed to this approach is how active we are as therapists during the session. We talk a lot; we interrupt frequently. This follows our idea that the goal of therapy is change, not expression of emotions or thoughts. Most traditional approaches to therapy rest upon the assumption that if the therapist allows or facilitates the clients expressing their true feelings, positive change will result. In marital therapy, this proves to be a very troubling stance. Couples are usually expressing their feelings and points of view quite vocally by the time they get to a therapist's office. The way they are expressing those feelings and thoughts, however, have not solved the problem. Most often, their expressing those things have become part of the problem. Clients can end up doing exactly what they have been doing at home—it just costs them more money in our office!

Because we typically do brief therapy and because we are so active, we take great care to ensure that both partners feel heard and validated. This can be a challenge in couple therapy. Acknowledging one partner's views or feelings can alienate the other partner, if he or she gets the sense the therapist is agreeing with the other or is taking sides in the conflict. We bypass this problem by acknowledging each person's point of view and feelings, while filtering out several troublesome kinds of communications, such as:

1. *Blame.* Blame means attributing bad intentions or bad traits to another (or oneself): "He does that because he wants to undermine me"; "She just wants to have everything her way"; "He is narcissistic"; "She's controlling."

2. *Invalidation.* This means undercutting the other person's confidence in his or her own feelings and perceptions: "You're not really mad at me, you're mad at your ex-wife and taking it out on me"; "It's no big deal. I don't know what you're so upset about."

3. *Stalemating.* Closing down the possibilities for the relationship or either partner to change. This can be done by attributing unchangeable characteristics to one's partner (or oneself) or to the relationship. It can also be done by predicting the worst for the relationship or the partner's future actions: "He'll never change"; "There's no hope for this relationship."

4. *Vagueness.* Words and phrases so general as to lend themselves to misinterpretation or misunderstanding—we call these packaged or empty words. "Packaged" suggests they are like packages that have some specific contents, but the contents are not clear until the words are unpacked with specifics. "Empty" implies that they are empty of specific meanings until the person speaking them fills in the specifics: "We just don't communicate"; "You don't show me any respect"; "She talks down to me."

These aspects of couple communication are like potholes. They can be jarring to the marriage and the therapeutic journey and may even cause a breakdown if they are severe and persistent enough. So, we steer for that narrow path between agreeing and acknowledging without closing down possibilities or blaming.

We avoid those potholes by reflecting each person's communication, while subtly altering it to filter out blame, invalidation, and closed-down possibilities. "He does that because he wants to undermine me," gets reflected as, "So you've thought he's tried to undermine you at times." "She just wants to have everything her way," becomes, "In your view, she wants things her way much of the time." "He is narcissistic," could be reflected as, "You think he's been pretty self-absorbed or selfish at times." "It's no big deal. I don't know what you're so upset about," gets reflected as, "For you, it seemed like no big deal and nothing to get upset about it. For her, it was a big deal and you don't yet understand why."

Another way to filter out blame, invalidation, and closed-down possibilities is to get people to be specific. We typically do this by helping people explain what they mean, by talking in what we call "videotalk." Videotalk entails describing something by detailing what that something would look like and sound like if one could see or hear it on a videotape. If we hear, "He is narcissistic," we would ask the person, "Can you give an example of a time when he was doing something that gave you the sense he was narcissistic?" If he said, "She's controlling," we might ask him, "If we could follow you two around with a videotape, what kinds of things would we see her do when she is what you call controlling?"

Like many marital and family therapy approaches, ours focuses on changing patterns. We search for troublesome patterns of interacting we can observe during the session and for reports of out-of-session problem patterns. What patterns do we try to change? Repetitive patterns of action, interaction, communication, perception, and thinking, which are not working according to one or both of the partners. Our theory is not a normative one, which prescribes what true "healthy" marriages involve, so we rely on the couples or one of the partners to indicate which of their patterns is troubling. We cue in on the ones they complain about and leave the others alone, unless they involve clear danger (as in violence, sexual abuse, affairs—which, with AIDS, can be lethal these days—etc.).

We call what we do "changing the patterns of doing and viewing" (O'Hanlon & Wilk, 1987; O'Hanlon & Weiner-Davis, 1989; Cade & O'Hanlon, 1993). How do we accomplish this changing of the doing and viewing? During the session, we use humor, stories, and the interviewing techniques detailed above. Between sessions or after the session, we use task assignments designed to break up usual patterns of interaction or perception.

One last element of our approach deserves mention here. We tend to focus on our clients' strengths and interests to help provide solutions and tap into their expertise and motivation. For example, the couple in this interview are both aspiring writers. We use that in several ways. First, we try to tap into their creativity. Second, since they are writers, we use writing as a metaphor for organizing some of our conversation with them.

COAUTHORING A LOVE STORY: TRANSCRIPT OF THE SESSION

BILL: We'll just have you introduce yourselves—first names—and then we'll talk a little, but before that, I just want to say that we've talked up here, and this is being audiotaped, and if for any reason, you don't like this afterwards, and you don't want it on tape then we'll have them go back and erase that part of the tape. And, also, we've said that you don't have to say anything that you're not comfortable saying in front of this group, that we don't need to know every little detail about everything that's happened. We don't know what Linda [their friend] has told you about what we might do here, but anything you want to say in terms of what we're going to focus on here.

PAT: Thank you again for being willing to do this. Just maybe pick a problem or two that we can deal with during our hour here. So, a little quick introduction.

DONA: Do you want anything more than my name?

PAT: Well, I've found out we both went to KU [University of Kansas], so we've being talking about that, and so did Linda, so we've got several Jayhawkers here.

DONA: My name is Dona, it's D-O-N-A, Dona.

JAMIE: My name is Jamie.

BILL: Okay, great! I think of this as a consultation, not even that you have to have a problem, but sort of like a tune-up, if you want to have that. Probably what it would be nice to focus on is some places where things haven't gone so well in your relationship at moments and where you would like them to go differently in the future.

[Giving them the message that this could be a tune-up both decreases the magical expectations some couples may have that this session will solve all their problems instantly and puts things in more health-based, rather than pathology-based, terms.]

DONA: Okay.

BILL: Either one of you can bring up one of those or you may have discussed what you'd like to bring up here.

DONA: We haven't really talked about it too much, but I'll start.

BILL: Yeah.

DONA: I think I do look upon this as more of a tune-up. I don't think we are having really terrible problems. We've been together for nine years and actually married for about seven or eight, I kind of lose track.

BILL: About the same as us.

DONA: Yeah, right. And it's a second marriage for both and . . . um . . .

PAT: Now, are there kids?

DONA: Yes, not together. I have three grown children and Jamie has a son who's 14.

BILL: Living with you at this point?

DONA: No.

BILL: Comes to visit occasionally?

JAMIE: Every other weekend.

BILL: Every other weekend, okay.

DONA: And I think that one of the things that we want is to keep getting along, because I think we had a really unique relationship when we began and it's still unique but it's harder to keep it that way, I guess. And I think we both have some problems with each other right now. Part of the problem I think I would define as work-related. I'm not working (*laughs*) . . . I'm not working full time, I've been a teacher, and I had a very good job, which I had to resign from when we moved to the Cape about four years ago. I didn't have to, I chose to. I was commuting to X, I don't know if some of you know where that is, and we live in Y, and it was just a very long, arduous commute, which I did for three or four months and said, you know I just can't keep doing this.

PAT: Yeah.

DONA: And I had a job that I really liked, and I made a nice salary, which we were very comfortable having and since then it hasn't been so nice because I've tried a number of things. I did real estate for a while, but the market was really terrible, and I have a part-time teaching job in night school but it's, of course, not going on during the summer and . . .

BILL: So that's put a financial strain . . .

DONA: So it's, yeah.

PAT: Plus missing the affirmation of having a job and structure in your life and . . .

DONA: It's, yeah, I think a lot of that for me is I'm just really, really angry that the job situation is the way it is, and you know I can't really find anything well-paying. I've looked for a lot of jobs and applied for them and even had interviews, and it's frustrating to me.

PAT: So that's kinda gone along with some of the things that used to go on in your relationship—dropping out in some ways. Like what sorts of things did you used to do that you look back on and say, "That was really great, when we used to do that"?

[Here we are searching for what used to work better for them, for two reasons. One is that reminding them of those times might ease some of the current tensions by reevoking some better feelings than recent ones and may remind them that they could do more of those early activities. The second reason is that we often get a sense of what the couple's relationship will be like when they are finished with therapy. Here, we could make an initial guess that they will be going out to dinner more, going to plays, or going on trips, perhaps.]

DONA: *(laughs)* Well, I think we felt a lot freer about going out to dinner, going to plays, going on trips. We've sort of . . . we want very much to go to Belize, Jamie has taken scuba diving, and I'm all for it, and I don't think we can right now, so we sort of get into snarls about that. And he works and he is providing, and I have never really been totally supported. Even in my first marriage, I worked. Then, I was divorced. So, I find this really hard, just kind of philosophically, to—I mean, I should relax and enjoy it and be glad that he can do it, I think, but it's an issue.

PAT: Sure.

DONA: For both of us.

BILL: So somewhat just the financial strain of, and then that cuts back on some of those things that you wouldn't have to think so much about or decide between the going out to dinner or the trip to Belize or whatever it may be. It certainly impinges upon that. How about the relationship between the two of you and how you two have talked about this stuff or dealt with it? Because if the job situation doesn't change, the money situation doesn't change, which it may not, given the economy, who knows. President Bush tells us it's going to improve a great deal in the near future, so if you put your faith in that that'd be great. *(laughter)* And I'm sure it's going to improve and there are going to be lots of jobs created . . .

PAT: But so far . . .

BILL: But so far, given if that's a pipe dream and if it doesn't work out so much like that, how about the moments that you two have talked about this kind of stuff. Money-related stuff or job-related stuff, or the moments when you have settled back and said, this is okay. So tell us about . . . I guess what we search for are two things. One is how are things working, even with the strains of this situation, and how are things not working with the strains of the situation and then try to get more of the stuff that's working to happen instead of the stuff that doesn't work. We're sort of going to reorient you. Maybe because you haven't talked a lot, yet, Jamie, we can pick on you. That is, tell us about those moments you think that you two have worked it out pretty well, given the financial strains. How have you done that? When you've talked about or gone to do things or planned something . . . those moments when it worked well, when you thought, this was okay, we still have the financial strains, but this is pretty good how we dealt with it. Do you remember . . .

[Here we are searching in the past for solutions that they have found naturally in their relationship.]

JAMIE: I think there are many moments in which it's not an issue at all, but always in the background there's this stress level that was never present before. And I think that contributes to both of us being more irritable and testy with each other, and that certainly didn't help me because I'm sort of ornery anyway. So that added stress just makes me snap at different times, probably more quickly and be less tolerant of things that, you know, have always been present in the relationship, but somehow are magnified when there is a background radiation of stress or worry and that kind of thing.

[In response to our query about solutions, Jamie has gone back to talking about the problem. Gently, Bill steers him back to talking about the solutions. Problem descriptions will emerge throughout the session, but without this interspersal of solutions, an unbalanced picture may emerge and the couple may get discouraged or begin to argue during the session.]

BILL: Okay, so tell me one of those moments when you snapped or you two got into it some way and then somehow you moved out of it. It's those things that I'm looking for in terms of the resources. How have you two managed at those moments when it's gone better? If we could follow you around with a videotape—this is one of our metaphors—so, if we followed you around with a videotape at those moments when there's not much snapping occurring, even though the background radiation of the irritation of the money strain is there. Or you've gotten into it, and you're having a disagreement that's more than just snapping at each other a little. You've gotten into it but somehow, at that moment, something shifts and you talk about it in a way that's more partnership than alienation. If you can, describe what we could see on the videotape at those moments.

JAMIE: I think, at some points, what happens is if some little thing happens that starts an argument, which could be anything really, uh, the kitchen is messy that bothers me, I say, "Goddammit, why don't you clean this off!" Or I just storm around and do it myself. Okay, that's really nothing. However, if Dona says, "Wait a minute, don't talk to me like that, don't lay this on me," and then I come back at her about it and say, "Wait a minute it's always like this," and start to say the "always" kind of statements . . .

[Jamie details one of their problem patterns.]

PAT: Those "always" words, yes.

JAMIE: . . . then I think that if neither of us yields or neither of us says, "Cool it, wait a minute," then we can continue. We hardly ever have screaming matches or anything like that. This is usually, kind of, here's the little thing that happens and now for the rest of that day we're mad, we're not friendly, we don't touch each other.

PAT: So what about the times when one of you does say, "Wait a minute, cool it"? How does that happen? I was thinking about Bill and I having an argument sort of like that. We were getting ready for the Christmas party, it's always a big, tense thing around the house, because I run a counseling center, and I usually have maybe 36 people or something for this Christmas dinner and . . .

BILL: We have to pass the white glove inspection.

PAT: A clean house once a year, you know, once a year it's clean. So now we've been doing this together for many years, and it's gotten to be much less of a problem, but I remember, last Christmas, we were starting to kind of huff and puff around and get kind of grumpy, and I just went over and put my arms around you and said, "Honey, look, you know it doesn't have to be perfect, it'll be all right." And somehow that just made it okay, so I'm sure you must have times like that. How do you get to that, hey, let's just chill out, it's not . . .

[Pat told a story here that both normalizes—we all have these kinds of struggles in marriage—and suggests a solution, which involves changing the pattern. Dona picks up on this immediately and responds that they use a similar solution.]

DONA: Well, I put my arms around him and everything's fine.

BILL: Well, one of the things that I have heard from both of you is that one of the things, if we could just follow you around with a video camera, and look back at those times, if there were more touching between the two of you, we'd probably say things are going a bit better.

DONA: We do touch quite a lot and we, when things are normal, we do.

BILL: If things have been tense, there's been less touching, you'd say?

DONA: Oh, absolutely, yeah.

BILL: They're sort of like, don't get your cooties on me . . . that kind of thing, all right, yeah.

JAMIE: Just withholding affection. I'm mad, therefore . . .

BILL: I'm not going to make physical contact with you.

DONA: I think, in the beginning, one of the things that I said that I really liked about Jamie was that he diffused my anger, but with his humor. I mean, a lot in the beginning. And I think that he still does, but it doesn't happen as often. We don't end up laughing as much as I would like to, as much as I think is important. He's really funny and I like his humor, and sometimes when I really am angry, I end up laughing, and I think that's just great, you know, but . . .

BILL: That lightens you both up at times, and so he's not as funny sometimes as years have gone on. You think, I used to like that, but recently you've gotten hooked in in a way that's not too great.

DONA: I think that, I mean, obviously the "always" and "never" words are . . . and I do try not to say "always" and "never," but in the heat of battle they do come out. And I think his method of chilling me out, you know, he'll say, you know, lighten up, or make me laugh and mine was more to go over and say, "I'm really sorry, I want to get along, let's try to get along." We really do want to get along. I mean, I think both of us really do. Sometimes we end up crying and hugging each other and saying, "This is so stupid." And, really, what we're arguing about is usually things that are pretty dumb, pretty insignificant.

BILL: A little humor and lightening up sometimes is what's helped you get in a better place, as well as physical contact and sort of getting you out of that anger stance or whatever. And that's happened less in recent times with this background of financial strain and just as the years have gone on, maybe.

DONA: I think some of it is just, you know, the passing of time.

BILL: And falling into patterns and things like that.

PAT: Well, the good thing is that a lot of these [things you] are saying, well, that's true for us, too. You know, we, humor gets us out of it, touching gets us out of it. The other thing that we use, and I don't know if this would be helpful, but sort of try it on, is we sort of cue for what is the change of a problem. Like one of us will say, "Do you have a request?" Also, to stay out of the global, saying things like, "Well, you're just a slob," those kinds of comments and . . .

[Here we normalize and tell stories to suggest new patterns.]

BILL: "You never clean up around here"—she lived to regret that one, actually. "Nobody cares about how this house looks but me. . . ."

PAT: All right, yeah.

BILL: And then, now with the kids—we have four kids, older ones and younger ones—and now, when the kids and I are cleaning up, we'll often say, "Nobody cares about how this house looks but me," and she thinks, "My God, why did I ever say that?"

PAT: But saying, you know, "Do you have a request, like so would you like for me to have the kitchen cleaned by this time every day," or, you know, and maybe even then compromising and saying, "Well I'm not willing to do that, but I'm willing to do this." I don't know, do you think that maybe that could be a phrase that you might use that would, sort of, shortcircuit the argument? I want to have some way to keep you from going on and on.

DONA: Right.

PAT: "Do you want me to do something?"

DONA: Yeah, I think that's a good suggestion.

BILL: There are two things that we distinguish between. Sometimes I just want [to be angry] so sometimes she asks me that question, and I say, "No, I just want to be angry." That's just, I realize I'm just trying to blow off some steam, and when she realizes that, it's a little easier for her. Okay, she's just supposed to listen, and I'm blowing off some steam.

PAT: And I can just say, "Thank you for sharing."

BILL: Yeah, right. That's our joke phrase, "Thank you for sharing." So sometimes I just want to be heard and then I'm upset, that's it. And sometimes there's actually something that I want you to do.

DONA: I think that Jamie often, I don't mean to speak for you, but sometimes he just wants to blow off, and I think I was better in the past about letting that happen. Now, I just get sucked into it, and I get so mad. The other day he said, "Why don't you get a job," and I just, you know, I mean I'm just devastated that I can't get a job and [. . .] instead of thinking well, he doesn't really mean that, you know he is never intentionally mean, but I forgot, and I just, ooooh, I was furious, and I came back and we really then got into it.

BILL: Right.

DONA: And he was upset and he felt stressed, and I sort of knew all that, but I just didn't let him rave. And I think that was really what he should have [done].

JAMIE: I think one of the things that has happened over time is that one of the strengths of our relationship was that I could yell and rant and Dona would sit back and let it go by, let go, it's over. Dona can be really, have emotional highs and lows and cry over things. So at one point that was a real strength. That was a way each of us could get out whatever it was that was inside, and it would blow over. But her emotional outbursts, crying over things that I look at, and I say this is pretty insignificant, bothers me sometimes, and my yelling bothers her sometimes. That was not the case previously, but now is. So now we need some other way, I guess, to get us out of that recurring pattern that is in one way a strength and in another way is a weakness.

BILL: Yeah, well, I would say it occurs to me from what you say that one of the ways is to remind yourself at those moments, it's like the tempest, you know, the storm that comes out of the sea, and you say we've just got to let it blow through. Your ups and downs, you know.

PAT: I'm sensitive like Dona. Bill calls me his mimosa plant. You know, those plants you touch and they fold in and withdraw?

BILL: You know those plants that fall down when you touch them and they go whooo. (folding in on himself)

PAT: Right.

BILL: A little mimosa. She goes from, "This is the worst relationship I've ever had" to, "Wow, I'm so in love with you, this is the greatest thing in the world."

PAT: Not quite that extreme.

JAMIE: I recognize the scenario.

BILL: So, and there are times when I do handle it poorly or when I get hooked into it, not that I shouldn't take it seriously, but I get hooked into if I feel it's a personal attack on me, it's very similar to the two of you. When I'm centered and when I'm thinking, you know, this is just Pat and this is what she's going through, and I can really support her for going through that. But when I start to take it personally and think that it's aimed at me or somehow a comment on me as a person, then I get defensive. You know, I say if you ever want to see me be the shittiest, pettiest that I can be just give me the message that I'm a shitty guy. If I don't have a sense that I'm to blame or getting the blame for it, then I'm fine. I went through a really bad time when I had screwed up in our relationship in a major way and, for a couple of years, I was much worse at being there for her because I think that that threw me off. So, how can you two remind yourself, you know, maybe a code word or a code image or something like that, that I can just let this person be whatever they are, and I don't have to fix it or react to it or correct them because they're attacking me? Somehow, how can you move back to humor and touching? These are three ways you've used to handle these things well. One is remind yourself like you did before not to get hooked in. Just support that person where they are now and not defend yourself from what they're saying. Second is to use humor, humor in a nice way rather than a sarcastic way like you have. Then the other one is to use physical touching to break the pattern and then you can get back to that good place. It seems to me those are the three things that you've already used that you can rehabilitate in some ways.

[The story both recognizes and normalizes their troubles and gives a guideline for avoiding blame. This is followed by a summary of previous solutions.]

PAT: So what would be a symbol that would help you kind of . . .

DONA: A symbol?

PAT: Yeah, something to kind of keep you on track, something that reminds you to not go back to patterns that don't work. A reminder.

BILL: How could you remind yourself at those moments when you have in recent times, even with the strain, how have you reminded yourself not to get hooked in? You've said he just rants and raves and that used to be okay with me and I would just let him do it.

[Focusing on exceptions to the problem reinforces what is desired.]

DONA: Well, I think before it was just, sort of, unconscious, I just sort of, you know, it was, I didn't have to remind myself to do it.

PAT: Yeah.

BILL: Right. I just have a suggestion that may work for you. Could you get a letter from him saying that it's okay for you not to have a full-time job at this point, and he knows you've made your best efforts.

[This symbol, which utilizes the couple's interest in written communication, would at least reduce the job conflict problem.]

DONA: Oh, that would be [a] help! If he would verbalize somehow his true feelings about this situation in a letter or, I mean, he does some, but he kind of, he really does vacillate a lot.

BILL: When he's feeling the stress and strains of the financial situations— maybe if we could get him to write a letter saying he knows you've made your best efforts at this point to get a full-time job and that he recognizes that it's President Bush to blame, not you (*to Dona*). Would you be willing to do that (*to Jamie*)? And then in moments when you're starting to feel like, "Oh, I'm such a terrible person because I haven't got a job and I've caused all this," you can just look at that letter and say, "I've got his signature right here, I don't have to feel badly about this."

DONA: Yeah.

BILL: "That I really have made efforts."

DONA: I'd like that. I would like that.

BILL: That could remind you not to get hooked and you could go back to that letter every once in a while just to not get freaked out and say, "Oh, my gosh, I have to defend myself because he thinks I'm such a bad person because I haven't made enough money." You know, when you keep saying, "I don't have a job," you do work inside the home as well as outside the home. I assume you are doing things at home. Now, I don't want to make any assumptions here, perhaps I'm going too far.

DONA: I do. I do the laundry.

BILL: You do the laundry. You know, actually we have a disagreement about that because I think I do the laundry, and Pat says, "You wash the clothes, you dry the clothes, and you fold Patrick's [our six-year-old's] clothes and your own clothes. I fold the sheets and my own clothes and Zachary [our 14-year-old] folds his." She has to make it very specific about who does what.

PAT: He does most of the laundry.

DONA: The laundry is entirely my domain.

BILL: Entirely your domain, so you work inside the home, as well as you work part-time outside the home, right?

DONA: Right.

BILL: And that's an ongoing thing?

PAT: During the school year.

DONA: Well, I do other things, too, I mean, I really do try to find work.

BILL: You bring in money in other ways. So it's not like you don't earn money at all.

DONA: Right.

BILL: You just don't bring in as much as you used to, as much as you'd like to or as much as both of you would like to.

[Here Bill is validating Dona's efforts and contributions, while acknowledging her dissatisfaction with the work and financial situation.]

DONA: And I don't have the structure of a job, which I think is very frustrating to Jamie. That, you know, I seem to be, and I am a lot freer to do things that I want to do that he can't do. We both write and this is another area of friction. If I could make money writing, I mean, I have made money, a little bit. If I could make a best seller, or write a bestseller, and he says do it, you know, do it, but then to do that it means that I'm really not earning anything, probably, or little and then there's this kind of needling about, you know, and I don't know this gets really complicated because he wants to write, too. He actually does write, that's his job, but he's written novels, and he'd like to do it again.

BILL: Right. But he's envious of the position you've got. He's saying, "I wish you were out there working full time and I could take time off . . . "

DONA: Right, absolutely.

BILL: . . . and, at times, he says, "Why don't you just do that and go for it?" and, at other times, when he's feeling financial strain or he's upset about something he'll say, "You haven't brought in any money this month"?

DONA: Or, "You're just gone gallivanting off, you've met your friends for lunch and la-di-da."

BILL: And you're not really working on that bestseller, you're not taking advantage of this time when you haven't got so many duties.

DONA: That's right, isn't it?

JAMIE: Yeah, I think that's a good characterization. Another part of the tension, I guess, comes from the fact that a lot of my work I do out of an office in our house. So if I am trying to concentrate and work and get something done as I'm looking out at a pond and the sun beating down and thinking about being on a boat and knowing that my partner is not really applying herself at that moment. It's exactly what you said in terms of sometimes I'm encouraging her and sometimes I'm saying just work in a Burger King, just get some money.

BILL: Yeah, get some bucks. So this is again something we talked about. Could the request be that you work at least 15 minutes or a half an hour a day on your bestseller, and if you did that that he'd get off your case and couldn't say anything about it?

DONA: I don't think 30 minutes would probably do it for him. Would you make a request?

JAMIE: Yeah, the request would be, write a bestseller.

PAT: We'd all like to write a bestseller, we're trying for that, too, but it's hard to control that, so it's better to ask for honest effort. Would an hour a day seem like a real effort or two hours?

JAMIE: Yeah, I think so.

PAT: An hour a day.

JAMIE: Some kind of consistency. I think if I saw that happening then I would be able to say to myself . . .

[Bill interrupts to make certain what Jamie says results in nonblaming.]

BILL: You feel better, well, we're under this financial strain now, but it looks like it's leading towards something. How about at least one proposal sent out per month? Or is there anything else like that?

DONA: God, don't make it too hard.

BILL: "Don't make it too hard." I'm not sure what's too hard.

DONA: (to Jamie) What do you want? What's your request?

PAT: Good!

[Pat wants to reinforce Dona's using this method of asking for a request and getting specifics from Jamie.]

JAMIE: Consistent behavior over time and one hour a day of writing activities.

PAT: Monday through Friday?

JAMIE: Yeah, an hour a day, Monday through Friday, would probably do it for me. I mean, that would be a commitment, because some of what I hear is, "I want to write." So show me 10, 20, 30 pages of something. I say, "I think this works. This is good, I like this, do something with it." And then it's, "Well now I think I'm gonna start a pizza company."

DONA: Oh, Jamie!

JAMIE: And the consistency is lacking . . .

DONA: Yank, yank.

BILL: Okay, but so can we get away from that talk, then, if it is acceptable to you to agree to do the consistent writing, he's gonna have to agree to shut up about the pizza company comments.

[We are trying to keep them on track to an agreement and shift away from blame and provocation. If Dona is making her effort, we will ask Jamie to make some of his own.]

BILL: So would one hour a day be acceptable to you? Would that be workable? Do you think you could keep it? Would you keep it?

DONA: Actually, it would be very good for me if he demanded that from me.

BILL: To have that structure from the outside.

PAT: Yeah, it's very hard to discipline yourself to write.

BILL: Okay, wait a minute, now. So I think because we're writers and we know this story as well, I think it would be great to have some consequences then for you, if you don't stick with it, and some consequences for him, if he brings up this shitty stuff about why don't you get a job when he's already told you he'll lay off that stuff, if he sees some consistent effort. So, consequences for him if he says these little digging comments and consequences for you if you don't keep your hour-a-day commitment. Now, I usually look for the consequences in what kind of things do you think you should do but you have trouble getting yourself to do besides the writing stuff, like writing friends, cleaning out the hall closet.

[Our goal is to strengthen the intervention and have a consequence, other than complaining, to apply if the clients fail to keep their agreements.]

DONA: I don't have any trouble with any of those. They fill in time.

BILL: They fill in time. That's distraction from having to write, right?

PAT: So, what may be a consequence that would be good for the relationship, like you have to give Jamie a back rub or something like this. So, maybe something that would go back to the relationship.

BILL: I kinda like that one.

JAMIE: Yeah, but is that a negative consequence?

BILL: It's a consequence, and she has to do something she usually puts off doing, I guess that's what I'm saying, and that we get more consistent on relationship-enhancing things that, you know, that if she flakes out on her writing she does something nice for the relationship, and you get some goodies out of it, so . . .

PAT: What would be a favor to you that she doesn't really love to do?

BILL: It could be household tasks, it could be a personal task. We don't have to be real specific.

JAMIE: We can make side agreements after the . . .

[Here, we are giving them the general idea and inviting them to fill in the details. This makes it a collaborative effort.]

PAT: Yeah, that's right.

BILL: You can say, well I really said that but that was a code word for this.

PAT: Code "back rub," back to the back rub. We'll just call it a back rub.

BILL: Back rub, yeah, or whatever it may be. Yeah, you can get explicit if you want, if you're loose, that's fine. Okay, so . . .

DONA: I was thinking of emptying the dishwasher or something.

BILL: Emptying the dishwasher, yeah, that's a good code word for that.

DONA: I hate that.

BILL: Yeah, you hate emptying the dishwasher, so, good. If you haven't done your hour, let's say by six o'clock at night, you have to empty the dishwasher in the next 24 hours. Does that sound okay?

DONA: Uh huh.

BILL: You can shift this around, I mean, you're smart enough to sort this one out. Just, that's the idea. Okay, now. If you do your snide comments after she's agreed to do her hour and she's been doing it consistently, if you do any of your snide comments like, "Why don't you bring in some bucks here instead of sitting on your ass or going out with your friends" or whatever it may be, "just gallivanting around . . . "

PAT: He probably talks nicer than that, Bill.

BILL: Fine. Um, so, if you make those comments then what would you have to do, in terms of enhancing the relationship or doing something that she usually wants you to do, but you don't do.

JAMIE: I guess we could select from, um . . .

BILL: A list of hundreds?

JAMIE: Back rubs or uh . . .

DONA: How about weeding the yard?

JAMIE: Weeding the yard, ooh, that's not bad enough, I don't think.

BILL: You don't think that's bad enough?

JAMIE: Now, how about, you know what I really don't like is the laundry.

DONA: Well, you don't do it, though.

JAMIE: Right, but I could do it.

BILL: So he would take . . .

JAMIE: If I'd come back at you with a nasty comment . . .

DONA: I don't mind the laundry, though.

BILL: Okay, so that's no good. You don't like to do it, but she doesn't mind doing it, so that's not a great enough benefit for the relationship or, you know, it's no big deal.

DONA: Well, let's just use code word "back rub" and we'll, we'll . . .

BILL: You'll fill in the details as you go. Something that you usually don't get around to doing, but it's great for your relationship or great for you.

DONA: I really would like more help in the yard. We have a boat now, and the yard is the last thing in the world he's interested in.

BILL: So, maybe it is that. It may not be hard enough for you, but it'd be great for her, and it might help just keep you on track in terms of not saying those comments. You have to figure out a formula. For every 15 minutes he rants and raves, he has to do 15 minutes of yard work, or for every one shitty little comment, he has to do 15 minutes of yard work. You work out that formula.

DONA: Does this get put down in writing or is this . . .

BILL: I think it's a good idea so you don't forget about it, you know, it's just a good idea.

DONA: I want to ask if we agreed that you were gonna write me the letter about your understanding? (*Jamie nods.*)

DONA: Right, and I'm going to write down that I agree to do the writing.

PAT: One hour a day, yes, Monday through Friday.

BILL: Yes, that's a good idea, again, by what time and make it realistic so that you know you'll do it, that you can do it, and that you check in every day and make sure you've done it. Because I know when you're a writer that it is very easy to slide.

PAT: Yeah, it's very easy to.

BILL: There are lots of invitations to sharpen the pencil, go clean the other room, or go out with the friends or anything to not sit down and stare at that blank sheet or the blank computer screen. I've written seven books, and I know about this.

PAT AND DONA: Yeah.

BILL: I'll do about anything not to sit my buns down and write. But once I get into it, it has its own energy. And then I don't want to do anything else for a while. So once you get into that mode you may write two or three hours in a day.

DONA: Write two or three bestsellers, I thought you were gonna say.

PAT: That'd be great, yes!

BILL: That's okay, too. Yeah, I think what Pat said is right, that you can write the bestseller, but getting it published and making it a bestseller is different, so that's why, I think that, you know, we have to declare that a request for a bestseller is unguaranteeable, so that's why it's best to stick to only activities. We ask people to only request activities towards that goal. This is a financial strain but at least I can see that we might be working our way out, because the writing is good and if she persists on it, it could be a bestseller, and that's going to take care of all these things. Okay, great. The other thing is that, when you get in the midst of it, it seems to me that there are a couple of things you can do is to rehabilitate what worked earlier on in the relationship—using humor, using touching.

[Here we clarified that requests have to be made in terms of something that can be checked and are within the other person's power to make happen.]

DONA: Right.

BILL: So, I suspect that probably what I would recommend is some combination of the two, that when he's saying something kind of shitty, you have to goose him or something like that. Something humorous, some humorous kind of touch or activity or whatever it may be, um, or just a hug or whatever it may be. I think, I liked the story Pat was telling earlier. She had a couple [. . .] this woman would rant and rave and say terrible things to her husband, and she would threaten to castrate him during a fight. And he just stood there, just sort of paralyzed with . . .

PAT: He'd never said anything back to her, like, "How dare you speak to me like that," or anything that you'd expect people to say. So I decided to meet alone with him and I said, let's just think of all the outrageous things you could do. Like if she's ranting and raving, if you could throw up, it would stop her, and then she'd jump back at least. Now he didn't do that, I couldn't have done that, either. I talked about that just to kind of get his mind loose. Then I said, "You could get a water gun and shoot her." He did that, she loved that. She has a good sense of humor, she thought that was really funny. I said, "You could hide under the table." This usually happened in the kitchen, so he hid under the kitchen table. That worked. She also thought that was funny. Then I said, "Why don't you just say, 'When you talk to me that way I'm gonna leave for a half an hour. It really upsets me.'" So he did that, too. She didn't think it was funny, but it did get her to stop. And then, the final thing was, I said, "You know, you've been married 23 years, have you ever said how this makes you feel?" And he hadn't, he'd never said, "Gee that really hurts me when you threaten to castrate me and say I'm not a man." So he did that, too, and it really shifted their relationship. So the idea is just doing something different, even if it's weird, like hiding under the table or getting a water gun.

[Pat's story illustrates being creative and changing one partner's part of a pattern to change the couple's pattern.]

BILL: Unexpected.

PAT: Yeah.

BILL: Unexpected. Introduce the unexpected. When in a dilemma, introduce novelty. So do whatever it could be that has humor in it, that's not mean-spirited but has humor in it, and it will break up the things. I remember a colleague of ours, Steve de Shazer, had parents who were having such a difficult time with one of their kids, and the kid was just oppositional and belligerent, you know, just really tearing up the household, and so the parents had tried all these behavioral programs and talking to the kid and everything, and finally the therapist just suggested every time the kid went out, they should do something crazy and unexpected that wouldn't be harmful or danger-ous. When he came back, and he would look for his underwear, he couldn't find them. Where were his underwear? They were always in the freezer. And he'd ask his parents, "Where are my underwear?" And they'd say, "They're in the freezer," and he would say, "Why are they in the freezer?" and they would just shrug their shoulders. Every time he left they would put his underwear in the freezer. And the kid was thinking, "What, my parents have gone psychotic. I don't know what's going on with them," but it sort of freaked him out, and he started walking a little more carefully around his parents. You know, psycho killers or something, because they would just put his underwear in the freezer. When in a dilemma, do something totally unexpected and totally different, and maybe something new will happen, rather than the same damn thing over and over again. So, I don't know.

DONA: I think that's a really good suggestion, because I, as you're talking, I think, you know, I really do get drawn into this, just terribly. And we end up just snarling at each other. We don't scream and beat on one another or anything like that, but it's not fun, it's not fun. And it's really hard to think, "Well, what made me laugh before?" I don't think he's quite as funny as he used to be. No, he's not, he's really worried. In the good old days, when we both had money, he wasn't as uptight and I understand that, but still, I would like to have that looseness that was there.

PAT: We had a discussion like this actually about five months ago, about, you know, "You're not as funny as you used to be, Bill"—and the interesting thing is he took the month of June off. He was very funny the month of June, so, you know, it had a lot to do with not being overwhelmed.

BILL: Now we're into July, and we're down the tubes. (*laughter*)

PAT: He's still fairly funny. Yeah, I do understand this. It's somewhat situational. So, my thought is I think maybe that will heal itself when you get this bestseller or when, you know, the money thing gets handled a little better. I really sense that you're gonna work that out.

[We have been normalizing and joining by telling them about our similar struggles.]

DONA: Well, I want to.

PAT: Yeah.

BILL: And you're both writers with creativity. It won't sort the money problem out in the interim; it'll just sort the relationship out in the interim, get you out of the patterns. Then, that'll support you, hopefully to get the money thing handled better. You'll feel more capable of writing that best seller or getting another kind of job or whatever it may be. You're capable of coping with the financial strain as it is at the moment. Because adding relationship strains to the financial strains makes it a lot harder to handle, I think. The other thing is, I read this book about men's liberation years ago, um, and they said that men feel the burden of being the financial womb of the family, that is, the nurturing of the family financially, and when there's enough money and there's not much of an issue about it, that's fine but when there's not, sometimes that old program kicks in that we got when we were growing up. You're gonna have to be responsible for the household finances and that somehow that furrows your brow, you know, and as I grow up and get more mature and responsible, which I fight tooth and nail. I go kicking and screaming into adulthood, still, at 39, I'm still kicking and screaming trying to fight it. I have those programs kick in that I'm supposed to be responsible. She's quite capable of earning a living, she earned a great living before I came along, much better than I did, and I still feel this burden of responsibility to make it. It's totally irrational, it's totally unconscious . . .

JAMIE: It's scary.

[Before, we showed some gender sensitivity by pointing out that Dona did work inside the home, as well as outside, when she (or Jamie) had minimized or dismissed that. Here we show some sensitivity to male issues, and Jamie seems to relate to what we're saying.]

BILL: Yeah, and I'm feeling the burden of it all and thinking, you know, if I don't do this then it's not gonna happen and that's totally crazy. She's a totally competent person to do that, and we can share that regardless. You know, we can share that responsibility, but I'm feeling it's on my shoulders, and I'm feeling that tension in the furrow of my brow. So maybe we can liberate ourselves from that, like women have been able to liberate themselves from ideas that they have to stay home and take care of everybody in the family and that's their job, and you still (*talking to Dona*), I'm sure, have some of that burden, like you have to take care of everybody emotionally or, you know, in some ways. But, you've freed yourself a lot from that, and I think we haven't freed ourselves so much from that. It's sort of kicked in at some point in my life, and I don't like it that I feel this. It's too grim, too grim.

PAT: I think I also felt some of that "man's" kind of responsibility then for the first two or three years we were together. I mean, I was a single parent, three kids, I only had child support for one of those kids, I had no alimony, and, you know, I felt a lot of that. Ugh, you know, I can't take a day off, I've got to work, because I, you know, I just get paid for the hours I work.

BILL: You still do feel that.

PAT: I do still feel that a little bit, yeah.

DONA: Well, I feel some of that, too. I feel that, you know, God, I worked all my life, and I've been through some really terrible financial struggles, and I don't want to go through any more, and, you know, too bad Jamie, I can't handle this. And I think, sometimes I think, you know, I'll just move to some other state where I could get a job, but he doesn't want to move, and then I get really angry because I don't really want to move, either, but I also sometimes think it's because of him and his child that we stay in Massachusetts, and if we could move somewhere else I could probably get a job. I mean, I'm pretty sure I could, although it's getting more and more difficult because I'm getting older, and that kicks in, too. But I think that I would work and then I think so, you know, it's just because we live in this stupid state that I can't get a job, and why don't we move somewhere else and then that gets a lot of anger. That's when I'm saying . . .

PAT: That might be a time when maybe the two of you could work out some kind of an agreement, like if I apply for this many jobs or something, 'cause one time Bill had a business with his mother that was a little computer-type business, where you could drop in and just use these computers. It was in the small town of Blair, Nebraska, and, um, no one was really trying hard to make this business go. Since I started a counseling center in '75 and I realized somebody has to be really committed to make a business go. So it was losing money, losing money, losing money. Finally, we made an agreement that if it lost so much money the next two months, that he would close the business, and of course his mother had to agree, too, but that worked out fine. So we had an agreement that if this doesn't happen by this date [. . .] I don't know how exactly you might want to apply that to this, but if I do this and this and this and this and I still can't get a job and then I apply over here, and if I can get a good job, but having a kid nearby . . .

[Here we were going for some sort of time or activity agreement, but it fizzled. Not every idea has to work out in a session.]

JAMIE: Well, to move would mean that we'd just be reversing positions, basically.

BILL: Yeah.

JAMIE: I would lose my job, my clients, my . . .

PAT: Yeah, right.

DONA: It doesn't make sense, really.

JAMIE: We can deal with the financial part of it if our relationship is on an even keel. That's the important thing to me, I think. And I like the idea of using the unexpected to break the patterns. The problem is the recurring patterns and going through the same routine, sort of Pavlovian.

PAT: Yes, right.

BILL: Well, I was saying earlier that I have a mentor in the brief therapy field. He said, "You can't expect a utopian ideal for your clients that go out after your therapy. They're not going to solve all their problems in life, they're gonna have struggles. They're gonna have problems, because life is just one damn thing after another." He said, "But the problem for people who come into therapy is life has become the same damn thing over and over again, so our job as therapists is to help people go from the same damn thing over and over again, back to one damn thing after another" [J. Weakland, personal communication, 1986]. So that's what we're saying, it's just the repeating of the drag kind of things that you both don't like that that's become the real drag. It's not that you won't ever have problems or struggles with money or whatever it may be, but if you can find new and creative ways of handling that or go back to some of the other ways you have, to rehabilitate those earlier ways, then it's not such a drag because it's not the same damn thing happening over and over.

[Here we're reassuring them that even with the plans we have made they should be prepared for some tough times. But we suggest that when they get stuck in repetitive patterns, they can get creative and change things.]

JAMIE: Uh huh.

BILL: And it does sound to me, as you said, that this is more in the realm of tune-up rather than basic relationship, you know, major problem. But it could turn into major problems if it lasts long enough.

[Calling it a "tune-up" reassures them and suggests the basic relationship is strong and good.]

DONA: Uh huh.

BILL: And right now it's in the tune-up phase, where if you can just introduce the unexpected and make some of these little changes, go back to some of the things that worked before, it sounds like things will be great and one of the two of you, one or both of you get those best sellers going. That'd be nice.

DONA: That would be nice.

BILL: And that was one of the dreams, I suspect, that you both had when you got together, at least some time after you got together, is supporting each other in that writing process and saying, "We can do it; you can do it." You can be the critic, say, "Yes this works; that's great," and go ahead and send that off. That's one of the values in your relationship. So I think this is a good sort of stopping place, if that's okay with you two. Remember when we said at the beginning if it's not okay with you for us to have this on tape, we'll erase it, and you can figure that out either now or tell us later.

DONA: I don't mind. (*Jamie nods.*)

BILL: It's okay with you, okay, good. And the other thing is they may have questions for us or for you, if you'd be willing to stick around for a few minutes. If you leave, we'll probably gossip about you when you leave, so you might as well stay around and see what the gossip is. I would appreciate it if you would stay around and let them ask us some questions. If they ask you anything that you don't want to answer, just say I pass on that one or whatever, you don't have to talk about everything.

[What follows is a discussion with participants in the workshop, who have been observing the session. We include this because it clarifies some issues and it continues the session. This process shows clients that we see them as competent and would like to have them as collaborators and consultants.]

OBSERVER: Thank you, Dona and Jamie, for being courageous enough to do this with us, and I'm impressed with the amount of love and sharing between you. I just was curious, Dona, have you invited Jamie to help you in any way with your job search?

DONA: Um, yes, uh huh, yeah, he's invited himself.

BILL: He didn't wait for that invitation to be issued. He said here's what you should do, you should . . .

DONA: He cuts out the ads and hands them to me and . . .

BILL: "How 'bout this, honey?" Yeah, right, very helpful. (*laughter*)

OBSERVER: I have a question about new behavior and breaking patterns. How do you decide when to give tasks for behavior that is absurd versus more normal?

PAT: I think just by the mood you're in, really. I don't know that we have a rule.

BILL: I have a sense that absurd would appeal to both of them.

PAT: Yeah, I mean they have a sense of humor, they have a playful streak.

DONA: I like the water gun.

BILL: The water gun, she likes the water gun.

PAT: Get the water gun on the way home, right.

BILL: So, you know, I think that you just give multiple choice options. Here's an absurd one, here's a regular one, you know, say, "This really hurts me," and which ones they light up at or which ones she says, "I hate the water gun," you know. So I think we let them decide, and we give multiple choice, some absurd, some commonsensical.

OBSERVER: I wonder if Jamie could say that he thought that his problems were heard . . .

JAMIE: Yes.

BILL: Your concern is maybe he didn't get heard as much as Dona did, yeah, okay. Your sense of things . . .

JAMIE: I feel fine about it. I think that we talked about some of the real issues in the relationship.

BILL: Good, okay, thanks for checking it out. Because we did sometimes talk about what she brought up earlier and went with that. I just had a sense that it was for you, too. You were going, "Yeah, that's it." We haven't talked about everything that's ever gone on between the two of us, but important things.

OBSERVER: Well, I wanted to add that I think you're a wonderful couple, I wish that I had wonderful couples like that.

PAT: Oh, yeah. I wish that, too.

BILL: Yeah, right, unfortunately some of them aren't so fun.

OBSERVER: I have one question. I feel like there's a teeny missing link, because I heard, Dona, that you said in the beginning that you had loved your job, it was an affirming job, and you were good at it, et cetera, et cetera, and it was in X, and I do know where that is. What inspired the move to the Cape?

DONA: A lot of people ask that. They ask, "Didn't you think about this?" Um, we just wanted to move to the Cape. We had discussed it from the beginning of when we first knew each other. We had both spent lots of time down here. We wanted to, we found a house that we really like, it seemed like the right time to do all that buying and selling of property, and so we did, we sort of plunged, a little sooner than we had actually thought we would, and . . .

BILL: Because you found a good deal on the house or something?

DONA: Yes, we found this house, and we were able to sell our house and the thing all worked out, and yes, I did think about what it would be like to commute, I just didn't know it was going to be quite as terrible as it was.

BILL: And this is where writers think they're going to write bestsellers.

DONA: Right, absolutely.

BILL: Out on the Cape.

DONA: Uh huh.

BILL: Definitely.

DONA: It could be a little closer to the water, but . . .

JAMIE: We both actually thought we could handle the long commute, that's what it came down to. I commuted . . .

OBSERVER: Uh huh. You both think you can have it all, and you didn't quite get it all.

DONA: No, we didn't quite get it all.

JAMIE: But at least we're not being machine-gunned out of our bedroom in Dorchester.

BILL: There is something to be said for that.

PAT: Really.

BILL: It's hard to write a bestseller with those holes in the wall.

OBSERVER: What was the most helpful part of this?

JAMIE: I didn't quite . . .

PAT: What was the most helpful, do you think, part of the session? If you know yet, actually.

JAMIE: What do you think? (*to Dona*)

DONA: Oh, I know. I liked having two of you, actually, and kind of relating your own thing. I think that's kind of unusual, it struck me as a little unusual to hear you . . .

BILL: That's right, it's against the law back here on the East Coast, I believe, for the therapists to say anything about themselves.

DONA: It is. It's very unusual.

BILL: It is unusual.

DONA: I don't know if it's against the law, but they don't do it.

BILL: It's against the therapist law.

DONA: But I like that. You may have been doing it so we would relax, maybe you don't do it . . .

PAT: No, we always do it.

DONA: But I found that different and that was very helpful to me.

BILL: Great, yeah. I think we do it partly to normalize, say, you know, "Things aren't so good, we have the same kind of stuff," and also to give ideas about alternative ways to handle it. Ways we've worked it out, ways other people have worked it out. We tell lots of stories about ourselves and about people that we have seen, and so storytelling is a big part of the therapy that we do. So, yeah, it was very deliberate.

[We are open about what we are doing to show respect and collaboration.]

DONA: I like that.

BILL: But, also, it just pulls things out. There were so many similarities between your situation and ours that were quite striking.

JAMIE: I think it also changes the dynamics, so that instead of one person listening, directing, it changes that somehow, and that the Burns and Allen routine helps, too, I think.

BILL: Which one is Burns?

PAT: Yeah, that's what I was thinking. I don't know if I want to be Gracie.

DONA: Stiller and Meara, maybe.

BILL: Yeah, Stiller and Meara, that's better.

PAT: That's the one. But you know I do think that that is one of our philosophies about therapy, is that we don't consider ourselves having all the answers and you're screwed up people, that kind of thing. We kind of think that this is an exchange where we can come to some collaboration, yeah.

BILL: It makes it more of a conversation, right.

OBSERVER: What do you think will make you do what you've agreed to do here?

BILL: What will get you to do it, writing it down?

[Bill restates the question because he did not like the phrase, "make you do." That could have invited them to rebel or given them a sense of being manipulated or controlled.]

JAMIE: We want to get along.

DONA: Yeah, I think writing it down is a good idea.

JAMIE: The basic motivation is we want to get along.

DONA: Uh huh.

JAMIE: Writing it down will give us a document that we can point to when we're being hysterical.

BILL: So, one thing is he says they're motivated to do it, that's one thing that'll get them to follow through. And the second thing is writing it down will just remind them. Can you imagine anything that would just get it to slip away?

DONA: Yes.

BILL: I'm talking about relapse prevention.

DONA: Time, you know, I think you do forget, you know, even . . .

BILL: That's why the writing it down would be important.

DONA: Right, uh huh.

BILL: Or maybe you can get a copy of this tape, maybe Linda will get a copy of this tape, or we can arrange to get a copy . . .

DONA: That would be nice.

BILL: . . . and you could listen to that. Okay. Well, we'll make a note, or would you keep us on track in terms of that, Linda, and make sure we can get a copy of it for you and that would be another way to remind you. If you ever get stuck, let's put in this damn tape and listen to what they had to say, or what we had to say at that moment.

DONA: I just thought of one thing, too, that speaking of tapes. When we, well, we had a commitment ceremony before we had a wedding ceremony, and we made a tape for that of music and when we put that tape on now, I mean that would do it, that would [be] all we'd ever have to . . . I just thought of that, we never do it in the middle of an argument, but if we did that would probably end it.

[Here Dona comes up with another pattern intervention that would remind them of their affection for one another and break the conflictual pattern. It appears she has incorporated some of the strategies we were suggesting during the session.]

BILL: If you're in the midst of it, you have to stop and listen to that for at least five minutes or something like that.

PAT: Wonderful.

JAMIE: Oh, that would really work.

BILL: Great.

JAMIE: I almost cry just thinking about it.

BILL: So sweet.

PAT: Really, if my day could be filled with couples like this, it would be so wonderful.

BILL: They all want to hire you and bring you back home so they can feel good about their marital therapy . . . hey, we want this couple, yeah. (*laughter*)

JAMIE: We're available.

BILL: Hey, you need the bucks, right? They'll come every week for the Cape Cod seminar, same problems, we'll see how the different therapists handle it.

JAMIE: Good idea.

BILL: We'll let the organizer of these workshops know that. These people are available for hire.

OBSERVER: If they had come to you in Nebraska for this, what would you recommend for follow-up with them?

BILL: I'd say, just going out and doing it and then having us check back with them or them check back with us in about a month and see how it's going.

PAT: Yeah, we probably wouldn't schedule another session. Or, if we did, we'd say we'll put this for six weeks down the road, and if you don't need it just cancel it, but please cancel a week in advance so we can fill it.

BILL: Yeah, they were so cooperative. I think they're motivated, they've got the idea.

FOLLOW-UP

Two and a half months later, we received a follow-up note from Dona. She wrote, "Things are going very well for us, we've gotten along so well since our 'tune-up' even though things have not improved on the financial front." Eight months later, she wrote, "Everything is going well for us although we've yet to hit the big money! However, life is pleasant and we're happy so I won't complain about [money]. In fact, we were able to take a week's vacation to the Keys in Florida that was great fun."

REFERENCES

Cade, B., & O'Hanlon, W. H. (1993). *A Brief Guide to Brief Therapy*. New York: Norton.

Hudson, P. O., & O'Hanlon, W. H. (1992). *Rewriting Love Stories: Brief Marital Therapy*. New York: Norton.

O'Hanlon, W. H., & Weiner-Davis, M. (1989). *In Search of Solutions: A New Direction in Psychotherapy*. New York: Norton.

O'Hanlon, B., & Wilk, J. (1987). *Shifting Contexts: The Generation of Effective Psychotherapy*. New York: Guilford.

Weiner-Davis, M. (1992). *Divorce Busting*. New York: Summit Books.

CHAPTER 10

Entering One Another's Worlds of Meaning and Imagination

*Dramatic Enactment and
Narrative Couple Therapy*

SALLYANN ROTH
RICHARD CHASIN

> Individuals are never entirely at the mercy of events so long as
> they retain the power to reconceive them.
> —MORSON AND EMERSON (1990, p. 230), on Bakhtin

The stories we create about our lives and relationships both arise from
and shape our experience (Bruner, 1986; Epston & White, 1992; Gergen
& Kaye, 1993; White & Epston, 1990). In this sense, our many life stories
are both our creations and our creators. They are the principal way that
each of us participates with others in the making and remaking of
ourselves as social beings. When the relationships we count on to sustain
and invigorate us are in trouble, however, we often feel ourselves to be
less agents in creating our own life stories than actors playing roles
shaped, if not scripted, by others, in dramas that consign us to unsatisfying repetitions or direct us toward some painful end. We experience
ourselves as so constricted in our couple that we cannot express or
perhaps even know our own complexity. Our sense of agency, capability,
and imagination is diminished; alliances that once energized us now
weigh us down. The past is experienced as fixed and foreclosed rather
than as in flux and open, more as an encased and permanent exhibit
than as a rich store of possibility to which we can return again and again
for material to create and revise our narratives and redesign our futures.

We are equal contributors to this chapter, as we have been to our previously published joint articles.

In these periods, we inhabit what Bakhtin, in writing about literature, calls "'small time': a present without perspective that separates us from the resources of real creativity . . ." (Morson & Emerson, 1990, p. 230). Confined within the stifling parameters of small time, we cannot engage in generative dialogue with our partners or even with parts of ourselves. Our self-stories seem inextricably and unhappily joined with those of our partner. Hope for meeting the other as other is diminished, if not entirely lost. With little cognitive or emotional horizon beyond the immediate, we cannot see ourselves or our situation from an outside position. There is no way out—or in.

When partners are at impasse in their relationship, their individual and couple stories have become predominantly narratives of limitation. How can they each develop narratives of possibility or gain the freedom and agency to create narratives of choice? How can they move from small time to its alternative, great time (Bakhtin, in Holquist, 1982)? How can generative dialogue replace routine exchanges? How can partners risk moving toward each other from positions of protective withdrawal? How can they become less reactive and more curious? How can they restrain impulses to persuade or dominate and, instead, enter respectfully and reflexively into each other's worlds of meaning and feeling? How can they come to experience themselves and the other not as closed and static, but as open and evolving—as unfinalizable (Bakhtin, in Holquist, 1982; Morson & Emerson, 1990)?[1]

In this chapter, we present a model for use at the outset of couple therapy or in consultation to an ongoing couple therapy.[2] The model employs a structured interview in which each partner creates a series of dramatizations, some corresponding to existing memory and meaning, others imaginatively revising that memory and meaning. All of the enactments are performed by the couple within the session.

We and some of our colleagues have worked effectively with this model for many years. Colleagues with differing approaches to therapy, differing styles of working, and differing theory bases have reported effective use of the model to us. In this chapter, however, we discuss the model in a narrative frame and as a demonstration of some principles and practices that we believe have applicability beyond the model itself. It illustrates some important ways that full entry into an "as if" or imaginary world (Iser, 1993), or a subjunctive mode (Bruner, 1986), or an experience of transgressing ordinary boundaries of time, place, and

---

[1]"Unfinalizable," a term used by Bakhtin, means indeterminate, open, endlessly full of possibility.

[2]This model, originated by Richard Chasin in 1982, has been further developed by Chasin, Roth, and colleagues in the subsequent years. A less fully developed version of the model with a different explanatory frame is described in Chasin, Roth, and Bograd (1989) and in Chasin and Roth (1990).

role (Iser, 1993; Morson & Emerson, 1990; Penn, 1982, 1985; Penn & Frankfurt, 1994; Tomm, 1987), can increase the possibility of entering a domain of experience in which conceptions of the past are alive and inexhaustibly rich in untapped meaning, where the future is undetermined, and where the present is the creative nexus between the changeable past and the changeful future.

With others whose work is based on a narrative metaphor (Epston & White, 1992; Freedman & Combs, 1993; Freeman & Lobovits, 1993; Weingarten, 1992; White & Epston, 1990; Zimmerman & Dickerson, 1993), we seek to help couples to expand the breadth and openness of the narratives they can develop both separately and with each other, as well as to strengthen their sense of agency through "vivid, robust experiences of alternative possibilities" (Freedman & Combs, 1993, p. 294). With those whose work is grounded in a social constructionist, language-based model (Andersen, 1987, 1992; Anderson & Goolishian, 1988; and others), we believe that meaning-making is "an intersubjective phenomenon, created and experienced by individuals in conversation and action with others and with themselves" (Anderson, 1993, p. 324).

Our work differs in some significant ways from that of many therapists whose work is guided by narrative ideas in a social constructionist frame. Our entry into individual narrative, into the meaning-making realm of the partners in a couple, occurs principally through engagement with the imaginary. Additionally, we rely more heavily on dramatization, on fully being in experience, than on verbal acts explaining and describing experience at some remove from it. Of course, being in conversation is also being in experience. However, conversation and dramatic enactment are different in that the latter almost always involves intense affect and full engagement of all senses and faculties as the clients live out highly evocative scenes, ordinarily from many standpoints and roles.

DESCRIPTION OF THE MODEL

In the model we present here, each partner scripts, and is the protagonist in, a number of dramatizations in response to specific questions from the therapist. In each enactment, the partner and the therapist conform to the protagonist's instructions; improvisation is restricted. Through role reversal, both partners ultimately play, at one time or another, most of the roles in all of the dramatizations, but especially roles in which they provide or receive fulfillment. The therapist plays all of the roles that seem destructive or disappointing.

The first enactments represent each partner's individual dreams for the couple's future. They are followed by scenes from the past. Specifically, one partner stages two emblematic episodes, a painful scene from childhood and, next, a related scene from the distant past of his or her family of origin. That partner then deliberately revises and reforms these scenes in order to dramatize the past as it "should have been." Following this series of past scenes by one partner, the other member of the couple creates and enacts a similar sequence of past scenes.

These dramatizations are the episodes of a therapeutic *Midsummer Night's Dream*, an adventure in alternate realities that includes imaginary experiences of a redeemed past and a memorable voyage into an ideal future. The power and complexity of these dramatic enactments can shift how the partners see what they have regarded as the fixed past and the inevitable future, can engender hope and vitality, and can provide a springboard for lasting change.[3]

The enactments are preceded by careful contracting and specific questioning that are designed to prevent each member of the couple from getting stuck in the accustomed stories of attack or complaint, to activate their individual strengths, to encourage the expression of their separate longings, and to heighten and contain the emotional force of the dramas to come.

The model's full structure is outlined in the following section. The needs of a particular couple, however, may contraindicate use of the model or may call for variations on this basic structure (Chasin & Roth, 1990; Chasin, Roth, & Bograd, 1989). Table 10.1 indicates important characteristics of each scene in the standard model; Table 10.2 exemplifies the sequence in which the scenes are enacted.

OUTLINE OF THE MODEL

Deciding Whether to Propose Use of the Model

Our first step is to decide whether to use the model with a specific couple. It works best for couples with longstanding difficulties who are committed to working things out with each other and who are generally honest and open about vital matters. We do not recommend using the model when it is likely that there is serious deception, lack of commitment, or any situation of overriding importance, such as an untreated major illness, significant substance abuse, or an active involvement of one member in a relationship that violates an implicit or explicit fidelity

---

[3]The entry into the imaginary and its transforming effect on those who voyage there together are not mere flights of fancy but can have expanding, enduring, and desirable impact. "But all the story of the night told over, / And all their minds transfigur'd so together, / More witnesseth than fancy's images / And grows to something of great constancy, / But howsoever, strange and admirable" (W. Shakespeare, *A Midsummer Night's Dream*, Act V, Scene I).

TABLE 10.1. Important Characteristics of the Enactments

Scene	Mood	Time	Dramatis personae	Protagonist authors scene and plays . . .	Roles that protagonist's partner is likely to play
A. Vision of a satisfying future	Fulfilled	Future	Protagonist and partner as a couple	All roles	Partner getting what he/she wants; self doing exactly what partner wants
B. Painful remembered past	Painful	Protagonist's childhood	Protagonist's family of origin	All roles	Partner and his/her family members, except those who appear to be the source of hurt or deprivation
C. Painful mythic past	Painful	Past too remote to be remembered by protagonist	Family of origin of one of protagonist's parents	All roles	Members of partner's family, one or two generations ago, except those who appear to be the source of hurt or deprivation
D. Painful mythic past transformed	Fulfilled	Same as above	Family of origin of one of protagonist's parents transformed	All roles	Members of partner's family, one or two generations ago, especially those who are most positively transformed
E. Painful remembered past transformed	Fulfilled	Protagonist's childhood	Protagonist's family of origin transformed	All roles	Partner and his/her family members, especially those who are most positively transformed

Note. In the structured sequence of enactments, the first partner creates his or her version of scene A, a satisfying future scene, following which the other partner creates another such scene expressing his or her wishes. Then, one partner creates past scenes B–E, following which the other partner creates his or her past scenes in the B–E sequence.

TABLE 10.2. Sequence of Enactments in the Case Example

Satisfying Future Scenes Enacted
Alice's satisfying future scene enacted
John's satisfying future scene enacted

Painful Childhood Scenes Enacted and Revised
John's past scenes
John's remembered painful childhood scene enacted
Painful mythic past scene: John's father's family of origin enacted
Transformed mythic past scene: John's father's family of origin rescripted
John's painful past scene transformed
Alice's past scenes
Alice's remembered painful childhood scene enacted
Painful mythic past scene: Alice's mother's family of origin enacted
Transformed mythic time scene: Amanda's mother's family of origin rescripted
Alice's painful past scene transformed

agreement between the partners. We try to learn about such possibilities in a brief telephone conversation, sometimes with the clients and sometimes with a referring therapist.

Agreements Made at the Start of the Session

The Pass Rule. In order to promote safe and voluntary participation, the therapist and clients agree on the "right to pass," that is, the right of each partner to refuse to answer any question or carry out any suggested activity without saying why. If the clients do not agree to the pass rule, the model cannot be used, since safety and noncoerciveness—necessary in any therapy—are especially important when clients new to a therapist or consultant are invited to participate in emotionally intense experiences.

Administrative Arrangements. Agreements about the length of the meeting and any use of audio or videotape are made at this point in the session.

Postponing Problem Statements. The therapist expresses a preference to the partners that they temporarily postpone statements of "the problem" until later in the meeting or until the next meeting. The therapist's preference, however, is posed only as a request or a suggestion and does not foreclose either client's option to open with a brief problem statement.

Descriptions of Individual Strengths and Resources

We invite each partner to name and describe his or her own individual strengths and personal resources independently of what the other partner may think. If a description is vague, we ask for more specificity; if it is highly specific, we ask for a more general statement.

Verbal Descriptions of Individual Visions for the Couple Relationship

Next we ask each partner to describe what might be happening between them if the relationship were already greatly improved in the way he or she wishes it to be.

Enactment of a Satisfying Future Scene

Each partner enacts a brief vignette in an imagined future, one in which his or her longings for the relationship have already been achieved. In these dramatizations, through a series of role reversals, the partners collaborate in dramatizing each other's individual vision.

Enactment and Revision of Painful Childhood Scenes

Each partner creates and is protagonist in a series of past scenes (outlined below). When they are completed, the other partner takes his or her turn at being protagonist in a similar sequence of past scenes.

A Painful Childhood Scene Enacted. Each partner concisely enacts a painful past experience, usually from childhood, in which his or her early unmet yearnings resemble the salient adult wish that is perfectly fulfilled in the enactment of the satisfying future for the couple.

A Painful Mythic Past Scene: One Parent's Family of Origin Enacted. That partner identifies a key hurtful figure in the prior scene and dramatizes an actual or imagined scene in the formative years of that figure, one that accounts for his or her later hurtful behavior. The key figure is usually a parent, but may be someone else. The episode is set in what we call *mythic time* or *time beyond memory*,[4] because the scene was not actually witnessed by the client but came down in family legend, or is grounded only in fragmentary information about the past.

A Mythic Past Scene Transformed: One Parent's Family of Origin Rescripted. The client then revises the prior scene to happen as it "should" have—helpful, not harmful; fulfilling, not depriving; protective, not endangering. The vanquished or neutralized villain in this scene is sometimes social, economic, or political oppression.[5] Some revised scenes focus not on larger systems, but on the interior of the family.

---

[4]The phrase "time beyond memory" was suggested to us by David Epston.

[5]Often these burdensome or harmful forces were so invisibly integral to a generally shared worldview that they could not be identified at the time. What family members learned may have become canonical, passed down through the generations unchanged even as economic, social, or political climate and family context became substantially different. The rescripted scene may involve a radical transformation of the course of history. It may also flow more subtly from the recognition that the exact lessons learned,

A Painful Past Scene Transformed: A Childhood Scene with a "Reformed" Parent. The client recreates his or her painful childhood scene as it might have gone if the parent had *actually* had the experiences enacted in the mythically rescripted scene.

Statements of "the Problem"

When clients have contracted to postpone describing the problem until after the enactments, the therapist offers each partner an opportunity to

- State succinctly his or her view of the problem in the relationship
- State how he or she views the problem in the relationship in light of what has happened in this meeting
- Say nothing at all

Deciding on a Next Step

The therapist and clients, and any consultant involved decide on a next step (a homework task, a next appointment, a suspension of meetings, and so on), on the basis of what has emerged.

CASE ILLUSTRATION AND DISCUSSION OF THE MODEL

The detailed application of the model can best be described through an extended case example. The example presented here, taken from a consultation session conducted by Sallyann Roth, includes key sections of dialogue (somewhat condensed and minimally altered for illustrative purposes), comments about technique, and general observations about the use of the model. These observations, though not systematic, are drawn from our own extensive application of the model and from direct feedback from clients and from colleagues who have used it.

Alice and John, a white, middle-class couple, were referred for consultation by their therapist,[6] who felt, as they did, that an otherwise extremely successful couple's therapy had not yet altered a particular

---

while useful or essential in their time, have become limiting as they have been carried forward to the present.

[6]The referring therapist, Louise Enoch, PhD, had worked with Alice and John from the time they had been separated, through times of tremendous strife, to the point of the consultation at which they were reunited and committed to each other and to doing things differently. They accepted the referral because of their tremendous trust in their therapist. We are grateful to Louise Enoch and appreciate her excellent clinical work both preceding and following the consultation. And we are grateful to the couple for their generous permission for all of us to learn from their work.

painful and repeating interaction that often left the partners feeling hopeless and disaffected with each other. The consultant asked for only minimal information about the impasse and the partners' background.

Deciding Whether to Propose Use of the Model

Prior to the consultation, the couple's therapist had explored the possibility of using this model with them and the partners had agreed to participate. For this reason, the illustration used here starts with the second step, the opening agreements.

Opening Agreements

Pass Rule

CONSULTANT: Many people have told me that the kind of meeting we plan to have here today works best for them when they feel that everything they do or say is completely voluntary. If you are asked to participate in any way that feels "wrong" to you—even a little bit—do you agree to say "no"? You needn't give a reason, just indicate that you wish to "pass" and we'll go on. If you are not fully ready at any time, I recommend that you pass. Do you agree?

JOHN: That's a big relief. I was worried that we might have to do things here that would be too hard.

ALICE: (*laughing*) Me, too. But if one of us passes, will we get enough from the meeting?

CONSULTANT: Yes. Actually, not "going along" can be very useful. If either of you "passes," it may help you feel safe and will allow me to feel less inhibited about what I ask. This way, you decide what's useful, and what you're ready for.

[Both partners accept this agreement.]

The "right to pass," originated by James Sacks (Lee, 1981), reduces clients' anxiety, enhances their sense of responsibility for and control of what happens in the session, and inhibits a common consultant–client dynamic in which the consultant takes or is given the "power" to know what is "right."

Administrative Arrangements

Next, the therapist negotiates all other contractual arrangements, such as length of session, confidentiality, and any use of audio or videotape.

John and Alice agreed to having a videotaped meeting of up to two hours, with ordinary confidentiality rules in effect.[7] The consultant assured them that all agreements would be revisited at the end of the meeting. For example, they could have the tape erased, leave it with the therapist to review, or take it home themselves. They would know better what they wanted to do with the tape after they knew what was on it.

Postponing Discussion of Problems

CONSULTANT: Most often, when partners come to a meeting like this, each one is prepared to speak about what brings them here. However, I like to work with couples in a way that does not start with problems. Some people find it too frustrating to put off saying what's wrong. Would it be all right with you to put some of the things you planned to say on hold until later?

ALICE: It's okay with me.

JOHN: Fine with me. I'm not all geared up.

Although most couples agree to postpone discussing problems, some people decide to talk about them first. If such early problem statements are kept brief, this model interview can still be effective.

Description of Individual Strengths and Resources

CONSULTANT: I'd like to meet each of you by learning two or three things that you really like about yourself. I'd like to know some of your enduring strengths, whether or not your partner would agree, and whether or not they are showing up in your couple relationship.

JOHN: Well, I'm a nice guy. People like me, I'm a funny guy, and I'm good at meeting people.

CONSULTANT: What is it about you that people respond to, that leaves them feeling that you are really nice?

JOHN: Usually I can find something in common to talk about with people. I ask them questions about themselves. When you listen to what people say, they like it. And I crack jokes, so people lighten up and tell me what's really going on.

[John speaks about his skills for about seven minutes.]

---

[7]This kind of meeting generally takes two hours. If it is necessary to work in shorter periods of time, the safest place to break the meeting is after the enactments of the longed-for futures.

CONSULTANT: Thank you, John. Alice, what are some of the things you like about yourself? How are you particularly skilled, resourceful, strong, or able?

ALICE: I'm really good with my kids.

CONSULTANT: What do you do, that someone might observe, that would show them how you are good with your kids?

ALICE: When they're real upset—even at me—I just listen and don't get upset myself. I try to listen and think about what they're feeling, or what is bothering them, and let them get it off their chests. [She continues in this vein for a while.] And I can be a lot of fun.

CONSULTANT: In what way?

ALICE: I like to try new things. I don't like to do the same things all the time.

CONSULTANT: Thank you, Alice. So, John, for you it's a light sense of humor, an ability to joke in such a way that people open up to you, and your genuine interest in others, that enable you to listen carefully to them. And for you, Alice, it's an ability to separate out "the problem" from a personal comment about you, to stay calm in the face of another's upset. And a sense of fun and adventure. Do I have it right? Anything you'd like to correct?

[Both Alice and John accept the consultant's summary statements.]

The early and deliberate focus on strengths has a powerful, beneficial effect on clients. They are usually surprised and relieved when asked to describe their strengths. Only rarely is a client unable to spell some out. The listening partner is usually silent, respectful, and interested.

In responding to the consultant's questions about strengths, clients often become animated, which suggests to us that they are not only describing skills, but are also reexperiencing their skillful selves. In later steps of the interview, when the therapist employs the same words and phrases that clients have used to describe their strengths, their recently recalled competence sometimes seems to be reactivated.

The celebration of strengths is especially empowering to couples who feel oppressed by larger social systems. These couples are often demoralized, feeling generally disrespected, for example, by service providers whom they experience as interested only in their difficulties and failings.

In addition to the more obvious benefits to the clients, the process of exploring strengths tends to prevent the therapist from adopting the problem-saturated view with which clients usually lead. This exploration of individual strengths also begins to separate out each partner's storyline from that of the couple. This disentangling of individual stories from the couple's joined stories is essential in enabling partners to hear themselves and each other differently.

Each Partner's Vision for the Relationship

CONSULTANT: The next question is, if things were already different in your couple—in exactly the way you, as an individual, want them to be—what would be happening between you that isn't happening now, or that isn't going the way you want it to go? This may be hard to answer. Most of us have more practice in describing what we don't want than what we do want. Please be specific. How would the two of you be with each other if your relationship were already better? Take some time to think about it.

JOHN: [in summary] When I come home from work, Alice is waiting for me. She comes to the door to meet me and greets me with a kiss. She is glad to see me. The children have eaten, and they have cleaned up. There are no chores to do, so we can go out to dinner together. We joke with each other about how well things are going, and we hold hands under the table.

ALICE: [in summary] We are comfortable together—at ease. We are doing separate tasks without bumping into each other. We talk about nice things, maybe memories, maybe things to look forward to.

Clients often stumble when approaching the less familiar activity of specifying their hopes, but ultimately they answer. The therapist keeps the clients to the task of saying what is yearned for, not what is wrong.

Satisfying Future Scenes Enacted

CONSULTANT: As you probably know from everyday misunderstandings, it's really easy to not "get" exactly what somebody means. So, partly for that reason, and partly because sometimes people learn more about their own wishes by actually playing them out, I propose that you each enact a very brief scene in which your wishes have already come true [see Table 10.2 for an outline of these scenes]. Alice, if you agree to do this, then in John's scene, you'll play your role as he scripts it, even if it is something you wouldn't ordinarily—or ever—do, and, John, in Alice's scene you'll play your role as she scripts it, even if what she designs is not what you would ordinarily—or ever—do. Your participation in these scenes does not constitute an agreement that you will *ever* do this again. These scenes need not be like what you have just described. Also, don't worry about not knowing how to act. I'll direct. I'll help. This is just to see what it would look like. Is this okay? (*Both nod agreement.*) Who's going to go first?

[John seems ready. Alice volunteers.]

CONSULTANT: What scene will illustrate your wishes, Alice?

Enactment is introduced as a way for the partners to develop more accurate knowledge of each other's dreams. The therapist does not mention its other potential advantages—for example, to stimulate wishful longing, broaden cognitive perspectives, interrupt customary unsatisfying interactions, desensitize fears, and, possibly, rehearse novel behavior. In our experience, an elaborate explanation that includes such details usually amplifies client anxiety. Our silence is not an attempt to obfuscate or to be opaque. Indeed, if a client asks for a more detailed explanation, we respond openly and fully.

Alice's Satisfying Future Scene Enacted

ALICE: I want to be outside. We are outside.

[She is planting flowers, and he is using a "weed whacker." She and John are working in the same physical space but are quite separate, sharing few words. They enjoy their separate work, and occasionally stop to admire each other's efforts. He brings her tea. As they go indoors, they kiss. In the enactment, they giggle a lot and seem embarrassed and awkward. The consultant tells them she will look away as they kiss, and does.]

CONSULTANT: Is this it, then? A sense of ease and comfort? (*Alice assents.*) You picked one of the hardest things to show because a lot of what happens for you is invisible, but it seems that the quiet, appreciative, and affectionate way that you are with each other is central. Is that right? (*Again she assents.*) Thank you. Can we switch to John's scene? (*She agrees.*)

John's Satisfying Future Scene Enacted

[John is walking in the door after work. Alice comes to the door to greet him with a welcoming kiss showing how happy she is that he is home. The children need no attention, nor does the house. Alice is excited about a big surprise she has planned; She bought tickets for them both to go to a hockey game, which he loves and she does not. At the game, she is the one who buys the hot dogs and beer so that he can enjoy the game without interruption. When they arrive home, she asks him what he wants her to wear, and when he says "the skimpy pink thing," she puts it on. The scene ends with a long hug as a stand-in for "a real passion kiss."]

CONSULTANT: Is that it then, John? (*He nods.*) Thank you. Notice your feeling. Remember it. In the future, it may be useful for you to recognize this feeling. Being welcomed emotionally, physically, being thought of when you are not there, enjoying loving companionship, having your wishes come first—these all seem important in your scene. Do I have it right? Did I miss something important, or misstate anything? (*John says no.*)

Until the scene is perfected, it is rehearsed over and over, with each partner playing both the role of the self and the role of the other in every step of the interaction, providing each with experiences from the perspectives of both roles. No matter how tedious and awkward the process may seem, successful enactment requires that each client experience precisely what he or she wants. This task is not completed until the scripted scene is played from beginning to end with each partner in his or her own role.

Occasionally, bias can be problematic for therapists directing wishful scenes. The therapist must accept the visions without judgment or skepticism, even if they seem sexist, offensive, insufficient, peculiar, or bewildering. There can be no editorializing; the therapist cannot be a drama critic or a social critic. We have asked the clients to do something difficult: to show their unabashed wishes, without explanation, without rationale, without even a practical context. We need to remember that the scenes are both exactly what they are and are also metaphoric representations of far-reaching longings.

Typically, partners in conflict are highly reactive, do not listen carefully or fully, and may respond in ways so often practiced, so habituated, that they are automatic. They may hold their own positions so tenaciously that they can scarcely contemplate another position and may make sharply negative attributions. Enacting their undefended yearning disarms and interrupts these patterns and introduces novel interactional behavior. The anxiety couples often feel in role-playing their visions for the future is sometimes manifested as hilarity or giddiness. Clients have told us that this reaction is sometimes related to their sense of high risk and exposure when specifying desires instead of criticisms.

Performing the exercise places certain unaccustomed requirements on the couple. As author, each partner must cease making requests by complaint or sullen silence, suppress the passive desire that the other partner will magically mind-read his or her needs, and suspend the belief that his or her wishes will be ignored, misunderstood, or refused. As cooperator in the other's scene, each partner must dismiss the presumption of knowing what the other wants, overcome the tendency to refuse a request before it is fully expressed, forego the unwillingness to experiment with what the other wishes, and check the urge to protest that the other's needs are either obscure or excessive. The very process of creating a scene of a wish fulfilled interrupts habits of attacking and complaining as it places each partner in a proactive stance rather than a reactive one.

As each partner listens openly to the other's dream and then experiences it from the position of both self and other, empathy, hope, and a sense of creative possibility may develop.

We have frequently found that future enactments seem to have rehearsal value. Although no couple has ever *exactly* reproduced an "ideal scene" at home, many clients have reported some significant behavior change after the session. For many, the experience of playing various roles in this psychodramatic future seems to expand the range of feeling and action they can imagine and perform (Moreno, 1978).

When first using this method, we were concerned that our initial focus on wishes would make clients feel that we were ignoring their distress. However, couples have told us that they experienced our opening inquiries about their yearnings for the relationship as directly attentive to their pain.

Painful Childhood Scenes Enacted and Revised

CONSULTANT: (*to both Alice and John*) You know, when each of you described your dream and you played it out, it seemed like it was about certain very specific things, and it may have also been, in a way, about things that are more complicated and mysterious. Yours, Alice, seemed to be about a certain comfort in being together without a whole lot of words having to be spoken. And yours, John, seemed to have a lot to do with really being welcomed, received, and touched with an open heart, having your wishes and pleasures in Alice's mind even when you weren't there. So, the next question is this: Think back in your life to a time long, long before you met each other when such wishes may also have existed. Perhaps when you were young children. There might have been a time, Alice, when you needed that kind of ease and comfort, casual conversation and quiet companionship. Separateness and togetherness. And, John, a time that you needed that kind of warm, physical welcome, thoughtfulness about your wishes, and companionship in your pleasures. So, go back in your mind—almost like rewinding a tape to older memories, much older memories—and ask yourself if any scene comes to mind when the quality of what you wanted here was just what you wanted and didn't get then. Whatever comes to you is just fine. Let me know whenever you've got something in mind. Just take a minute and

something will come. If more than one memory comes to mind or
if the kind of thing you are thinking of was embedded in the daily
life of your home, then any single example will be just fine. [See
Table 10.2 for an outline of these scenes.]

One reason the therapist guides the client to the distant past is to
avoid reenacting an incident that directly involved the partner in any
way. A more important reason is that we seek to stimulate clients to
reimagine and reconstruct themes that are woven into their full life
narratives, not merely into accounts of their adult relationships. Therefore, we ask each partner to work with a relevant scene from their early
lives. However, we do not limit the request to a scene from childhood
because significant "early" events may be located in adolescence or
early adult life.

In response to our invitation to bring up a past scene, clients usually
bring up one of those singularly paradigmatic or endlessly repetitive
childhood episodes that has become a keystone in the construction of
dominant themes in their life stories.

John's Painful Childhood Scene Enacted

[After both indicate that they are ready, John begins. The consultant asks
Alice to pull her chair back so that she is physically removed from the
central action.]

JOHN: When I was a kid, we always went camping. I used to pretty much
    come and go from the campsite, and it never made much difference
    to my parents whether I came back or not. It was frightening. I even
    had my own tent.

[The consultant asks John which parent will be key, as they have only
enough time to work with one parent today. He selects his father, James.
She helps him to develop the scene through role reversal, with the
therapist playing James. In this scene, John leaves the campsite at night,
without being asked where he is going or when he is coming back. The
only notice James takes of him is to remind him of an undone chore.
When the scene has been developed, John is invited to step back and
observe it. Alice plays the role of 12-year-old John, and the consultant
plays John's drunk and distant father. John, as observer, is asked, "What
does young John need right now?"]

The therapist uses the "mirror technique," in which the protagonist
leaves the scene and observes others enacting it (Starr, 1977). This is
meant to provide a fresh view with a broader perspective than one has
when playing a role in the scene itself.

The past scene is often one the partner has heard about, and it may well have been brought up in an accusatory episode ("You are just like my . . ." or, "You are treating me as if I'm your . . ."). When the scene is played out, it is important for the therapist, not the partner, to take the role of any person described as having been neglectful or hurtful. This role may well be one in which the partner has already been cast. We were initially surprised to find that casting the therapist in a negative role seems not to disrupt the nascent therapeutic relationship. In fact, the more accurately the therapist portrays the negative role, the better understood the client feels.

Since the selected past scene is generally held by the protagonist as an emblematic event in the construction of his or her life story, it is also a potential key to powerful and far-reaching transformative possibilities, particularly when role-played and witnessed by a partner. Enactments of the recalled painful past are brief, because we believe that extending them might reinforce problematic patterns.

Painful Mythic Past Scene: John's Father's Family of Origin Enacted

CONSULTANT: What do you know about your father's history that explains to you how he could have acted this way, not attending carefully to his own son?

JOHN: I don't have a clue. I don't even know if I'd recognize a picture of his father. My dad, James, told me his father was a tough guy and I would've liked him. Dad lived in a separate apartment, upstairs. My grandmother even rented it as an apartment after he left home, but it was my father's room growing up.

[A new scene is set up and developed. John plays James at age 11, upstairs in the family home, alone and lonely, feeling that nobody cares about him. Alice then briefly takes this role, experiencing James's isolation and loneliness. John plays his grandfather, Jeremy.]

Transformed Mythic Past Scene: John's Father's Family of Origin Rescripted

[John, playing James at age 11, designs and enacts the interaction he thinks that James most needed from his father, Jeremy. In this re-formed scene, Jeremy spends time with James, goes for a walk, shares a soda, and is generally interested in him. In doing this scene, Alice and John each spend time enrolled as the nurtured son and the nurturing father, James and Jeremy. The scene ends when Jeremy (played by Alice), is giving time and attention to James, played by John.]

The parent's reformed family history scene is developed until it satisfies what the client imagines his parent would have needed. In such scenes, the therapist steps back and is less central to the action. The partner is cast in a protective or healing role, often as a magically transformed grandparent. In group psychodrama this role is called the "reformed auxiliary" (Sacks, 1978). The reformed episode is the action equivalent of Milton Erickson's hypnotic incorporation of a healing person into the client's memory, a technique designed to enable the client to move to a future that seemed unachievable without this experience (Erickson, 1954; Haley, 1973). In family therapy terms, a nurturing or healing experience replaces a neglectful or hurtful one in the family history. Strictly speaking, in the storyline of the drama, it is not the client who has experienced care and healing, but the client's parent, enabling that parent, in the next enactment, to provide what the client yearned for as a child and still yearns for now.

A dimension is added in this and the next step in our method in that the key "healing" role is played by the current partner who, in troubled couples, is often seen as neglectful, hurtful, or depriving in the present. At the remove of prior generations and childhood, even partners at impasse can usually play fulfilling and healing roles for each other, often giving and receiving the kind of care that they seek in their lives together.

John's Painful Past Scene Transformed

CONSULTANT: (*to James, played by John*) You have been cared for in just this way by your Dad, you've gone for walks, talked, had sodas together, and he's had his hand on your back affectionately like this many, many times. James, you have had all of this with you, as you grew up, and you now have a 12-year-old son of your own. You are camping, and John seems to be getting ready to leave the campground by himself. What does he need?

[John scripts and enacts a scene in which James, his father, makes a companionable plan to go with him to the sporting-goods store. James is concerned and even scolding when John is late, and there is an easygoing camaraderie, including casual, physical touch. Alice plays John as the young person receiving this care. They then reverse roles; the scene ends with the transformed James, played by Alice, affectionately headed to town with the young John.]

The therapist typically asks the protagonist to demonstrate the healing actions to be provided by the transformed parent before the partner takes the parent's role and gives these fulfilling responses to the protagonist, who is in role as him or herself as a young person.

When a partner takes the role of fantasy protector or healer in the other's family history, the "helping" partner perceives the other's current pain from a fresh standpoint, has an experience of effectiveness usually not granted to him or her, and thereafter may have access to a wider range of responses to the partner's current distress. The "healed" partner has an experience that may reveal ways that the current problem is amplified by the echoing past, is freed from the monolithic image of the partner as frustrator, and receives a precise and vivid memory marker of gratification to replace a vague image of what fulfillment might be like. Both partners usually experience renewed hope for their relationship.

Alice's Painful Childhood Scene Enacted

[The following dialogue represents virtually all of what was said in Alice's past scene.]

ALICE: When I think of coming in and not feeling comfortable, I think of the first time—after my mother married my stepfather—I came in the house and they'd been fighting. They were screaming and they were bleeding . . .

CONSULTANT: Bleeding, literally?

ALICE: Bleeding.

CONSULTANT: Both of them?

ALICE: Yup. And there was broken furniture on the floor, and broken dishes all over.

CONSULTANT: Each one of these pillows will represent something smashed, cracked, or bloody. What are they?

ALICE: Pea soup all over, stains on the wall, a dented pan.

CONSULTANT: (*tossing a pillow on the floor*) This pan is bashed in. Anything else?

ALICE: All the silverware's on the floor, and chairs are broken, legs off.

CONSULTANT: (*adding another pillow to the pile on the floor*) This chair has its leg off.

ALICE: The phone's pulled out.

CONSULTANT: Have you ever seen anything like this in your life?

ALICE: Never.

CONSULTANT: And what's going on inside you?

ALICE: I'm scared. And my brother and sister are saying, "It's all right. Everything's all right. Ma's okay." And then my mother comes out, and I see her face all cut.

CONSULTANT: And what happens when you see her face?

ALICE: I want to run. I want to leave. My God! What happened? I just want to go outside.

Painful Mythic Past Scene: Alice's Mother's Family of Origin Enacted

CONSULTANT: What do you know or imagine about your mother's upbringing that helps you to understand why she might have been in such a situation?

ALICE: I don't know, except I know that her mother and father didn't bring her up, her grandmother did. The grandparents wouldn't give my mother back to her parents. They were baby-sitting, and they just kept her. She had two brothers who were brought up by her actual parents. She always felt like an outsider. My mother was always angry that her parents didn't fight for her, that they didn't go and just take the baby back.

CONSULTANT: (*to Alice's mother, Amanda, as a baby, played by Alice*) Why have your parents left you here?

ALICE: I don't understand why my mother doesn't come and get me. It must be something I did—or something I didn't do.

Transformed Mythic Past Scene: Amanda's Mother's Family of Origin Rescripted

[Alice's mother (the baby Amanda) is played by John, as Alice plays Amanda's mother, Abigail. The consultant takes the role of Abigail's mother, Adelaide.]

ABIGAIL: (*Amanda's mother, played by Alice*) I'm taking Amanda home, she belongs with me.

ADELAIDE: (*Amanda's grandmother, played by the consultant*) But you've left her here for so long. You don't really want her. You can't have her!

ABIGAIL: (*played by Alice*) I'm not leaving without her.

ADELAIDE: (*played by the Consultant*) Well, you're going to have to take her from me.

ABIGAIL: (*played by Alice*) Well, I will then. (*She does.*)

[The scene is replayed with John taking the role of Abigail.]

ABIGAIL: (*played by John*) Get your hands off my daughter!

ADELAIDE: (*played by the Consultant*) But wait a minute, wait a minute. You left her here! She's mine!

ABIGAIL: (*played by John*) Too bad, she's coming home with me now—forever.

CONSULTANT: (*as self, to Abigail, played by John*) How come you came and got her?

ABIGAIL: (*played by John*) Because I love her. I couldn't see her . . .

ADELAIDE: (*played by the consultant, to Abigail, played by John*) You hardly even know her. She's just a baby.

ABIGAIL: (*played by John*) But she's my daughter. (*Abigail grabs her daughter, Amanda, played by Alice, and holds her close for a long time..*)

CONSULTANT: (*to Amanda, played by Alice*) Is this about right?

AMANDA: (*played by Alice*) Yeah. This is nice.

Alice's Painful Past Scene Transformed

CONSULTANT: Now, Amanda, hang onto that feeling of being loved and cared for, because you're going to need it. You're going to grow up and you're going to have a daughter who needs some things from you. And let's see what happens. You've got eight children, your husband has died, and you learn that the man you have now married doesn't treat you well. But you have had this (*consultant indicates the holding*), quite a lot of it. And you know that you're special in your mother's eyes and heart, really special. So, let's see what happens.

AMANDA: (*played by Alice*) I'm going to kick him out.

CONSULTANT: All right. Do it. I'll take Ed's role.

AMANDA: (*played by Alice*) Ed, you're history!

ED: (*played by consultant*) What do you mean? You just married me! You're my wife!

AMANDA: (*played by Alice*) Not this way I'm not.

ED: (*played by consultant*) What can I do?

AMANDA: (*played by Alice*) Stop drinking. Never hit me.

ED: (*played by consultant*) I'll stop drinking tomorrow.

AMANDA: (*played by Alice*) No, . . . no. No, I'm not going to live this way. I'm just not going to do it. You have to go. I want an instant divorce.

ED: (*played by consultant*) You asked for it. I'm never coming back.

AMANDA: (*played by Alice*) Okay.

CONSULTANT: (*as self to Amanda played by Alice*) Now, what does your daughter, Alice, need? She just walked in on this chaos. You've just thrown Ed out.

AMANDA: (*played by Alice, speaking to the childhood Alice, played by John*) This is never going to happen again. You'll never have to see anything like this again. (*She giggles nervously.*)

CONSULTANT: (*to Alice as herself*) I can see that this has been really hard. It's probably easier to joke about it than to do it straight because it's so hard. Reverse roles. I'll be Ed again. You, Alice, become yourself at age 13. You, John, become Amanda and throw Ed out, get your instant divorce. Convince Alice that this is over. That it will never happen again. Give Alice what she needs.

AMANDA: (*played by John*) That's it, mister! You're out of here. You're history.

ED: (*played by consultant*) Hey, what do you mean? Hey, you're my wife.

AMANDA: (*played by John*) You're out of here. . . . Go on. (*pushes Ed out of the house*)

ED: (*played by consultant*) I'll never drink again!

AMANDA: (*played by John*) I don't care if I ever see your face again. Get out of here! You're a loser! (*closes door on Ed*) Alice, oh my God, I wish you'd never had to see anything like this in your life. That's never going to happen again because that bum is never showing his face in this house again. I'm never ever going to let you feel that frightened again. (*He moves toward her, enfolds her in his arms, as she sobs and holds him close.*)

Statements of the Problem

CONSULTANT: (*to couple*) Now, if you want to, this is a time for you to talk about problems, but you may prefer not to. You may want to mention a problem you brought in, or to say something about a problem in the light of what we've done here today, or to say nothing at all. Whatever you do is fine; you don't need to do the same thing.

[John chooses to pass; Alice chooses to respond.]

ALICE: When John was doing his scenes, I could see how lonely he was and he is so gregarious all the time that I don't picture him that way—lonely—at all. I think he's much more able to deal with people and get along than I am, and yet, I can see now, in ways that I don't usually think about, why I'm so important to him in his day-to-day life. And I, as a person—I'm not used to the affection that he gives me. It's hard for me to—I didn't grow up in an affectionate household so it's, sometimes—I just don't know how to deal with it.

Frequently, the partners are stimulated, even a bit bemused, by the rapid sequence of brief enactments of the past and present, the recalled and imaginary, the painful and relieving. They often have not yet explicitly spoken of their difficulty. At this point, when offered such an opportunity, they frequently pass. Often, both partners feel hopeful and closer, having just shared emotionally powerful and constructive experiences, and prefer to savor the mood rather than spoil it with complaints. If they do choose to describe their problems, they tend to present them with less acrimony and despair and with greater softness than we believe they would have prior to the work of the session. The attitude is generally one of collaboration, not blame.

Closing

We are often asked what the therapist should do next after using this technique with the couple. We think that this intervention, like all others, needs to be seen in the full context of the evaluation, treatment, or consultation, and that the therapist should use what has transpired in this session to decide with the clients what will happen next. We find that experience of this structured process—the safety of the right to pass, the review of strengths, the dramatic enactments of past and future—may open new options for the therapy just as it may open new options for the couple's relationship.

Three Months Later

Alice and John continued in couple therapy with the referring therapist. Three months after the consultation, having recently viewed a videotape of the session, they came to the consultant's office to sign a release. At that meeting, the consultant asked if they would be willing to share their experience of the consultation, to say what was useful and not useful to them, and to make suggestions for change. They agreed and Alice spoke of how, immediately following the consultation meeting, she had started noticing that John "really craved attention." And she said that, at first, she had tried to be conscious of welcoming him home warmly, but that had tapered off. The conversation continued:

JOHN: I had forgotten all those things that happened to her, and how I loved her because of the person she became in spite of them—not really forgotten, but, it was out of my mind. We had always been close, but somewhere along the line we shut each other out from the vulnerable sides of ourselves. And when we fought we'd get down and dirty. We'd do the worst things to each other.[8]

---

[8]Eighteen months after the consultation the therapist revealed to the consultant that the partners had told her that, before the consultation, they had felt pretty good about each other and had come to understand each other, but that there were a few last hurdles to get over. Their comment to her about the effect of the consultation was that it had helped them over the last hurdle and had gotten them emotionally connected and ready to contemplate ending therapy.

ALICE: Now, we still fight, we have our differences, but we handle them a bit better. We discuss it, let the person think about it—

JOHN: (*to Alice*) You said it very well in the car on the way home from the session. At first, we were both really quiet, then about one third of the way home, Alice, you said, "You know, we do the absolutely worst thing to each other when we fight." And she was right. What we used to do was. . . . She would ignore me. She wouldn't say a word to me. She would totally shut me out. And me, I would smash things around the house and yell and scream. And we had gotten into this habit where that's what we did. Yup, she'd stop talking, and I'd throw an ashtray. So we talked about it. And I thought, "What are we doing? What are we doing to our own kids?" So now I can tell Alice really tries. She starts to close down, and then she says to herself, "Nooo, I'm not going to shut him out," and I pick up an ashtray, and I start, and then I say, "No, there has to be a better way," and I stop myself. And because we don't fight like that, the anger level doesn't go up to where it used to.

ALICE: That day was so emotional for me, doing it, and later watching the tape of it. I was so nervous. I hate role-playing. We've been in a lot of counseling, and we've talked about our parents. But to go the next step, to their parents and grandparents, that really took me off guard. I didn't have pat answers, things I've known my whole life. It opened up a new part of me.

JOHN: I'd never thought about my father at all, what he went through. I never thought how it was almost the same thing that I went through. I'd never thought about it from *his* side. So now I think, I don't want to do this to my children.

THE MODEL IN A NARRATIVE FRAME

The case demonstrates the use of the model and illustrates the general approach of blocking the habitual and reawakening and reinvigorating the imaginary to generate fresh, emotionally forceful, and evocative experiences. We see this model as one of a growing set of experiential methods finding application within an evolving social constructionist narrative theory base (Chang, 1993; Freeman & Lobovits, 1993).[9] While most therapeutic work applied within this theory base has relied primar-

---

[9]Highly imaginative enactment is not new in couple therapy. A most creative and familiar early example is Papp's "choreography" (1976, 1990). However, there has been a drift away from action methods in couple therapy, particularly in approaches that stand on a social constructionist narrative theory base.

ily on conversation as the medium of exchange and action, our model relies on in-session dramatic experiences whose great emotional force, strangeness, and variety enliven the partners' sense of possibility and capacity to create and to feel expansively. Through cooperative participation in the active–imaginary, the partners create with each other liberating scenes that are entered into memory, along with the new meanings they generate and organize.

In the session, each partner spends time in the standpoint of witness, reflector, author, and actor, positions that each call into being their own perceptions, ideas, and feelings. In the enactments, both partners enrole deeply in, and play many parts in rapid succession, embodying through these roles modes of feeling, speaking, and relating that differ from what is customary for them.[10] Both the standpoints and the roles expand possibilities for feeling, expression, and interaction once the partners resume their own real-life roles.

By deep immersion in many roles in a number of scenes, each partner comes to know something of the authoring partner's version of what every person or character they play has experienced, might have experienced, or might someday experience in the relational contexts that have been played out. In this way, the partners come to know each other in their stories by approximating their experience of others. Each role-played scene permits each partner to know something of the other's story in a way that parallels how each knows his or her own story—that is, from the inside. It is not merely seeing another's view or hearing another's voice. It is a taste of "being" who others are, were, might have been, or could be. Through these roles, each partner enters into rich, highly textured relational fields with their accompanying complex stories. The old monologic accounts of themselves and their couple cannot withstand the confluence of the many perspectives, many voices, and subjective experiences occasioned by participating in these enactments.

The enactments get the partners into motion with each other and make space for respectful not-knowing, wondering, and inquiring (Roth, 1993). In these ways, they encourage openness where there was closure, a sense of the indeterminate where much seemed prescripted. They have emotional as well as cognitive impact. As Schieffelin (1993) reports in a very different context, "the performance . . . becomes life, no less than life is reflected in the performance; the vehicle for constructing social

---

[10]In the illustration above, for example, the partners played 16 roles each: partner, partner's wished-for partner, gratified self, self as injured or neglected child, self as gratified, attended-to child, own re-called parent, own re-formed parent, parent's parent in time beyond memory, parent's re-formed parent, parent as child, partner as injured child, partner as gratified child, partner's parent as child, partner's re-formed parent, partner's parent's re-formed parent, and wise/caring observer.

reality and personal conviction appears to be just as much drama as rational thought" (p. 292).

Through dramatic enactments, each partner can begin to know more and to know less about themselves, each other, and what is possible in their relationship. In other words, the multiplicity of experiences, which carries great imagistic variety, emotional range, and narrative weight, provides partners strong impetus to be curious, to be open, and to recognize and welcome the unfinalizability of themselves, the other, and their relationships.

ACKNOWLEDGMENTS

We thank our generous colleagues and friends whose conversations with us have enriched and expanded our thinking in this chapter: David Epston, Jill Freedman, James Griffith, Sheila McNamee, Peggy Penn, Carole Samworth, and Kathy Weingarten.

REFERENCES

Andersen, T. (1987). The reflecting team: Dialogue and meta-dialogue in clinical work. *Family Process, 26*(4), 415–428.

Andersen, T. (1992). Reflections on reflecting with families. In S. McNamee & K. J. Gergen (Eds.), *Therapy as Social Construction* (pp. 54–68). London: Sage.

Anderson, H. (1993). On a roller coaster: A collaborative language systems approach to therapy. In S. Friedman (Ed.), *The New Language of Change: Constructive Collaboration in Psychotherapy* (pp. 323–344). New York: Guilford.

Anderson, H., & Goolishian, H. A. (1988). Human systems as linguistic systems: Some preliminary and evolving ideas about the implications for clinical theory. *Family Process, 27*(4), 371–393.

Bruner, J. (1986). *Actual Minds, Possible Worlds.* Cambridge, MA: Harvard University Press.

Chang, J. (1993). Commentary on J. Freedman & G. Combs, Invitations to new stories: Using questions to explore alternative possibilities. In S. Gilligan & R. Price (Eds.), *Therapeutic Conversations* (pp. 304–308). New York: Norton.

Chasin, R., & Roth, S. (1990). Future perfect, past perfect: A positive approach to opening couple therapy. In R. Chasin, H. Grunebaum, & M. Herzig (Eds.), *One Couple, Four Realities: Multiple Perspectives on Couple Therapy* (pp. 129–144). New York: Guilford.

Chasin, R., Roth, S., & Bograd, M. (1989). Action methods in systemic therapy: Dramatizing ideal futures and reformed pasts with couples. *Family Process, 28*(1), 121–136.

Epston, D., & White, M. (1992). *Experience, contradiction, narrative and imagination: Selected papers of David Epston and Michael White.* Adelaide, Australia: Dulwich Centre Publications.

Erickson, M. H. (1954). Pseudo-orientation in time as a hypnotherapeutic procedure. *Journal of Clinical and Experimental Hypnosis, 2,* 261–283. Reprinted in J. Haley (Ed.) (1967), *Advanced Techniques of Hypnosis and Therapy: Selected Papers of Milton H. Erickson, M.D.* (pp. 369–389). New York: Grune & Stratton.

Freedman, J., & Combs, G. (1993). Invitations to new stories: Using questions to explore alternative possibilities. In S. Gilligan & R. Price (Eds.), *Therapeutic Conversations* (pp. 291–303). New York: Norton.

Freeman, J. C., & Lobovits, D. (1993). The turtle with wings. In S. Friedman (Ed.), *The New Language of Change: Constructive Collaboration in Psychotherapy* (pp. 188–225). New York: Guilford.

Gergen, K. J., & Kaye, J. (1992). Beyond narrative in the negotiation of therapeutic meaning. In S. McNamee & K. J. Gergen (Eds.), *Therapy as Social Construction* (pp. 166–185). London: Sage.

Haley, J. (1973). *Uncommon Therapy: The Psychiatric Techniques of Milton H. Erickson, M.D.* New York: Norton.

Holquist, M. (Ed.). (1982). *The Dialogic Imagination: Four Essays by M. M. Bakhtin.* Austin: University of Texas Press.

Iser, W. (1993). *The Fictive and the Imaginary: Charting Literary Anthropology.* Baltimore, MD: Johns Hopkins University Press.

Lee, R. (1981). Video as adjunct to psychodrama and role-playing. In J. L. Fryrear & R. Fleshman (Eds.), *Videotherapy and Mental Health* (pp. 121–145). Springfield, IL: C. C. Thomas.

Moreno, J. (1978). *Who shall survive? Foundations of Sociometry, Group Psychodrama and Sociodrama.* New York: Beacon Press. (Originally published in 1953)

Morson, G., & Emerson, C. (1990). *Mikhail Bakhtin: Creation of a Prosaics.* Palo Alto, CA: Stanford University Press.

Papp, P. (1976). Family choreography. In P. J. Guerin (Ed.), *Family Therapy: Theory and Practice* (pp. 465–479). New York: Gardner Press.

Papp, P. (1990). The use of structured fantasy in couple therapy. In R. Chasin, H. Grunebaum, & M. Herzig (Eds.), *One Couple, Four Realities: Multiple Perspectives on Couple Therapy* (pp. 25–48). New York: Guilford.

Penn, P. (1982). Circular questioning. *Family Process, 21*(3), 267–280.

Penn P. (1985). Feed-forward: Future questions, future maps. *Family Process, 24*(3), 299–310.

Penn, P., & Frankfurt, M. (1994). Creating a participant text: Writing, multiple voices, narrative multiplicity. *Family Process, 33*(3).

Roth, S. (1993). Speaking the unspoken: A work-group consultation to reopen dialogue. In E. Imber-Black (Ed.), *Secrets in Families and Family Therapy* (pp. 268–291). New York: Norton.

Sacks, J. (1978). The reformed auxiliary ego technique: A psychodramatic rekindling of hope. *Group Psychotherapy and Psychodrama, 23,* 118–121.

Schieffelin, E. L. (1993). Performance and the cultural construction of reality: A New Guinea example. In S. Lavie, K. Narayan, & R. Rosaldo (Eds.), *Creativity/Anthropology* (pp. 270–295). Ithaca, NY: Cornell University Press.

Starr, A. (1977). *Psychodrama: Illustrated Therapeutic Techniques.* Chicago: Nelson Hall.

Tomm, K. (1987). Interventive interviewing: Part II. Reflexive questioning as a means to enable self-healing. *Family Process, 26*(2), 167–183.

Weingarten, K. (1992). Consultations to myself on a work/family dilemma: A postmodern, feminist reflection. *Journal of Feminist Family Therapy, 4*(1), 3–29.

White, M., & Epston, D. (1990). *Narrative Means to Therapeutic Ends.* New York: Norton.

Zimmerman, J., & Dickerson, V. (1993). Separating couples from restraining patterns and the relationship discourse that supports them. *Journal of Marital and Family Therapy, 19*(4), 403–413.

CHAPTER 11

Staying Simple, Staying Focused
Time-Effective Consultations
with Children and Families

STEVEN FRIEDMAN

Two stories are worth telling to give the reader some background on my thinking about the process of psychotherapy. The first experience happened many years ago when I was working with a four-year-old boy and his mother, in regard to the boy's encopresis. In spite of many months of "treatment" and much time spent in the complex and cumbersome process of hypothesizing about the reasons for the child's behavior, the boy continued to crap in his pants. The boy and his mother finally decided (wisely, I might add) to go it on their own. About a year later, I ran into the mother and timidly asked how her son was doing. The mother told me that several months after our last contact, she told her son that if he started using the toilet instead of his pants, she would buy him a new pair of fancy sneakers. Apparently, overnight, her son started usually the toilet and has not messed his pants since!

The second story is a more personal one. Several years ago, my wife and I were moving a couch from the living room upstairs to the basement. In so doing, we got the couch lodged in the hallway. The more we pushed and pulled, the more the plaster chipped away from the walls and the more securely lodged the couch became. Fortunately for us, we have a neighbor, a retired engineer, whom we tend to call on at such times. He surveyed the situation, trying to suppress a sly smile that expressed the thought, "Well, look what the two of you have gotten into this time." After spending a minute or two examining the scene, without putting his hands on the couch at all, he went to one spot on the couch and simply and gently pressed it. The couch easily and swiftly moved from its fixed position and was dislodged.

As psychotherapists, we often become enamored with theories and explanations. At times, this search for explanations leads us into a complex jungle of ideas and hypotheses, immerses us in an interminable morass of blame and dysfunction. Too often, we push and pull only to find ourselves more dug in and defeated; too often, we blame clients for their "resistance" or "untreatability" rather than gain some needed perspective in finding a more useful and gentle leverage point to create opportunities for movement and change. To do this effectively and efficiently requires the therapist to allow him or herself to "become distracted by important information" (Philip Hill, personal communication, November 1986) and, by so doing, stay simple and stay focused. Therapy, even in the face of complex problems, can be effective and simple if only we allow our attention to wander toward those points that open the way for movement and change.

The situations described above, among others, led me to see the usefulness of dispensing with elaborate hypothesizing and, instead, to put my energies into constructing solutions with clients that lead directly to the clients' goals. I envision my job as minimizing the client's dependency on the therapeutic relationship and maximizing the client's resourcefulness and self-sufficiency in more confidently and effectively moving along the road of life.

In this chapter, I will provide several clinical examples of the flexible use of multiple frameworks in doing time-effective therapy with children and families. The clinical work presented took place in a suburban center of a large health maintenance organization, the Harvard Community Health Plan. Keeping in mind that there are a variety of perspectives and possibilities in approaching any clinical situation, I work to "stay simple and stay focused" and to tailor my approach to the unique needs and goals of the family. My work emphasizes solutions and possibilities and incorporates and integrates aspects of the narrative model (e.g., "externalizing the problem") and the use of a reflecting team process. Since a single method may not be effective in helping a particular family achieve their objectives, drawing on a variety of approaches allows the necessary flexibility to enable the family to reach their goals in a time-effective manner.

In many instances, a goal directed, solution-based, and optimistic perspective about change can rapidly lead to a successful outcome (e.g., Friedman, 1989a, 1989b, 1989c, 1990). At other times, a problem-saturated story becomes so dominant in the life of the person/family that they neglect to notice or acknowledge other descriptions or stories. My job then is to make space for those alternative stories to emerge (Friedman, 1992; 1993b). One method for doing so involves objectifying and "externalizing the problem" as a force outside the person/family, which is interfering with them achieving their goals (e.g., White, 1992; White & Epston, 1990). The therapist joins with the person/family to find alternative or preferred behaviors, which prevent the continued intrusion of this force on their lives. Children, especially, seem to enjoy the playful nature of this kind of conceptualization and actively and eagerly take on the challenge of liberating themselves from a powerful external force (e.g., Durrant, 1989; Friedman, 1991). Throughout the therapy process, I find it useful to maintain a solution-focused perspective (e.g., Berg, 1994; Berg & Miller, 1992; de Shazer, 1985, 1988, 1991; O'Hanlon & Weiner-Davis, 1989) utilizing client generated resources, building on any existing presession change, amplifying "exceptions" to the problem, and supporting the client's efforts to take steps in a positive direction.

In addition, the introduction of a reflecting team offers a forum that opens space for new options to emerge (Andersen, 1991). The reflecting team acts as a symphony of diverse voices offering the family multiple perspectives on their dilemma (e.g., Andersen, 1991; Davidson & Lax, 1992; Hoffman-Hennessey & Davis, 1993; Mittelmeier & Friedman, 1993) or as an audience to amplify and embody changes (Brecher & Friedman, 1993). Each of these approaches, separately and in combination, are useful and productive avenues for generating successful outcomes in a variety of clinical situations.

Since my goal is to "keep it simple," it is important that I develop at least one "customer" relationship (Berg, 1989); that is, find one family member who is ready to take action. If none of the people with whom I am sitting are customers for change, I need to either work with the client(s) in ways that will enable him or her to become a customer or find a customer in the larger system (e.g., a grandparent, a worker from the Department of Social Services, a probation officer, etc.). Since it is often the parents who are initiating contact, the child or adolescent, in most instances, comes to therapy as a "visitor" or "complainant." As we will see, in such situations, one can work with the parents alone or playfully engage the child in a way that enables him or her to become a customer as well. The more customer relationships that exist, the more likely is the family to achieve a positive outcome in a relatively brief period of time. Following a brief outline of guiding assumptions (after Friedman & Fanger, 1991), several clinical examples will be presented, illustrating the usefulness of a "stay simple, stay focused" approach.

GUIDING ASSUMPTIONS OF POSSIBILITY THERAPY

1. *Learn to be distracted by important information*, especially evidence of change and success.

2. *Maintain a cooperative/collaborative posture,* a stance of naive curiosity, optimism, and respect for the client and his or her request. Rather than thinking of ourselves as experts who have privileged knowledge about how to create change, we do better to consider those with whom we work as the experts and, thus, develop and nurture a sense of curiosity and inquisitiveness about their lives and relationships. By not imposing our own solutions and preferred outcomes, we show respect for the complexities of peoples' lives and offer them the opportunity to determine the direction of therapy.

3. *Keep your assumptions simple* and avoid elaborate explanatory thinking and hypothesis generation (O'Hanlon & Wilk, 1987).

4. *Take the client seriously,* and *stay focused on the client's goal.* What is the client's vision of "success"? This is a request based, consumer-driven therapy that places priority on the *client's* preferred outcome.

5. *Keep your expectations realistic,* and help *frame a successful outcome in clear observable terms.* Too often, we set our goals and expectations too high and find ourselves overwhelmed with the complexity and enormity of the problems we are facing. Since a small change creates the possibility for larger changes, by thinking small we can maximize chances for success and create a more hopeful context for change, which leaves both the family and ourselves in a more empowered position. The goal is simply to create opportunities for the person/family to take small steps in a positive direction.

6. *Build on client solutions, resources, and competencies, and generate optimism regarding change by assuming a hopeful, future-oriented stance. View language as a key to therapeutic change.* Therapy is a special kind of conversation, in which dialogue leads to the generation of new meanings, understandings, and options for action (Anderson & Goolishian, 1988). Since change is inevitable, "change talk" can be promoted by focusing on a description of positive futures and by amplifying already occurring *exceptions* to the complaint (de Shazer, 1988, 1991). By asking about times when the complaint does not happen the door is opened to a conversation about "what works" rather than "what doesn't work."

7. *Respect people's resources and creativity,* and never underestimate their capacity for creating more hopeful and satisfying lives. *Time is an ally* (Hobbs, 1966). Since change occurs outside our offices, we need to be respectful of, and sensitive to, amplifying these changes. Seeing families on an intermittent basis (e.g., every two, three, or five weeks) has added to my growing respect for the impact of those events occurring outside my office that are quite "therapeutic."

8. *Introduce novel perspectives and generate tasks and homework that involve the client in "doing something different."* Novelty is an important ingredient in doing time-effective therapy (Budman, Friedman, & Hoyt, 1992). It is useful to rapidly (preferably in the first session) offer some

new perspective or view on the issues presented. One way to introduce novelty is through "experiments" that can be suggested to the family.[1]

9. *Make each session count.* Helping people achieve their goals as rapidly as possible is both practical and ethical (Hoyt, 1990; Hoyt, Rosenbaum, & Talmon, 1992). While maintaining respect for the complexity of a situation, the *goal is to act simply* (Gurman, 1992). This means looking for openings for change and exploring novel alternatives. People often get bogged down in doing "more of the same." The introduction of some novel element can help destabilize these patterns.

10. *Define a successful outcome as requiring hard work,* and *applaud the client* on small steps taken in a positive direction (Berg & Miller, 1992; de Shazer, 1988).

CLINICAL ILLUSTRATIONS

Ordeal Therapy: Leah Grows Up

The Johnsons were struggling with helping their four-year-old daughter negotiate several major developmental transitions. The approach taken here was simple and straightforward. I built on ideas that the parents generated and fed these back in the form of suggested tasks. The parents were seen on four occasions over a two-month period. The first three meetings were one-half hour in length, and the final meeting lasted 15 minutes. Four-year-old Leah was not toilet trained and was sleeping in her parents' bed. The initial referral from the pediatrician mentioned that the "parents need help in setting limits and dealing with a very anxious child." I never met with Leah.

Session 1

THERAPIST: Maybe you can tell me, so I can understand, what you were hoping to accomplish coming here?

MOTHER: I think, as far as I'm concerned, my daughter is very, very nervous and very shy, and she's almost four and she will not potty train. Another big issue, which is our fault, is that she sleeps with us at night. The main issue for me. . . . I don't know what steps to take to help her make the transition to get into her bed, to potty train . . .

THERAPIST: (*looking for "exceptions"*) You're talking about wanting to help her make some developmental transitions. . . . Has she always slept with the two of you? Was there ever a time this wasn't happening?

---

[1] Rather than *prescribing* or *imposing* tasks on the client, my work involves *offering* or *suggesting* ideas that are constructed out of the clinical conversation. Since any conversation has the potential to be one of imposition or of mutuality, it is incumbent on the therapist to cooperate with the client in generating a mutually agreeable plan of action.

FATHER: It's hard to say. From the day she was born, she didn't go to bed 'til one A.M. And one of us would be up holding her or rocking her just to keep her quiet, because she would fuss all the time. Then she would finally go to sleep and be up two hours later. We finally decided to put her in our bed so we could all get some sleep.

MOTHER: He did most of the work with that. Because I'd get so upset with her that he'd just take over.

THERAPIST: (*curious about, "Why now?"*) What is it now that has you thinking that it's time to do something about this?

MOTHER: I think where she's getting older and has to break away, I realize I'm not helping her.

[When asked where they want to begin, the toilet issue or the sleep issue, the parents go on to say they prefer to start with the potty training since they feel this will be easier to resolve. I learned that the parents were especially anxious about their daughter's potty training because she was due to begin a preschool program in two weeks, and the school required that the children be trained. The parents clearly wanted to help their daughter overcome this developmental hurdle. I also learned that the parents, when Leah needed to either move her bowels or urinate, had been putting diapers on her, at her request. From listening to the parents, I became convinced that Leah was ready to give up her diapers and just needed some firm encouragement to do so. The mother mentioned the idea of simply removing the diapers altogether, but was unsure about trying it. I carefully assessed their motivation, talked with them about the phenomenon of one-trial learning and told them a story about another family with whom I had worked successfully. In that situation, when the parents got rid of the diapers the child achieved success quickly and was very proud of his accomplishment of using the toilet "like a big boy." After this discussion, I suggested that they consider giving away all the diapers but one, and let Leah know that this will be her last diaper and that it will be her choice whether to "make" in her pants or use the toilet. The parents agreed to do this and I asked them to call me in a few days with an update on their success. I emphasized my confidence that their efforts would have a positive outcome. The mother called three days later to say that they had been successful and that they were ecstatic about how quickly and matter-of-factly their daughter responded.]

Session 2

This session took place two and a half weeks later.

THERAPIST: Well, I heard a good report. How has that been going and how did you accomplish it? [I direct attention to what the parents did that enabled this change to occur.]

FATHER: We went home that night and told her we weren't going to buy her any more diapers. She only had a couple left and . . . one morning we just put her pants on . . . and she's been going [to the bathroom] ever since.

THERAPIST: That's remarkable! She didn't yell and scream and cry for a diaper?

FATHER: No.

THERAPIST: Wow!

MOTHER: I was surprised.

THERAPIST: What was her reaction to using the toilet?

FATHER: It's like she's been doing it for years.

[During the past week, Leah also began attending preschool, and the mother described some difficulties separating on the first two days of school. However, by the third day, the mother reported some improvement: "She didn't hang on to me and cry, and she kissed me goodbye."]

THERAPIST: It's impressive what you've been able to do in helping her get over two big developmental hurdles, using the potty and the transition to preschool. The next frontier then is the bed . . . [I compliment the parents on successfully managing to help their daughter through two major developmental transitions in a very brief period of time and move the focus to their next objective.]

MOTHER: (*laughing, but expressing her trepidation about moving into the sleep arena*) You'll have to sedate me and put me somewhere because I don't know if I can handle it . . .

[The father went on to mention that he once slept on the floor in his daughter's room to help her get used to her bed but gave this up after a short period. It was apparent to me that these parents were willing to make real sacrifices to help their daughter. I then suggested an approach to help their daughter sleep in her own bed. I framed this as an important step that would require some temporary sacrifice on the part of the parents. I presented this idea in such a way that the focus became "sharing the burden" rather than on the sacrifice itself. The reader will recognize the introduction of an "ordeal" (Haley, 1984) as a way to rapidly create change in the desired direction.]

THERAPIST: You could always try taking turns sleeping on the floor in her room. So you'd share the responsibility. But it would also require a commitment to staying there initially with her through the night to help her acclimate.

MOTHER: Maybe she wouldn't mind if we alternated.

THERAPIST: It's just a matter of taking turns and allowing her to not get fixed that it has to be one of you. It helps her to be a little more flexible. It can be Daddy one night, and Mommy the other. . . . What do you think about the timing of this? [Having presented the idea and gotten their agreement, I offer the parents an opportunity to tell me when they would choose to implement this plan.]

FATHER: Do you think we should wait a couple of weeks 'til she acclimates to the preschool?

MOTHER: That would probably make us feel better . . . waiting a bit. Maybe we should wait two weeks. . . . She did a lot better at preschool today.

THERAPIST: Well, each day will get better. Having these two positive experiences, getting out of the diapers and the preschool transition under her belt may make this [next step] easier. [I offer the parents reason for hope.]

MOTHER: Yes. She'll think she can do it.

THERAPIST: Yeah.

[Later in this session]

THERAPIST: And the sooner she can make the transition to her own bed, the sooner you can have your bed back . . . your privacy . . . and she can have hers.

[The parents describe how uncomfortable it is right now with their four-year-old daughter sleeping in the middle of the bed.]

FATHER: You're afraid you're going to roll over on top of her.

THERAPIST: That arrangement is unfair to you and to her. So, if you keep in mind how nice it will be to have your own bed back, this will be an incentive to push on this.

MOTHER: It will.

FATHER: Definitely.

[The parents agree to wait two weeks before implementing this plan and we schedule a meeting in one month.]

Session 3

THERAPIST: I'm eager to hear how your experiment worked.

FATHER: It's going well, I guess. But the floor is feeling very hard. We started a week ago Friday night.

[The father describes spending the first night on the floor. Leah went right to sleep. She got up one time to go to the bathroom and then asked to sleep in the parents' bed. The father said, "No," and when she started to cry, the father gave her his hand to hold and she fell right back to sleep.]

FATHER: That's the only real complaint she's had. She really hasn't complained since.

THERAPIST: You've been alternating?

FATHER: Every other night.

THERAPIST: Okay. Have you stayed there the whole night?

FATHER: A few times we've come out to watch TV but one of us would go back and spend the night there.

THERAPIST: So each of you, on the nights when the other is sleeping in Leah's room, get to have your bed to yourself.

MOTHER: Yes. (*laughing*)

THERAPIST: So, that's a step up from flailing little arms and legs . . . but sleeping on the floor is not easy either.

FATHER: Some nights it's okay. But other nights you can't move when you try to get up.

THERAPIST: I'll bet.

[Later in the session, the parents informed the therapist that they're ready for this ordeal to end—a very positive sign.]

MOTHER: We want to make the move now.

THERAPIST: What's the next move? [I offer them a chance to state their goal.]

FATHER: Getting out of the room and back to our own bed.

MOTHER: Yes.

THERAPIST: It's been about ten days [of implementing this plan]?

FATHER: Just about.

MOTHER: Do we just tell her tomorrow night we're out of there?

THERAPIST: You sound ready.

MOTHER: I'm really ready.

THERAPIST: Well, it's only been ten days, a relatively good ten days . . . where she's gotten used to sleeping in her own bed . . . and she's gotten up to use the bathroom. But she's still relying on having someone there, close by. [I express my ambivalence about moving too quickly.]

MOTHER: Do we break it now or keep going?

THERAPIST: When you're sleeping on the floor, are you looking forward to the next night?

[I want to further assess and cultivate their motivation.]

MOTHER: Yes!

THERAPIST: It feels good [to be in your own bed].

FATHER: You bet.

THERAPIST: The next step is a big one. You've taken a number of steps already, helping Leah grow up and be more independent, and you've done it successfully. And this is a big one, like the diapers and the preschool. What could you anticipate at this point or in the near future if you give up staying with her in her room at night?

FATHER: We already told her that "soon no one will be in here with you." What I think will happen is she'll wake up and then come running into the living room or the bedroom and want to sleep in our bed. And if we tell her to go back to her room she'll probably say, "No." That's what I think she'll probably do.

THERAPIST: What do you [mother] think?

MOTHER: It seems that when he and I get together on an issue, like with the toilet training and said, "This is how it's going to be," she responds. Before, he'd say it and I'd say it and it didn't work. So, if we get together on this one and say, "You need to sleep in your own room," well, it might work.

THERAPIST: Do you want to do something gradual or something more drastic? [Again, I offer the parents a choice but with the implications that they will do something.]

MOTHER: I don't know.

THERAPIST: The idea is to make this a successful experience for her. The most important thing here is your sense of her potential readiness to tolerate this transition. That's something you can tell better than anybody. It would be better to keep sleeping on the floor, not more comfortable, for two more weeks, maybe less, if there was a sense she wasn't ready yet. If the chances for success are not so good, I think it's better to continue to make this sacrifice that the two of you are making to get to the point where you're going to be successful— than take a chance of it not working. [I emphasize my ambivalence about the timing and, in so doing, support the parents as the best ones to decide about when to move ahead.]

FATHER: We could stick pillows under the blanket and make her think we are there. (*laughter*)

THERAPIST: So, it's a matter of gauging her readiness. You've been moving along very quickly on these other things [toilet training; preschool transition] and now she is sleeping in her own bed. It's a lot of positive steps that have happened. It's hard to gauge about moving too quickly here. I know it's unpleasant sleeping on the floor, but I wonder if continuing to do that as a temporary sacrifice is worthwhile for a little while longer. On the other hand, it's uncomfortable being on the floor, and she may be getting used to having one of you there.

MOTHER: That's just it. Right.

FATHER: She could fool us and not complain. [Here the father has shifted from the negative scenario he presented earlier to one of increased optimism.]

[We discuss some midrange alternatives such as each parent trying to leave the daughter's room once every third night and returning to the parental bedroom. I leave it up to the parents to decide how to proceed. Before stopping, we also discuss how much Leah has changed over the past two months. I learn that Leah is doing gymnastics and doing very well at it. I tell the parents: "She's growing up and you're helping her."]

Session 4

This session takes place two weeks later.

THERAPIST: Well, tell me what's happened here over these two weeks.

FATHER: We've made out real good.

THERAPIST: Yeah. Tell me.

FATHER: We started out with doing every third night that one of us would not stay in Leah's room. She did it on Thursday night and that was it—no problem.

THERAPIST: How long were you in there with her?

MOTHER: 'Til she fell asleep.

FATHER: And then the next night, I tried it, but she kept waking up. Then Sunday we told her "go off to bed. We'll be along in a little while" and she went right in and went to sleep and we haven't been back since.

MOTHER: (*laughing*) She's wonderful! She also goes to the bathroom by herself at night.

THERAPIST: How have you done this? You've made so many changes so quickly. [I share my pleasure with the parents' accomplishments.]

MOTHER: I don't know. (*laughing*) We're surprised.

THERAPIST: So, you're off the floor and back in your own bed. You've got the bed to yourselves for the first time in four years!

MOTHER: She's done great.

THERAPIST: Wow! The diapers, the preschool, the sleeping . . . and she's doing good with all of it. How are you doing with all these changes?

MOTHER: Well, they've been painful, but we're thankful.

THERAPIST: That's wonderful!

MOTHER: It's worked out well.

THERAPIST: You've really done a great job helping her make these changes. . . . So what would you say is the most positive part of the changes that have happened?

MOTHER: Her independence.

FATHER: You can tell she's more independent.

THERAPIST: Have you celebrated this in some way? This deserves some kind of a celebration. . . . Are we finished then? Does that take care of what you came here about? [Having accomplished the goals originally discussed, I ask the parents if they are satisfied with the outcome.]

MOTHER: I think so.

FATHER: Yeah.

THERAPIST: Well, I'm certainly going to remember what you've been able to accomplish. It will be an inspiration to other families who are dealing with things like this.

About six months after the final session, I got a call from the mother requesting marital therapy. Leah continued doing well and was described as a very independent little person. The parents, in spite of any marital difficulties, were able to pull together successfully in dealing with their child. This successful experience in therapy, in fact, may have made it easier for them to call when the marital issues required attention.

Fear Busting: Matthew Outwits the Monsters

With children, the use of a narrative framework can lead to a playful and yet highly focused treatment (e.g., Durrant, 1989). The pediatrician's referral on eight-year-old Matthew noted that he "has fears; won't sleep in own room; sleeps on couch in living room near parent's bedroom; talks about monsters and ghosts; not willing to be apart from us [parents] for any length of time; has nightmares." Matthew came bursting into my office with his parents and immediately began telling me about the monsters that lived in his house. The more questions I asked the more detailed and elaborate his stories became. I found myself having trouble following his train of thought. His parents also seemed bewildered by this "crazy talk." Not long before the parents scheduled this appointment with me, they had seen another therapist who diagnosed Matthew as having a "dysthymic disorder" and recommended medication, which the parents refused. This therapist had also engaged Matthew in "play therapy," in which he would have Matthew draw pictures of the monsters and tell stories about them.

Both the mother and father were at their wit's end about how to deal with Matthew's crazy talk and his regular nightmares and were concerned that his fears masked a real depression, which would require individual psychotherapy. As we talked, it became clear that the fears were wreaking havoc on everyone in the family. I asked the parents what would happen "after the miracle," and they replied that Matthew would be "happier and more at ease with himself and would tell a straight story that didn't include ghosts and demons."

The more I talked with Matthew about the demons, the more he would become agitated and illogical in his speech. My homework assignment for the family, at the end of this initial session, was for the parents to note and keep track of the influence of the fears on various aspects of Matthew's life as well as how the fears affected their lives. I also asked the parents and Matthew to note those times when the fears were not successful in wrecking havoc on the family, times when Matthew was able to successfully persist in some activity in the face of the fears.

At the next session (two weeks later), I learned that the fears were significantly influencing both Matthew's life (e.g., he would not go upstairs in the house by himself; he would avoid involvement in peer activities and want to be at home, etc.) and his parents' lives as well (i.e., they were constantly worrying about him). The parents also reported that Matthew had gone to the dentist on his own; he had gone upstairs by himself when his father had requested he get something; and he even went down into the cellar on one occasion by himself. Matthew reported that he had gone to an amusement park with his class and while on some of the rides had "beat the fears."

I then met with Matthew individually and talked with him about ways to outwit these fears that had become so intrusive in his life. Did he want a life free of fears? Did he want a life where he wasn't a slave to the fears, a life of his own, where *he* would make decisions and not the fears? He agreed he would like such a life. I suggested he might try the "marble test" as a way to outwit the demons that were plaguing him (adapted from Ross, 1960): "Find some marbles of various colors. Taking about six or seven in your hand, you approach the monster and ask it to tell you how many different colored marbles you have in your hand. A real ghost will be able to give you an accurate number. But if the ghost is not able to guess the number of marbles then it will disappear." Matthew liked this idea and agreed to try it. I also talked with him about his nightmares, which he said were very similar each night, ending in the same scary way. I asked Matthew if he could develop a new ending to the nightmare, something different than the usual scenario (Goleman, 1992). He indicated his willingness to try this and even had an idea for a new ending. At the conclusion of the session, I met with the parents and asked them to continue to notice when Matthew outwitted the fears. I also reviewed the plan that Matthew and I had discussed, that is, the use of the "marble test" to outwit the fears and the development of a new ending to his nightly dream.

In our next appointment, a month later, Matthew reported that he was no longer having nightmares but that the "marble test" worked only some of the time. There had been some ghosts that could accurately guess the number of marbles he had in his hand. I said that these ghosts must be very strong and powerful and would require an even greater challenge to outwit them. Matthew and his parents were pleased that he was no longer having nightmares, and the teacher at school had noticed Matthew becoming more involved and active in class. I talked with Matthew about becoming a "fear buster" and what it would take to outwit these powerful fears. He told me he had some ideas that he wanted to try at home. The parents had also decided to no longer allow Matthew to sleep in the living room and, with his help, converted the den to his bedroom and moved the den area to his old bedroom upstairs. The parents had also been requiring Matthew to be more independent and self-sufficient in getting himself dressed.

At our final meeting, one month later, the parents reported that Matthew was sleeping through the night in his new bedroom and was not having nightmares. He was more willing to go upstairs by himself to play his Nintendo game, which was now in the new den and seemed "less fearful . . . more down to earth . . . less into fantasy." Matthew told me how he modified the marble test in such a way that ghosts could not guess the number accurately. I commended him on his abilities to effectively outwit the ghosts. At the end of the session, I presented Matthew with an official "fear buster" certificate (see White & Epston, 1990). The teacher had continued to remark to the parents on changes she was observing in how independent Matthew was becoming. A follow-up call one month later indicated that Matthew was continuing to do well.

Temper Taming: Rose Finds Her Voice

The next clinical situation reflects a family's immersion in a problem-saturated narrative and the efforts of a therapist and her team to help liberate them from this demoralizing reality. Twelve-year-old Rose was described as oppositional and strong-willed. Rose's temper would take over when she didn't get the response she wanted from her parents, plunging the whole house into chaos. These daily battles between Rose and her parents left the parents feeling frustrated and helpless. The mother had been calling the therapist almost daily for the past several weeks. These episodes had been going on for the past year. Rose had been previously diagnosed with an "attention deficit disorder" and medication had been prescribed. The medication did not alleviate the difficulties the family was experiencing. The consultation session described was arranged by the therapist (Cynthia Mittelmeier) to generate some new ideas to help this family free themselves from their helpless and demoralized position. In the room with the therapist during this session was the author–consultant, and behind the one-way mirror was a reflecting team. The therapist and consultant attempted to externalize "the temper" as a force that was interfering with family harmony and togetherness.

[About 10 minutes into the session]

CONSULTANT: What sort of things have you [parents] been doing that you've had some success with? [I look for successes.]

MOTHER: Well, I learned a real important lesson this past week. As you know, we tried a number of behavior modification programs without much success. When we act as policemen. . . . Well, let me give you an example. Rose came home from school the other day, and she was hostile. And she had a plan she wanted to do that was unacceptable to me—to go uptown on her bicycle at 4:30 P.M. It was too far away and too late . . . so I said, "No, that's not going to happen." So Rose gets angry. Now we have two problems; she doesn't understand why she can't do these things and now she's acting out. Telling her to take a time-out just doesn't work in these situations. . . . What I thought about was that using the behavior modification plan we're taking away a privilege or isolating her because of a behavior. We're putting ourselves in a position of almost being policemen. And those kind of controls are really not effective. Instead of losing privileges when you're bad, we've moved to earning privileges. Everything is earned.

CONSULTANT: So the policing is not the role you want to be in.

FATHER: It's like we're *taking* all the time. . . . Well, it [the new system] worked out well last night.

THERAPIST: [focusing on what worked] How did you do it last night?

FATHER: We asked Rose to help out and then she would earn the right to watch the TV show she wanted.

MOTHER: We're always separate. It's Rose over here and we're over there. We have a big problem with "mouth" [disrespectful behavior] . . . a really bad problem and I get angry after one and a half or two hours of listening to how . . . "I wish you were dead . . . I'd like to spit on your grave." That's the kind of things that we hear almost on a daily basis. But we want to back away from the situation that is all confrontational. Rose is a willful person . . .

CONSULTANT: It's not so much policing Rose, but policing "the temper" and that's something, Rose, that you can work on with your parents. The temper gets in the way between you [Rose] and them. You know what I mean? [I bring the conversation back to the need for a team effort to challenge "the temper," rather than a perspective that makes Rose the "problem."]

MOTHER: Once the temper is there, it's very difficult to make a difference. We tell her, "We want to help you," but it ends up being "us versus you."

CONSULTANT: The only way that this can work is with a team effort. There really has to be a temper taming team that makes this work.

FATHER: At night, I'm usually with Rose. She asked to watch her favorite TV show that is on from 8:00 to 8:30. When it was over, she wanted to watch the next show that was on. I said, "No . . . you've earned the right to watch only the eight o'clock show and after that it's time for bed." So I was reading in the other room . . . and when I went back in, Rose was watching the next show. In the past, there would have been screaming . . . and even though she wanted to watch it, she went off calmly to bed. She said, "Fine." It was really great.

CONSULTANT: How did you do that, Rose? My guess is the temper would have been around at that time. I'm trying to understand how you prevented the temper from taking over at that point. [I want to understand how Rose challenged the temper and allowed her voice to be heard.]

ROSE: I didn't feel the temper coming around.

CONSULTANT: That's incredible. Wow!

MOTHER: Yesterday we had a great day. I explained to her that she had to earn privileges. She can't assume she can just do things.

THERAPIST: What are you looking for that lets you know you can give her a privilege?

FATHER: It would be nice to have a day when we get along. We're not looking for perfection or anything. We expect a few little things to happen. No matter how she acted before, she expected that this was her right and that this was her right . . . and that's not the way it is in the real world.

MOTHER: Tiger temper can ruin it for her. Rose is a very strong-willed person.

CONSULTANT: Your mother is saying that you're a strong-minded person.

ROSE: I am.

CONSULTANT: How could I tell you were strong-minded . . . that you have a mind of your own? Do you talk up at school or with your friends if something is bothering you?

ROSE: Yes, I will.

THERAPIST: How come your mother thinks you're such a strong-minded person? Because you have your own ideas about things? How do you think she came up with that idea?

ROSE: I don't know.

CONSULTANT: When you want something, do you say it pretty clearly?

ROSE: Yes.

CONSULTANT: Okay, so that would be one way she'd know. I think because you're such a strong-minded person that's one thing the temper doesn't like. The temper likes to be the strong one. The temper likes it to be easy. And it sounds like there's been a time when the temper had it pretty easy. It sounds, though, like things are changing a little bit. You're not being a slave to the temper, because a slave does what the temper wants. But you're not that kind of person who's going to just do what the temper tells you to do. Do you know what I mean?

ROSE: I think so.

CONSULTANT: How long do you think it will take before you're not cooperating with the temper? Two weeks, three weeks? [The goal is presented, while the timing is left to Rose.]

ROSE: I think it will take a while.

CONSULTANT: Six months, four months?

ROSE: I don't know. (shrugs shoulders)

CONSULTANT: It's hard to know, but you think it will take a long time. Other people have been pleasantly surprised about how quickly these changes can happen. But, when you're in the middle of it, it feels like it's going to take a long time. I'm wondering if Rose can give the temper a message that change is about to happen, to get it prepared. Rose, do you understand? To prepare the temper so it gets ready to leave. You could put a sign up in the house, "This way out" . . . an exit sign, I don't know. It may be that because the temper has been around so long it won't go away unless it gets a tough message.

MOTHER: Can I ask a question? Rose, do you want the tiger temper to leave?

ROSE: Yes.

CONSULTANT: That's an important question. . . . I'm wondering if this is a good time to take a break to hear from the team. Is that okay with you? (*to parents*)

FATHER: Yes, sure.

MOTHER: Okay.

[The therapists, Rose and her family move to a position behind the one-way mirror and the team moves in front of the mirror.[2] Rose, her family, and the therapists listen as the team has a reflecting conversation.]

SALLY: I was thinking how Rose moved from "temper talk" to "Rose talk" and that, more and more, the temper isn't having a voice in what she says and what she does. First, the temper was stealing her voice and, now, I get the feeling that she's stealing back her voice from the temper. And I'm wondering if the temper is feeling a little unhappy . . . "I'm losing my place in this family . . . and maybe I want to act up and tempt Rose again . . . because I enjoy bossing her around." When a temper is desperate, it tries to pull some dirty tricks and I'm thinking that we can all fall for a tricky temper.

AMY: I was impressed about the times Rose was not letting the temper be in control. But there may be times when she doesn't realize this, and that is how the rest of the family can be helpful . . . noticing and pointing out those times when Rose's in charge. The situation with the TV is a good example of how she was in charge, not the temper.

SALLY: The temper wasn't talking, Rose was talking.

AMY: Maybe Rose didn't think that was such a big deal, but I was really impressed.

MADELINE: I wonder if the temper is trying to confuse her into thinking it will take her a long time, but maybe it will take a lot less time to get the temper out of her life.

___

[2]Team members included Sally Brecher, LICSW, Amy Mayer, PsyD, Madeline Dymsza, LICSW, and Edward Bauman, PsyD.

EDWARD: I wonder if her parents can help by noticing when the temper is fading.

SALLY: Yes. I wonder if Rose and her parents can sit down and talk about when the temper isn't in control of Rose and her voice, and when the times are going well for her. Because I think the temper really has her saying things she doesn't mean like, "I don't care." That doesn't sound like Rose. And Rose's parents have found ways this week to get on top of the situation, and they should be commended. They haven't let the temper push them around, and Rose's not letting the temper push her around. My feeling is we're seeing real progress . . . real change.

[Reflecting team and family change places]

THERAPIST: I wonder what fit for you in what the team said and what didn't fit. Who wants to start?

MOTHER: I will. It's nice to see a different perspective of what you've experienced. It's nice to hear a positive message. One thing I heard was that the real Rose is not the same Rose we see when she's angry. This is important for me to remember because I take it personally.

FATHER: They seemed to be impressed with last night, with Rose cooperating. It was nice and they felt positive about it, which is good. It gives me hope.

CONSULTANT: You mentioned the step the team noticed about the TV situation. The fact that Rose had her own voice in this situation and wasn't being influenced by the temper, what does that tell you about the future?

FATHER: Hope! Maybe we can change this around. It was a nice feeling. I went to bed feeling calm. It wasn't an hour of screaming. . . . It was nice to be able to say, "No" and get cooperation.

CONSULTANT: And you saw that that was possible.

FATHER: Yes. Right. It was. It was nice.

[At this point in the session, Rose had tuned out the conversation and responded to questions with, "I don't know . . . I didn't hear anything."]

MOTHER: (to Rose) What do you remember about what they were saying about your voice and the temper's voice?

ROSE: They were saying that they heard my voice and not the temper's.

CONSULTANT: The goal here is really for your voice to get stronger and the temper's voice to get smaller and smaller. One of the benefits you have is that you are growing and getting stronger but the temper stays the same—so, really, the temper gets smaller and smaller and your voice gets stronger and stronger. (I demonstrate with my hands.)

THERAPIST: I was wondering if there is something your parents can do in helping you tame the temper?

ROSE: I'm not sure.

CONSULTANT: I'm wondering if it would be valuable to have a sign. If your parents see the temper sneaking around they can grab the sign, hold it up, post it up—"temper in the area."

ROSE: It would be kinda embarrassing in front of my friends.

CONSULTANT: Yeah. Well, it wouldn't have to be up all the time.

ROSE: (*laughing*) If my friends were over, I could just see my mother come marching along with a sign . . .

CONSULTANT: What I think would also be useful is tracking those times when Rose's voice is being heard without it being influenced by the temper.

MOTHER: Yeah. I would like to not listen anymore to the temper. Because I feel I get really hurt when I hear that voice. I think I need to say, at that point, for my own self-respect, for our relationship, I don't want to listen to that voice, because it's not you talking. And I'm going to walk away at that point.

CONSULTANT: That sounds like a good idea.

For three months following this session there have been no major "blow-ups" between Rose and her parents. The therapist has seen the family twice since this meeting and the door was left open for future contacts as needed.

In the clinical situation presented, the family was engaged in an externalizing conversation that enabled them to pull together to not cooperate with a powerful external force (i.e., "the Temper") while creating upset in the family. The 12-year-old child became engaged in, and intrigued by this idea. She was also able to "save face" in regard to her behavior and be supported as a part of the solution rather than a part of the problem. The parents were able to distinguish Rose's voice, which they wanted to hear more of, from the temper's voice, and were able to view Rose's behavior less personally.

"Externalizing the Problem" with a Twist: "Ghosty" Is Gone

Often in working with children and families, I find it necessary to rethink my approach in response to feedback from the family. In the following clinical situation, in addition to "externalizing the problem," I introduce a novel and playful element as a way to interrupt a pattern that had become established. This combination of approaches leads to a successful outcome.

Five-year-old Kevin came to my office with his mother because "Kevin is always angry and directs this to his mother." The mother, a single parent, was at a loss about how to discipline Kevin who "was ordering her around." Kevin admitted that he "gets mad a lot" and that he and his mother get into "bickering" at times. The mother felt it was Kevin's behavior that "set her off." I suggested that Kevin draw a picture of "Ghosty," which was the name he had given for the "angry monster" that lives in his house, and we set another appointment.

At this next session, Kevin brought his picture, and we discussed how Kevin could get control of his life back from this "uncooperative monster" that was creating trouble in the household. I suggested that Kevin and his mother develop a chart and track, for each day, whether Kevin or "Ghosty" was in charge. I challenged Kevin to show that he could have a life free from the influence of "Ghosty," a life where he would not be a slave to the monster. He seemed to enjoy this discussion and appeared eager to give it a try.

At our next meeting, the mother reported that there had been no progress. She had been using the chart for two weeks now and felt like Kevin was "not concerned if Ghosty wins." In light of what she was saying, I decided to shift gears and look more closely at the cycle of interaction that was occurring in the mornings that led to most of the upset. The mother described how Kevin would procrastinate ("space out") in the morning and would look to her to help him get dressed and ready for school. We talked about "Ghosty" being very effective in holding on to Kevin and not letting him go about his business in the morning. The mother needed time in the morning to get herself ready for work and found Kevin's slowness infuriating. The mother, as a way to facilitate Kevin getting ready in the morning, was setting out his school clothes the night before on the couch in the living room. Somehow, even though the clothes could always be found in this same spot, Kevin would dilly-dally around, lie down on the couch, and "space out."

In an attempt to introduce novelty into this routine, I suggested that the mother vary the location of his clothes each morning in a way that required that Kevin actively search for them. She was to find a new place to put his clothes each day. We discussed how, if he failed to get ready on time, he would need to go off to school in his pajamas. I asked him if he had a pair of pajamas that he wouldn't mind wearing to school. He adamantly said, "No."

At our next appointment, the mother reported that Kevin was more cooperative in the morning and did not have to go to school in his pajamas. He was ready on time in the morning, sometimes even before his mother. Kevin, with a big smile on his face, announced, "'Ghosty' is gone!" The mother also added that she and Kevin were having more fun together. No further appointments were made.

Building on Presession Change: Rico Frees Himself from Drugs

In many clinical situations, family members have already made changes (and seen improvement) prior to the initial appointment (Weiner-Davis, de Shazer, & Gingerich, 1987). In these instances, the therapist comments on and amplifies those steps taken that indicate that change, in a positive direction, is already happening . Therapy becomes a process of amplification of already demonstrated steps toward a positive outcome.

A 16-year-old young man, Rico, had been using marijuana and cocaine over at least a three-month period prior to our initial contact. Rico had been stealing money and jewelry from his parents to get drugs. Rico and his friends were also involved in stealing cars to get money for drugs. Rico's drug use came to light when the parents became suspicious about money missing from the house and from their bank account. I received a call from Rico's pediatrician, who had him take a urine screen, which turned out positive for cocaine. He admitted to the pediatrician that he was using cocaine and marijuana and indicated that he wanted to stop. The pediatrician asked me to set up an appointment with the family. The family was seen on three occasions over a four-week period. In the two weeks that had passed from the time Rico met with the pediatrician and the family's appointment with me, Rico reported no drug use. An opportunity existed, therefore, to build on this positive development.

Session 1

THERAPIST: Do your parents know what's been going on?

RICO: Yes. I've told them

THERAPIST: What drugs were you using?

RICO: Cocaine and marijuana.

THERAPIST: How were you using the cocaine? Was it smoked, injected?

RICO: No. Sniffed.

THERAPIST: Not crack?

RICO: No. We used to put cocaine in the marijuana. It's called an "*ouli.*"

THERAPIST: How long has this been happening . . . have you been using?

MOTHER: Excuse me, do you (*to Rico*) want to talk alone without us first?

THERAPIST: I know your parents are here and it may be uncomfortable but . . . it's in the past now, and I'd like to hear from you.

RICO: About three months, on and off.

THERAPIST: Your friends are into that?

RICO: Yeah. At parties and stuff like that.

THERAPIST: How did this come to light?

FATHER: Well, some things were missing in the house, like money and other stuff. That's the way it started to come up, the whole situation. And he admit it. What, about a month ago or so?

RICO: Yeah.

[The parents went on to describe how Rico's drug use came to light. Money and jewelry were found missing from the home. Rico, at one point, took his mother's bank card and withdrew $300. The parents, when they became suspicious, confronted Rico about the missing money. Rico acknowledged he took it.]

FATHER: I was ready to beat him up because I was upset. He know what I was going to do. So he had no choice but admit it. And he asked me for help.

THERAPIST: He did.

FATHER: I spoke with a cop friend of mine, and he tried to help me out the best he could. He told me to call here. Rico admitted he used the $50 to buy stuff. They taken advantage of him. They only gave him baking powder.

THERAPIST: So he got taken.

FATHER: At that point, at that moment, it tied up my hands because he admit it and he asked me for help.

THERAPIST: That's the important thing. So, what are you doing now [to help Rico]? I'm trying to understand what are you doing now. You're watching in terms of the money?

FATHER: We have to. Right now, I cannot trust him. No way. With the things going on. Okay, I feel bad like I said, but I have to hide the money. I have to lock my door because—maybe he is trying to calm down and all—but if he's dealing with friends, I've got to be careful.

THERAPIST: It's part of what has to happen now. For your parents to help you, they really have to tighten things up here. Stay on top of where you go and what you do. That's got to be done.

FATHER: Well, I don't know if he understands what I try to tell him almost every day, but I wish he just stop and think about what we're going through. Rico, it's not easy, son. Because if you want to believe it or not, I'd like to kick your ass, but you've got my hands tied because you want help. So, if you just give me the opportunity to help you, things will be okay.

THERAPIST: So what are you doing, Rico, that's helping you to be able to resist that urge to get involved [with drugs]?

RICO: I've been staying home.

THERAPIST: Just trying to stay home more, so you're not in a situation to be tempted. Yeah. But how about at school. You're going to see some of the kids?

RICO: No. They don't go to school.

THERAPIST: So you don't run into them there.

FATHER: This is outside kids. He been doing pretty good since he had the drug test done.

THERAPIST: When was that?

FATHER: It is almost two weeks. If he keeps doing this kind of thing [coming home after school and not using drugs] he'll build up the confidence. I can't say I have confidence now. . . . I can't say that. No.

MOTHER: I give him less money. Before I gave five dollars a day, now I give three.

THERAPIST: That's very good. These are the kinds of things your parents have to do.

[In the section to follow, I use "scaling" questions (Berg & de Shazer, 1993; Berg & Miller, 1992; Kowalski & Kral, 1989) as a way to both assess Rico's confidence in overcoming his drug use and to provide an opportunity for him to amplify his thinking about the benefits of creating a drug-free life. Rico expresses his thinking publicly (with his parents as witnesses). By "going public," Rico not only articulates the steps needed to overcome the drug problem but gives his parents confidence in his abilities to free himself from drugs.]

THERAPIST: Tell me something, Rico, I'm trying to understand how confident you are about your ability to be stronger than these drugs. And let's say a 10 is you have the most confidence you're not going to be a slave to these drugs, and a 1 is you've got no confidence at all. Okay? Where would you put yourself at this point? I know it's early in the [recovery] process.

RICO: I would say an 8.

THERAPIST: An 8—okay. That's pretty confident, pretty confident. What gives you that feeling of confidence that you will not be a slave to the drugs? What makes you feel like you're an 8? What goes into making you feel like an 8 instead of a 5 or a 4?

RICO: I was thinking, a while back when I said I needed help, "What's the use of using it?" It's not going to do nothing. I was thinking that. I spoke to a friend of my mother's who told me that he used to use it [drugs] in Puerto Rico. I remember him saying, you don't need to use it. It will bring you nowhere. And that's true, you know. I seen a lot of friends of mine that recently got out of jail from using that stuff . . . got caught selling.

THERAPIST: So, you've seen some of the problems you can get into with it [drugs]. What else have you been thinking that makes you as confident as an 8 about not cooperating with the power of those drugs?

RICO: I just stopped hanging with those people.

THERAPIST: So you made a decision not to hang with that crowd, that group.

RICO: Uh-uh.

THERAPIST: How can you manage that? Aren't they going to call you, come looking for you?

RICO: Well, they have. I do see them. I knew them for so long. I know when they come around, I know what time, so I try to prevent not being there when they have money. I remember, two days ago, they had a half-ounce of weed. I was coming home from school and they asked me if I wanted to and I said, "I can't. . . . I want to stop this stuff."

THERAPIST: You told them.

RICO: I told everybody that I know. A few of them laughed. A few said that's good. I told them I was going to a program. And I just told them I was getting a blood test every week. Just to get them off my mind.

THERAPIST: Right.

RICO: They said, "Are you sure?" "Yeah," I said. "I'm sure," and then they wanted to go for a ride, and I went home. I knew that they would be coming back, and I went home and my father was there, and he was cooking and stuff and I said to him, "I'm bored, let's rent some movies." That's why. I knew if I didn't do something I was going to have an urge to do it [use drugs]. I would think about it twice.

THERAPIST: Right. Okay. So you were having that feeling of being bored and where other times you would be tempted to move in the direction toward the drugs, you spoke to your dad.

RICO: Yeah. I said, "Let's rent a movie. I'm bored. Let's go somewhere."

THERAPIST: "Let's do something." Yeah.

RICO: I knew if I just stood in the house and I was bored, my father would end up saying go outside or go to a friend or something. I know he ain't thinking about what I was going to do. But I would sneak away, and they'd probably be smoking the weed, marijuana, and I'd probably end up doing it. So as soon as I got home, my father started cooking, I said, "Let's rent some movies."

THERAPIST: (to Father) Okay, did you know what was going on with Rico or did you think he was just asking to rent some movies?

FATHER: No, no. I had a feeling what's going on. So I said, "Yeah. Okay. No problem. Let's go [get the videos]."

THERAPIST: So you responded. So that's one way your parents can help you, you know.

FATHER: An example right now that I can think of . . . I think it was last Saturday. I went to Boston. I see a big group of friends of his in the neighborhood, and I tell my wife, I don't really want to go to Boston but I'm going to go and I took Rico and his brother with me. I don't like the air there. [The father had a sense of possible trouble in the neighborhood.]

THERAPIST: This beginning time is the hardest. I think you've made a lot of positive steps; telling those kids you don't want to use anymore is a big step. Being able to walk away from a situation like you did. And being sensitive to your own feelings inside that you're tempted and to figure out another plan is another way to know. [I emphasize how difficult this process is and support and acknowledge the positive steps that Rico has already taken to rid his life of drugs.]

FATHER: I said to Rico, "I'll make time, anytime." I say, "Rico, I don't ask you to say goodbye to these guys completely. You cannot do that. To tell them you cannot be their friend because they do that. But, when you see that they're going to do something wrong, you get the hell out of there." It's hard. I always expected the best from him . . .

THERAPIST: Yeah. I know. You're fortunate your parents are in there for you, trying to help in any way they can. At this point, the simplest way to go is to continue doing what you and your parents have started. I think you'll be able to manage it at this level and not need a formal program. But, there are other options. That you're at an 8 in how confident you feel makes me optimistic. What do you think would have to happen for you to feel like a 9? to get from an 8 to a 9?[3]

RICO: To get to a point . . . that I can make my friends stop asking me to be hanging with them. If they can understand what I'm trying to do. So far, some of them have stopped already [putting pressure on me], and two of them are thinking of going into a program, too.

THERAPIST: Okay.

RICO: Because one of them had an overdose and I told him I was getting into a program. And he said, "I want to do that, too."

THERAPIST: You're helping those other guys, too, because they see someone

[3]Since a scale implies movement on a continuum, scaling questions provide a means to assess where the client places him or herself on some important dimension and a "visible" yardstick with which to monitor progress (Kowalski & Kral, 1989).

say, I'm not going to let these drugs ruin my life. So they say, "If Rico can do it, maybe I can do it." Obviously, your interest is in helping yourself. But they'll probably be some kids who keep pressuring you.

RICO: Yeah. They'll keep it up.

THERAPIST: Because they don't want to be alone in doing this. You know. So, to get to a 9, you stop being asked.

RICO: Yes. The thing that I do . . . when they're coming around and when they get money . . . and sometimes I'll hear, "I'm going to get real bombed out today." So I ask, "What time you getting bombed?" So I start to go home. This week they were smoking bomb, weed, strong.

THERAPIST: On the one hand, it's a temptation to know all of this, but, on the other, it's making you stronger. Those outside forces will always be there.

FATHER: Yes.

[I then ask the parents to scale their confidence in Rico having a drug-free future. Since their confidence levels are lower than Rico's, I ask Rico what he would need to do to bring their confidence levels up.]

THERAPIST: So, it's going to be your job to figure out how you're not going to get pulled back into it. And you've shown you're able to do that. It takes some strength. So that makes me very confident. . . . Where would you (*to father*) put yourself on a 1 to 10 scale? How confident are you in Rico's ability to not let these drugs push him around, where a 10 is most confident?

FATHER: I don't know. (*The father translates my question into Spanish for his wife.*)

MOTHER: 6

THERAPIST: So, you're more skeptical. You're a little more cautious.

MOTHER: Yeah. Right now, he's very good. He can do it. But he can also change his mind like that [quickly]. So I give 6.

THERAPIST: How about you? (*to Father*)

FATHER: About the same.

THERAPIST: A 6?

FATHER: Yeah.

MOTHER: I've been very nervous. Not sleeping, because of all this. It's tension. If I get home and I don't find him there, I start worrying.

THERAPIST: Your parents are at a 6, so they're not as confident as you are. What do you think you can do that's going to help them get to a 7, from a 7 to an 8? What are they going to need to see that will be helpful to them?

RICO: I'm really not sure. So far, what I've been doing . . . is not thinking about what is going to happen tomorrow. I just take it day by day.

THERAPIST: That's important.

RICO: I think about my schoolwork when I'm in school, not where are they. I don't be thinking where will they be now.

THERAPIST: Okay. And you used to be distracted by that stuff.

RICO: Yeah. At times, I could be anywhere and I'd make a phone call and find out, "Oh, we're going to get some stuff," okay.

THERAPIST: The drug stuff was foremost in your mind then, and now you're not thinking that way. What can you do if you come home and your dad is not there, like he was the other time. What can you do?

RICO: So far this week, he's been working late. So, the only thing I do is be with this guy [an adult and his friend]. They're cool. I'll talk to them, play cards and then I go home.

THERAPIST: So instead of being by yourself you go to a friend's house . . . that makes sense.

RICO: Those people know I used to use it, and they tell me you shouldn't hang with them [the other kids].

THERAPIST: They support you. You're safe there. Rico is thinking very clearly about this. I'm impressed. I see kids who are trying to get off drugs who don't think so clearly about this. I'm impressed. And you've already taken a lot of steps and done a lot of thinking.

MOTHER: This week . . . I'm more happy.

FATHER: Every night either she or I get up at 1 A.M. or 3 A.M. to check that he's in his room. It's hard, because I get up at 5 A.M. [for work].

THERAPIST: I don't think you're going to have to do it for long but, at this point, I think you're right. You've got to do it. It's part of what will help Rico. I think the two of you are doing well, trying to help your son. I'd like to set up another time to meet. Okay?

[A meeting is scheduled for one week later.]

Session 2

[I met with Rico for most of the session, with his mother joining us for a few minutes at the very end.]

THERAPIST: How have you been doing over this period?

RICO: Good.

THERAPIST: Were there situations this week when you were feeling tempted [to use drugs]?

RICO: No.

THERAPIST: You were bored sometimes?

RICO: Yeah. But not tempted.

THERAPIST: Did that surprise you?

RICO: Yeah. Because yesterday I was watching a movie, a Spanish movie. It had kids smoking weed. And I was laughing, camping on them.

THERAPIST: I see.

RICO: It shocked me. I thought I would have the urge, but I didn't. I thought, "It's stupid, don't do that." I think I'm doing well with my situation. The movie makes it [the drug scene] look interesting. . . . It's a strong movie. You see the stuff right there and they're sniffin' it.

THERAPIST: So it was right there in front of you.

RICO: I was just laughing.

THERAPIST: You could step back. You didn't feel part of that movie. [I emphasize Rico's ability to get perspective and distance.]

RICO: I didn't feel part of it. It was stupid. I was laughing.

THERAPIST: Have you run into any of the guys [who use drugs]?

RICO: Yesterday. One of them who use to sell, I saw him yesterday. I was like, "How you doin'?" . . . and I went off.

THERAPIST: They're letting you be.

RICO: Little by little, they're letting me be. They use to call and we would get together and we'd just be chillin', just be relaxed, watching TV and all of a sudden they say, "We'll be right back," and they bring some stuff out . . . coke or something.

THERAPIST: So now you're just not putting yourself into that situation.

RICO: No. As I said, I'm taking it day by day. . . . I tell people I'm in a program and they check my blood. I'm trying to clean myself up. A friend of mine from Puerto Rico told me as soon as they find out you do drugs your respect is just thrown away. That really hurt me. I noticed that some people who knew I was doing drugs were hitting on me, calling me "basehead" and all this stuff. I didn't even freebase [smoke purified cocaine].

THERAPIST: So you lose respect in the community [by using drugs].

RICO: Yeah.

THERAPIST: Would it be helpful to have a urine test once in a while?

RICO: Yeah. That would be nice. It would prove the point that I can do it.

THERAPIST: Okay. I'm trusting your word that you're taking these steps

now, so it's up to you. If you think it would help to know you have
to come in and get checked out . . . we can do it.

RICO: Yeah.

THERAPIST: Okay.

RICO: My parents were saying it's harder for them to get confidence in
me again.

THERAPIST: So this would help build confidence for them to see some
results on a test.

RICO: I would like that.

[To further solidify Rico's plan for a drug-free future, I ask him to tell
me what advice he would give a friend who was thinking about getting
involved with drugs.]

THERAPIST: If you had a friend who was getting involved with drugs, what
would you tell them? What advice would you give?

RICO: I've been doing this with some people. I would explain to them
every detail that goes into it. You would get a little urge, and then
five minutes later, you want more. You find something or jump
somebody to get it. I could control myself that far. I never hurt
someone. So I tell them everything that is into it and they be like,
"It makes you a fiend, you always want more" and I say, "Yeah, man
. . . it's real bad for you. Just don't do it."

THERAPIST: What other steps do you think you need to take? What other
temptations might come up?

RICO: Parties. If I go to a party—I don't go that much. My father doesn't let
me. He knows what type of people are there. If I go to a party, there's
always going to be a group of people smoking marijuana. Probably
half of the whole room will leave. Hopefully, I will pull through that.

THERAPIST: Half the group will leave. What do you mean?

RICO: All the boys might leave and go outside and smoke weed. They'll
go one-by-one but you know what's happening.

THERAPIST: And there's a group left in the house that doesn't do it.

RICO: Yeah.

THERAPIST: What would you do?

RICO: I think I can handle it.

THERAPIST: It sounds like you're really giving yourself respect and getting
respect from other people by staying off of drugs. . . . Have your
parents asked you to pay back any of the money [you took]?

RICO: No. But I want to. I feel bad. I want to pay them back every little
cent I took.

THERAPIST: You may not be able to do it now, but at another point when you're working, you can do it.

RICO: I feel real bad about it. I blame the stuff [the drugs].

THERAPIST: It [drugs] can really pull you in to doing things you don't want to do.

RICO: My parents just want me to clean my system out and do good in school, but I don't feel satisfied by that.

THERAPIST: It will be a nice thing to be able to give the money back to them, besides your being off drugs.

[I excuse myself and go to the waiting room and ask the mother to join us.]

THERAPIST: Rico continues to do well, and it really has taken a lot of energy and effort on his part. We were talking earlier about how important it is for you and your husband to watch carefully.

MOTHER: I still wake up in the middle of the night and look [to see if Rico is in his bed].

THERAPIST: That's good.

MOTHER: I watch him closely.

[I encourage the mother to continue being vigilant with regard to Rico, and we discuss Rico's wish to have periodic urine screens to help demonstrate his progress and build up trust with his parents. Another meeting is scheduled in 12 days to follow up on Rico's progress.]

Session 3

THERAPIST: (*to Rico*) How have you been doing?

RICO: Great.

MOTHER: Great. Yeah. Very great. (*She pats Rico on the back proudly.*)

THERAPIST: Let me hear about situations that have come up that you needed to find a way to handle.

RICO: A few days ago—I told my father about it—a friend of mine was going to a party and she needed someone to go and baby-sit. Two other boys said they would go. And I said yes [I'd join them]. Later, they said they were getting weed. I said, "Why are you doing it?" They said, "It's the weekend, why not?" Then she invited me, and I said, "Oh, no, I don't want to go . . . they're going to smoke marijuana and I'm in a program." And she said, "That's all right . . ." As soon as I got home, I told my father.

THERAPIST: Have there been other situations that have come up?

RICO: No. That's the only time I came close. I told my father I could've gone and come back quick. But I left. And the next day I saw them [the boys] again, and they were telling me they really got bombed. And I said, "That's good for you."

THERAPIST: So, you could listen . . .

RICO: I could listen, but it doesn't affect me.

THERAPIST: That's wonderful. That's really not easy to do.

All subsequent urine screens have been negative. A follow-up call three months later indicated that Rico now saw himself as "at least a 9," and his parents were proud of his accomplishment. Rico had reconnected with a church youth group and was dating a young woman who was supportive of his not using drugs.

CONCLUSIONS

Doing time-effective possibility therapy is more that just implementing a set of techniques. While opening up new choices or options, the therapist must also create a climate of acceptance and hope, where the client's dignity and resources are respected. At times, this involves listening to the family's problem-saturated story. By hearing and acknowledging that story, the therapist can pave the way for developing new and more empowering narratives.

The framework discussed here exemplifies a collaborative, respectful, and strength-oriented therapy (Friedman, 1993a; Friedman & Fanger, 1991). It emphasizes the benefits of nonpathologizing approaches to the therapeutic process and places the client as a coparticipant in constructing time-effective solutions. A therapy of possibility and empowerment invites the client to envision future options, to develop alternative stories, and to experience a sense of personal agency or efficacy. The therapist guides and structures the therapeutic conversation such that the family, rather than becoming immersed in problems and constraints, is afforded opportunities to re-vision their predicament in ways that emphasize possibilities and offers hope for the future. Operating from a narrative of hope and optimism, with a view toward the future, can go a long way in making the therapeutic endeavor not only a more positive and useful experience for the family, but also a more time-effective one.

REFERENCES

Andersen, T. (Ed). (1991). *The Reflecting Team: Dialogues and Dialogues about the Dialogues*. New York: Norton.

Anderson, H., & Goolishian, H. A. (1988). Human systems as linguistic systems:

Preliminary and evolving ideas about the implications for clinical theory. *Family Process*, 27(4), 371–393.

Berg, I. K. (1989). Of visitors, complainants and customers. *Family Therapy Networker*, 13(1), 21.

Berg, I. K. (1994). *Family-Based Services: A Solution-Focused Approach*. New York: Norton.

Berg, I. K., & de Shazer, S. (1993). Making numbers talk: Language in therapy In S. Friedman (Ed.), *The New Language of Change: Constructive Collaboration in Psychotherapy*. New York: Guilford.

Berg, I. K., & Miller, S. D. (1992). *Working with the Problem Drinker: A Solution-Focused Approach*. New York: Norton.

Brecher, S., & Friedman, S. (1993). In pursuit of a better life: A mother's triumph In S. Friedman (Ed.), *The New Language of Change: Constructive Collaboration in Psychotherapy*. New York: Guilford.

Budman, S. H., Friedman, S., & Hoyt, M. F. (1992). Last words on first sessions. In S. H. Budman, M. F. Hoyt, & S. Friedman (Eds.), *The First Session in Brief Therapy*. New York: Guilford.

Davidson, J., & Lax, W. D. (1992). Reflecting conversations in the initial consultation. In S. H. Budman, M. F. Hoyt, & S. Friedman (Eds.), *The First Session in Brief Therapy*. New York: Guilford.

de Shazer, S. (1985). *Keys to Solution in Brief Therapy*. New York: Norton.

de Shazer, S. (1988). *Clues: Investigating Solutions in Brief Therapy*. New York: Norton.

de Shazer, S. (1991). *Putting Difference to Work*. New York: Norton.

Durrant, M. (1989). Scaring fears: Making exceptions to problem behaviour meaningful. *Family Therapy Case Studies*, 4(2), 15–31.

Friedman, S. (1989a). Brief systemic psychotherapy in a health maintenance organization. *Family Therapy*, 16(2), 133–144.

Friedman, S. (1989b). Child mental health in a Health Maintenance Organization: A family systems approach. *HMO Practice*, 3(2), 52–59.

Friedman, S. (1989c). Strategic reframing in a case of "delusional jealousy." *Journal of Strategic and Systemic Therapies*, 8(2–3), 1–4.

Friedman, S. (1990). Towards a model of time-effective family psychotherapy: A view from a Health Maintenance Organization (HMO). *Journal of Family Psychotherapy*, 1(2), 1–28.

Friedman, S. (1991). Toward a wellness model of time-effective family psychotherapy. *Family Psychologist*, 7(2), 23–24.

Friedman, S. (1992). Constructing solutions (stories) in brief family therapy. In S. H. Budman, M. F. Hoyt, & S. Friedman (Eds.), *The First Session in Brief Therapy*. New York: Guilford.

Friedman, S. (Ed.). (1993a). *The New Language of Change: Constructive Collaboration in Psychotherapy*. New York: Guilford.

Friedman, S. (1993b). Escape from the Furies: A journey from self-pity to self-love. In S. Friedman (Ed.), *The New Language of Change: Constructive Collaboration in Psychotherapy* New York: Guilford.

Friedman, S., & Fanger, M. T. (1991). *Expanding Therapeutic Possibilities: Getting Results in Brief Psychotherapy*. New York: Lexington Books/Macmillan.

Goleman, D. (1992, June 24). Tormented by nightmares? Rehearse a different ending. *New York Times*, p. C14.

Gurman, A. S. (1992). Integrative marital therapy: A time-sensitive model for working with couples. In S. H. Budman, M. F. Hoyt, & S. Friedman (Eds.), *The First Session in Brief Therapy*. New York: Guilford.

Haley, J. (1984). *Ordeal Therapy*. San Francisco: Jossey-Bass.

Hobbs, N. (1966). Helping disturbed children: Psychological and ecological strategies. *American Psychologist, 21*(12), 1105–1115.

Hoffman-Hennessey, L., & Davis, J. (1993). Tekka with feathers: Talking about talking (about suicide). In S. Friedman (Ed.), *The New Language of Change: Constructive Collaboration in Psychotherapy*. New York: Guilford.

Hoyt, M. (1990). On time in brief therapy. In R. A. Wells & V. J. Giannetti (Eds.), *Handbook of the Brief Psychotherapies*. New York: Plenum.

Hoyt, M. F., Rosenbaum, R., & Talmon, M. (1992). Planned single session therapy. In S. H. Budman, M. F. Hoyt, & S. Friedman (Eds.), *The First Session in Brief Therapy*. New York: Guilford.

Kowalski, K., & Kral, R. (1989). The geometry of solution: Using the scaling technique. *Family Therapy Case Studies, 4*(1), 59–66.

Mittelmeier, C. M., & Friedman, S. (1993). Toward a mutual understanding: Constructing solutions with families. In S. Friedman (Ed.), *The New Language of Change: Constructive Collaboration in Psychotherapy*. New York: Guilford.

O'Hanlon, W., & Weiner-Davis, M. (1989). *In Search of Solutions*. New York: Norton.

O'Hanlon, B., & Wilk, J. (1987). *Shifting Contexts: The Generation of Effective Psychotherapy*. New York: Guilford.

Ross, N. W. (Ed.). (1960). The subjugation of a ghost. In *The World of Zen*. New York: Random House.

Weiner-Davis, M., de Shazer, S., & Gingerich, W. (1987). Building on pretreatment change to construct the therapeutic solution: An exploratory study. *Journal of Marital and Family Therapy, 13*(4), 359–363.

White, M. (1992). Deconstruction and therapy. *Dulwich Centre Newsletter, 3*, 21–40.

White, M., & Epston, D. (1990). *Narrative Means to Therapeutic Ends*. New York: Norton.

CHAPTER 12

Solving the Unknown Problem

ERIC GREENLEAF

> ... and if we think by imagining signs and pictures, I can give
> you no agent that thinks.
> —WITTGENSTEIN (1958, p. 6)

This work is an ongoing improvisation in psychotherapy, an attempt to harmonize themes from ancient and modern practice. The rhythms for the piece come from the old music of hypnosis and dreams, practiced in many cultures and revived in modern times in the work of Freud (1935), Erickson (Rosen, 1982), and White and Epston (1990), among others. You will recognize them as "metaphorical communication" and "visualization."

The ensemble that performs here are members of my six-month long hypnotherapy class, each an experienced psychotherapist with a different repertoire of skills. We play various themes with a "reflecting team" motif (Andersen, 1991), in which solutions are developed collaboratively. In our practice, we have "passed the trance" from one member to the next, using a faceted crystal as a focus, and developed solutions to human dilemmas by passing an image from person to person. This improvisation is a method in much modern therapy. You may hear echoes of "strategic therapy," "psychodrama," and "therapeutic rituals" in our composition (Haley, 1987).

The method of composition involves a radicalization of some signature assumptions in therapy, a "going to the root or foundation of something." This method has been used in producing the spare, lovely pieces of the Milan Team (Boscolo, Cecchin, Hoffman, & Penn, 1987) as they "go to the root" of strategic therapy. Here, we radicalize the notion of "unconscious mind," taking seriously the assumption that this "mind" cannot be consciously known and the insight of Erickson's that this "mind" can be utilized in a positive manner.

Imagine hypnosis as a sort of conversation, which enables the discussants to imitate all manner of felt human experience. Imagine, too, that the language of this conversation is dreamlike; that it is pictorial and emotive. Now, suppose that these pictures express relationship. As Bateson (1972, p. 56) says:

> A dream is a metaphor or tangle of metaphors. . . . A metaphor compares things without spelling out the comparison. It takes what is true of one group of things and applies it to another. . . . The dream elaborates on the relationship but does not identify the (original) things that are related.

I'd claim that "dream language" provides proper understandings of human events, especially those we cannot speak about in common language and do not wish to speak about to patients in "therapeutic" language. Dreams are what the Tibetans call *rang-snang*, "one's own thought-forms or visions," and they are, I think, perfect structural representations of complex experiences. This is true whether the dreams are spontaneous or are made up spontaneously in the therapist's office.

If we adopt the convention that what is unsayable in the common language is "unconscious," we may still wish to communicate about relationship. We may wish to do so without inventing "technical" terms for the discussion, such as "codependent," or "ego-syntonic." We may wish to do so without presuming "meanings" for the symptoms, inhibitions, and anxieties we exhibit. We may be led to use the language of images to discuss and resolve "unconscious problems." "Solving the unknown problem," requires an evocation and resolution of images; and of metaphor. Add to these ideas the common intuition that the solution often "lies within the problem"; then we have the suggestion to imagine a solution as it comes forth from the image of the (unknown) problem.

> We need language more to tell stories than to direct actions. In the telling, we create mental images in our listeners that might normally be produced only by the memory of events. . . . Mental images should be as real as the immediately experienced real world. (Jerison, 1976, p. 99)

To realize the solution we follow a rule of thumb: "Treat the imagined situation as real," and propose possible courses for action, which would obtain if the situation were actually occurring: practical advice, not magical advice. This advice may be proferred by a therapist, by the client, by the family, or by the team, just as interventions and directives are constructed in modern therapies. The task is to utilize a person's own competence to allow change to occur.

A main principle is to complete the dramatic action of the dream, the imagined event, using a person's own images. These dramatic actions may be thought of as a sort of "thought experiment" in the development of possible solutions. Another principle might be termed "conservation of imagery," the attempt to relate to all aspects of the image and to involve them in prospective solutions. (A fuller discussion of this sort of active imagining can be read in Greenleaf, 1977.)

Modern therapies employ the conventions of narrative description to describe their work (White & Epston, 1990), and the work of *this* therapy may be thought of as conversations in and with the language of the unconscious: dream images. The conversation concludes as the problem resolves.

"Passing the trance," is a hypnotic simile for the discussion that occurs in a reflecting team or consultation. Hypnosis, as a prime metaphor for "unknown solutions" and for the utilization of "the unconscious mind," can be applied to an "unknown problem." The practice of hypnotherapy has always been "solution-oriented," from the work of hypnoanesthesia in surgery and pain control through the early work of Freud (1935, p. 27), who said,

> Anyone who wished to make a living from the treatment of nervous patients must clearly be able to do something to help them. My therapeutic arsenal contained only two weapons, electrotherapy and hypnotism . . .

In the week prior to the class you will read of, we practiced passing the trance to each other. This was the first experience each member had had in hypnotizing another person. The form of the trance was to focus attention on a faceted crystal, close the eyes comfortably, and allow the hypnotist to lightly lift the subject's hand. Then, the subject would hypnotize the next person in a like manner.

We then posed a question for the next class: to consider solving an unknown problem that has been interfering in life. We considered some metaphorical expressions of the "unknown" in solving human problems: the engineer's "black box" and the photographer's darkroom. In the former, inputs and outputs can be described, but the workings of the connections between them remain obscure. In the latter, a negative is placed in a series of solutions in a darkroom. After it is passed through these solutions, it emerges as a positive image.

Therapists wishing to use these themes in their work should listen to the music of images and practice developing them in cooperative conversations. An excellent first book of practice is Furman and Ahola's (1992) *Solution Talk*. The "Beethoven quartets" of the genre are represented by the work of Milton Erickson (Rossi, 1980).

In the class that follows, we began with a discussion of women and power, and of the feelings that were developed in the course of inducing a trance, of "being the hypnotist." Then we returned to the unknown problem. The following is the piece we improvised on December 7, 1990.

THE LADY OF THE LAKE

ERIC: I wanted to catch up a little with what people's experiences were last week, if I can, and then go on from there, because I still would like to be on the track of this unknown problem. What do you recall that was of interest?

HELEN: I felt very anxious about being first in line and turning to Clem and hypnotizing him and passing the trance around and wondering if I could do that. I did go into trance and felt that anxiety. It was such a strange experience, because I thought I was in trance, but I could still feel the anxiety. I did get calmer and more trusting that I could do my task of being a hypnotist, and when I turned to Clem, I felt like I was bringing some of that trance with me and not being so worried or so self-conscious about it. . . . I felt that I shared that induction around the room, and what I noticed was a more intense kind of curiosity and noticing, as people did the inductions and went into trance. I had this sense of more freely and openly looking at people and really looking and taking it in . . . and then I really listened—this kind of quiet, open nonintrusive listening, which is really being aware, and I really liked that. It seemed kind of like a surprise to me.

The other thing I noticed during the week—I just wondered the other day if it was related to that unknown problem—was that I took care of a lot of little details that were hanging, like just personally. I meditate every day, and a lot of that came to me while meditating, remembering. Even today I remembered to go for that tape to bring it back here. So I had a lot of little experiences of little things that sometimes I'll think of and feel like I don't have time to do them. But I just did them.

When we left here last week, Kathy and Marilyn and maybe you, Ann, were walking in front of me, and I said, "Hey, you guys! We did it. We hypnotized them!"

MARILYN: We assured one another that we hadn't been pretending.

ERIC: Really?

HELEN: So that was really helpful to me, too. I think that really put me over into the camp of believing that I can do it.

ERIC: How about you, Ann? What was it like for you?

ANN: Well, I felt the experience was cumulative. (*general laughter*) I couldn't see straight. I really felt, from the very first, as we passed it around that I had to stop listening; otherwise, I would be really uptight when it came to Cathy's turn to do it to me. I was very anxious, too, about passing it on: I didn't know what would happen— what would actually happen. I had lots of doubts about what would happen. But what I recall during the experiencing was actually going back to the beaches of Hawaii, actually being there. It was just very, very clear, and that's where I was. I figured it was a cumulative experience with everybody talking about it, and it became more and more crystallized and refined until it was just an absolute clear picture.

What I was thinking about during the week, as well, was that solution to an unknown problem, and not knowing where the picture will bridge that unknown problem. Where will it meet? Where is it in that picture, that crystal-clear picture that I have in my head of the beach? The unknown problem: Where will it meet? It actually pops into my head almost every day. I find it so interesting, the unknown problem. Heavens to Betsy, I have so many at this point! It would be nice to have a solution, rather than knowing I have all these problems and looking for a solution.

ERIC: Yes, that's one corollary of this, for sure.

ANN: I have been talking a lot about all these problems that I have, wondering if maybe I shouldn't be talking about them and hoping that somehow a solution would emerge. Maybe I shouldn't be so interested in problems, because if I'm not maybe I'll forget they are problems, and maybe they will become unknown problems and be duly addressed. It's really crazy.

ERIC: I like this idea of the unknown problem so much, partly because it's another way of talking about the metaphor of unconscious mind or unconsciousness. Remember the psychoanalytic version of things, in which you get a problem because something falls into your unconscious. You repress information or feelings or desires or memories, or your whole childhood is unknown to you. Thereby, you get an unknown problem. But, if you think about the way we've been working hypnotically, with the unconscious as a kind of resource, you could drop something like your problems into the unconscious and get them solved in just that same way. You could say, "Well, this isn't too bad; I'll just drop that in." It's like a stock pot: "This looks like leavings, but I don't want to throw it away; I'll just toss in in"; and pretty soon it develops its own flavor, and you can use it to make sauce.

HELEN: In the 12-step programs, that's what they call "letting go."

ERIC: Yes. You give it up to the higher power, or you drop it into the unconscious mind. "I can't handle this so I'll give it over to God"; or, "I can't get anywhere with this so I'll become unconscious of it and it will work itself out". That's kind of the approach Ann is taking with this; I think it's a very interesting one. Now, calling something "unconscious" is usually thought of in a kind of personal way, or else archetypically, like the Jungian way. . . . But there is another, I think accurate way of thinking about the unconscious. Things which are unconscious are also impersonal, social and interpersonal things. Your family feeling when you were a child may qualify as something unconscious: You know what it sort of feels like; if you were there again you would recognize it; but it would be very hard to put into words. What is the feeling of all of you together at the dinner table? But it has a very particular feel to it—just like odors: . . . you know the smell of a particular place in a more intricate kind of way than your language allows you to describe. You know the difference in the smell between the chocolate in Dove bars and the chocolate in Häagen-Dazs ice cream, but it would be very hard to describe. So where you have an experience without a personal concept or word for it, that's also unconscious. The feeling between you and your friend when you were hypnotizing her is hard to put into words. Or, the assumptions that you have by growing up female or male in this culture . . . that's unconscious, too. What I am trying to reach for is that the culture and the interpersonal events are unconscious; we don't have good ways of describing them. We talk about our background: "My mother was that way, my father was this way, my sister was that way, my grandmother . . . et cetera," but there are very few words to describe how everybody was all together, which is what you would need to become conscious of those sorts of issues.

If you grew up in an alcoholic family, let's say, you don't have very clear words for that whole system, so you can surprise yourself by understanding something by observation, which you didn't have a handle on. You say, "Oh, I see, it can be different." A kid will go into households where drinking is not an issue, the parents will have a glass of wine at dinner, the bottle gets put away, and everyone plays Scrabble, and it's, "Oh! I never knew about that."

So this business of an unknown problem can be a simile for or similar to an idea of the whole background you come from. It's problematic because you have no way to talk about it that resolves it. . . . I like the notion of an unconscious solution better than I like even the one of an unknown problem.

ANN: Yes, finding an unconscious solution—solving the unknown problem.

ERIC: Cathy, what was it like for you this last week?

CATHY: It was interesting, Ann, when you said that it seemed cumulative, because by the time it got to Clem, I was gone. I felt so deep into something that I don't even remember what John said to me. And when Eric first said, "This is what we are going to do," at first I felt nervous, because, like you I felt, "Oh my God! I've got to perform. . . ." Instead of the one who is learning, I've got to be the one who has to accept some sort of responsibility. So I felt nervous, but as we went along I just let it go, and as I sat there I just went under and under and under, and I just kind of had that soft gaze, and I was here but not in any specific way. And by the time John got to me, it was very strange. It was like I was in this meditative trance, and I didn't want to come out of it. It felt like being asleep but being awake. I recalled a lot of physical energy, and he must have been saying something about my hand, because my hand got so tingly with energy, and heavy. . . . I don't remember what I said to you. I just felt like I just needed to talk. I completely forgot that there was a purpose, and I didn't remember until you just now said that there was this undefined problem. All of a sudden: "Oh yeah, that's right." I forgot there was a beach. I just was out of it. I couldn't tell you what John said to me, other than that I remember something about my hand. There was some focus that brought my energy into my hand and that crystal. It was a very intense experience that I don't really know how to describe.

ERIC: You are doing a good job. The soft gaze is like what Helen talked about: being able to watch without being so intent, or to observe oneself or what was going on, and then that feeling of going under, under, under—of doing that thing that Ann's been fooling with all week, which is kind of the boundary between consciousness and unconsciousness. "Where does the beach apply to something unknown?" is a story about going under, and at some point it's like where the eyes are closing, where you're hitting the water, and then where you're under; and then you go way under. It can feel that way, or it can feel like trying to approximate a boundary—to come close or to let something go into that. Those are all similar experiences. Or like just falling asleep when you're kind of daydreaming, and you don't know quite the moment but you feel yourself . . . or going under anesthesia. They are all like experiences.

CATHY: That soft gaze. . . . It was almost as if the soft gaze was turned inward. I felt like I left my body, except for my hand—like the only energy that was left was in my hand . . .

ERIC: . . . So I guess you learned how to do this, because you passed the crystal around to Ann, and she had a very powerful experience. And I remember that how you approached it was not remarkably differ-

ent from anyone else: You were not tongue-tied or at a loss for
movement or words; you handed it over, you told her what to do;
she started to do it, you spoke with her, and she had a very complete
kind of experience.

HELEN: I noticed, though, that your words just flowed. You were very
articulate. I was very moved and impressed. I thought you were
probably in trance . . .

CATHY: That's interesting. That really surprises me because I just felt like
I just let go. I really don't know what I said; I really don't.

HELEN: You'll enjoy watching the tape.

ERIC: It's very much like trying to remember what dance steps you danced
if you are just dancing and somebody says, "Boy, she can really
dance!" and you can't remember. It's not choreographed in that way;
but it's being in tune with the music, only this was like singing or
singing words.

CATHY: Yes, but this was different. I felt this to be a very, very profound
something. I checked out. It was a different experience. And it's
really interesting because I came to this class with all this uncertainty
about whether I could even experience this stuff, and it seems like
each time it's gotten more and more profound in terms of my
experience. Remember that you and I had a similar experience in
one induction where we thought we went to sleep? Well, in some
ways, I think I am going that deeply under, but I'm staying conscious;
there is a part of me that is staying conscious, whereas before I was
completely unconscious. Now, it's like having a foot in both worlds.

ERIC: Yes, that's exactly what it is like. That's that boundary where, for want
of a better expression, you are consciously unconscious. It's very
pleasing; it's a very powerful sensation; and that's the one you're
aiming at. Helen's description is good again about when you're doing
therapy or observing and you're nonintrusive, and things are just
moving along between you and the other person in an unselfconscious
kind of way. And you are pursuing a similar goal together, so that
you're being helpful without having to adjust yourself a lot, and the
other person is also being helped without your having to do much, . .
. Then what developed in you was individual. It didn't exactly follow
what John aimed at; and Ann didn't exactly follow what you aimed at;
it was a cooperative effort. Marilyn, what happened with you?

MARILYN: I also felt a cumulative effect, being the last person, and I did
my various trips—I just did my various Marilyn things. I was also
nervous; I got to be nervous the whole time. (*general laughter*) I also
had this dual sense of feeling the cumulative trance but also the
nervousness; and that was very strange for me; to feel that experi-

ence of being in trance and being nervous at the same time was novel. And I was also observing, watching. It seemed to me that each person added their own little flavor when they did it: how they do stuff, how their minds work, how the words of each of us come through. And I was trying to say to myself, "Stop observing so much; just stop worrying." There was all this chatter, all those committee members in there chattering away. Also, my back was really hurting me at the time. . . . There was also this awareness that at some point I was going to have to turn to you, and I was going to have to perform and put the teacher in trance. (*long general laughter*) But you approached me with such purity of intent—and you were just you, being here with me—that the rest just kind of dropped away. And I got very entranced with the different facets of the crystal, looking at the colors. I really wanted to look at all the objects in the room through them. That was mostly what I was fixated on. I remember doing the other various bits of it all.

ERIC: Can I put in a parenthetical comment here, because that's so nicely said? What you just described is what's meant by "utilization" in hypnotherapy. That is to say, you sit there before you hypnotize, looking at things every different possible way, being like Marilyn; your mind works that way. You look at the different possible seating situations and sensations and what went before and what will go next, and you're looking at things from different angles. Ann gives you a hypnotic induction, which allows you to use that style as a skill instead of feel it as a symptom, because then you start looking at the different facets of everything and looking at everything's different facets in order to help you meet your goals, whatever they may be. (In this case they are sort of unknown goals.) That enables you to utilize the thing that was bothering you without your having to change; that is, you don't have to become single-minded. Instead, you can use this ability to look at all the different angles and facets and enjoy it. It's a great talent.

MARILYN: Yes, it was very enjoyable. I don't really remember; things got lifted and all, but there wasn't much more to it than that. Still there was a sense of well-being, and that was very pleasurable, and then it was my turn to pass to you. I was just aware of the fear (*expressive gesture, general laughter*), and at one point when I went to lift your wrist my hand was so icy cold in comparison.

ERIC: I didn't notice . . .

HELEN: . . . There was this really nice sort of duet where he dropped his hand and you held your hand out and he dropped the crystal in it . . .

ERIC: So everybody did splendidly ... oh, what about the unknown problem?

MARILYN: I have no idea. Another part of me was realizing I always come to this class after couple's therapy, and we have some very known problems that are taking up a lot of space in my life. Again, when we were going around the room I was thinking, "How can I do this paradoxical thing, to make this known problem become an unknown problem, because I want to find a solution?"

ERIC: And what did you think? Let's take a break for a short while, and then we'll come back and do more about this.

ANN: You could get me into this dream.

ERIC: That's true ... this is really a kind of induction of dreams, if you don't mess with a person's imagery or language too much. Ann's dream of the beaches in Hawaii: if that were told as a dream instead of as a trance, and all the involvement that came with it ...

CATHY: I kept a dream journal while I was studying with Eric. I never do that, but what was very interesting was that all the dreams somehow tied together as one long, all-encompassing story, which I didn't anticipate at all. Sort of like the image that you talked about (maybe it was your image, Helen)—the whirlpool. Somehow it all connects because it's all down this same funnel, surrounding this central issue. It's just a powerful way to work with metaphors and ways to just hook right in immediately to a person's personal image ... without them having to know what it means.

HELEN: You didn't have to know what it meant?

CATHY: Yes, and I kept thinking, "Okay, all right, fine, but what does that mean?" And what I got, but not until the very end, was this sensation of understanding without the language—the same thing you were talking about earlier—the experience of knowing, resolution—experiencing the resolution and just knowing—that and letting go of my need to intellectualize it, rationalize it, put into little categories and boxes and file it away. It was a very different sort of experience.

HELEN: That makes me think: I said I don't remember dreams, but what's happened is different. I wake up, and I'm not quite awake, and I have this knowing about this dream, and I feel like I go, "Oh!" about this dream, and I go back to sleep. I never remember the next day. I vaguely remember the dream; I never remember what that knowing was.

ERIC: You don't remember what you knew, but you remember knowing it. That is what you're both describing. That's the experience that I'm referring to by those words, "solving the unknown problem." You feel something's solved or resolved but you don't know what it was. You can't say what the trouble you were having was within the dream. You can't remember the dream itself, but you can remember that you know how it resolves, sort of like knowing how to play the piano; or you know how to hypnotize her but you don't know how you did it.

HELEN: It's like a new knowing or a surprise? It seems right. I feel . . . go back to sleep. Sometimes, I don't even remember what happened, or I think, "Oh, I want to remember this," but I can't remember what that enlightenment was.

ERIC: That's right, but that's built into the experience because you were reorganizing unconsciously, you might say. If you take a physical analogy: You don't know what you were doing wrong, but now you are not doing it wrong any more, so the ball gets where you throw it or you keep the beat while you're drumming. You didn't know what was wrong. . . . You've had this experience, I know, when you dance: doesn't feel right, doesn't feel right, doesn't feel right, you try different things, and then it feels right. But you may not be able to say what was wrong in the first place, because again either the language is poor for the way you put your foot this way instead of that way, or maybe there's no exact position for it. You can't say, "Now in your fourth position you ought to have flexed more," because you weren't in a fourth position; you were at some funny angle. So, you have to figure it out without the language for it, usually by trial and error of a kind, until it feels right. I think that's the way that many, many important problems are solved when they're solved.

MARILYN: I had a dance teacher who taught metaphorically, and we had common metaphors, but, when I look back, the language seems so imprecise. What did it mean to "lift" or to "get lighter" or imagine this happening with the front and that happening with the back? . . .

HELEN: I had that experience with a friend of mine coaching me in my ever-failing golf tournament. He kept telling me I was picking the club up, and I didn't know what he meant until I saw it on video; then, "Oh!" I could see it immediately; I saw it but I couldn't feel it.

ERIC: Yes, or if Cathy were teaching hypnosis she would talk about a "soft gaze," and everyone would glaze over; they would not know what it meant. But you [Helen] would kind of get a hint of it, because you think, "Oh yes, I look very intently and sometimes people get uncomfortable; then last week I was kind of looking around and nobody got uncomfortable." What was the difference?. . . . It's imprecise, it's allusive: It points to but it does not define. If you say to your kid, "I love you," that word could mean at the moment, "Oh, what a surprise: You came home and you cleaned your shoes before you came in." It could mean a lot of different things, the referent could be very widespread, but you know when the person got it right, and you felt love. So a lot of the words that are metaphorical in that sense we use as though they were technical. I know if I love someone; I know if I don't for sure; but if I use the words "lift up" and you use the words, we are talking about different experiences probably. And "hypnosis" likewise, which is a technical sounding term but only means "pertaining to sleep"; that's all it means; I looked it up yesterday.

ANN: As you were talking I was thinking also about what you said earlier: If you could talk about it, it becomes more conscious. But, if words are so imprecise, then you really are unconscious. . . . I'm thinking of clients who insist on talking about their understanding of an experience, and they beat it to death. . . . I thought, well, maybe they need clearer understanding of it; but, when you talk about words being imprecise anyway, we know very little.

ERIC: They might need a feeling of resolution—"Ah! I understand that"— the way people in recovery programs feel when the word "codependent" is first used. They say, "Oh, that's what I've been going through!" Or people who meditate are told about Zen sickness. They say, "Oh, I feel weird; I couldn't concentrate; I have Zen sickness." Zen sickness is what happens when you meditate; codependence is what happens when you relate to people. . . . But it's interesting that people have a faith in explanations that won't quit, as though giving the reason for something were a solution to a problem; and I've always been very puzzled by that, as though if you could give words to it you could solve it. I think you can re-solve it—you can feel okay about it and not question it any more—but real understanding is a whole different matter, I think more like what Ann and Cathy were saying. You know it or you know how to move, but your explanation for it is going to lag way behind that feeling of resolution.

Now, this known problem of yours: Could I say without being too far off the mark that we could say it had something to do with self-presentation of power and balance in the relationship? The known part of the problem has something to do with the way two people get along? (*pause*) Maybe it doesn't.

MARILYN: No, it doesn't. It has to do with when two people choose to be together.

ERIC: If two people choose to be together . . .

MARILYN: . . . then what? That's my formulation.

ERIC: Okay, let's suppose that that's the way the problem is expressed,

and that the unknown part of it has something to do with the way.
. . . I'll just make this up if you don't mind, for the purpose of an
exercise. Suppose that you have one person of the two-person
relationship taking all the responsibility. One person says, "Well, I'm
the hypnotist; I've got to make your tummy feel better" or, "I've got
to decide whether to be in the relationship or out of it." And let's
suppose that the unknown part of that is the part the other person
plays, that the decisions are also interpersonal in a funny way. This
is just to say that there is an unknown part of the problem.

Now roughly, roughly, roughly, let's say it's a question of how a
person resolves that matter of continuing a relationship or leaving
it or something like that. Suppose that's all we know. Or suppose we
know even less; suppose we just know what I knew with this couple
this morning: They come in and, they say, "We're having trouble in
our marriage." Suppose that's all the mention you get: "Things have
changed between us." Sometimes people are vague, not intentionally, but because that's the closest they can get, and they're fair-
minded, and they say, "There's something different in our marriage"
or, "We've grown apart"—things that people say in long relationships
when they don't want to get into all the details. "There's a problem."

And let's say that we have the kind of odd faith that the solution
is somewhere within the problem. Somewhere within the body of
the dancer is the solution to the matter of putting her feet right,
assuming that there is a way this dance can be done. We'll assume
we have a solvable problem, a resolvable problem. Okay, so far?

We don't know quite what the problem looks like. Four of us
don't know very much about the problem at all, and the fifth
person may or may not know a lot about it. The woman of this
couple that had been married for 40 years told me a story in the
first session. The story was told to exemplify her husband's critical
nature. She has a two-year-old grandchild. She said to the little boy,
"Let's make some cookies." The husband said, "Oh, he's too small
to be able to make cookies." She said, "We're going to do it anyway.
After all, a two-year-old can pour the eggs into the batter after I
crack them; he can stir them up, not perfectly, but he can really
give them a good stir; and he can plop them on the pan." They
went ahead and they baked the cookies, and everyone ate them
with great gusto.

So let's say that there's this problem, but we don't exactly know
what it's like. If you dreamed about a problem and you didn't know
what it was, what would it look like? What's an image of an unknown
problem? You can see that it's there, but you cannot see what's in it.
You see the couple before you, but you don't know what went into
40 years of marriage.

HELEN: A lake. I imagined a lake, a body of water. I couldn't see the fish or the rocks.

ERIC: Okay, you don't know what's under. You see the surface; you see the water, the expanse of it, but you don't know what's in it.

MARILYN: I had an image of a fog, also over a body of water. So, it was both the water and the fog, and things sort of dimly emerging, but I couldn't make out what they were. There were things behind the cloud.

ANN: I had a cloud like a black fire creating smoke. I couldn't see through it. It was framed by white, but it was black.

CATHY: I closed my eyes to try to figure out what this would look like. I saw the image of sort of a combination . . . who is that artist? Escher . . . this thing that comes in, and then you can't tell which one's the black side and which one's the white side, like the image of the Rorschach. Is it a woman? Is it a vase? And you can't tell. That was my image of the problem.

ERIC: Very nice. He'll draw birds turning into fishes, and you can't tell where the birds turn into fishes. I think, because it's Marilyn's image, let's say it's a lake. . . . It's a lake. Now suppose that the solution to this problem comes out of the lake and appears when the fog clears. Suppose you take a look and see what it looks like.

HELEN: Well, I had an instant image when you said "the solution." It was the image of a woman—a woman's body—this very classical, statuesque, tall woman's body coming up out of the lake. I couldn't tell if it was a statue or if it was a woman.

ERIC: And how is she dressed, or is she dressed?

HELEN: There's the sense of nudity, but she is draped in something gauzy, something around her. You can't see her features.

ERIC: Can you see her hair? Short, long, dark, light?

HELEN: It's long. Dark or light? I really can't tell. I really can't see. It's sort of misty, sort of pale, light.

ERIC: Is she carrying anything, or is she unadorned and unencumbered?

HELEN: She's not carrying anything. She's unadorned and unencumbered. It's a very powerful figure, a very strong . . . horrible woman.

ERIC: No kidding, that is a surprise. She's just standing straight up? Does she gesture at all?

HELEN: Turned sort of and looking straight ahead.

ERIC: And the mood about her beside powerful: Is there another feeling you sense about her?

HELEN: Light. There's a sense of light, light coming from her.

ERIC: Now suppose that you pass that image of her to Ann and see what happens with it. You can do that by handing it to her if you like. And suppose you say what you see or feel when you look at this woman and what she does.

ANN: I also see a sword in the lake and this jewel. Everything is glistening as though there's a bright light behind it. She is immersed in the lake as if she's just standing there.

ERIC: And what's the feeling that she conveys to you now?

ANN: It's kind of . . . a feeling of comfort.

ERIC: So there's power and brilliance and comfort, too. Go on.

ANN: Yes, as if all the answers were contained. I feel comforted by the image.

ERIC: And do you see her face, her hair or her gestures?

ANN: Brilliant yellow hair and kind of wavy; kind of serene; no striking features of any kind; no strong feeling, emotion, or anything like that. It's more . . . presence.

ERIC: Do you see her facial features at all—whether her eyes are open or closed, or if her mouth has any particular expression?

ANN: Her eyes are open. Her features are delicate. Her skin is very . . . smooth . . . pretty, very pretty.

ERIC: And what is she doing with the sword? Is she holding it or looking at it or . . .

ANN: No, she's not doing anything with it. It is just there beside her. Light's really reflecting off it. It's sort of part of her and sort of there with her.

ERIC: Now suppose you hand the image to Cathy and see what she says.

CATHY: I can see this woman's statuesque figure coming marching out of this lake. Actually, I can't see the boundaries of the lake, so it feels like an expansive body of water; I have no sense about where it ends or where it begins. I see the sword kind of lying across the top of the water within her reach. I see the way the light from the sky glitters off of it, radiates off of it. I can't see her yellow hair as clearly. It's very interesting, because when she looks out across the horizon there are beautiful golden lights in the distance. They're not necessarily lights from a city or anything, but there is just some beautiful light from a distance; light from the horizon casts a glow on the water.

The image of the woman, when I look closer at her, as you were asking Ann to do, was very odd. She was made of this substance that was very hard, like cement, but she didn't feel rigid. It was just solid and the temperature of it was almost cold, but not cold in an emotional sense; it was cool, but I don't get a feeling of detachment. I get a feeling of a very strong presence on this horizon or on this area. It is almost literally like a statue, and yet there is movement: There is grace, there is serenity, there is incredible wisdom and a very strong, nurturing care-taking sense. But, again, it's like your living room walls, Eric—the texture. It is solid, but you get a sense of softness here.

ERIC: And suppose you convey that to Marilyn.

MARILYN: I'm having a little trouble with this, because as soon as you began talking, I also got the lady of the lake and I had my own image of that, so it's a bit hard to let that one go and fit in your images.

ERIC: You can have them both.

MARILYN: [I see] also a lot of glistening and shimmering light off of her; also, that sense of being a statue, so ideal, almost inhuman. I don't feel the nurturing part as much as the truth part. So there is water that's running off of her; she comes up with all that power, and there's water running off of her, and everything is glistening as well as the jewels and the sword. Actually I saw a chalice; she came up with this chalice.

ERIC: Do you swim?

MARILYN: Do I? So-so. Yes, sort of.

ERIC: Suppose you swim out to the middle.

MARILYN: To her?

ERIC: Yes, unless she will stroll over to you.

MARILYN: No, she's set out there. She sort of comes up like on a dolly or something and down again. (*pause*) Okay, I'm about there. . . . Okay. . . . She is a little bit scary to get close to. She is a very imposing figure, so I want to keep my distance. I want to get close enough to experience her, but not too close—just a little bit farther out.

ERIC: Suppose you go a little bit closer than you think is prudent, just a little bit, just a little bit closer, if that's okay. It's like making a movement that's a little bit like reaching towards imbalance, but you know you can sustain it—sort of like being on a point.

MARILYN: I start to have a feeling of sharing in her power. It's frightening, but also, just looking, I feel some of that. It's like a movement to her or something I'm partaking of.

ERIC: Closer still.

MARILYN: I'm too frightened by her: She's got a chalice in one hand and a sword in the other.

ERIC: Well because she's so occupied (*general laughter*) you might have to get a move on. . . . She can't swim, but you sort of have to keep your distance.

MARILYN: But these are heavy objects, and she is no one to mess with. She brooks—I don't know what that word means—she brooks, she allows no wishy-washyness, no hesitation.

ERIC: That's kind of a truth function, so you are safer with her if you move directly.

MARILYN: If I move directly, then I have to move either toward her or away from her.

ERIC: Toward her is a good idea. Breathe deeply and use everything you know.

MARILYN: (*weeps for a while, then laughs*) I want to get the hell out of here.

ERIC: I appreciate your honesty. That is the truth, isn't it?

MARILYN: That is the truth.

ERIC: But since you've come this far . . .

MARILYN: I was going to say, before, because she'll permit no lies: That's the truth. (*pause*) I'm done.

ERIC: Oh no you're not. I don't think so. I think you'll know when you are. Not quite yet. It was a good try though. You have to remember: You're out in the middle of a lake, and it's a long swim back. You'll need all your strength to go back, so in that funny way, you are compelled to go a little closer.

MARILYN: There are ripples moving out from her still from that powerful entrance, and . . . they are pushing me a little bit away, and I have to stroke over to get closer; I have to use my own energy to get closer. (*long pause*) So I am very close to her, a couple feet away from her. She's just waiting. I'm supposed to do something, but I don't know what. And she's going to disappear; I only have a short period of time.

ERIC: What would you like to do?

MARILYN: Nothing that I can think of.

ERIC: Suppose you get close enough to get up out of the water. You could put your hand on the sword and pull yourself up, or hold onto the cup and pull yourself up.

MARILYN: Okay, I'm standing in the water. Everything's very crystalline clear.

ERIC: Can you see into the chalice?

MARILYN: Yes.

ERIC: What does it look like?

MARILYN: It's glazed . . . red . . . something cold in the bottom. It could go on forever.

ERIC: The feeling of looking into it?

MARILYN: Awe and curiosity and a desire to find something.

ERIC: And when you put your hand on the sword?

MARILYN: It felt like all the energy that Cathy was talking about—tremendous energy. It's sort of hard to get a grip on it with all the jewels and stuff—nubbly little sharp things; they hurt. At the same time, there is so much energy—almost too much energy.

ERIC: And when you hold the chalice in your other hand, how does that feel?

MARILYN: (*long pause*) It's like my conundrum: It's wisdom and love, how to hold them both.

ERIC: Hold them both. Just breathe easy and slow and keep your head up. Breathe nice and slow and just wait. (*long pause*) What do you notice?

MARILYN: There's some sense of circuitry. I connect these two disparate pieces. I feel calm and powerful.

ERIC: And your body feels how?

MARILYN: Solid. A little bit upset, but mostly at peace.

ERIC: Suppose you let the feeling of peace ripple through you.

MARILYN: I just had a thought. Somebody, having looked at my astrological chart many years ago, was talking about how one of my difficulties in working with groups was that I was such an absolutist: that I worked, I talked, cooperation, but absolutely, and was always looking critically. . . . I just seemed to be able to apply those thoughts to what is happening in this relationship: I'm absolutist in my conceptualization of how everything has to be.

ERIC: Now what do you feel like?

MARILYN: Like opening my eyes and getting the attention off of me.

ERIC: Do you want to swim back or stay out there?

MARILYN: I want to acknowledge the lady somehow.

ERIC: You might ask her name so you can ring her up if you want to. Does she have a woman's name?

MARILYN: She is just the lady of the lake.

ERIC: Does she have a name?

MARILYN: I don't know it.

ERIC: Ask her.

MARILYN: Nah, I don't want to ask her. But I can ring her up.

ERIC: As long as you know the way to contact her.

MARILYN: Thank you. . . . I don't know what to do with it now.

ERIC: Comments or questions? I take it you would not like to talk about this right now?

MARILYN: I don't care. No, I could.

HELEN: I feel excited, and lots of feelings. Most amazing to me was that our image of this woman was similar, because as you described it, that's what I saw, too. I also had a very similar image. I didn't see a sword and a chalice; I saw her right hand out like this (*holds her hand out straight*) and her left arm (*holds her other hand at the side*) with sort of the functions of a sword and a chalice.

ERIC: The one hand pointing to truth?

HELEN: With light coming out.

ERIC: And the other by her side?

HELEN: And the other. . . . When I swam, I wasn't really afraid; I was curious, and I swam out in front. It felt kind of powerful pointing at me, so I moved to the nurturing side. There was a little platform, and I climbed up and sat there and felt pretty good right there.

    The other thing that kept coming forward for me was a very powerful, powerful dream I had about twenty years ago. I was standing on top of a mountain or hill looking at this huge yellow moon. I stretched my arms out to the moon and to the light, and I got filled up with the light of the moon. I was standing on this; then I turned around. It's the most wonderful . . . I can't describe this feeling of total fullness of light. Then, I turned around and looked over this vast dark landscape like the desert. I couldn't see anything out there, but I was just glowing. I could hear these voices out there—people saying, "Look at her! There she is!" and coming toward me. In my dream, I got very scared and I ran, and it was sort of like hiding my light under a bushel. I felt such a terribly sad feeling to run away from that, but it was so terrifying to me to be the beacon, to be the light. And talking about power there is this sense of being more able and more willing to be full of light or to be the power.

ERIC: And you can see the courage it took to move that little bit in the water, because it is so terrifying when you approach that, that you really had to swallow hard and stay with it. It takes enormous courage. You were just sitting in a living room, but the interior of that dream is so powerful, and the awesome feeling that everyone described, where you are stunned by the power of it, or her.

CATHY: I noticed that, for me, I either had to participate in your vision and allow myself to let go of any of my own notions about it—to just participate in yours (I don't mean you specifically, Marilyn)—or to allow my experience. I had to make the choice, and so my experience was very different when I was going into it myself. It was like when I couldn't see the yellow hair, but when you were talking about it, I could. When I took it on myself, it was a different experience.

What I wanted to say was that I really felt very moved by sharing your experience. It was in my own way, but I participated with you and felt the struggles, and it felt very intense: It felt very personal, very intimate, and I felt that I went there with you . . . I shared something with you. I felt very awed by your willingness in participating in it and your strength to be able to accept the challenge when you clearly identified some caution and some strong hesitancy. You allowed yourself to be sort of coaxed by Eric, encouraging you to go a little closer, to check things out, and it was just a wonderful experience to witness this. Even though it was in my mind, witnessing your experience, even though you were just sitting in a room and I was just sitting across from you, there was a very real journey that you were going on and going through, and it felt powerful.

ERIC: Side by side with that, you had some other experience of your own, too. What's that?

CATHY: . . . Part of me was detaching so that I could again appreciate your role as the therapist working with her. In other words, I let go of my own experience of the statue when I participated with her. It was very powerful and personal, and it was me. In fact, here it is: It was me. When I was envisioning the statue, I was the statue. It wasn't me looking at her, but I was experiencing it . . .

ERIC: And you had the sword, as well? Anything in the other hand? Oh, the sword was off to the side, so your hands were free. Did your body feel like the way you described, or more like the way Marilyn's did?

CATHY: It felt like this (*touches the wall*), and cool like this, not cold.

ERIC: Cool and soft in appearance, but firm. And then is there a way to describe the emotion you felt standing there?

CATHY: I felt very powerful; I felt very wise; I felt very knowing, very tolerant—maybe that was a better word—nurturing, too, but tolerant, as though I could look off at anything, and even if I felt that what was happening was not what I thought was optimal, there was a tolerance, a knowing that it would work itself out. . . . There was just something that I experienced, just wise and tolerant and at peace, and contemplative but not in any kind of intense way—just that soft focus, but all-encompassing, as though I was observing the world.

ERIC: Like that brightness that you both described at the horizon. And the fog was very bright. And, also, the feeling of peace that you described, when the two hands were together and both energies were consonant, when you were accepting of or tolerant of what there was. Ann?

ANN: I was very much into the image, and when you started to tear, I did, too. It was as if we shared the experience. It was really incredible. I was thinking, also, of that point where, you know, I do cry with my clients. That's how I felt. And I was feeling, as Eric said to approach her because she wasn't going to stroll over to meet you, I walked on water, too, to meet her. You went swimming; I walked on water to meet her, and it surprised me. As you approached her, there was this fear of feeling strong emotion. I felt a strong emotion with you, and I did cry.

As you tried to find a way to approach her, to get closer to her, to experience her, my experience drifted off to focus on the sword. Because when you talked about the sword and the jewels and how difficult sometimes it was to climb out—because it was difficult to grab, because it was so bumpy with the jewels—I saw that. And, for me, the sword was the most striking; it wasn't the woman at the time. And when you talked about the chalice, looking into the chalice, the chalice was very heavy; so I took the sword, and I brought it inside me and I saw it inside me. And as I thought about it, what I felt, more symbolically, was wisdom, because the woman was a statue, and, therefore, for me her face. ... Yes, it was beautiful, but it was perfect, and that's not real to me, and so I couldn't take a reading. But I could take in the sword for some reason, and that maybe is a solution for me—my solution to the unknown problem ... whatever that means.

ERIC: Yes, the feeling of truth is interior; it's inside you.

ANN: ... When I'm being the woman capable of connecting, it's the sword. I don't know whether there's a name for it or not, but I can see the jewel and the tapering. As you say, it's the experience that is called the solution, whatever that is. But that was my experience—very powerful. I felt the sharing and going with you, being frightened with you and being awed, if that's what you felt; but of course, for myself, it was just being overwhelmed by the image; and I could focus on the sword and take that with me. The chalice was too heavy; it was too gaudy, too ornate, too heavy; but the sword felt right. Interesting.

CATHY: I forgot that we had an unknown problem again. (*general laughter*)

ERIC: I don't know what it is.

ANN: We all have a solution now; what are we going to do with it?

MARILYN: We can't find a problem. (*Isis, Eric's cat, has been sitting close to Marilyn throughout the afternoon. She stretches, and walks out of the room.*)

ERIC: Well, as though it were an aspect that you wouldn't know. (*pause*) Isis the cat was very patient with you, Marilyn. She stayed and stayed and stayed. She's a gentle cat, used to having her own way. (*pause*) Any questions about this from the point of view of hypnosis, before we stop? Any oddities or questions?

ANN: Well, what is striking to me is the sharing of the images and the emotions. Is there a healing effect or anything that happens if you share that, even if you don't talk about it?

CATHY: This feels to me almost like a more powerful way to work in a therapeutic sense than to work with hypnosis. This is what I like. I love watching Eric work with someone and there is a dialogue; because the thing I don't really care for in hypnosis is that there doesn't seem to be a dialogue. And that is the interesting piece that I struggled with for a while: At the end, part of me wanted to talk about it and figure it out and come to some sort of resolution or conclusion, but there was something that had just happened that I needed to just let sit. In fact, once you said to me, while you were doing this very type of work with me on a dream image, "Go to sleep; sleep on it," while I was sitting in a chair working on it. I thought, "Oh boy, okay," and I did and I came up, and it was all fresh again and there was more material.

ERIC: See, Cathy is kind, too. She thought, "Well that's really stupid. But, okay, it seems to make sense to him. I'll try it." It's awfully nice of you.

CATHY: But it worked, and I guess what I just want to say is that this seems to me from the experiential point ... and from the therapist's position, to be a very powerful way to work with people. You can deal with issues without having to identify them, and in a very powerful, personal, impacting way; at least that's what it felt like for me, and this seems like something that I could use in my own work—in my own sessions with families or people—more comfortably than hypnosis.

ERIC: Yes, although I swear to you on Erickson's book that this *is* hypnosis, and this is the way Erickson did it, too, for that matter [Rosen, 1982]. If you just read transcripts like in that book, they are conversations. You don't get the full impact of that in a group, but, for example, in the tape that I played of working with one person, you sure get a conversational feel to it.

The interesting thing to me is that the standing of the person with the troubles, in this case whatever you are trying to sort out in your life with your partner, is very elevated here. Everyone feels the bravery of the person who is troubled, the inventiveness, the beauty of the feeling of that person.

My conviction, from doing this a lot, is that if you walked in somewhere with a group of sympathetic people and said, "Look, I'm having this trouble with my partner. Here's the trouble: That guy or woman is this, this, this, and I am this, this, this, and I can't decide," there would be a very big mix of feelings toward you or around you. One would be sympathetic, but one would also be thinking, "Gee, what could she do? Maybe she should do this. Where did this come from?" There would be the confusion of multifaceted views.

This way, you had many different emotions in a short span of time, and everyone was right along with you in her or his own particular way. It was a very equal sort of experience, so that you weren't the identified patient in a bad sense. You were somebody heroically pursuing something very difficult. It's a whole different sense.

And so everyone got to remember heroic instances (*looking around the room*): You've taken the sword. You become the woman. You remembered that marvelous dream and the courage it took to stand in the full moon and feel filled that way and be seen to be doing that.

This is the difficulty we talked about at the beginning today—the difficulty of being visibly the person with power, and, especially as a woman, being seen to be powerful in that way, or being seen to be decisive, or being seen to tell the truth and stay with it, to have the interior truth, or to offer an unfathomable mystery. . . . These are very powerful experiences, which you share very naturally if you are in the dream together, or passing around the crystal—same thing; whereas if you hear it as a set of problems some poor person has, "Oh God, I've got troubles with my girlfriend or boyfriend," it's very hard to feel as thoroughly as Ann did here. You tend to make distinctions instead of cooperative kinds of approaches.

CATHY: And it feels to me like the person, in this case you, Marilyn . . . my observation of you is coming from a powerful place where you are in control of the image and what you are going to do with it, as opposed to someone who could sit there and tell this story and say, "Oh poor me, poor me" or, "Gee, I don't know what I'm going to do."

ERIC: Or, "What's the matter with me? I can't decide" or any of those kinds of things.

CATHY: It completely bypasses that, and I just see your strength and your struggle, your participation in that in a decisive, meaningful [way] where I get a sense of you as being in control of things.

ERIC: And of being powerful. I think that's fair to say: By your expression

of feeling and what you decided to do by agreeing to go further and
so on, you have a powerful and positive effect on everyone, and
everyone feels gracefully able to participate.

See, you don't run into the things that you would identify as
codependent problems in working this way, like who is helping
whom and who is doing what, because nobody benefited more than
anybody else. Everyone is equally and gracefully moved. Another
thing I like is that each person is demonstrably individual; your
experience and yours are individual. Even though they are very close
in feeling, you wouldn't mistake one for the other. Yours is clearly
Helen's way, and yours is clearly Marilyn's, and each of ours is our
own in that way.

MARILYN: I am trying to remember what you [Eric] suggested or asked,
when you [Helen] first came up with the lady and with the female
figure. Do you remember?

HELEN: What do you see? You are looking at the lake, and what do you see?

ERIC: Yes, what do you see? You'll see the solution.

MARILYN: You said?

CATHY: I think you did suggest that something would come up out of the
lake.

HELEN: Did you see a woman as a solution?

MARILYN: Yes.

ERIC: The solution to the unknown problem would appear as a something.

ANN: I saw just a parting of my cloud as a bright light and then put the
woman onto the original.

MARILYN: I saw the woman, I said the lady of the lake, and then you
said . . .

HELEN: When you said, "Something will come up out of the lake," I didn't
have my eyes shut; that was just there.

ERIC: It's really convincing and interesting that way. I always think that
people spend so much time . . . in the kind of psychotherapy we are
all taught to do, you could spend weeks and months trying to identify
the problem and its origins and searching into yourself and, "What
are you not facing?" I've heard beginning therapists say things like,
"What are you afraid of looking at in yourself?" and, "What are you
running from?" as though there were some kind of dark, unconscious, horrible thing that you couldn't get in touch with and, "Maybe
it's a memory; did something happen to you when you were little?"
All of which may be true of a person; but you just *saw* it, and then
it's so convincing, because then what comes out of your unconscious
is this marvelous dream, these very sympathetic feelings, your sense

of yourself as a woman and person. And all of that comes, not as a kind of scraggly, difficult matter but as something you can start to use. That's why I like this, too. It's so immediate that it's convincing. You are not thinking, "Well, I wonder if it's this or that; well, I can't really decide because it's this on this end and that on that end." You just grabbed it with both hands and said, "There it is," and once you did that . . .

That's why I like this, either with a naturally occurring dream or one you make up by looking for it. It pops up. If you have the black box with the lid open, it is what comes out. It's not Pandora's box but the box with the solution . . . and the solution to the problem comes out because the solution is down in the unknown problems; and it really is, too, in a real way. Even though people give lip service to that, you can experience it.

FOLLOW-UP

In June of 1993, I spoke with Marilyn by phone. She told me that she is still with her partner, and that they have bought a house together. She says that she is happy.

REFERENCES

Andersen, T. (Ed.). (1991). *The Reflecting Team: Dialogues and Dialogues about the Dialogues*. New York: Norton.

Bateson, G. (1972). *Steps to an Ecology of Mind*. New York: Aronson.

Boscolo, L., Cecchin, G., Hoffman, L., & Penn, P. (1987). *Milan Systemic Family Therapy: Conversations in Theory and Practice*. New York: Basic Books.

Freud, S. (1935). *An Autobiographical Study* (J. Strachey, Trans.). New York: Norton.

Furman, B., & Ahola, T. (1992). *Solution Talk: Hosting Therapeutic Conversations*. New York: Norton.

Greenleaf, E. (1977). Active imagining. In J. L. Singer & K. S. Pope (Eds.), *The Power of Human Imagination: New Techniques of Psychotherapy*. New York: Plenum.

Haley, J. (1987). *Problem-Solving Therapy*. San Francisco: Jossey-Bass.

Jerison, H. J. (1976). Paleoneurology and the evolution of mind. *Scientific American, January*, 90–101.

Rosen, S. (Ed.). (1982). *My Voice Will Go with You: The Teaching Tales of Milton H. Erickson, M.D.* New York: Norton.

Rossi, E. L. (Ed.). (1980). *The Collected Papers of Milton H. Erickson on Hypnosis*. New York: Irvington.

White, M., & Epston, D. (1990). *Narrative Means to Therapeutic Ends*. New York: Norton.

Wittgenstein, L. (1958). *The "Blue" and "Brown" Books*. New York: Harper & Row.

CHAPTER 13

Solution-Focused Therapy with a Case of Severe Abuse

YVONNE DOLAN

A stalking, rape, and assault survivor, Cindy came to therapy requesting help in overcoming symptoms of severe depression exacerbated by extended and horrific physical, emotional, and sexual abuse. The process of pursuing legal charges against the perpetrator had taken her nearly three years, and she was feeling emotionally depleted and suicidal. Cindy described a past history of six psychiatric hospitalizations for depression. Her previous treatment had included a series of electric shock treatments. While these details were respectfully noted by the therapist in response to Cindy's self-description, they were not emphasized in her therapy. Rather, a solution-focused approach (Berg, 1994; de Shazer, 1982, 1984, 1985, 1988; de Shazer, Berg, Lipchik, Nunnally, Molnar, Gingerich, & Weiner-Davis, 1986; Lipchik & de Shazer, 1986; O'Hanlon & Weiner-Davis, 1989) was taken. The purpose of this chapter is to illustrate how some methods of solution-focused therapy can be used to effectively treat the results of severe trauma.

Victims of severe abuse, whether it be physical, emotional, or sexual, tend, as a natural psychological defense response, to develop a rigid associational compartmentalization in reference to traumatic experiences (Dolan, 1985, 1989, 1991). This compartmentalization begins when the victim dissociates from the experience of the abuse at the time of its occurrence. Such dissociation is understandable since, many times, it is the client's only means of psychological survival. If left untreated, this dissociation and resulting compartmentalization tends to recur later in life whenever the client is thinking about the original trauma, responding to new trauma, or experiencing events that are literally or symbolically reminiscent of a previous trauma. Consequently, the trauma survivor is unable to access and utilize much needed internal resources at the very times they are most needed. One way to understand associational compartmentalization is in the everyday tendency for thoughts to trigger related associations. As a client observed, "When things are going well, in my relationship with my husband, or in my life in general, I tend to be aware of his virtues, and the memories of other times in my life when things have gone well. On the other hand, when we are fighting, I tend to remember all kinds of examples of his shortcomings, the difficult times we have had in our relationship, and all the other things that have gone badly and painfully in my life. When I am thinking of positive things, it is hard to remember the negative and vice versa."

Associational compartmentalization, if not corrected, prolongs the negative perceptual and behavioral consequences of the abuse indefinitely. This compartmentalized way of thinking tends to be more rigid in victims of trauma, and the difficulties Cindy describes typify this phenomenon. Specifically, Cindy describes herself as literally having "amnesia" for her resources. Following a depressive episode, she tells the therapist, "I need to set up some systems so that I don't develop amnesia for the good things in my life."

Solution-focused work with survivors of severe abuse is multifaceted, and extended discussion of various issues is available in Dolan (1991). In the following excerpts, taken from three consecutive weekly sessions, the reader will find illustrations of how solution-focused therapy can be an effective tool for empowering clients to overcome rigid compartmentalization and other symptoms of post-traumatic stress in order to assist them in moving forward towards a more satisfying future.

The client had been seen by the therapist (who in this case was Charles Johnson, MSW) on four previous occasions with his Solution Group team. The approach, in which the team sits behind a one way mirror, consults with the therapist, and asks questions and gives messages, was influenced by and is similar to the Milwaukee Brief Family Therapy Center team model. The four sessions with the team in which Cindy was seen previously focused on strengthening Cindy sufficiently so that she could testify against the perpetrator in court. The sessions excerpted here took place shortly after her successful court testimony. Although Cindy was seen without the team in these sessions, the therapist still used the previous positive effects of the team's predicting their being favorably impressed by Cindy's continued progress.

The following excerpts, taken from transcripts of the three consecutive sessions with Cindy, illustrate how techniques derived from solution-focused therapy can be effective for treatment of severely traumatized clients.[1]

[1]Since no mention of contingency arrangements for suicidal feelings is made within the transcripts excerpted here, I want to clarify that the therapist and client had already established an agreement that the client could and would immediately telephone him or his on-call service if she was in any danger of hurting herself.

SESSION ONE

[Since the goal of previous sessions had been to prepare the client to withstand court testimony, and this goal has now been accomplished, the therapist begins this session by asking the client for a redefinition of the therapeutic goal.]

THERAPIST: How would you know this session was helpful? What do you think would be most helpful?

CLIENT: Maybe some validation. It's like he's revictimizing me again. He might only get three months in jail . . .

[Now the therapist begins a line of questioning intended to help the client provide herself with some validation. The assumption is that, out of respect, any meaning attached to the client's statements should be elicited from her, rather than applied by the therapist, and, by extension, self-validation should be elicited from the client, rather than arbitrarily given by the therapist.]

THERAPIST: What does it say about you that you've held on for nearly three years in pursuit of justice, what does that say about you?

CLIENT: That I'm tenacious, that I did not buckle under pressure.

THERAPIST: What kind of person doesn't buckle under pressure?

CLIENT: Someone that is strong, has a good sense of their values. Somebody that wants to make things better for herself, even if it gets worse first. Someone who just wasn't going to take it lying down.

[Now the therapist asks the client to define what difference this self-validation makes.]

THERAPIST: And what difference does knowing that about yourself make for you?

CLIENT: I think once I'm fully recovered and not even feeling fear of [the perpetrator] or anyone related to [the perpetrator], I'll have less fear of failure in any endeavor, I'll be more willing to take risks like in writing a book . . .

[The therapist now shifts to solution-defining questions.]

THERAPIST: What would be some of the signs to you that you're healing from this?

CLIENT: A month will go by, and I will suddenly wake up and realize that I didn't think about anything that's happened to me.

THERAPIST: Didn't think about anything at all?

CLIENT: I won't flash back to violence. I'm not filled with rage at injustices. . . . You know, I'll start seeing that other side, that there's even life beyond advocacy.

THERAPIST: Really. Tell us more about that.

CLIENT: I think that, uh, you know, the things that I've been working on politically now and with a domestic violence support group, really it's like a catharsis for me. It helps me get over it. And I know that somewhere out there it's beyond getting over it. And eventually I'm going to move onto things other than advocacy. I think that advocacy will teach me more things about myself than what to do about this. I just see it another empowerment path. I don't see it as the end.

[The therapist now pursues further clarification through systemic solution-focused questions:]

THERAPIST: Anything else that would let you know that you are healing?

CLIENT: Yeah. I would feel safe to have sex again. (*pause*) Because I don't right now. It's too scary to make myself that vulnerable. And not to have the fear of flashing back during sex. I also think that other people might tell me. . . . Input from other people, you know. That other people might tell me that, "Gee, it's really nice to see you've really got beyond this." I think that I'll reach that point, and it will be obvious to them.

THERAPIST: How will it be obvious to them?

CLIENT: Because it just won't be the subject of discussion that I bring up anymore.

THERAPIST: What will you be talking about instead?

CLIENT: Oh, well, normal things that everybody else talks about, whether its goofiness or more serious stuff. You know, like everybody else talks about. I mean, people out there talk about sports and movies and politics and life dreams and goofy gossip and you know . . .

THERAPIST: Well, those are some good things.

CLIENT: I want to get to the point where I can experience [happiness] without it being related to victories with things that are related to [perpetrator].

THERAPIST: What would be going on if that happened? I'm curious.

CLIENT: Well, I'd be happy 'cause I got a letter from my grandma, or you know one of my favorite movies that I never thought would make it to network TV is on. Or, you know, taking an exhilarating swim or a nice sunset or things that I just want to open myself up to, experience like that.

SESSION TWO

[Instead of immediately asking the client what is going better, for the purpose of identifying exceptions to the problem, the therapist first asks a neutral question. In working with severely traumatized clients, I have found that in some, but not all cases it is important to begin with neutrality, rather than immediately pursuing a proactive line of questioning. This avoids the potential risk of inadvertently trivializing or discounting the client's suffering. However, at first opportunity, the therapist respectfully shifts emphasis to the resources and potential solutions inherent in what is better about today than yesterday. I believe that to spend more time than necessary on descriptions of the client's pain, rather than the pursuit of the solution to the pain, would be just as disrespectful and trivializing as failing to acknowledge the pain in the first place.]

THERAPIST: How are you doing?

CLIENT: Better than yesterday. Yesterday was real rough.

THERAPIST: What makes today better than yesterday?

CLIENT: I'm running errands with a friend of mine. She dropped me off. Yesterday, I was closed in all day avoiding people. Pretty rough last night.

THERAPIST: Do I need to know something about that?

[Rather than assuming that he should focus on the problem of yesterday's depression, the therapist instead asks the client whether he needs more information about it.]

CLIENT: Well, I was suicidal last night.

[Taking the client's cue, the therapist now asks for more information. As a result, the therapist and client now define a different problem, that of dealing with a bully.]

THERAPIST: What was going on?

CLIENT: Just neighborhood crap and spiraling thinking, and the bully in the complex was throwing her considerable weight around and . . . just that, I feel like I went from one asshole to another. And this woman, I got like five hang-up phone calls from her yesterday, and she's going around intimidating everybody. And she filed a false pot-smoking complaint against one of my friends. And my friends who have resolved to stand up to this . . . bitch, quite frankly, have now lost their resolve because they have children. And they figure if she is vindictive enough to call the cops and say so-and-so was seen smoking pot outside, then she's vindictive enough to make anonymous calls to social services and make false allegations of neglect and abuse.

THERAPIST: Okay, I want to get back to you. So you were feeling suicidal last night. That was kind of one state that you were in.

CLIENT: Yeah.

THERAPIST: And how are you today?

CLIENT: Tired and low energy. Not very cheerful.

[The therapist now returns to solution-focused questions designed to help the client identify any useful existing or potential solutions inherent in the difference between today and yesterday.]

THERAPIST: And what is your perception of what makes today different than yesterday?

CLIENT: Well, I called my friend Jo . . . and you know, she spent about an hour and a half on the phone with me last night and helped me to calm myself and . . . having her support. And she kind of helped put some things back into perspective about the bully in the apartment complex, too.

THERAPIST: How was it helpful for you?

CLIENT: I guess it helped validate me when I didn't have the strength to validate myself.

THERAPIST: And what difference did that make when you felt validated by some outside source?

CLIENT: It just made me feel like I wasn't going nuts, that this indeed was happening and that other people saw it. And other people were, like me, were not willing to be intimidated by her, unlike the other residents, who understandably chickened out. And, you know, Jo is a very astute person and has only met this bully once and yet was able to lay a lot of observations on the line that were on the mark. And she also kind of helped me see a bit of sense of humor about the situation.

THERAPIST: Really? Tell me about that.

CLIENT: Oh, just, you know, because this bully has been telling everybody, "You better tell Cindy to watch her ass because I'm ready for a big confrontation with her." Which is not a good time for me right now, because my depression has been so up to the surface. And I just know that I'm vulnerable. And . . . Jo made suggestions like, make 3-by-5 cards, and if she decides to confront me, Okay, [I] whip these cards out of the purse, and oh yes, and so.

[At this point the therapist takes a moment to joke with the client. While there is no direct therapeutic purpose to the humor, it serves to enhance a context of warmth and friendliness that I have found to be helpful in allowing a use survivors to feel safe in therapy settings.]

THERAPIST: That's how Ronald Reagan ran the presidency for eight years: 3-by-5 cards.

CLIENT: (*laughs*) Really? That's scary!

THERAPIST: Sure.

[The client now begins to spontaneously describe a possible solution to her problem.]

CLIENT: But you know, and if she . . . I have nasty cards. Like, if she starts getting nasty, I have nasty cards and, "Oh are you going to back-stab me again like you did on May 22nd, 1992?" And then, mention four or five of those things and, "Hey Linda, it's up to you, do you want to push it that far? Because, if you do, I've got the cards for it!" And we just had some jokes about her alcoholism, you know, because when she drinks, she gets bolder. And laughing about coming out and saying, "Gee, Linda, it's 10 A.M. and how many drinks have you had?"

THERAPIST: So even in the midst of this depression, you were able to grab on to some humor. What do you think that means that you were able to do that?

CLIENT: That I have a lot of strength and inner resources, and that after I felt validated I was able to see the lighter side of something I had been viewing very darkly.

THERAPIST: Uh huh. Well, let's do some measurement here. Let's say a 1 is so depressed that you're a rock, a slug, or whatever. And a 10 is like you'd be Mary Tyler Moore on angel dust . . . so happy. (*client laughs*) Where were you on that scale before you talked to your friend Jo?

CLIENT: Oh my God, I was right on the brink of 1.

THERAPIST: And after you talked to Jo?

CLIENT: About a 2½.

THERAPIST: And how about right now?

CLIENT: About a 4.

THERAPIST: About a 4. And so you've gone from a 1 to a 4 in, would you say, less than 24 hours?

CLIENT: Yeah.

THERAPIST: What do you make of that? How did you do that? I'm curious.

CLIENT: Well, I think I got down so low that I was, like, really scared. And my Mom was, like, threatening hospitalization, and that had something to do with it, too, because I promised myself I would never go into the state hospital again. And I'm just relieved to snap back. And I think that although I felt totally out of control, I could recognize that I haven't been this low for about a year and a half. And I could recognize that, even though I get this low and it's really scary, I could recognize that I'm able to pull away from it.

THERAPIST: So there is something to be learned from it?

CLIENT: Yeah.

THERAPIST: And what would that be?

CLIENT: That I have more control over it than I think I do. And that I need to set some systems up in place so I don't develop amnesia about the good things in my life. Like Jo was also suggesting 3-by-5 cards where I write down all the good things I've done in my life and powerful moments. It was bad yesterday. I did not eat, period. Cried and cried and cried. And it was like I developed this amnesia or something. And just felt like I didn't have the strength to do any self nurturing things like spend time . . . or play relaxation tapes or anything. It was all I could do to try and keep my mind off of things and that was a big battle, too.

THERAPIST: So did Jo come over spontaneously?

CLIENT: Today?

THERAPIST: No, last night.

CLIENT: I called her about 10:45.

THERAPIST: So you were down, and still able to call someone.

CLIENT: Right.

THERAPIST: What do you make of that?

CLIENT: That I have good self-preservation instincts. I was feeling really, like, spontaneous or, I'm trying to think of the word, when you get to that point where you're just not thinking and you say to yourself, "If there is one more thing, I'm going to blow my brains out . . ."

THERAPIST: And?

CLIENT: And, I reached that point and I said, "No! No! No! You're not going to push yourself over the edge." And that's where I called her.

THERAPIST: Cindy, is it different for you not to push yourself over the edge?

CLIENT: No. I always kind of hit that brink and then I pull myself back. Because no matter how dark things get in my depression, I instinctively know that something about the next day will be better. And that some people will be very sad at my leaving and. . . . It's really good, too: Every time I get that suicidal, I really want to leave behind a note explaining why. . . . And usually these explanations would take up six pages. And I don't have the energy to crank out a six-page suicide note. It's goofy, but I never want to commit suicide without leaving this lengthy, well-worded explanation as to why and ... (*laughs*) I always get to the point that when I am feeling that suicidal I just don't have the wherewithal to sit down and write something like that. It's absurd.

THERAPIST: Well, I don't know if it is absurd. I think that is very fascinating, that you can't do that without leaving this big note. What does the big note mean?

CLIENT: Well, in all honesty, the note always means placing blame and taking blame away. Placing blame on the situation and the people. And usually when I am feeling suicidal it's because I am feeling so angry and so helpless and powerless in a situation. So part of the note would be placing blame on the events or people that I'm so agitated about and the other part is to console and reassure loved ones that they had nothing to do with my decision. 'Cause, you know, I was suicidal last week, and had told my Mom about it. And the look in her eyes, even the next day after I had told her, really pointed to me how traumatic it would be for her.

THERAPIST: What would you be doing differently if you were a 5? You're a 4 now?

CLIENT: Probably take a shower. 'Cause I've been out and about today. I'd take care of some business, make a couple of phone calls I need to make. And would feel more confident in going home if the bully is waiting to ambush me. No matter where it happened, I would make that ground my turf. That kind of thing. It's something I've really been grappling with, Charlie. I don't understand it. It's like, in some ways I've really been growing by leaps and bounds, metaphysically, spiritually, physically, intellectually, politically, socially. And then, in juxtaposition, there's this other part of me that's really as low as I was a year and a half ago.

THERAPIST: So you kind of have these two states?

CLIENT: Yeah.

THERAPIST: The one state—or the 1.5 state, I guess we should call it. And what would we call the other state?

CLIENT: Potential for 10 and bursting the edges of 8.

THERAPIST: So, call it an 8 state?

CLIENT: Yeah.

THERAPIST: Well, let's talk about it. Can we talk about that a little bit?

CLIENT: Yeah. It's, like, I get real angry with myself for being depressed, like I feel just awful and start chastising myself, "You have the power to control this, why are you creating this?" And I just don't feel like

I have the strength. I mean deep, deep down I know I can do it. I mean I *know* I can do it. And I don't know what it is in me that doesn't allow myself to do it. The depression fulfills some needs for me or else I wouldn't be so reluctant to give it up.

THERAPIST: I'm kind of curious about that because you've told me that you are on disability. And one of the things you were frightened about was losing the disability, and. . . . How depressed do you have to be to be convinced that you could keep the disability?

CLIENT: Right.

THERAPIST: How undepressed or antidepressed can you be without losing your disability? Can you be an 8 without losing your disability?

CLIENT: I think so. Unless, the local TV station follows me around with a camcorder and sees me leaping in the streets or something.

THERAPIST: Exactly. Yeah, I'm curious about that 8 state. And what are the influences that go into having you be in that state, that 8 state?

CLIENT: Lots of self-talk.

THERAPIST: Self-talk?

CLIENT: Yeah, and lots of self-nurturance and doing the right things for myself. Working with my planet [a self-hypnosis technique], doing relaxation techniques, keeping myself busy, and always expanding my growth and experience, but still allowing myself to have time to kick back and take a break. It's like a true balance.

[The "planet" is an associational cue (Dolan, 1985, 1989, 1991) based on the client's ability to use a technique in which she fixes her gaze on a little marble and vividly imagines and experiences the safety and security of being within that very lovely peaceful environment depicted within the marble, a safe "planet," where all is well and nothing can harm her. She was taught this in the first of her previous sessions in front of the team. For a detailed discussion of the use of similar associational cues for treatment of trauma symptoms see Dolan (1991).

THERAPIST: How do you do the self-talk, and what do you mean by that? And how does it happen when you do it?

CLIENT: Just giving myself validation. You know, what you're doing is the right thing, or a pat on the back like "you really dealt with that situation or that person appropriately and maturely." Seeing very nasty things about people but viewing it from the viewpoint of "pat on the back, good for you for seeing that, that's their problem and not yours," which is just the opposite of what I do when I'm depressed. Just being my own best friend.

THERAPIST: Is there a trigger that gets you into the self-talk?

CLIENT: It just kind of seems to happen automatically.

THERAPIST: So, it's unpredictable?

CLIENT: I think ultimately it isn't but . . .

THERAPIST: Ultimately it isn't. Tell me more.

CLIENT: Well, I mean I just feel that I need to look at what error it is that this depression fills my needs. I don't mean staying depressed to stay on disability. I mean looking at what needs the depression fulfills. I just know if I'm really honest with myself, I have the capability to not make feeling good an unexplained wispy little thing that I can't seem to grasp. I know its graspable and it's within reach. But, you know, when I'm in the pits of despair, I mean it's just like not even having the energy to write a suicide note, I don't have the energy to go to my purse and pull my marble out [the device for soothing self-hypnosis described earlier] . . .

THERAPIST: So, I'm curious. Do you know . . . when you start to spiral down? Can you predict that?

CLIENT: Yes. Most of the time.

THERAPIST: Most of the time.

CLIENT: Yeah.

THERAPIST: And what are the predictive states for that?

CLIENT: Like an outside stressor will happen. And then, sometimes, I'm actually able to see it as an outside stressor, and, like, I'll tell myself, "This is not important and deserving of your time and attention right now." This is exactly what happened yesterday. I woke up yesterday feeling good, and I was going to go take care of some business and go work at my brother's office for a while. And I had even taken a shower and laid out an outfit to put on. And then there was new crap in the apartment complex, an outside stressor. And I basically told myself it's not worthy of your attention, you're going to finish getting dressed and call Mike and see if this is a good time to come down to the office. And then there was this noise and people were screaming at each other.

THERAPIST: So. . . . what would you call that? Was that a tip, was that a hint that . . .

CLIENT: Yeah, it was a hint, it was like, "Try to keep things in perspective and don't let this detract from your goals today." There were more outside stressors. And I just started in gradations giving into it . . . hang up phone calls and all that. And then I was just . . .

THERAPIST: So there were times in the past when you've licked that spiraling down.

CLIENT: Yeah.

THERAPIST: Can you tell me about that?

CLIENT: Uh, just similar kinds of situations. I'm actually able to shelve it and put it into perspective. Have the big perspective picture and just look at from the point of view that this is simply not worthy of my attention. And one thing that Jo said to me, you know. She said, "This is a major thing in your life right now, dealing with this bully, but," she said, "when you're 83 years old and looking back on your life, if you even bother to think about the incidents, you're going to think about how you grew as a person, how you dealt with this bitch and, if anything, about how she aggravated you." So, although I don't always think about it, specifically in terms of this old Cindy looking back, it's that big picture perspective.

THERAPIST: That's interesting. There's this 8 state and there's this 1.5 state. There's this depressed state and there's this antidepressed state, isn't there?

CLIENT: Yeah. The 8 state seems to be much more involved with the big picture.

THERAPIST: Yeah. What do you think the odds are, if you could predict in the next week this 1.5 state?

CLIENT: You mean predicting its occurrence?

THERAPIST: Yeah.

CLIENT: I think that there's still a potential for it and it's just so bizarre, Charlie. I just had this flash on some of the things that depression does for me. Sometimes, it the only way I can assert to others, leave me alone, absolve me of responsibilities.

THERAPIST: What does the other state do for you, the antidepressed state?

CLIENT: In the first place, I'm just more capable of taking on responsibilities. I'm also capable of saying I don't want to become involved with this particular thing because of whatever—I've got too much going on, it's not that interesting, whatever.

THERAPIST: So either state lets you have a boundary? It kind of creates boundaries for you?

CLIENT: Yeah.

THERAPIST: I was curious about what state you would rather be in to get away from things. Or, to put distance between yourself and things. In the 8 state pretending to be in the 1 state, in the 1 state, or maybe in the 8 state, just being in the 8 state? What would be the best for you in terms of not taking so much out of you and enhancing your life?

CLIENT: 8 in the 8.

THERAPIST: 8 in the 8.

CLIENT: Or maybe 8 in the 1.

THERAPIST: 8 pretending [to be] 1?

CLIENT: Yeah, when necessary. Because, being a 1, I feel that it's life-threatening and it jeopardizes so many things, the goofiest of things, like, I haven't gone grocery shopping for two weeks and so I'm out of food. Being an 8, or an 8 masquerading as a 1, I'd still get things done and I would feel better about being assertive in a more clear and forthright way.

THERAPIST: Makes a lot of sense, doesn't it?

CLIENT: It's kind of hard to talk about, to be real honest with you about it, because these are things that I would not ever discuss with anyone.

THERAPIST: Yeah, I want you to know I really appreciate you doing that. As always, you're very articulate about yourself and your states . . . and it's very heartfelt stuff. I appreciate that about you. . . . (pause) I've got some homework for you. So . . . here's the homework. It's going to be kind of extensive, is that okay?

CLIENT: Yeah.

THERAPIST: What I want you to do is this . . . I want you, and this is the suggestion your friend Jo gave you, which I really agree with. I would like you to make up one set of cards, self-talk cards. Now the state I would like you to make this up in is not a 1.5 state. I would like you to be in at least a 5 state when you write them.

CLIENT: When I write them.

THERAPIST: Yeah, and what I'd like are those things about you that really convince you that you have this inner strength. And I don't want you to fill out the whole card. Just flash cards that you can use to remind yourself.

CLIENT: Okay.

THERAPIST: Then, I'd like you to write something that a friend of mine calls a "Rainy Day Letter" [Dolan, 1991]. This is a letter to yourself, into the future. And I think this should be from a 6, a 7, or an 8 state. And remember those postcards we've all heard about, "Dear so-and-so, Dear Cindy, having a great time, wish you were here"? What I'd like you to do is write to yourself [in the future] in a 1.5 state from an 8 state, something like, "Dear Cindy, here's what it's like to be in this 8 state right now. Wish you were here." Just so you don't have amnesia for what it can be like. So, write about the things you're doing and enjoying, like the things with your dog, your friends, the sun, how you feel about yourself . . .

CLIENT: (*laughs*) That's real interesting.

THERAPIST: Yeah, so it's like a postcard from yourself to your future from your past, which will also be your future. It's kind of interesting. And, I'm almost getting myself confused here . . . if you feel yourself slipping or unbalanced just a little bit, I want you to get out the flashcards and use them. Keep flashing through them. So I want you to use that. And I want you to use that Rainy Day Letter in case of emergencies. I want you to seal it, and I want you to put it in your purse. And the last thing, and this is just optional. What I'd like is for you to do things with the 8 and the 8 pretending to be 1 and the 1.5. I'd like you to think about those things and how you could best use them for yourself.

[Here the therapist utilizes the client's previous relationship with the team for encouragement and support.]

Therapist: And know that I and the team continue to be amazed by these two states . . .

SESSION THREE

[In this session, after the therapist begins by mentioning some observable and presumably positive changes in the client's behavior and appearance, it is the client who immediately shifts to a solution-focused direction which focuses on identifying and describing the solutions that she has experienced since the previous session as a result of her homework.]

THERAPIST: I'm fascinated by this, Cindy, quite honestly. And I want to get your homework, but you . . . look really different than you did last session. What's going on with you? 'Cause you look really different. Your makeup looks different. Your hair looks different. What's different for you?

CLIENT: The homework really helped.

THERAPIST: Can you tell me about that?

CLIENT: A lot. A lot. Well some of the homework I started working on as soon as I left here last week. And some of it I did Tuesday and finished off yesterday. And I've had a lot of, like, contemplation time. And, yesterday, when I finished my cards, I kept going through them, and . . . what I think I need to do for myself is, because what you had told me was look at these cards when you're slipping, and what I've seen is that I should look at them all the time.

THERAPIST: What difference did the homework make for you?

CLIENT: It reminded me of my strengths and my goals and who I truly am, not even ego, but who I am spiritually and soul-wise, who I am. And it put some things in perspective. And I've been real successful this week at setting boundaries for myself and setting boundaries for others. ... And that kind of helped ground me. And the cards helped bring that through. And it felt good to set boundaries with people.

THERAPIST: What difference did that make?

CLIENT: The cards helped me to stick to the boundaries I set, but also to make it easier for myself and the other person . . .

THERAPIST: Did you bring the cards?

CLIENT: (*begins digging in purse for cards*) It really calmed me down with that bully that lives in the complex. She just tried playing a nonverbal game with some heavy implications. I recognized what she was trying to do.

THERAPIST: So, what weapon did you use to do that?

CLIENT: Well, if I'd been down, I would have gone back inside. Instead, I stayed on my friend's porch. I was aware of her but I just continued my conversation with my friend. I will not let her browbeat me into my apartment.

THERAPIST: So, what do we call this?

CLIENT: Boundaries. One of the cards says, "This is my turf." And I remember thinking of that. This is a postcard I wrote to myself:

Dear Cindy, I wish you were here. I've been having a wonderful time doing things that make me feel good.

Here are my flashcards:

I have the love and support of family and friends.
Baki bird [her dog]
Whatever I'm seeking in life, it's seeking me.
I'm aligned with the infinite spirit.
I will command and radiate respect.
This is my turf.

and I underlined *my turf*, that's a real boundary setter.

Warriors rest between battles.
54321 [relaxation exercise]
I am accessing my personal power.
I am an ex-victim.
I love myself.
I am strong and resilient.

THERAPIST: I'm fascinated that you referred to yourself as an ex-victim. This is the first time I've heard you say this. How did this come about?

CLIENT: It really came about after I got out of this last depressive funk. Because, I saw that I was victimizing myself with—especially with—the condo bully. And you know I still do it, I still hide behind my drapes. I do not feel safe in opening them. And I still check my car for nails and bombs [because of stalker] before I enter it. And I think that I'll do that for a long, long time. And part of me really resents it, but part of me feels that it's necessary for my safety. But the rest of it—I'm tired of it. I'm tired of the not answering my phone, screening my calls, I'm tired of the, "Oh, gee, it's dark outside, and I'm afraid to walk across the courtyard and visit with my neighbor."

THERAPIST: So the tiredness, getting tired of things lets you be an ex-victim.

CLIENT: Yeah. I got fed up with how I was allowing it to affect my life. In all honesty, I'll play up the victim part to a point during the sentencing part. To a point. Because I want that judge to understand how I have been affected. And I really want to put emphasis on that. But, at the end, I am going to tell the judge, and I know that [the perpetrator] and his attorney are not expecting this, that I am going to tell the judge that I am not invested in remaining a victim. That I have done my best to get on with my life and make something positive out of this terrible experience. And I'll tell him that I volunteer for the Domestic Violence Coalition, and I'm going to tell him that it was empowering, my involvement with the Stalking Bill, was empowering. I want [the perpetrator] to hear that because that's setting a boundary like, "Screw you, you don't have that grip over me anymore." But I also want the judge to see that. Because sometimes people sympathize with victims, but there is a part of them that is really disgusted, and I don't want that judge to be disgusted with me. I want him to see these are all the terrible things [the perpetrator] has done. This is how it affected my life. Some of these things are still affected, but I am NOT, and I am going to use the phrase, I am *not* invested in being a victim anymore. Because, I don't want that judge to be disgusted with me and think, "Well she's going to cry and be a victim for the rest of her life."

THERAPIST: I'm going to ask you about a confidence scale. A 1 is you have no confidence that this will last beyond right now. And 10 is so confident that this stuff is over with that you can't even remember it ever happening to you. Where are you on that scale?

CLIENT: Part of me says 5, and that's the more insecure part, and then another part of me says 8, if I really stick with it and work hard at it.

THERAPIST: Which do you favor?

CLIENT: Well, I definitely want to be an 8.

THERAPIST: Do you feel that you know more about being an 8 this week than you did last week?

CLIENT: Definitely.

THERAPIST: So, when I see you next, what will be going on for you to be an 8?

CLIENT: Well, I need to go through the cards everyday. And there are some other things I need to do that I've been doing this week, that I need to continue to do. Not to grow complacent about my spirituality, to actively practice it, and to not be as rigid with myself.

THERAPIST: If you're not being rigid, what would you do?

CLIENT: I wouldn't be my worst critic. I would give myself some room to be flexible, which I did. I mean, my nails look like shit, and I thought, "What is more important? Do you want to have immaculate looking nails or do you want to relax and do some embroidery?" That kind of thing. And just continue to be aware of my boundaries.

THERAPIST: And if you dropped into the 6-to-5 area what would you need to do?

CLIENT: Look at the cards, and practice some of those things on the postcard, go out and walk the dog, hang out with the friends, if it's warm, go swimming. And eat.

THERAPIST: Yeah, that's important. How are you different now [than when you were depressed earlier in your life]?

CLIENT: I'm more self-aware and mature and seasoned. I have more self confidence now. . . . Just everything is much better. Kind of like my decision to be an ex-victim, I can be an ex-mental patient. And, I still need to work on being an ex-victim, but it feels good to know that I can experience real unpleasant things and, although it can take some time, that later down the road, I can use those experiences to my advantage, like a propeller to move further in life and change and growth.

THERAPIST: That's pretty inspiring.

CLIENT: Yeah. It is. . . . I can't think of any specific jokes but I've even been able to laugh at [the perpetrator] lately. . . . I don't find my self-identity in what has been done to me, but who I am as a result of being on the other side of what's been done to me. And it's getting past. Remember last time, we talked about being an 8 and still utilizing the 1? Because we had some real long honest conversations about my depression. And how I used it, sometimes, to set boundaries and what-not. And I think that it's the same thing with the domestic violence. Don't play off of the shock value because that stuff shocks people sometimes. Don't play off of sympathy. I don't need to reveal that about myself for those reasons. And I think that, say, I had a new friendship, waiting to reveal it, saying only incidentally that I experienced this, gives you the message that I'm over it.

THERAPIST: So how will people be experiencing you when this happens?

CLIENT: Parts of who I was six or seven years ago, only more mature, extroverted, gregarious, real energetic, good sense of humor, but capable of the social niceties when those other qualities aren't appropriate.

FOLLOW-UP

Following the three sessions described, therapy with Cindy was successfully terminated, and no further sessions were held. In follow-up interviews, 12 months and 18 months later, Cindy continues to function well and has not required additional therapy.

DISCUSSION

Solution-focused techniques employed included constructive systemic individual questions (Lipchik & de Shazer, 1986) and scaling questions (Berg, 1994; Berg & Miller, 1992). The therapist also included solution-focused homework assignments, such as writing postcards and letters to help identify and later elicit resources. The homework assignments were derived from the client's descriptions of recent life experiences.

Scaling was especially effective in empowering Cindy to overcome the rigid associational compartmentalization that kept her dissociated from needed resources in times of crisis. For example, by labeling her suicidal state as a 1.5, and her resourceful state as an 8, it was possible for her to elicit useful behaviors and self-talk from herself at the times when these were most needed to intervene in her depression and other symptoms exacerbated by her posttraumatic stress. As the above case demonstrates, solution-focused therapy can be employed as a powerful tool for empowering survivors of abuse and other traumas to move forward toward a satisfying future.

REFERENCES

Berg, I. K. (1990). *Solution-Focused Approach to Family Based Services*. Milwaukee, WI: Brief Family Therapy Center.

Berg, I. K., & Miller, S. (1992). *Working with the Problem Drinker: A Solution-Focused Approach*. New York: Norton.

Berg, I. K. (1994). *Family Based Services: A Solution-Focused Approach.* New York: Norton.

de Shazer, S. (1982). *Patterns of Brief Family Therapy: An Ecosystemic Approach.* New York: Guilford.

de Shazer, S. (1984). The death of resistance. *Family Process, 23*(1), 11–17.

de Shazer, S., (1985). *Keys to Solution in Brief Therapy.* New York: Norton.

de Shazer, S. (1988). *Clues: Investigating Solutions in Brief Therapy.* New York: Norton.

de Shazer, S., Berg, I., Lipchik, E., Nunnally, E., Molnar, A., Gingerich W., & Weiner-Davis, M. (1986). Brief Therapy: Focused solution development. *Family Process, 25*, 207–222.

Dolan, Y. (1985). *A Path with a Heart: Ericksonian Utilization with Resistant and Chronic Clients.* New York: Brunner/Mazel.

Dolan, Y. (1989, Winter). Only once if I really mean it: Brief treatment of a previously dissociated incest case. *Journal of Strategic and Systemic Therapy.*

Dolan, Y. (1991). *Resolving Sexual Abuse.* New York: Norton.

Lipchik, E., & de Shazer, S. (1986). The purposeful interview. *Journal of Strategic and Systemic Therapies, 5*(1–2), 88–89.

O'Hanlon, W., & Weiner-Davis, M. (1989). *In Search of Solutions.* New York: Norton.

CHAPTER 14

Tales of the Body Thief
Externalizing and Deconstructing Eating Problems

JEFFREY L. ZIMMERMAN
VICTORIA C. DICKERSON

Who is the "body thief"? Perhaps, in an insidious way, we are. Those of us who live in Western cultures, where anorexia seems to have the strongest foothold, see the individual as the center of meaning and often do not notice how our preferences have been shaped by cultural discourse. We have been subjected to normalizing judgments (Foucault, 1979, 1980) and evaluated as objects. We have also been recruited into a process Foucault calls "subjectification," where we operate on ourselves to reach the specifications set by the culture (e.g., women and thinness). We are taught to know ourselves through these specifications and not through what our own experience tells us to value. No wonder most women who are gripped by anorexia tell us they are enacting their own individual preference. Furthermore, anorexia seems to reflect many of the techniques of power that are in evidence when one group dominates another: techniques of isolation, evaluation (through surveillance and comparison), and promotion of a lack of entitlement to one's own experience. These notions of isolation, evaluation, disentitlement, and

---

We have borrowed our chapter title from Anne Rice's recent installment in her vampire series, but this chapter is about another thief: anorexia. Not only did the metaphor catch our eye, but also we noted the cultural conditions that were reflected in the original vampire story; we can see how this story may have helped create a culture of fear and persecution. Similarly, if we take note of the patriarchal culture in which we live, we see reflected a continual assertion of men's notions of how thin a woman's body should be. This story of thinness seems to have the effect of creating an ongoing experience of fear and persecution for many women, and serves to support the status quo of male domination.

a shaping cultural discourse, are directly reflected in the way we organize our clinical work and formulate our questions when working with young women whose connection to their bodies is being stolen by anorexia. We are sensitive to how easy it is, as people and as therapists, to participate inadvertently in supporting the status quo of the culture.

Most treatment of anorexia seems to play into anorexia's hands. This treatment is based on notions of individual defects (e.g., the inability to grow up or to take charge of one's life). Such constructions support the notion of an individual or family genesis of the problem. Because of this, many therapists inadvertently recreate the conditions that support anorexia by using the tactics that anorexia itself employs. These tactics include hospitalization resulting in isolation of the person, ongoing evaluations (of the person and of weight), and removal of the person's entitlement to her own experience (e.g., by suggesting she no longer knows what is going on). Gremillion (1992) suggests that the traditional psychiatric approach, the traditional therapies, and many family therapies, replicate the conditions of anorexia for women. Individual approaches attempt to teach rational control (privileging an objective, male perspective) over so-called "irrational process" (feelings from a female perspective), such as guilt, feelings of inadequacy, and subjective experience, including bodily sensations. In effect, further self-domination is not only encouraged, it is insisted upon through acts of power used to control the person. These acts of power, Gremillion suggests, are justified by the person's "underlying weakness." This weakness is seen through the objective methodology of science, rather than seen as *produced* by this methodology, as Gremillion and others, including the authors (Zimmerman & Dickerson, in press-a), would suggest. Psychiatry constructs the female body as weak and impulsive, a reflection of both a cultural construction and the construction anorexia uses to encourage young women to dominate themselves. A final point Gremillion raises is that anorexia represents the ultimate extreme of rebellion and conformity. Perhaps this may address the question David Epston (personal communication, 1993) often asks his clients: "Why does anorexia attempt to destroy the best women of their generation?" (i.e., keeping their voice, as will be discussed later in the chapter). These women want to assert their knowledge and abilities, but are limited to the cultural arenas of food and bodily shape.

Narrative therapists have taken a very different approach to this work, based on a very different understanding of the problem. The perspectives that shape one's thinking have real effects on people and on the therapist (Dickerson & Zimmerman, in press). Using a narrative metaphor represents a radical shift in perspective. Instead of using a metaphor (physical), in which individuals are seen as machines with weaknesses and defects, or a metaphor (biological), in which families are seen as organisms in which symptoms have functions, a narrative meta-phor (White & Epston, 1990) situates the problem in the discourses that culturally and personally have become an influence in the person's, or family's, life. There is also a radical shift from viewing "facts," which mental health professionals discover, to viewing them as artifacts of the models and metaphors "experts" use to organize what they see. Instead of discovering the facts, a narrative point of view suggests that facts are created. This shift is consistent with social constructionist (McNamee & Gergen, 1992) and postmodern (Kvale, 1993) views currently in favor in social psychology and intellectual thought.

White (1986) suggests that the social context in which anorexia occurs allows women to have authority only in areas such as food and thinness. Women are thus encouraged to subjugate their authority in broader contexts and in relationships with men. In general, women are encouraged by the culture to give up their opinions, to be loyal to other's wants, and to feel guilt when they violate these rules. In some families, for various reasons, these specifications seem to operate to an even greater extent than others. White suggests that anorexia encourages parents to have a greater involvement in their child's life, further inviting the child to have involve-ment with anorexia. White (1991) supports a process of questioning that first helps the woman to notice the effects anorexia is having in different areas of her life (social, emotional, intellectual, physical). He then explores the effects anorexia is having on the person's interactions with others, including addressing issues of ongoing evaluation (comparison) and how anorexia demands isolation and secrecy. Next, White asks questions about anorexia's requirements for the young woman's interaction with herself. These might include specific acts (e.g., self-surveillance and policing), as well as attitudes or conclusions that anorexia has created about the person. This process of interviewing has the effect of deconstructing these prac-tices by bringing forth the cultural, social, and familial contexts that helped create and support them. ("Deconstruction" is a term White [1991, p. 27] defines as "procedures that subvert taken for granted realities and prac-tices.") In short, the invisible becomes visible, and the client is helped to further distance from anorexia's requirements. Raising questions for the client about her interest in challenging the problem and helping the client to notice unique outcomes (e.g., experiences that were at odds to ones that followed anorexia's requirements), leads to a conversation about anti-ano-rexia and the beginning of a new story.

David Epston (personal communication, 1993), in an attempt to create a social context that supports very different notions for women (an anticontext), has developed what he calls the Anti-Anorexia–Anti-Bu-limia League. The archives of the League consist of letters David has written clients and they have written to him, as well as videotapes of sessions. In sharing the archives and by questioning clients about what they think about what others in the League have said, David creates a context not only where different ideas for possibilities for women exist, but where members contribute knowledge that helps other members access alternative knowledges.

Carol Gilligan's understanding of "voice" for women (Gilligan, 1982) and her discussions with young adolescent girls (Brown & Gilligan, 1992; Gilligan, Lyons, & Hanmer, 1990; Gilligan, Rogers, & Tolman, 1991) have led her to the conclusion that young adolescent girls are "losing their voice" or coming to "not know what they know." This loss of voice for young adolescent girls points to a subjugation of women by the normative cultural (Bruner, 1990, calls this "canonical") discourse for women in a patriarchal society. We also believe that parents might inadvertently cooperate with the prevalent patriarchal discourse. The implications are that parents would see their daughters as needing to respond in certain more acceptable "feminine" ways. These then become dominant stories about girls that are constitutive, inviting them to respond in ways for which they see no other options.

Our work is strongly influenced by Michael White and David Epston. We are beginning to develop our own Anti-Anorexia League, as well as using the New Zealand archives to assist in discussing issues with our clients. We have also found it helpful to use Gilligan's metaphor of "voice" to ask questions about entitlement and address the gendered context that supports anorexia.

THE CLINICAL QUESTIONS

The basic ideas about anorexia that we have presented in these opening paragraphs are reflected in our clinical questions, evidenced in the following clinical vignettes. The specific flow of the questions is in response to the client's experience, so they vary from interview to interview. The areas we try to address include:

1. A full picture of the influence of the problem over the person's life
2. Isolation and secrecy created by the problem
3. Experience of evaluation in family and social domains and with respect to cultural specifications for women; how anorexia replicates this experience
4. Notions of the self created by the problem and by the culture; habits recruited into; fears that support the problem and guilt for disobeying it
5. Ways the problem has stolen the person's voice; how entitlement is discouraged by family and social invitations and by cultural

prescriptions; the relationship between losing one's voice and vulnerability to anorexia and bulimia. It is critical to bring forth the person's preferences in this area. It is also important to separate the cultural prescriptions, which might lead to losing one's voice and vulnerability to anorexia and bulimia (It is critical to bring forth the person's preferences in this area. It is also important to separate the cultural prescriptions, which might lead to losing one's voice, from personal preferences, i.e., having a voice.)

6. Anti-anorexic and anti-bulimic steps, attitudes, and areas untouched by the problem

Further sessions are informed by catching up on anti-anorexia activities in any sphere. Further sessions also use League tapes to generate and support alternative knowledges and to further deconstruct the problem. We suggest that, particularly given the nature of the problem, the person's opinions, not the therapist's, are privileged and given the most air time. At the same time, anorexia and its tricks must be confronted with questions.

We have also been experimenting with questions about self-domination and self-assertion, such as the following:

- What bodily functions have you been forced by anorexia to dominate?
- Where did you learn these tactics of domination?
- What other aspects of yourself has anorexia gotten you to assert yourself against?
- What invitations exist for you to assert yourself against yourself rather than others?

We also find it useful to ask questions about the stories anorexia has created about the intentions of other persons in the young woman's life and vice versa. A narrative metaphor suggests that people create stories to justify their actions as the only ones possible given certain mitigating circumstances (see Zimmerman & Dickerson, in press-b, for a more complete discussion of this). Examples of these questions include:

- What ideas does anorexia put in your head about your daughter as a person?
- How does that affect what you do?
- What does anorexia tell you about what your parents are after?
- How does that affect you?
- Do you notice any times when they seem to be after something different?

In general, in narrative therapy, if the work is not proceeding one may:

1. Not have a problem relevant to the person, or consonant with their experience. Issues such as lack of entitlement, evaluation, and isolation are more important to the client than weight gain and can be focused on as the problem.

2. The client might not fully notice the effects of the problem. Again, this is the danger of restricting the problem definition to one sphere, like weight loss.

3. The unique outcomes, or anti-anorexic steps and areas (David Epston refers to these as "counter-practices"), are not engaging the client's experience. It is only through the engagement of alternative *experiences* that new meaning is created.

CLINICAL VIGNETTES

In the first example (Jackie), we illustrate work with a young woman who has had a long history with anorexia, and we demonstrate the questions one might ask in an initial session. In the second example (Valerie), we show work with parents, again in an opening session, this time with a young woman whose career with anorexia is much shorter. The third example (Beth) portrays work with a young woman who has come back to the therapist to discuss her victory over bulimia, and thus shows some of the work retrospectively, through the eyes of the client.

Jackie

This is a transcript from a first session with a young woman (age 15) who already had a "career" of anorexia (three years duration). In the preceding year, she had four hospitalizations for anorexia. Jackie says that she traces the turning point of anorexia's total dominance of her to her first hospitalization.

THERAPIST: [Reviews what he knew from phone conversation with mom.] What would help me is to hear from you what you see as the problem or problems. Do you see anorexia as a problem, or what?

JACKIE: I don't know. I don't want to be fat. When I lost more and more weight, I felt better. Every time I went to the hospital, when I've left I've lost even more weight. I was in the hospital the majority of last year. I don't want to keep losing out on things at school.

THERAPIST: Do you think of anorexia as a name for this problem, or do you have another name?

JACKIE: I don't know. I am afraid of being fat. That's what we talked about in the hospital. I guess anorexia is what they call it.

THERAPIST: Would it be all right to use it now, or would that be uncomfortable?

JACKIE: It's fine.

[We find it useful to "name" the problem. Calling it "anorexia" allows a later use of "anti-anorexia."]

THERAPIST: So the anorexia affects you in a way that being fat seems like the worst thing in the world?

JACKIE: Well, I am really afraid.

THERAPIST: That's a primary effect of anorexia? . . . it makes you afraid?

JACKIE: I don't know. I don't really enjoy eating anymore. It's more like a punishment to me. I don't know. I see others, friends eat, but . . . I don't really like to.

THERAPIST: So that's one of the effects of anorexia being around in your life. It has stolen your enjoyment of food. It has turned food into a punishment.

JACKIE: Yes.

[Naming "anorexia" also allows the therapist to ask questions that map the effects of the problem on her life and on her relationships. As indicated above, this gives a full picture of the influence of the problem.]

THERAPIST: I'm interested in some of the other ways anorexia has had effects on your life. (*writing*) It creates a fear of being fat. It has taken away your enjoyment of food. It has turned food into a punishment. It gets you into a cycle of feeling better when you lose. What would be your words to describe it?

JACKIE: I feel really strong and have energy.

THERAPIST: Like a high from it. It gives you highs when you cooperate with it. Energy and happy feelings.

JACKIE: Yes, that is how I feel.

THERAPIST: What else? The anorexia put you in the hospital how many times? Four?

JACKIE: Nine times. Some were short, almost monthly. A few were longer.

THERAPIST: It put you in the hospital and into the hands of doctors. Have they, in turn, taken over some of your life?

[Jackie and her mom came to see the therapist (JZ) because they thought the hospital team was too oppressive.]

JACKIE: Being in the hospital, I was watched whatever I did. Being on the unit made me more nervous about food. I think it made me much worse to be around others. I saw girls who were skinnier than me. We would compete with each other. I don't think they should have us all together. I felt gross if I wasn't the smallest.

THERAPIST: You mean the anorexia has you compete to see who is thinner?

JACKIE: I was constantly watching others and looking at myself.

THERAPIST: Would it be fair to you if I said the anorexia gets you to engage in constant comparison with others and in surveillance of yourself? You are forced to compare yourself with others and watch yourself. Would it be fair to say that is one of the effects of the anorexia? (*Jackie nods.*)

[These questions go directly to the issues of evaluation and self-surveillance.]

THERAPIST: Are you also saying being on the unit made it easier for anorexia to have that effect, getting you to engage in self-monitoring? Self-torture? Would you go that far?

JACKIE: I'm not sure if it's completely torture. I want to be thin. I also feel that way around my sister. Everyone complimented my sister about being so thin. Everyone looked at me like I was different. My family would say, "Look how pretty your sister is." [Note: Jackie, pre-anorexia, enjoyed softball and "boyish" activities.] My sister told me I need to lose weight and start acting like a girl if I want people to like me.

THERAPIST: So your sister's comment made you vulnerable to anorexia. Once anorexia moved in, it got you to compare yourself to others, not just to her. I had someone in here recently who told me that the way anorexia worked on her was that she was never allowed to feel happy; that was an effect for her. What do you think about that for yourself?

JACKIE: Sometimes I feel really awful, mostly about the way I look. I'm not sure why, but I feel awful when I don't think I'm small.

THERAPIST: You feel it. What words would you use to describe how anorexia makes you feel when you don't think you are small enough?

JACKIE: Like a cow.

THERAPIST: It makes you feel gross.

JACKIE: Yes.

THERAPIST: The anorexia gets you to engage in comparisons with others. What effects has this had on your relationships? Has it created distance?

JACKIE: Not necessarily distance. I do have some relationships with friends at school. There *was* a friend who teased me about how I looked, and I reacted.

THERAPIST: So it had some effect on that relationship. Does anorexia have some effects on your having friends?

JACKIE: Sometimes there is like a wall there. I have them, but I can't do certain things with them, especially last year being in the hospital.

THERAPIST: This wall that anorexia makes between you and your friends—do you think it's a good thing or a bad thing? What's your thought about that?

JACKIE: Well, I've been told it's not so good.

THERAPIST: I'm not interested in what you've been told. I'm interested in what you really think.

JACKIE: It's fine with me. I don't know. People always say, "Why don't you just go and eat with them; you don't have to eat that much."

THERAPIST: They make it sound like that would be a simple thing to do.

JACKIE: Right. It's not!

[Jackie's response here is indicative of how dominant and oppressive anorexia is, given the cultural specifications for women.]

THERAPIST: So, what would you say is anorexia's effect on your friendships—hurts in that way, helps, no difference?

JACKIE: No real difference, except when a whole bunch decides, "Let's go and get a bite," and I can't. Maybe it makes for a small distance.

THERAPIST: Would you say it's inconvenient?

JACKIE: I guess I miss some of those times when they go out and eat or get together to cook something.

THERAPIST: You miss the camaraderie, the opportunity for connection. Do I have that right?

[This comment refers to the isolating effects of anorexia.]

JACKIE: Yes.

THERAPIST: What do you think of the comparison thing the anorexia forces you to engage in—is that a problem? Is it uncomfortable, annoying, or okay?

JACKIE: Oh, I guess it's okay. Sometimes I do get tired of thinking about it.

THERAPIST: It gets old. (*Jackie nods.*) . . . I'm interested in other ways anorexia affects you. What effect does it have on your attitude to yourself? Does it affect the way you feel about yourself?

JACKIE: Mostly in how I look. All of the time I think how bad I look.

THERAPIST: What should I call this?—a state of constant negative self-evaluation?

JACKIE: I do feel awful. For a while, I just didn't feel good enough to want to do anything. I didn't think I could do the things I used to.

THERAPIST: So anorexia stole certain activities from you. Like what?

JACKIE: I used to play softball and really was good at it. Being in the hospital made it hard, and then the doctors said I couldn't play because my weight was too low.

THERAPIST: So what do you think about that?

JACKIE: I don't know. I wish they wouldn't watch me so closely. I don't think it's right. When they take all the things away that I care about, that makes it harder to have any motivation to beat the problem.

THERAPIST: So anorexia got doctors to monitor you, and they took away things you enjoy. This is in addition to getting you to monitor yourself. Who has been harsher with you—the doctors or the anorexia in how it gets you to treat yourself?

JACKIE: About the same. Maybe the doctors.

[As suggested above, many treatment plans inadvertently support the conditions that have created anorexia. This seems to be Jackie's experience here.]

THERAPIST: Who has made you feel worse about how you look—the doctors or the anorexia?

JACKIE: Not sure. Both have.

THERAPIST: Who has been more restrictive—the doctors or the anorexia? That's what I hear from others. Anorexia's worst trick is that it gets others to control your life. (*Jackie looks sad.*) . . . Are you tired of this? I know anorexia is difficult to resist; but I wondered how you were feeling about it.

JACKIE: A little tired, but I'm not sure I want to be rid of it.

THERAPIST: What would be your estimate, roughly, of how much of you has separated from anorexia and how much it still influences you?

JACKIE: Roughly 25% tired of it.

THERAPIST: What has gone into that 25%? Like, I notice you've been out of the hospital during the summer. Would that be evidence of that 25%?

[Jackie went on to describe how she talked to people from school and realized what she had lost out on last year. Jackie said she wanted to have fun, that was an important goal. To have that, she said, she was willing to fight anorexia to maintain her weight.]

Jackie was followed for six months by the therapist (JZ) on an every other week basis (her request). These sessions uncovered an alternative history for Jackie, one in which she had a strong voice and was considered the rebellious one (although at puberty this was strongly discouraged by her father and extended family). Jackie would prefer to have that voice resurrected. The therapist and Jackie noticed areas where she asserted her voice in school. Watching tapes of the Anti-Anorexia League, Jackie decided anorexia's purpose was to isolate and control her. Jackie, after three months, brought food to share and ate in front of friends for the first time in years (we called this "Freedom Day"). She then ran for student government and won. She began spending more time with friends and more time out of her room, even at home. She began to eat more (this was never discussed, her mom told the therapist) and to eat in the kitchen. She also began to confront her father's verbal abusiveness (her mother began confronting this, as well). She was beginning to consider other possibilities about herself, including social ones and being more talkative. She got a summer job. When looking at a League tape, after questions by the therapist, she decided that anorexia was unachievable perfection, isolation, self-criticism, and she is noticing anti-anorexia practices in these areas. She has had no further hospitalizations.

Jackie's Comments

[Jackie made the following comments after a reading of the transcript and the above description of the development in her life.]

THERAPIST: What reaction do you have to hearing the transcript and the summaries?

JACKIE: When people have a problem, you hear about it; it's weird to think it was me. The answers came from me, but they sound typical of what you hear others say.

[After a six-month interval, this reading of the transcript from the first session allowed Jackie to notice the anti-anorexia steps she had taken over that time period.]

THERAPIST: What effect does that have?

JACKIE: Just weird.

THERAPIST: What about hearing the list of accomplishments?

JACKIE: Weird hearing them all at once. They didn't feel like accomplishments. Just life.

THERAPIST: Hearing them all at once is it easier to think of them as accomplishments?

JACKIE: Maybe. I guess so. Winning student government. Working in a job.

THERAPIST: What do you think someone will think of you when they read the list?

JACKIE: Don't know.

THERAPIST: What if I told you my guess is they'd be quite impressed? Would it surprise you?

JACKIE: Yes. You don't think about it as having accomplished so much.

[What followed was a discussion about the strength involved in taking those steps, particularly when anorexia is still affecting her life. Also, there was some talk about meeting with her parents, to get her dad to begin creating space for her to assert her strength more directly at home.]

THERAPIST: One thing I notice is how anorexia takes this talent of self-assertion and turns it against you. It gets you to assert yourself against your own body. Do you notice this talent?

[An important distinction is being made here: a special talent at the service of the person, or that talent having been taken over by the problem. This comment is intended to support an alternative knowledge—anti-anorexia step—of Jackie using the talent for herself.]

JACKIE: I do know if I set my mind to something, I'm always determined, I always do it. I make sure I do it!

THERAPIST: Do you like that about yourself?

JACKIE: Yes.

[There followed a discussion about self-assertion and anorexia's invitations in her life.]

Jackie most recently decided that she was able to manage the anorexia on her own—that the gains she made were due to her and not the therapist. Meanwhile, her parents are being seen to work on issues of entitlement and evaluation as they affect their relationship with Jackie. Dad has taken more responsibility for certain effects and feels good about this. The parents, the therapist, and Jackie have agreed to a modified occasional contact with Jackie by letter, phone, and a once-in-a-while session.

Valerie

The next clinical situation is quite different. Valerie is also 15, but, unlike Jackie, has been affected by anorexia for only about five months. The family retained authority over their own lives and searched for an approach that did not describe Valerie or themselves in pathological ways and used hospitalization only as a very last resort. Their search took some time, as they sampled some of the traditional offerings before coming to this therapist (JZ). The transcript illustrates questions that were asked of the parents in a first (family) session. Valerie's comments are also important in this example. In general, we like to see the whole family first, and then follow up with individual sessions. The amount of future family sessions is determined by how quickly family members separate from the habits that *inadvertently* support the problem.

[The conversation picks up at a point where Mom is talking about the anorexia pattern not having had time to develop for Valerie, because they caught it before it could.]

THERAPIST: How about you, have you found ways not to participate in anorexia's pattern? Anorexia likes to pull parents in as well.

[We have found it is important to separate parents, as well as the young woman, from the problem and its effects. We focus instead on their attempts to have influence *over* the problem.]

MOM: I think the best thing to do is back off, and they seem to do better. But that's the hardest thing to do.

VALERIE: Why don't you back off more then?

MOM: There are certain health problems that are an issue. You see a person not eating the things they are supposed to be eating. Protein is a biggie.

THERAPIST: That's a tough one. You know for a parent to realize the only way not to make it worse is to back off—that's a hard one.

Dad: You feel it's your responsibility.

THERAPIST: Yeah.

VALERIE: Why don't you back off and let me do it?

THERAPIST: (*to parents*) I think anorexia depends on wanting to terrify you into submission by getting you to participate by putting her under your gaze.

THERAPIST: (*to Valerie*) Who do you think monitors you more closely, anorexia or your parents? Who watches you more closely?

VALERIE: I don't know—about equal.

THERAPIST: I think one of anorexia's main means of control is to engage people like Valerie into an ongoing sense of evaluation and monitoring. So if it can get you to do it also (*speaking to parents*), it can turn around and say to her (*whispering*), "Your parents are on your back all the time; don't listen to them." At her age, she is a vulnerable target for that kind of talk. So how did you manage to back off, despite the fear? Because I don't think that's easy.

MOM: It worked.

THERAPIST: That's a pragmatic answer. (*laughing*)

[Here it is important to notice steps the parents have taken in an anti-anorexia direction, fighting anorexia's invitation to take control.]

MOM: You know, I still don't back off completely. It concerns me, when she is having problems with her stomach, that she goes from the morning, when she eats her breakfast, until 2:30, when she gets home from school, without having anything to eat. That concerns me.

THERAPIST: Yeah.

MOM: You know, she's got some problems. She's got some medical issues that need to be taken care of. We got into it the other day before she went to school. It's not that I'm being unsympathetic, but it's pretty hard to be sympathetic when a person is taking a hammer and banging themselves in the head with it. You know what you need to do to take care of it. Do it.

VALERIE: I'm not asking you for sympathy. I'm asking you to leave me alone.

MOM: Yet you want sympathy when you're not feeling good a few minutes before school is starting.

VALERIE: I'm not asking for sympathy.

THERAPIST: Yeah, it's tough. I think, as a parent, it's a very hard thing to back off. That would be the hardest thing for me to do. I can't think of a harder thing for me to do. It does seem to be, in my experience, the thing that weakens, that has a weakening effect, on anorexia.

MOM: Well, I just notice that I . . . it seems like before when I was the most scared and I was trying to make sure she ate or drank something every couple of hours because she was dehydrated, she had problems covering up as a result of that, and I finally got it through my head that you can put it in front of them but you can't force them. She knows that if you do this to yourself and it gets to the point where we have to take you to the hospital and feed you with a tube, then that's what we are going to do. And you have to realize, I think, that it's almost out of your hands when it gets to that point. You will do what you have to do.

THERAPIST: What you want, I think, is for Valerie to notice that anorexia is the guardian of the concentration camp she is in, not that you are the guardian of the concentration camp she's in.

[Anorexia's effect on parents is often to put them in the position of guards, or those who watch over. This contributes to anorexia's power of surveillance, evaluation, and a concentration camp experience.]

THERAPIST: So even if it means that anorexia manages to put her in the hospital or takes her summer away or some of her school away or gets doctors in a position of dominating her, like Jackie found, she has got to be able to see that it's anorexia doing it, not you doing something. Sometimes it takes that. I'm glad you're on to it, though. Maybe you'll write a book someday on how to handle fear and do what helps. That's a book a lot of parents would get some benefit out of.

[Also, we find it useful to talk to clients as consultants, utilizing the parent's expertise to assist others who are struggling against anorexia's tricks.]

THERAPIST: (to Mom) Anything else you want to say about the problem?

MOM: No.

THERAPIST: (to Dad) What are your thoughts? Do you want to add anything, or do you have a different perspective on something?

DAD: I have a lot of similar observations. For me, one of the things that stood out in my mind is trying to talk rationally or using logic to work—it doesn't.

THERAPIST: No, I find it doesn't either.

DAD: Emotionally, I am stable, flat. Very little ups and downs. But I had the first shouting match of my life with her. No logic anywhere. I've taken the course to back off. She has got to deal with it. I've done some reading. I've found the more you push, the more the barriers go up.

THERAPIST: You become the bad guy instead of anorexia being the bad guy.

[This is a comment intended to show how anorexia recruits others into its influence.]

DAD: It's really tough.

THERAPIST: I don't doubt it.

MOM: You want to nurture them, you want to feed them, you want to make sure they're not going to get sick.

VALERIE: Isn't it simple to say that the more you back off the more likely it is that I will eat more?

MOM: It took me a while to get there. I'm not completely there yet. When you're eating all the things . . .

VALERIE: If I eat when she backs off, why doesn't she stay backed off?

MOM: One of the things I have a problem with, Valerie, is that I think you are in somewhat denial about what you think—that you think you are just fine the way you are now. You do have a weight that we are trying to achieve—to follow the doctor's orders. Maybe we have to stop listening to that—I don't know. All I know . . .

THERAPIST: It just doesn't work to be in any kind of guardian position. That's not to say these aren't serious things. I can tell you've already noticed it hasn't worked helping her to try and notice those things herself. I'm going to ask her about it when I get to her. So you notice when you back out, she takes more responsibility for herself. It may not be as much as you like . . .

[The therapist is again noticing the parent's efforts and encouraging the parents to continue to notice the good effects their efforts are having.]

MOM: I'm assuming. I don't see her eat that much, but her overall state of mental health seems a bit better, so I'm assuming she's doing what she's telling me she's doing, and one thing I do know with Valerie is that she's a pretty honest person. I don't think she's deceitful. When I ask her something, I usually feel I get a pretty honest answer.

THERAPIST: Have either of you . . . I don't know where you are at about this . . . a lot of parents get sucked into the notion they're to blame for this. I don't know if you've tortured yourself with this. I hope not. I run into that a lot.

DAD: There's bound to be some of that. We are responsible for her home environment. So whatever degree we have contributed to it . . . maybe not that much.

[The therapist's comments reflect the power of evaluation that anorexia employs to get parents to indulge in self-blame.]

THERAPIST: (to Mom) How about you?

MOM: I thought about that, too. I thought about if I went back, what I would do differently. I don't know that there is anything. I try to be . . . I work out of my home, I've been there for the kids since they came into the world. I've worked my schedule around theirs and have been very actively involved in their school. I don't know that there's anything I would do differently.

THERAPIST: I'm really glad to hear that.

The therapist (JZ) had two individual sessions with Valerie after the family session. In the first, a picture of herself and her life before anorexia was solicited. This included less isolation and more comfort with people, having energy, being happy, and being a little rebellious. The importance of her having her own mind was made clear to both Valerie and the therapist. She clearly preferred this picture to the anorexia-dominated one. In the next session, she reported she had been fighting more directly with her mom. The therapist and Valerie watched a tape, selected from the Anti-Anorexia League archives, in which a young woman talked about anorexia, its rules, and her efforts to escape them. Valerie then concluded that it felt good to disobey anorexia (and mom). She also reported that her parents love her more than anorexia does and have her interests more at heart. She said that anorexia makes one feel fat when one is really thin. She discovered a time when she was able to listen to herself and eat when she was hungry. She realized she was able to unmask what anorexia was doing to her. The next session was with her mom, who reported that Valerie was eating now, had gained weight, and no longer felt the need for therapy. Mom was having some difficulty, nevertheless, with the way Valerie was asserting her wishes to be her own person (the degree of rudeness and the hurt it brought), but responded, after some questioning, that she preferred this way to Valerie asserting herself in anorexic ways.

Mom's Comments

[These comments were made after hearing transcript read several weeks after the first session.]

THERAPIST: Is there anything you would like to comment on regarding that conversation?

MOM: I came to the realization that the worst thing that could happen is that we would have to hospitalize her and feed her with a tube. When I let myself agree to this, I could back off, because I was ensured she would live. I realized that in talking more it was making it worse, so I was able to back off. In doing that, that's when things started turning around. She began taking responsibility and fighting it more. She fed herself more.

THERAPIST: (*later on in session*) What about the question I asked you several weeks later: "Would you rather she assert herself with anorexia's help or more directly, but in a rude way?"

[This questions reflects an intention to call attention to Valerie's "voice," her learning to speak for herself and stand up for herself in life. If anorexia has stolen her voice, then asserting herself, separate from anorexia, is a sign of having reclaimed her "voice."]

MOM: I still feel the rudeness is unpleasant, *but* the anorexia can kill her.

[Mom then told a story of Valerie threatening her with not eating and how she turned down the invitation to respond and gave the responsibility back to her daughter. This led to a discussion of what Valerie might really want. Mom told the therapist that she had created more space for Valerie to assert her wants directly.]

Beth

The final case example involves Beth, who at the time of the session was 21 years old. The therapist (JZ) had seen Beth for 12 sessions (once a week), two years before this interview. When first seen, Beth was bingeing and vomiting four to six times a day. She had just finished her sophomore year at an Ivy League school. When last seen, Beth had significantly reduced bulimia's influence over her. Beth requested therapy this time, two years later (after graduating from college), because she wanted to work on relationship issues and prevent bulimia from making any significant comeback in the stressful periods that were to come for her. What is illustrated here is a portion of the first session where Beth was catching the therapist up on the last two years and telling about her escape from bulimia.

[Beth was reviewing her junior year. At this point in the interview, she had started talking about the competing relationship demands on her self, her boyfriend, D, and her twin sister. She had come to the realization she needed to break up with her boyfriend.]

THERAPIST: Is there a relationship in your head—there is one in my head—between being for D or your family and bulimia?

BETH: Yes.

[This question reflects the tendency for women to give themselves up for others, a tendency that bulimia then can take advantage of.]

THERAPIST: Would you say something about this? I hope to show this tape to other potential League members.

[The therapist had explained something of the Anti-Bulimia League, and Beth agreed to contribute the tape; the League was a new development since the work done two summers before.]

BETH: This is what happened to me the last few years. The summer I was seeing you, I got incredibly angry with my mother, and then it was my father, and later it was my sister and D simultaneously. And, oh, before that, early in the school year, I made a promise to myself about December 25th. That's when I wrote you the letter. I stopped cold turkey and decided it was so easy to go on. And, when I did throw up it was because I was letting myself—"Okay, you can throw up."

THERAPIST: That's a different level of control.

BETH: Yes, it was a very different level of control. I mean, I was ecstatic and no one could understand it. I was cured. I was throwing up three to four, then less than two times a week, instead of four to six times a day. It was not that much of a greater step to go cold turkey on the 25th.

THERAPIST: Let me catch up. How did you make that first step? What words of wisdom do you have for others?

[Focusing on taking anti-bulimia steps and accessing the person's agency in this process invites the young woman to notice further steps.]

BETH: [Talking about telling a story to a friend of a friend who just got into bulimia] I don't know if you remember, but I had just bought a pair of skates.

THERAPIST: I remember.

BETH: I mean I still have those skates. Everyone says, "Beth you should get a new pair of skates." It was a freedom thing for me. I was healing myself. The momentum kept going. I stopped throwing up for a day, and I was so happy.

THERAPIST: Why were you happy, specifically?

BETH: Because I had done it for a day—that was a major thing. And, I think that kind of positive reinforcement thing helped me. Also, as I stopped more and more, I felt a lot better. I didn't know that lightheadedness and headaches weren't normal. I didn't know I was feeling sick.

THERAPIST: The side effects of bulimia.

BETH: Skating helped me, and then I started to feel really empowered.

THERAPIST: [Shares his experience that the women he sees seem to have the experience of being empowered by anorexia and bulimia] What difference does it make to be empowered by yourself and not anorexia and bulimia?

BETH: When I was in high school, I lived my life to please everyone else. Plus, to please me, I danced and lost weight, but I had to be the best to please my teacher. It was empowering, I had my little secret, my tool, and it was working for me. I don't know when it stopped. It did work, gave me the ability to be thin and eat with my friends. It was when—I was throwing up one to two times a week—I had a rule that any more was sick. I think when it started possessing me, and I didn't know it. [Beth goes on to describe the process of bulimia taking control by increasing the situations it appeared in and her not being able to stop and being afraid to try.] I thought college would help, but it didn't. It got worse. One of the worst things about telling my parents was that I became "bulimic." All trust was gone. . . . All the people I loved the most were telling me I didn't know what was going on. All my confidence was gone.

THERAPIST: One of the evils of bulimia is that it encourages parents to act that way.

BETH: [Tells a story about a friend of hers and how she hoped her parents would treat her, not like a sick person] By the time I came here, I was beginning to take control. I needed to do something. I was really depressed and sick and tired of being so unhappy. One thing that you told me that I really value and still always think—you said, "Beth, you are right," and I said, "Wow!"—because everyone I loved was telling me I was wrong for the last year, and I believed it. I remember thinking: I know I am right, but everybody I love tells me I'm wrong, so I must be wrong. That's where I lost it. So, all of a sudden to say I am right, my solutions do work, that's the empowering thing. So, when I said I won't throw up for an entire day, that's a big thing.

THERAPIST: Right.

BETH: That was really empowering. Eating safe foods was the next step. I hadn't done that for years. I also started—and this sounds weird—when I was skating or running, listening to music I loved and doing a mantra to myself: "I love you, Beth; I love you, Beth." [In school, Beth described dancing in a show, something she loves as a way of having her own space. She stopped running and became busy, separate from D, and with other than academic activities.] February 1st, I broke up with D. I was doing everything I could to make his life happy, and I was still getting: "Why didn't you do this, why didn't you . . . ?" And finally, I was so angry, and about my sister, and all of a sudden I went, "Oh, my God, my father and sister . . . don't mess with me here . . . he's really messing with me . . ."

THERAPIST: Did breaking up with D affect the bulimia?

BETH: At that point, I was already free. However, I think I broke up with him long before I broke up. He accused me of this many times.

THERAPIST: Because it was abusive? He wasn't letting you be you.

BETH: Yes, it was very abusive. I arranged my schedule so I couldn't be with him very much.

Interview about the Interview

[This session was conducted at the end of the summer after reading the above transcript with her.]

THERAPIST: Beth, you talked about being angry at various people you had significant relationships with, when I asked you about the relation-ship between being for others and bulimia. Could you clarify this?

BETH: I was thinking about living my life for the people I loved and simultaneously living my life for myself (dancing, school, work). But, I had this "should" to achieve. I wanted to be for myself, but I felt guilty about not attending to my family or my boyfriend. I learned to identify what I want and separate this from shoulds and from others. This way, I can then take control (and not have bulimia take control), being in touch with myself enough to act instead of react out of fear.

THERAPIST: (*later on in the interview*) You said you would die an old maid if you can't find a man on your own terms.

BETH: Yes, I feel okay with contradiction. I can hold complex feelings toward others and still feel worthy in my feelings. If that's not okay with them, they are not okay with me. Bulimia comes in when I'm feeling scared, and I don't have the energy to separate things out. It goes back mostly to entitlement in relationships and then perhaps to some evaluation issues.

[Gilligan's work with young women on the edge of adolescence suggests that women tend to disconnect from their own experience for the sake of relationship. Here, Beth is indicating a reversal of that process. She has reconnected with herself and is able to handle complex feelings.]

THERAPIST: Was breaking up with D a step to coming to this position?

BETH: The realization I can make it on my own I had always had, with my sister before, then D. Breaking up with D I realized, "*I'm* doing this; *I'm* making decisions."

THERAPIST: When bulimia is around, then, you know it means you need to take some action. But it's seductive; it says that it's the answer.

BETH: I think it *is* the action. It is seductive. It's a help when it's an alarm clock, and in how it forced me to think about my life in a way. Now I have a sense of power, control, and grace.

[Beth left the area at the end of the summer—1993—to begin her first semester of medical school. She felt more confident about her own voice in relationships and about being able to continue to manage bulimia.]

CONCLUSION

In general, we find this work very rewarding. When young women accept our invitation to be a presence in their own lives, to use their voice, to act in an empowered way, it is exciting to witness. Intervening in the ways described above has led to the empowering responses recorded here, indicating that women can be present to themselves, their lives, and their relationships. We also believe it is critical to develop programs for young women, preferably at the junior high level, to help them develop pre–anti-anorexia and anti-bulimia and pro-voice strategies. It is during this time in their lives, at the edge of adolescence, that they seem to be especially vulnerable (Gilligan, 1990).

Specifically, we would like to highlight the following.

1. The difference between fighting anorexia that has been around a short time (Valerie) from anorexia that has been around a long time (Jackie) is enormous. Some of this could be explained by the effects of starvation, which creates cognitive "fuzziness." However, Valerie had lost a considerable amount of weight, enough to produce some starvation effects. Therefore, we believe most of this difference is due to the way the traditional psychiatric system has replicated the conditions that encouraged the anorexia in the first place, and then replicated the tactics of the anorexia itself. This process has the effect of the anorexia getting more powerful and creating stories about authority figures (therapist, parents) that render their input as less significant. Often, this process begins with a psychiatric takeover of parents, who are told not to control their child's eating, and then the psychiatric system turning around and controlling it in even more harsh ways. If someone is going to control the young person, we believe it should be the parents more than therapists. If the anorexia is so powerful that the situation is acutely life-threatening, a collaboration could occur between parents and medical doctors to briefly hospitalize for weight gain to remove the acute threat. They (parents, doctors) could say that they won't let anorexia kill her and keep the weight gain separate from the therapy. (For example, in the transcript, Valerie's mom had said they could leave her be and hospitalize her if anorexia proved to be too powerful.) Nevertheless, we think the key is to create the conditions where the young person would take charge of the problem (in the way that we are more broadly defining it) and her life herself.

2. A focus on narrative suggests looking at the meaning-making process that each person in the system is engaged in. In families with adolescents (Dickerson & Zimmerman, 1992, 1993), the young person is attempting to narrate her own story, separate from the parents' story for her. By extension, before young adolescent girls can begin to narrate their own stories, they must first "know what they know," keeping or reclaiming their voice in order to see that they can even have a story. Valerie, and even Beth, could be thought of as engaged in a process of trying to reconnect with their own voices and with their families in a new way. Jackie seemed to have given up that effort and was allowing the voice

of anorexia to do most of the narrating. In the process of therapy, one can see her beginning to shift toward narrating her own story again. We believe the effects of the traditional involvement of the psychiatric system is to encourage further rebellion against the system's point of view. The psychiatric narrative does not leave much room for young people to create their own meaning. Rather, this "overspecialized" narrative creates a condition, which, as Bruner (1990) suggests, invites rejection of meaning.

The justification aspects of narrative, which we referred to earlier in this chapter, have not been fully shown here. One can see, however, how Valerie's parents saw no option but to take control, not really wanting to, but not believing that it was Valerie's intention to do so. We are finding that questions that bring forth these stories about the other's motivations and intentions are quite useful. Jackie's justification for why she was acting the way she was had less to do with the stories of significant others than with cultural prescriptions. In these types of situations, we think it is critical to use the Anti-Anorexia–Anti-Bulimia League extensively to provide examples of young women challenging these ideas and offering other possibilities. Coming from League members, the process has quite a different effect than coming from parents or therapists.

3. Using the League in a way that connects the person's anti-anorexic steps, actions, and attitudes with other League member's ideas, provides a powerful form of support for developing alternative stories. The combination of externalizing the problem, unmasking the lies that the culture creates as truths (i.e., deconstruction), constructing a story that is more empowering to the client (with less negative effects), and supporting it by circulation of knowledge with the League, is quite powerful. The book that David Epston (1993) is writing along with his League members should provide further help to those of us working in this way.

4. We have not commented much about Beth, because we believe her comments stand on their own. We would likewise encourage you to ask your clients to comment on and evaluate their experiences in therapy.

REFERENCES

Brown, L., & Gilligan, C. (1992). *Meeting at the Crossroads*. Cambridge, MA: Harvard University Press.

Bruner, J. (1990). *Acts of Meaning*. Cambridge, MA: Harvard University Press.

Dickerson, V. C., & Zimmerman, J. L. (1992). Families with adolescents: Escaping problem lifestyles. *Family Process, 31*, 341–353.

Dickerson, V. C., & Zimmerman, J. L. (1993). A narrative approach to families with adolescents. In S. Friedman (Ed.), *The New Language of Change: Constructive Collaboration in Psychotherapy* (pp. 226–250). New York: Guilford.

Dickerson, V. C., & Zimmerman, J. L. (in press). A constructionist exercise in anti-pathology. *Journal of Systemic Therapy.*

Epston, D. (1993). *Sharing of Anti-Anorexia–Anti-Bulimia League Archives.* Unpublished manuscript.

Foucault, M. (1979). *Discipline and Punish: The Birth of the Prison.* Middlesex, England: Peregrine Books.

Foucault, M. (1980). *Power, Knowledge and Selected Interviews and Other Writings.* New York: Pantheon Books.

Gilligan, C. (1982). *In a Different Voice.* Cambridge, MA: Harvard University Press.

Gilligan, C. (1990, Fall). Joining the resistance: Psychology, politics, girls and women. *Michigan Quarterly Review, 29,* 501–536.

Gilligan, C., Lyons, N., & Hammer, T. (1990). *Making Connections.* Cambridge, MA: Harvard University Press.

Gilligan, C., Rogers, A., & Tolman, D. (1991.) *Women, Girls, and Psychotherapy.* Cambridge, MA: Harvard University Press.

Gremillion, M. (1992). Psychiatry as social ordering: Anorexia nervosa, a paradigm. *Social Science Medicine, 1,* 57–71.

Kvale, S. (1993). Postmodern psychology: A contradiction in terms? In S. Kvale (Ed.), *Psychology and Postmodernism* (pp. 31–57). Newbury Park, CA: Sage.

McNamee, S., & Gergen, K. J. (Eds.). (1992). *Therapy as Social Construction.* Newbury Park, CA: Sage.

Rice, A. (1992). *The Tale of the Body Thief.* New York: Knopf.

White, M. (1986). Anorexia nervosa: A cybernetic perspective. In J. Elka-Harkaway (Ed.), *Eating Disorders* (pp. 117–129). New York: Aspen.

White, M. (1991). Deconstruction and therapy. *Dulwich Centre Newsletter, 3,* 21–40.

White, M., & Epston, D. (1990). *Narrative Means to Therapeutic Ends.* New York: Norton.

Zimmerman, J. L., & Dickerson, V. C. (in press-a). Narrative therapy and the work of Michael White. In M. Elkaim (Ed.), *Panorama des Thérapies Familiales.* Paris: Editions du Seuil.

Zimmerman, J. L., & Dickerson, V. C. (in press-b). Using a narrative metaphor: Implications for theory and clinical practice. *Family Process.*

Selected Bibliography

Adams, J. F., Piercy, F. P., & Jurich, J. A. (1991). Effects of solution-focused therapy's "formula first session task" on compliance and outcome in family therapy. *Journal of Marital and Family Therapy, 17,* 277–290.

Ahlers, C. (1992). Solution-oriented therapy for professionals working with physically impaired clients. *Journal of Strategic and Systemic Therapies, 11,* 53–68.

Allen, J. (1993). A reply to "A physicist's reactions." *Transactional Analysis Journal, 23,* 48–49.

Andersen, T. (Ed.). (1991). *The Reflecting Team: Dialogue and Dialogues about the Dialogues.* New York: Norton.

Anderson, H., & Goolishian, H. A. (1988). Human systems as linguistic systems: Evolving ideas about the implications for theory and practice. *Family Process, 27,* 371–393.

Anderson, H., & Goolishian, H. A. (1990). Beyond cybernetics: Comments on Atkinson and Heath's "Further thoughts on second-order family therapy." *Family Process, 29,* 157–163.

Andreas, C., & Andreas, S. (1989). *Heart of the Mind.* Moah, UT: Real People Press.

Andreas, C., & Andreas, T. (1994). *Core Transformation: Reaching the Wellspring Within.* Moab, UT: Real People Press.

Aponte, H. J. (1992). Training the person of the therapist in structural family therapy. *Journal of Marital and Family Therapy, 18,* 269–281.

Atkinson, B., & Heath, A. (1989). Solutions attempted and considered: Broadening assessment in brief therapy. *Journal of Strategic and Systemic Therapies, 8,* 56–57.

Atwood, J. D. (1993). Social constructionist couple therapy. *The Family Journal: Counseling and Therapy for Couples and Families, 1,* 116–130.

Auerbach, C. (1985). What is a self? A constructivist theory. *Psychotherapy, 22,* 743–746.

Bandler, R. (1985). *Using Your Brain—For a Change.* Moab, UT: Real People Press.

Bandler, R., & Grinder, J. (1975). *The Structure of Magic.* Palo Alto, CA: Science & Behavior Books.

Bandler, R., & Grinder, J. (1982). *Reframing.* Moab, UT: Real People Press.

Bandura, A. (1977). Self-efficacy: Toward a unifying theory of behavioral change. *Psychological Review, 84,* 191–215.

Bartley, W. W., III. (1978). *Werner Erhard.* New York: C. N. Potter/Crown.

Bartley, W. W., III. (1985). *Wittgenstein.* Chicago: Open Court.

Compiled by Michael F. Hoyt

Bateson, G. (1972). *Steps to an Ecology of Mind.* New York: Aronson.

Bateson, G. (1979). *Mind and Nature: A Necessary Unity.* New York: Bantam.

Bateson, G., Jackson, D. D., Haley, J., & Weakland, J. H. (1956). Toward a theory of schizophrenia. *Behavioral Science, 1,* 251–264.

Bateson, M. C. (1989). *Composing a Life.* New York: Plume.

Beavers, W. R., & Hampson, B. (1990). *Successful Families.* New York: Norton.

Beck, A. T. (1976). *Cognitive Therapy and Emotional Disorders.* New York: International Universities Press.

Beck, A. T., Freeman, A., & Associates. (1990). *Cognitive Therapy of Personality Disorders.* New York: Guilford.

Belensky, M. F., Clinchy, B. M., Goldberg, N. R., & Tarule, J. M. (1986). *Women's Ways of Knowing: The Development of Self, Voice, and Mind.* New York: Basic Books.

Berg, I. K. (1989, January/February). Of visitors, complainants and customers. *Family Therapy Networker.*

Berg, I. K. (1990). *A Guide to Practice: Constructing Solutions in Brief Therapy.* Milwaukee: Brief Family Therapy Center.

Berg, I. K. (1994). *Family Based Services: A Solution-Focused Approach.* New York: Norton.

Berg, I. K., & de Shazer, S. (1993). Making numbers talk: Language in therapy. In S. Friedman (Ed.), *The New Language of Change: Constructive Collaboration in Psychotherapy* (pp. 5–24). New York: Guilford.

Berg, I. K., & Hopwood, L. (1991). Doing with very little: Treatment of homeless substance abusers. *Journal of Independent Social Work, 5,* 109–119.

Berg, I. K., & Miller, S. D. (1992). *Working with the Problem Drinker.* New York: Norton.

Berger, P., & Luckman, T. (1966). *The Social Construction of Reality.* New York: Irvington.

Bergman, J. (1985). *Fishing for Barracuda: Pragmatics of Brief Systemic Therapy.* New York: Norton.

Bergner, R. M. (1993). Victims into perpetrators. *Psychotherapy, 30,* 452–462.

Berne, E. (1972). *What Do You Say after You Say Hello?* New York: Grove Press.

Bischof, G. P. (1993). Solution-focused brief therapy and experiential family therapy activities: An integration. *Journal of Systemic Therapies, 12,* 61–73.

Blackstone, P. (1987). Loving too much: Disease or decision? *Transactional Analysis Journal, 17,* 185–190.

Bloom, B. (1992). *Planned Short-Term Psychotherapy.* Boston: Allyn & Bacon.

Bly, R. (1990). *Iron John: A Book about Men.* Reading, MA: Addison-Wesley.

Boscolo, L., & Bertrando, P. (1993). *The Times of Time.* New York: Norton.

Boscolo, L., Cecchin, G., Hoffman, L., & Penn, P. (1987). *Milan Systemic Family Therapy: Conversations in Theory and Practice.* New York: Basic Books.

Bouchard, M. A., & Guerette, L. (1991). Psychotherapy as a hermeneutical experience. *Psychotherapy, 28,* 385–394.

Brasher, B., Campbell, T. C., & Moen, D. (1993). Solution oriented recovery. *Journal of Systemic Therapies, 12,* 1–13.

Briggs, J., & Peat, F. D. (1989). *Turbulent Mirror.* New York: Harper & Row.

Bruner, J. (1986). *Actual Minds, Possible Worlds.* Cambridge, MA: Harvard University Press.

Bruner, J. (1987). Life as narrative. *Social Research, 54,* 11–32.

Buber, M. (1958). *I and Thou.* New York: C. Schribner's Sons.

Budman, S. H., & Gurman, A. S. (1988). *Theory and Practice of Brief Therapy.* New York: Guilford.

Budman, S. H., Hoyt, M. F., & Friedman, S. (Eds.). (1992). *The First Session in Brief Therapy*. New York: Guilford.

Cade, B., & O'Hanlon, W. H. (1993). *A Brief Guide to Brief Therapy*. New York: Norton.

Cameron-Bandler, L. (1985). *Solutions: Practical and Effective Antidotes for Sexual and Relationship Problems*. San Rafael, CA: FuturePace.

Campbell, J. (1983). *The Way of the Animal Powers*. New York: Harper & Row.

Capra, F. (1991). *The Tao of Physics* (3rd ed.). Boston: Shambala.

Carnegie, D. (1981). *How to Win Friends and Influence People*. New York: Simon & Schuster. (Originally published 1936)

Castaneda, C. (1971). *A Separate Reality*. New York: Simon & Schuster.

Castaneda, C. (1972). *Journey to Ixtlan*. New York: Simon & Schuster.

Charny, I. W. (1992). *Existential/Dialetical Marital Therapy: Breaking the Secret Code of Marriage*. New York: Brunner/Mazel.

Chasin, R., Grunebaum, H., & Herzig, M. (Eds.). (1990). *One Couple, Four Realities: Multiple Perspectives on Couple Therapy*. New York: Guilford.

Chasin, R., & Roth, S. (1990). Future perfect, past perfect: A positive approach to opening couple therapy. In R. Chasin, H. Grunebaum, & M. Herzig (Eds.), *One Couple, Four Realities: Multiple Perspectives on Couple Therapy* (pp. 129–144). New York: Guilford.

Chasin, R., Roth, S., & Bograd, M. (1989). Action methods in systemic therapy: Dramatizing ideal futures and reformed pasts with couples. *Family Process, 28*(1), 121–136.

Chopra, D. (1988). *Return of the Rishi*. Boston: Houghton Mifflin.

Clifton, D., Doan, R., & Mitchell, D. (1990). The reauthoring of therapist's stories: Taking doses of our own medicine. *Journal of Strategic and Systemic Therapies, 9,* 61–66.

Coale, H. W. (1989). Common dilemmas in relationships and suggestions for therapeutic interventions. *Journal of Strategic and Systemic Therapies, 8,* 10–15.

Combrinck-Graham, L. (1987). Invitation to a kiss: Diagnosing ecosystemically. *Psychotherapy, 24,* 504–510.

Combs, G., & Freedman, J. (1990). *Symbol, Story, and Ceremony: Using Metaphor in Individual and Family Therapy*. New York: Norton.

Connell, G. M., Whitaker, C., Garfield, R., & Connell, L. (1990). The process of in-therapy consultation: A symbolic-experiential perspective. *Journal of Strategic and Systemic Therapies, 9,* 32–38.

Cottone, R. R., & Greenwell, R. J. (1992). Beyond linearity and circularity: Deconstructing social systems theory. *Journal of Marital and Family Therapy, 18,* 167–177.

Covey, S. R. (1989). *The Seven Habits of Highly Effective People*. New York: Fireside/Simon & Schuster.

Cronen, V. E., Johnson, K. M., & Lannamann, J. W. (1982). Paradoxes, double binds, and reflexive loops: An alternative theoretical perspective. *Family Process, 20,* 91–112.

Dass, R., & Gorman, P. (1985). *How Can I Help?* New York: Knopf.

Davidson, J., & Lax, W. D. (1992). Reflecting conversations in the initial consultation. In S. H. Budman, M. F. Hoyt, & S. Friedman (Eds.), *The First Session in Brief Therapy* (pp. 255–281). New York: Guilford.

Dell, P. (1986). In defense of "lineal causality." *Family Process, 25,* 513–521.

Dell, P. (1987). Maturana's constitutive ontology of the observer. *Psychotherapy, 24,* 462–466.

Deming, W. E. (1986). *Out of the Crisis.* Cambridge, MA: MIT Press.

Derrida, J. (1976). *Of Grammatology.* Baltimore, MD: Johns Hopkins University Press.

de Shazer, S. (1982). *Patterns of Brief Family Therapy.* New York: Guilford.

de Shazer, S. (1984). The death of resistance. *Family Process, 23,* 79–93.

de Shazer, S. (1985). *Keys to Solution in Brief Therapy.* New York: Norton.

de Shazer, S. (1988). *Clues: Investigating Solutions in Brief Therapy.* New York: Norton.

de Shazer, S. (1989). Wrong map, wrong territory. *Journal of Marital and Family Therapy, 15,* 117–121.

de Shazer, S. (1991). Here we go again: Maps, territories, interpretations, and the distinction between "the" and "a" or "an." *Journal of Marital and Family Therapy, 17,* 193–195.

de Shazer, S. (1991). *Putting Difference to Work.* New York: Norton.

de Shazer, S. (1994). *Words Were Originally Magic.* New York: Norton.

de Shazer, S., & Berg, I. K. (1985). A part is not apart: Working with only one of the partners present. In A. S. Gurman (Ed.), *Casebook of Marital Therapy* (pp. 97–110). New York: Guilford.

de Shazer, S., & Berg, I. K. (1992). Doing therapy: A post-structural re-vision. *Journal of Marital and Family Therapy, 18,* 71–81.

de Shazer, S., Berg, I. K., Lipchik, E., Nunnally, E., Molnar, A., Gingerich, W., & Weiner-Davis, M. (1986). Brief therapy: Focused solution development. *Family Process, 25,* 207–222.

Dickerson, V., & Zimmerman, J. (1993). A narrative approach to families with adolescents. In S. Friedman (Ed.), *The New Language of Change: Constructive Collaboration in Psychotherapy* (pp. 226–250). New York: Guilford.

DiNicola, V. F. (1993). The postmodern language of therapy: At the nexus of culture and family. *Journal of Systemic Therapies, 12,* 49–62.

Dolan, Y. M. (1985). *A Path with a Heart: Ericksonian Utilization with Resistant and Chronic Clients.* New York: Brunner/Mazel.

Dolan, Y. M. (1991). *Resolving Sexual Abuse: Solution-Focused Therapy and Ericksonian Hypnosis for Adult Survivors.* New York: Norton.

Driscoll, R. (1984). *Pragmatic Psychotherapy.* New York: Van Nostrand.

Duncan, B. L. (1992). Strategic therapy, eclecticism, and the therapeutic relationship. *Journal of Marital and Family Therapy, 18,* 17–24

Duncan, B. L. (1992). Strategy and reality: A comment on Goolishian, Anderson, and Held. *Journal of Marital and Family Therapy, 18,* 39–40.

Duncan, B. L., Parks, M., & Rusk, G. S. (1990). Eclectic strategic practice: A process constructive perspective. *Journal of Marital and Family Therapy, 16,* 165–178.

Duncan, B. L., Solovey, A. D., & Rusk, G. S. (1992). *Changing the Rules: A Client-Directed Approach to Therapy.* New York: Guilford.

Durrant, M. (1993). *Residential Treatment: A Cooperative, Competency-Based Approach to Therapy and Program Design.* New York: Norton.

Durrant, M., & White, C. (Eds.). (1990). *Ideas for Therapy with Sexual Abuse.* Adelaide, South Australia: Dulwich Centre Publications.

Easty, E. D. (1981). *On Method Acting.* New York: Ivy Books/Ballantine.

Edelstien, M. G. (1990). *Symptom Analysis: A Method of Brief Therapy.* New York: Norton.

Efran, J. S., Lukens, R. J., & Lukens, M. D. (1988, September/October). Constructivism: What's in it for you? *Family Therapy Networker*. (Reprinted in R. Simon, C. Barrilleaux, M. S. Wylie, & L. M. Markowitz [Eds.], [1992], *The Evolving Therapist: Ten Years of the Family Therapy Networker* [pp. 265–277]. New York: Guilford.)

Efran, J. S., & Schenker, M. D. (1993, May/June). Book review: A potpourri of solutions. *Family Therapy Networker*, pp. 71–74.

Efron, D. (Ed.). (1986). *Journeys: Expansion of the Strategic-Systemic Therapies*. New York: Brunner/Mazel.

Efron, D., & Veenendaal, K. (1993). Suppose a miracle doesn't happen: The non-miracle option. *Journal of Systemic Therapies, 12*, 11–18.

Ellenberger, H. F. (1981). *The Discovery of the Unconscious*. New York: Viking.

Ellis, A. (1990). Is rational-emotive therapy (RET) "rationalist" or "constructivist"? In W. Dryden (Ed.), *The Essential Albert Ellis* (pp. 114–141). New York: Springer.

Ellis, A. (1992). First-order and second-order change in rational-emotive therapy: A reply to Lyddon. *Journal of Counseling and Development, 70*, 449–451.

Ellis, A. (1993). Constructivism and rational-emotive therapy: A critique of Richard Wessler's critique. *Psychotherapy, 30*, 531–532.

Ellis, A. (1993). Another reply to Wessler's critique of rational-emotive therapy. *Psychotherapy, 30*, 535.

Epston, D. (1990). *Collected Papers*. Adelaide, South Australia: Dulwich Centre Publications.

Epston, D., & White, M. (1992). *Experience, Contradiction, Narrative and Imagination: Selected Papers of David Epston and Michael White, 1989–1991*. Adelaide, South Australia: Dulwich Centre Publications.

Erickson, M. H. (1954). Pseudo-orientation in time as a hypnotic procedure. *Journal of Clinical and Experimental Hypnosis, 6*, 183–207.

Erickson, M. H. (1980). *Collected Papers* (Vols. 1–4, E. Rossi, Ed.). New York: Irvington.

Erickson, M. H., & Rossi, E. (1979). *Hypnotherapy: An Exploratory Casebook*. New York: Irvington.

Erickson, M. H., Rossi, E., & Rossi, S. (1976). *Hypnotic Realities*. New York: Irvington.

Estes, C. (1992). *Women Who Run with the Wolves: Myths and Stories of the Wild Woman Archtype*. New York: Ballantine Books.

Evans, P. (1992). *The Verbally Abusive Relationship*. Holbrook, MA: Bob Adams.

Farber, A. (1981). Castaneda's Don Juan as psychotherapist. *Advances in Descriptive Psychology, 1*, 279–304.

Farrelly, F., & Brandsma, J. (1974). *Provocative Therapy*. Cupertino, CA: Metapublications.

Fisch, R. (1990). The broader implications of Milton H. Erickson's work. *Ericksonian Monographs, 7*, 1–5.

Fisch, R., Weakland, J. H., & Segal, L. (1982). *The Tactics of Change: Doing Therapy Briefly*. San Francisco: Jossey-Bass.

Fish, V. (1991). Still disputing the menu, still not trying the food: Constructivist complaints at the discourse deli. *Journal of Marital and Family Therapy, 17*, 197–199.

Foucault, M. (1975). *The Birth of the Clinic*. New York: Vintage.

Foucault, M. (1978). *The History of Sexuality: An Introduction*. New York: Pantheon.

Foucault, M. (1980). *Power, Knowledge and Selected Interviews and Other Writings.* New York: Pantheon Books.

Frankl, V. E. (1963). *Man's Search for Meaning.* New York: Washington Square Press.

Freedman, J., & Combs, G. (1993). Invitations to new stories: Using questions to explore alternative possibilities. In S. Gilligan & R. Price (Eds.), *Therapeutic Conversations* (pp. 291–303). New York: Norton.

Freud, S. (1937/1964). Constructions in analysis. In J. Strachey (Ed. and Trans.), *The Standard Edition of the Complete Psychological Works of Sigmund Freud* (Vol. 23, pp. 256–269). London: Hogarth Press.

Friedman, S. (1992). Constructing solutions (stories) in brief family therapy. In S. H. Budman, M. F. Hoyt, & S. Friedman (Eds.), *The First Session in Brief Therapy* (pp. 282–305). New York: Guilford.

Friedman, S. (1993). Does the "miracle question" always create miracles? *Journal of Systemic Therapies, 12,* 71–72.

Friedman, S. (1993). (Ed.). *The New Language of Change: Constructive Collaboration in Psychotherapy.* New York: Guilford.

Friedman, S., & Fanger, M. T. (1991). *Expanding Therapeutic Possibilities: Getting Results in Brief Psychotherapy.* New York: Lexington Books/Macmillan.

Friedman, W. (1993). Memory for the time of past events. *Psychological Bulletin, 113,* 44–66.

Furman, B. (1990, May/June). Glasnost therapy: Removing the barriers between clients and therapists. *Family Therapy Networker,* pp. 61–63, 70.

Furman, B., & Ahola, T. (1991). The "never-ending story": Or, the problem as solution. *Australian and New Zealand Journal of Family Therapy, 12,* 53–55.

Furman, B., & Ahola, T. (1992). *Solution Talk: Hosting Therapeutic Conversations.* New York: Norton.

Gale, J., & Newfield, J. (1992). A conversation analysis of a solution-focused marital therapy session. *Journal of Marital and Family Therapy, 18,* 153–165.

Gell-Mann, M. (1994). *The Quark and the Jaguar.* New York: Freeman.

Gergen, K. J. (1982). *Towards Transformation in Social Knowledge.* New York: Springer-Verlag.

Gergen, K. J. (1985). The social constructionist movement in modern psychology. *American Psychologist, 40,* 266–275.

Gergen, K. J. (1991). *The Saturated Self.* New York: Basic Books.

Gergen, K. J. (1994). Exploring the postmodern: Perils or potentials. *American Psychologist, 49,* 412–416.

Gergen, K. J., & Gergen, M. J. (1983). Narratives of the self. In T. R. Sabin & K. E. Scheibe (Eds.), *Narrative Psychology: The Storied Nature of Human Conduct.* New York: Praeger.

Gilligan, C. (1982). *In a Different Voice.* Cambridge, MA: Harvard University Press.

Gilligan, C., Roger, A., & Tolman, D. (1991). *Women, Girls, and Psychotherapy.* Cambridge, MA: Harvard University Press.

Gilligan, S. (1987). *Therapeutic Trances: The Cooperation Princple in Ericksonian Hypnotherapy.* New York: Brunner/Mazel.

Gilligan, S., & Price, R. (Eds.). (1993). *Therapeutic Conversations.* New York: Norton.

Gleick, J. (1987). *Chaos: Making a New Science.* New York: Penguin Books.

Goffman, E. (1986). *Stigma: Notes on the Management of Spoiled Identity.* New York: Simon & Schuster.

Goolishian, H. A., & Anderson, H. (1987). Language systems and therapy: An evolving idea. *Psychotherapy, 24,* 529–538.

Goolishian, H. A., & Anderson, H. (1992). Some afterthoughts on reading Duncan and Held. *Journal of Marital and Family Therapy, 18,* 35–37.

Goolishian, H. A., & Anderson, H. (1992). Strategy and intervention versus nonintervention: A matter of theory? *Journal of Marital and Family Therapy, 18,* 51–5.

Gordon, D. (1978). *Therapeutic Metaphors.* Cupertino, CA: Metapublications.

Gordon, D., & Meyers-Anderson, M. (1981). *Phoenix: Therapeutic Patterns of Milton H. Erickson.* Cupertino, CA: Metapublications.

Goulding, M. M. (1985). *Who's Been Living in Your Head?* (rev. ed.) Watsonville, CA: Western Institute for Group and Family Therapy Press.

Goulding, M. M., & Goulding, R. L. (1979). *Changing Lives through Redecision Therapy.* New York: Grove Press.

Goulding, R. L., & Goulding, M. M. (1978). *The Power Is in the Patient.* San Francisco: TA Press.

Greenburg, D. (1976). *How to Be a Jewish Mother.* Los Angeles: Price/Stern/Sloan.

Greenburg, D. (1987). *How to Make Yourself Miserable.* New York: Random House.

Greenburg, D., & O'Malley, S. (1983). *How to Avoid Love and Marriage.* New York: Freundlich Books.

Greenleaf, E. (1973). Senoi dream groups. *Psychotherapy: Theory, Research and Practice, 10,* 218–222.

Greenleaf, E. (1977). Active imagining. In J. L. Singer & K. Pope (Eds.), *The Power of Human Imagination: New Techniques of Psychotherapy* (pp. 167–196). New York: Plenum.

Greenleaf, E. (1994). On the social nature of the unconscious mind: Pearson's Brick, Wood's Break, and Greenleaf's Blow. *Ericksonian Monographs, 10.*

Grinder, J., & Bandler, R. (1976). *The Structure of Magic* (Vol. 2). Palo Alto, CA: Science & Behavior Books.

Grof, S. (1975). *Realms of the Human Unconscious.* New York: Viking.

Grove, D. R., & Haley, J. (1993). *Conversations on Therapy: Popular Problems and Uncommon Solutions.* New York: Norton.

Gustafson, J. P. (1986). *The Complex Secret of Brief Psychotherapy.* New York: Norton.

Gustafson, J. P. (1992). *Self-Delight in a Harsh World: The Main Stories of Individual, Marital, and Family Psychotherapy.* New York: Norton.

Gustafson, J. P., & Cooper, L. W. (1990). *The Modern Contest.* New York: Norton.

Haley, J. (1963). *Strategies of Psychotherapy.* New York: Grune & Stratton.

Haley, J. (1973). *Uncommon Therapy: The Psychiatric Techniques of Milton H. Erickson, M.D.* New York: Norton.

Haley, J. (1976). *Problem-Solving Therapy.* New York: Harper.

Haley, J. (1984). *Ordeal Therapy.* San Francisco: Jossey-Bass.

Haley, J. (Ed.). (1985). *Conversations with Milton H. Erickson, M.D.* (Vols. 1–3). New York: Triangle Press/Norton.

Haley, J. (1989). *The First Therapy Session: How to Interview Clients and Identify Problems Successfully.* San Francisco: Jossey-Bass.

Haley, J. (1993). *Jay Haley on Milton H. Erickson.* New York: Brunner/Mazel.

Hammerschlag, C. (1988). *The Dancing Healers: A Doctor's Journey of Healing with Native Americans.* New York: Harper & Row.

Hart, M., & Stevens, J. (1990). *Drumming at the Edge of Magic.* New York: HarperCollins.

Havens, L. L. (1976). *Participant Observation.* New York: Jason Aronson.

Havens, L. L. (1986). *Making contact: Uses of Language in Psychotherapy.* Cambridge, MA: Harvard University Press.

Havens, R. A. (Ed.). (1989). *The Wisdom of Milton H. Erickson* (Vols. 1 & 2). New York: Paragon House.

Held, B. S. (1992). The problem of strategy within the systemic therapies. *Journal of Marital and Family Therapy, 18,* 25–34.

Herr, S. J., & Weakland, J. H. (1979). *Counseling Elders and Their Families: Practical Techniques for Applied Gerontology.* New York: Springer.

Hillman, J. (1975). *Re-visioning Psychology.* New York: Harper & Row.

Hillman, J., & Ventura, M. (1992). *We've Had a Hundred Years of Psychotherapy and the World's Getting Worse.* New York: HarperCollins.

Hine, M. (1993). On reading the Stamford papers on constructivism: A physicist's reactions. *Transactional Analysis Journal, 23,* 45–47.

Hoffman, L. (1988). A constructivist position for family therapy. *Irish Journal of Psychology, 9*(1).

Hoffman, L. (1990). Constructing realities: An art of lenses. *Family Process, 29,* 1–12.

Hofstadter, D. (1980). *Godel, Escher, Bach: An Eternal Golden Braid.* New York: Vintage.

Hopkins, T. (1982). *How to Master the Art of Selling.* New York: Warner Books.

Hopwood, L., & Taylor, M. (1993). Solution-focused brief therapy for chronic problems. *Innovations in Clinical Practice: A Source Book, 12,* 85–97.

Hoyt, M. F. (1979). "Patient" or "client": What's in a name? *Psychotherapy: Theory, Research and Practice, 16,* 16–17.

Hoyt, M. F. (1985). "Shrink" or "expander": An issue in forming a therapeutic alliance. *Psychotherapy, 22,* 813–814.

Hoyt, M. F. (1990). On time in brief therapy. In R. A. Wells & V. J. Giannetti (Eds.), *Handbook of the Brief Psychotherapies* (pp. 115–143). New York: Plenum.

Hoyt, M. F. (1994). Managed care, HMOs, and the Ericksonian perspective. *Ericksonian Monographs, 10.*

Hoyt, M. F. (in press). Brief psychotherapies. In A. S. Gurman & S. B. Messer (Eds.), *Major Systems of Psychotherapy: Theory and Practice.* New York: Guilford.

Hoyt, M. F. (1994). *Brief Therapy and Managed Care: Selected Papers.* San Francisco: Jossey-Bass.

Hoyt, M. F. (Ed.). (1994). *Constructive Therapies.* New York: Guilford.

Hoyt, M. F. (in press). Is being "in recovery" self limiting? *Transactional Analysis Journal.*

Hoyt, M. F., Rosenbaum, R., & Talmon, M. (1992). Planned single-session therapy. In S. H. Budman, M. F. Hoyt, & S. Friedman (Eds.), *The First Session in Brief Therapy* (pp. 59–86). New York: Guilford.

Howard, C. S. (1991). Culture tales: A narrative approach to thinking, cross-cultural psychology, and psychotherapy. *American Psychologist 46,* 187–197.

Hudson, P. O. (1993). *Making Friends with Your Unconscious Mind: The User Friendly Guide.* Omaha, NE: Center Press.

Hudson, P. O., & O'Hanlon, W. H. (1991). *Rewriting Love Stories: Brief Marital Therapy.* New York: Norton.

Humphreys, K. (1993). Expanding the pluralist revolution: A comment on Omer and Strenger (1992). *Psychotherapy, 30,* 176–177.

Hyde, L. (1979). *The Gift: Imagination and the Erotic Life of Property.* New York: Vintage/Random House.

Johnson, L., & Miller, S. D. (in press). Modifications of depression risk factors: A solution-focused approach. *Psychotherapy.*

Joyce, T. A., & Taylor, V. L. (1990). Mastering words and managing conversations: Therapy as dialogue. *Journal of Strategic and Systemic Therapies* 9(4), 21–28.

Jung, C. G. (1966). The practice of psychotherapy. In *The Collected Works of C. G. Jung* (Vol. 16, R. F. C. Hull, Trans.). Princeton, NJ: Princeton University Press.

Kaminer, W. (1992). *I'm Dysfunctional, You're Dysfunctional: The Recovery Movement and Other Self-Help Fashions.* New York: Vintage.

Keeney, B. P. (1983). *Aesthetics of Change.* New York: Guilford.

Keeney, B. P. (1990). *Improvisational Therapy.* St. Paul, MN: Systemic Therapy Press.

Kelly, G. A. (1955). *The Psychology of Personal Constructs* (Vols. 1 & 2). New York: Norton.

Kershaw, C. J. (1992). *The Couple's Hypnotic Dance: Creating Ericksonian Strategies in Marital Therapy.* New York: Brunner/Mazel.

Kiser, D. J., Piercy, F. P., & Lipchik, E. (1993). The integration of emotion in solution-focused therapy. *Journal of Marital and Family Therapy, 19*(3), 233–242.

Kleckner, T., Frank, L., Bland, C., Amendt, J. H., & Brant, R. (1992). The myth of the unfeeling strategic therapist. *Journal of Marital and Family Therapy, 18,* 41–51.

Kopp, S. B. (1972). *If You Meet the Buddha on the Road, Kill Him!* New York: Bantam.

Kowalski, K., & Kral, R. (1989). The geometry of solution: Using the scaling technique. *Family Therapy Case Studies, 4*(1), 59–66.

Kral, R. (1987). *Strategies That Work: Techniques for Solution in the Schools.* Milwaukee, WI: Brief Family Therapy Center.

Kral, R., & Kowalaski, K. (1989). After the miracle: The second stage in solution-focused brief therapy. *Journal of Strategic and Systemic Therapies, 8,* 73–76.

Kral, R., Schaffer, J., & de Shazer, S. (1989). Adoptive families: More of the same and different. *Journal of Strategic and Systemic Therapies, 8,* 36–49.

Kris, E. (1956). The personal myth. *Journal of the American Psychoanalytic Association, 4,* 653–681.

Kuhn, T. S. (1970). *The Structure of Scientific Revolutions* (2nd ed.). Chicago: University of Chicago Press.

Laing, R. D. (1967). *The Politics of Experience.* New York: Pantheon.

Laing, R. D. (1970). *Knots.* New York: Pantheon.

Laing, R. D. (1971). *The Politics of the Family.* New York: Pantheon.

Laird, J. (1989). Women and stories: Restorying women's self-constructors. In M. McGoldrick, C. M. Anderson, & F. Walsh (Eds.), *Women in Families: A Framework for Family Therapy.* New York: Norton.

Lankton, C. R., & Lankton, S. R. (1986). *Tales of Enchantment: Goal-Oriented Metaphors for Adults and Children in Therapy.* New York: Brunner/Mazel.

Lankton, S. R., & Erickson, K. K. (Eds.). (1994). The essence of a single-session success. *Ericksonian Monographs, 9,* 1–164.

Lankton, S. R., & Lankton, C. (1983). *The Answer within: A Clinical Framework for Ericksonian Hypnotherapy.* New York: Brunner/Mazel.

Lazarus, A. A. (1993). Theory, subjectivity and bias: Can there be a future? *Psychotherapy, 30,* 674–677.

Lederer, W. J., & Jackson, D. D. (1968). *The Mirages of Marriage.* New York: Norton.

Lethem, J. (1994). *Move to Tears, Move to Action: Solution-Focused Therapy with Women and Children.* London: BT Publishers.

Levenson, E. A. (1972). *The Fallacy of Understanding.* New York: Basic Books.

Lifton, R. J. (Ed.). (1974). *Explorations in Psychohistory.* New York: Simon & Schuster.

Lightman, A. (1993). *Einstein's Dreams.* New York: Warner Books.

Linehan, M. M. (1993). *Cognitive–Behavioral Treatment of Borderline Personality Disorder.* New York: Guilford.

Linehan, M. M. (1993). *Skills Training Manual for Treating Borderline Personality Disorder.* New York: Guilford.

Lipchik, E. (1993). "Both/and" solutions. In S. Friedman (Ed.), *The New Language of Change: Constructive Collaboration in Psychotherapy* (pp. 25–49). New York: Guilford.

Lipchik, E. (1994, March/April). The rush to be brief. *Family Therapy Networker,* pp. 34–39.

Lipchik, E., & de Shazer, S. (1986). The purposeful interview. *Journal of Strategic and Systemic Therapies, 5*(1), 88–89.

Lipchik, E., & de Shazer, S. (1988). Purposeful sequences for beginning the solution-focused interview. In E. Lipchik (Ed.), *Interviewing* (pp. 105–117). Rockville, MD: Aspen.

Lomas, P. (1973). *True and False Experience.* New York: Taplinger.

Lyddon, W. J. (1990). First- and second-order change: Implications of rationalist and constructivist cognitive therapies. *Journal of Counseling and Development, 68,* 122–127.

Lyddon, W. J. (1992). A rejoinder to Ellis: What is and is not RET? *Journal of Counseling and Development, 70,* 452–454.

Lyddon, W. J. (1992). Cognitive science and psychotherapy: An epistemic framework. In D. J. Stein & J. E. Young (Eds.), *Cognitive Science and Clinical Disorders* (pp. 171–184). New York: Academic Press.

Lyddon, W. J. (1993). Contrast, contradiction, and change in psychotherapy. *Psychotherapy, 30,* 383–390.

Madanes, C. (1981). *Strategic Family Therapy.* San Francisco: Jossey-Bass.

Madanes, C. (1984). *Behind the One-Way Mirror.* San Francisco: Jossey-Bass.

Madanes, C. (1990). *Sex, Love and Violence.* New York: Norton.

Mahoney, M. J. (1991). *Human Change Processes: The Scientific Foundations of Psychotherapy.* New York: Basic Books.

Mahoney, M. J., & Lyddon, W. J. (1988). Recent developments in cognitive approaches to counseling and psychotherapy. *Counseling Psychologist, 16,* 190–234.

Maslow, A. H. (1968). *Toward a Psychology of Being* (2nd ed.). Princeton, NJ: Van Nostrand.

Mathews, B. (1988). Planned short-term therapy utilizing the techniques of Jay Haley and Milton Erickson: A guide for the practitioner. *Psychotherapy in Private Practice, 6,* 103–118.

Maturana, H. R. (1988). Reality: The search for objectivity or the quest for a compelling argument. *Irish Journal of Psychology, 9*(1), 25–5.

Maturana, H. R., & Varela, F. J. (1987). *The Tree of Knowledge.* Boston: Shambhala.

McGoldrick, M., Pearce, J. K., & Giordano, J. G. (Eds.). (1982). *Ethnicity and Family Therapy.* New York: Guilford.

McNamee, S., & Gergen, K. J. (Eds.). (1992). *Therapy as Social Construction.* Newbury Park, CA: Sage.

Meichenbaum, D. (1992). Stress inoculation training: A twenty-year update. In P. M. Lehrer & R. L. Woolfolk (Eds.), *Principles and Practices of Stress Management* (2nd ed., pp. 373–406). New York: Guilford.

Meichenbaum, D., & Fitzpatrick, D. (1993). A constructivist narrative perspective on stress and coping: Stress inoculation applications. In L. Goldberger & S. Breznitz (Eds.), *Handbook of Stress.* New York: Free Press.

Meichenbaum, D., & Fong, G. (1993). How individuals control their own minds: A constructive narrative perspective. In D. M. Wegner & J. W. Pennebaker (Eds.), *Handbook of Mental Control.* New York: Prentice Hall.

Melges, F. T. (1982). *Time and the Inner Future: A Temporal Approach to Psychiatric Disorders.* New York: Wiley.

Miller, D., & Lax, W. (1988). A reflecting team model for working with couples: Interrupting deadly struggles. *Journal of Strategic and Systemic Therapies, 7*(3), 17–23.

Miller, S. D. (1992). The symptoms of solution. *Journal of Strategic and Systemic Therapies, 11,* 1–11.

Miller, S. D. (1994). The solution conspiracy: A mystery in three installments. *Journal of Systemic Therapies, 13,* 18–37.

Miller, S. D., & Hopwood, L. (1994). The solution papers: A comprehensive guide to the publications of the Brief Family Therapy Center. *Journal of Systemic Therapies, 13,* 42–47.

Millman, D. (1984). *Way of the Peaceful Warrior: A Book That Changes Lives.* Tiburon, CA: H. J. Kramer.

Minuchin, S., & Nichols, M. P. (1993). *Family Healing: Strategies for Hope and Understanding.* New York: Simon & Schuster/Touchstone.

Molnar, A., & de Shazer, S. (1987). Solution-focused therapy: Toward the identification of therapeutic tasks. *Journal of Marital and Family Therapy, 13,* 349–358.

Molnar, A., & Lindquist, B. (1989). *Changing Problem Behavior in Schools.* San Francisco, Jossey-Bass.

Moore, R., & Gillette, D. (1990). *King, Warrior, Magician, Lover: Rediscovering the Archetypes of the Mature Masculine.* New York: HarperCollins.

Moore, T. (1992). *Care of the Soul.* New York: HarperCollins.

Moore, T. (1994). *Soul Mates: Honoring the Mysteries of Love and Relationship.* New York: HarperCollins.

Morgan, M. (1991). *Mutant Message.* Lees Summit, MO: MM Company.

Moyers, B. (1993). *Healing and the Mind.* New York: Doubleday.

Murphy, M. (1972). *Golf in the Kingdom.* New York: Viking.

Napier, A. Y., & Whitaker, C. A. (1978). *The Family Crucible.* New York: Harper & Row.

Neill, J., & Kniskern, D. (Eds.). (1982). *From Psyche to System: The Evolving Therapy of Carl Whitaker.* New York: Guilford.

Neimeyer, G. J. (Ed.). (1993). *Constructivist Assessment: A Casebook.* Newbury Park, CA: Sage.

Neimeyer, G. J., & Lyddon, W. J. (Eds.). (1993). Special issue: Constructivst psychotherapy. *Journal of Cognitive Psychotherapy, 7*(3).

Neimeyer, R. A. (1993). An appraisal of constructivist psychotherapies. *Journal of Consulting and Clinical Psychology, 61,* 221–234.

Neimeyer, R. A. (1993). Constructivism and the problem of psychotherapy integration. *Journal of Psychotherapy Ingegration, 3,* 133–158.

Neimeyer, R. A., & Neimeyer, F. G. (1990). Constructivist contributions to psychotherapy integration. *Journal of Integrative and Eclectic Psychotherapy, 9,* 4–20

Nunnally, E. (1993). Solution focused therapy. In R. A. Wells & V. J. Giannetti (Eds.), *Casebook of the Brief Psychotherapies* (pp. 271–286). New York: Plenum.

Nylund, D. (1992). Escaping a co-dependent lifestyle: A systemic/cybernetic approach. *Family Therapy Case Studies, 7*(1), 41–47.

Nylund, D., & Corsiglia, V. (1993). Internalized other questioning with men who are violent. *Dulwich Centre Newsletter, 2,* 30–35.

Nylund D., & Corsiglia, V. (1994). Becoming solution focused forced in brief therapy: Something important we already knew. *Journal of Systemic Therapies, 13*(1), 1–8.

O'Hanlon, W. H. (1987). *Taproots: Underlying Principles of Milton Erickson's Therapy and Hypnosis.* New York: Norton.

O'Hanlon, W. H. (1991). Not strategic, not systemic: Still clueless after all these years. *Journal of Strategic and Systemic Therapies, 10,* 105–109.

O'Hanlon, W. H., & Hexum, A. L. (1990). *An Uncommon Casebook: The Complete Clinical Work of Milton H. Erickson, M.D.* New York: Norton.

O' Hanlon, W. H., & Martin, M. (1992). *Solution-Oriented Hypnosis: An Ericksonian Approach.* New York: Norton.

O'Hanlon, W. H., & Weiner-Davis, M. (1989). *In Search of Solutions: A New Direction in Psychotherapy.* New York: Norton.

O'Hanlon, W. H., & Wilk, J. (1987). *Shifting Contexts: The Generation of Effective Psychotherapy.* New York: Guilford.

Omer, H. (1993). Quasi-literary elements in psychotherapy. *Psychotherapy, 30,* 59–66.

Omer, H. (1993). Short-term psychotheapy and the rise of the life-sketch. *Psychotherapy, 30,* 668–673.

Omer, H. (1994). *Critical Interventions in Psychotherapy.* New York: Norton.

Omer, H., & Strenger, C. (1992). The pluralistic revolution: From the one true meaning to an infinity of constructed ones. *Psychotherapy, 29,* 253–261.

Paglia, C. (1991). *Sexual Personae.* New York: Vintage.

Paglia, C. (1992). *Art, Sex, and American Culture.* New York: Vintage.

Palazzoli, M. S., Cecchin, G., Prata, G., & Boscolo, L. (1978). *Paradox and Counterparadox.* New York: Jason Aronson.

Papp, P. (1980). The Greek chorus and other techniques of paradoxical therapy. *Family Process, 19,* 45–57.

Parry, A. (1991). A universe of stories. *Family Process, 30,* 37–54.

Pearce, J. C. (1971). *The Crack in the Cosmic Egg.* New York: Julian Press.

Peller, J., & Walter, J. (1993). Celebrating the living: A solution-focused approach to the normal grieving process. *Family Therapy Case Studies, 7*(2), 3–7.

Penn, P. (1982). Circular questioning. *Family Process, 21,* 267–280.

Penn, P. (1985). Feed-forward: Future questions, future maps. *Family Process, 24,* 289–310.

Peters, T. J., & Waterman, R. H., Jr. (1982). *In Search of Excellence.* New York: Harper & Row.

Polster, E. (1987). *Every Person's Life Is Worth a Novel.* New York: Norton.

Polster, E., & Polster, M. (1976). Therapy without resistance. In A. Burton (Ed.), *What Makes Behavior Change Possible?* New York: Brunner/Mazel.

Prochaska, J., DiClemente, C., & Norcross, J. (1992). In search of how people change: Application to addictive behaviors. *American Psychologist, 47*(9), 1102–1114.

Puig, A. (1992, November/December). The *stuck* client and the solution-focused assessment. *EAP Digest,* pp. 22, 43.

Quick, E. (1990). The strategic therapy planning worksheet. *Journal of Strategic and Systemic Therapies, 9,* 29–33.

Quick, E. (1994). Strategic/solution-focused therapy: A combined approach. *Journal of Systemic Therapies, 13,* 74–75.

Rabkin, R. (1977). *Strategic Psychotherapy.* New York: Basic Books.

Rasmussen, P. T., & Tomm, K. (1992). Guided letter writing: A long brief therapy method whereby clients carry out their own treatment. *Journal of Strategic and Systemic Therapies, 11,* 1–18.

Ray, W. A., & Keeney, B. (1993). *Resource Focused Therapy.* New York: Brunner/Mazel.

Real, T. (1990). The therapeutic use of self in constructionist systemic therapy. *Family Process, 23,* 255–272.

Rhinehart, L. (1976). *The Book of est.* New York: Holt, Rinehart & Winston.

Ring, K., & Kelley, H. H. (1963). Comparison of augmentation and reduction as modes of influence. *Journal of Abnormal and Social Psychology, 66,* 95–102.

Rogers, C. R. (1961). *On Becoming a Person.* Boston: Houghton Mifflin.

Rosen, S. (1982). *My Voice Will Go with You: The Teaching Tales of Milton H. Erickson.* New York: Norton.

Rosenbaum, R. (1982). Paradox as epistemological jump. *Family Process, 21,* 85–90.

Rosenbaum, R. (1990). Strategic therapy. In R. A. Wells & V. J. Giannetti (Eds.), *Handbook of the Brief Psychotherapies* (pp. 351–404). New York: Plenum.

Rosenbaum, R., Hoyt, M. F., & Talmon, M. (1990). The challenge of single-session therapies: Creating pivotal moments. In R. A. Wells & V. J. Giannetti (Eds.), *Handbook of the Brief Psychothreapies* (pp. 165–189). New York: Plenum.

Rosenberg, E. H., & Medini, G. (1978). Truth: A concept in emergence. *Contemporary Psychoanalysis, 14*(3), 424–434.

Rosenthal, R., & Jacobson, L. (1989). *Pygmalion in the Classroom.* New York: Irvington.

Russell, R., & Laing, R. D. (1992). *R. D. Laing and Me: Lessons in Love.* Lake Placid, NY: Hillgarth Press.

Russell, R. L., & Van Den Broek, P. (1992). Changing narrative schemas in psychotherapy. *Psychotherapy, 29,* 344–354.

Sabin, T. R., & Scheibe, K. E. (Eds.). (1983). *Narrative Psychology: The Storied Nature of Human Conduct.* New York: Praeger.

Solovey, A. D., & Duncan, B. L. (1992). Ethics and strategic therapy: A proposed ethical direction. *Journal of Marital and Family Therapy, 18,* 53–61.

Sandelowski, M. (1991). Telling stories: Narrative approaches in qualitative research. *Image: Journal of Nursing Scholarship, 23,* 161–166.

Satir, V. (1988). *The New Peoplemaking.* Mountain View, CA: Science & Behavior Books.

Schafer, R. (1983). *The Analytic Attitude.* New York: Basic Books.

Schafer, R. (1992). *Retelling a Life: Narration and Dialogue in Psychoanalysis.* New York: Basic Books.

Schnarch, D. M. (1991). *Constructing the Sexual Crucible: An Integration of Sexual and Marital Therapy.* New York: Norton.

Seeman, J. (1987). Toward a model of positive health. *American Psychologist, 44,* 1099–1109.

Segal, L. (1986). *The Dream of Reality: Heinz von Foerster's Constructivism.* New York: Norton.

Selekman, M. (1991). The solution-oriented parenting group: A treatment alternative that works. *Journal of Strategic and Systemic Therapies, 10,* 36–49.

Selekman, M. D. (1993). *Pathways to Change: Brief Therapy Solutions with Difficult Adolescents.* New York: Guilford.

Seligman, M. (1990). *Learned Optimism.* New York: Knopf.

Selvini Palazzoli, M., Boscolo, L., Cecchin, G., & Prata, G. (1980). Hypothesizing, circularity, neutrality: Three guidelines for the conductor of the session. *Family Process, 19,* 2–12.

Sheehy, G. (1974). *Passages: Predictable Crises of Adult Life.* New York: Dutton.

Sheehy, G. (1981). *Pathfinders.* New York: Bantam.

Shilts, L., Rudes, J., & Madigan, S. (1993). The use of solution-focused interview with a reflecting team format: Evolving thoughts from clinical practice. *Journal of Systemic Therpaies, 12* 1–10.

Siegel, B. S. (1986). *Love, Medicine and Miracles.* New York: Harper & Row.

Siegelman, E. Y. (1990). *Metaphor and Meaning in Psychotherapy.* New York: Guilford.

Singer, J. L. (1974). *Imagery and Daydream Methods in Psychotherapy and Behavior.* New York: Academic Press.

Sluzki, C. E. (1992). Transformations: A blueprint for narrative changes in therapy. *Family Process, 31,* 217–230.

Smith, M. B. (1994). Selfhood at risk: Postmodern perils and the perils of postmodernism. *American Psychologist, 49,* 405–411.

Sontag, S. (1966). *Against Interpretation.* New York: Farrar, Straus & Giroux.

Speed, B. (1991). Reality exists, OK? An argument against constructivism and social constructionism. *Journal of Family Therapy, 13,* 395–410.

Spence, D. P. (1982). *Narrative Truth and Historical Truth: Meaning and Interpretation in Psychoanalysis.* New York: Norton.

Steiner, C. M. (1974). *Scripts People Live: Transactional Analysis of Life Scripts.* New York: Bantam.

Stevenson, H. C., & Renard, G. (1993). Trusting ole' wise owls: Use of cultural strengths in African-American families. *Professional Psychology: Research and Practice, 24,* 433–442.

Strayhorn, J. M. (1988). *The Competent Child: An Approach to Psychotherapy and Preventive Mental Health.* New York: Guilford.

Suzuki, S. (1970). *Zen Mind, Beginner's Mind.* New York: Weatherhill.

Talmon, M. (1990). *Single Session Therapy: Maximizing the Effect of the First (and Often Only) Therapeutic Encounter.* San Francisco: Jossey-Bass.

Talmon, M. (1993). *Single Session Solutions.* Reading, MA: Addison-Wesley.

Tannen, D. (1990). *You Just Don't Understand: Women and Men in Conversation.* New York: Ballantine Books.

Taylor, S. E. (1990). *Positive Illusions.* New York: Basic Books.

Tomm, K. (1987). Interventive interviewing: Part I. Strategizing as a fourth guideline for the therapist. *Family Process, 26,* 3–13.

Tomm, K. (1987). Interventive interviewing: Part II. Reflexing questioning as a means to enable self-healing. *Family Process, 26,* 167–183.

Tomm, K. (1988). Interventive interviewing: Part III. Intending to ask lineal, circular, strategic and reflexive questions. *Family Process, 27,* 1–16.

Tomm, K. (1989). Externalizing the problem and internalizing personal agency. *Journal of Strategic and Systemic Therapies, 8,* 54–59.

Turner, V., & Bruner, E. (Eds.). (1986). *The Anthropology of Experience.* Chicago: University of Illinois Press.

Varela, F., Thompson, E., & Rosch, E. (1991). *The Embodied Mind.* Cambridge, MA: MIT Press.

von Foerster, H. (1984). On constructing a reality. In P. Watzlawick (Ed.), *The Invented Reality* (pp. 41–61). New York: Norton.

Wallas, L. (1985). *Stories for the Third Ear.* New York: Norton.

Walter, J. L., & Peller, J. E. (1992). *Becoming Solution-Focused in Brief Therapy.* New York: Norton.

Walters, C., & Havens, R. A. (1993). *Hypnotherapy for Health, Harmony, and Peak Performance: Expanding the Goals of Psychotherapy.* New York: Brunner/Mazel.

Waters, D. B., & Lawrence, E. C. (1993). *Competence, Courage and Change: An Approach to Family Therapy.* New York: Norton.

Watts, A. W. (1961). *Psychotherapy East and West.* New York: Pantheon.

Watzlawick, P. (1976). *How Real Is Real?* New York: Random House.

Watzlawick, P. (1984). (Ed.). *The Invented Reality: How Do We Know What We Believe We Know?* New York: Norton.

Watzlawick, P. (1988). *Ultra-Solutions, or How to Fail Most Successfully.* New York: Norton.

Watzlawick, P., Beavin, J. H., & Jackson, D. D. (1967). *Pragmatics of Human Communication.* New York: Norton.

Watzlawick, P., Weakland, J. H., & Fisch, R. (1974). *Change: Principles of Problem Formation and Problem Resolution.* New York: Norton.

Weakland, J. H. (1993). Conversation—but what kind? In S. Gilligan & R. Price (Eds.), *Therapeutic Conversations* (pp. 136–145). New York: Norton.

Weakland, J. H. (1994). Metalogue: What is mental illness? With apologies and homage to Gregory Bateson. *Journal of Systemic Therapies, 13,* 70–73.

Weakland, J. H., & Fisch, R. (1992). Brief therapy—MRI style. In S. H. Budman, M. F. Hoyt, & S. Friedman (Eds.), *The First Session in Brief Therapy.* New York: Guilford.

Weakland, J. H., Fisch, R., Watzlawick, P., & Bodin, A. (1972). Brief therapy: Focused problem resolution. *Family Process, 13,* 141–168.

Weiner-Davis, M. (1990, April/March). In praise of solutions. *Family Therapy Networker* (Reprinted in R. Simon, C. Barrilleaux, M. S. Wylie, & L. M. Markowitz [Eds.] [1992], *The Evolving Therapist: Ten Years of the Family Therapy Networker* [pp. 173–179]. New York: Guilford.)

Weiner-Davis, M. (1992). *Divorce Busting.* New York: Fireside/Simon & Schuster.

Weiner-Davis, M., de Shazer, S., & Gingerich, W. J. (1987). Building on pretreatment change to construct the therapeutic solution: An exploratory study. *Journal of Marital and Family Therapy, 13,* 359–363.

Weingarten, K. (1991). The discourses of intimacy: Adding a social constructivist and feminist view. *Family Process, 30,* 285–306.

Wessler, R. L. (1992). Constructivism and rational-emotive therapy: A critique: *Psychotherapy, 29,* 620–625.

Wessler, R. L. (1993). A reply to Ellis's critique of Wessler's critique of rational-emotive therapy. *Psychotherapy, 30,* 533–534.

Whitaker, C. A. (1976). The hindrance of theory in clinical work. In P. J. Guerin (Ed.), *Family Therapy: Theory and Practice* (pp. 154–164). New York: Gardner Press.

Whitaker, C. A. (1989). *Midnight Musings of a Family Therapist.* New York: Norton.

White, M. (1984). Pseudo-encopresis: From avalanche to victory; from vicious to virtuous cycles. *Family Systems Medicine, 2*(2), 150–160.

White, M. (1986). Negative explanation, restraint and double description: A template for family therapy. *Family Process, 25*(2), 169–184.

White, M. (1989). *Selected Papers.* Adelaide, South Australia: Dulwich Centre Publications.

White, M. (1989, Summer). The externalizing of the problem and the re-authoring of lives and relationships. *Dulwich Centre Newsletter,* pp. 3–21.

White, M. (1992). Deconstruction and therapy. In D. Epston & M. White, *Experience, Contradiction, Narrative and Imagination* (pp. 109–151). Adelaide, South Australia: Dulwich Centre Publications. (Originally published 1991)

White, M., & Epston, D. (1990). *Narrative Means to Therapeutic Ends.* New York: Norton.

White, R. W. (1959). Motivation reconsidered: The concept of competence. *Psychological Review, 66,* 297–333.

Wile, D. (1984). Kohut, Kernberg, and accusatory interpretations. *Psychotherapy, 21,* 353–364.

Wittgenstein, L. (1958). *The Blue and Brown Books.* New York: Harper & Row.

Woolfolk, R. L. (1992). Hermeneutics, social constructionism and other items of intellectual fashion: Intimations for clinical science. *Behavior Therapy, 23,* 213–223.

Yalom, I. D. (1992). *When Nietzsche Wept.* New York: Basic Books.

Yapko, M. D. (Ed.). (1989). *Brief Therapy Approaches to Treating Anxiety and Depression.* New York: Brunner/Mazel.

Yapko, M. (1990). *Trancework: An Introduction to the Practice of Clinical Hypnosis* (2nd ed.). New York: Brunner/Mazel.

Young-Eisendrath, P., & Hall, J. A. (1991). *Jung's Self Psychology: A Constructivist Perspective.* New York: Guilford.

Zeig, J. K. (Ed.). (1980). *A Teaching Seminar with Milton H. Erickson.* New York: Brunner/Mazel.

Zeig, J. K. (Ed.). (1982). *Ericksonian Approaches to Hypnosis and Psychotherapy.* New York: Brunner/Mazel.

Zeig, J. K. (Ed.). (1987). *The Evolution of Psychotherapy.* New York: Brunner/Mazel.

Zeig, J. K. (Ed.). (1992). *The Evolution of Psychotherapy–The Second Conference.* New York: Brunner/Mazel.

Zeig, J., & Gilligan, S. G. (Eds.). (1990). *Brief Therapy: Myths, Methods and Metaphors.* New York: Brunner/Mazel.

Zeig, J. K., & Lankton, S. R. (Eds.). (1989). *Developing Ericksonian Therapy: State of the Art.* New York: Brunner/Mazel.

Zimmerman, J., & Dickerson, V. (1993). Separating couples from restraining patterns and the relationship discourse that supports them. *Journal of Marital and Family Therapy, 19,* 403–413.

Index